MORE ROOM IN A
BROKEN HEART

MORE ROOM IN A
BROKEN HEART

The True Adventures of
Carly Simon

STEPHEN DAVIS

PHOTOGRAPHS BY PETER SIMON

GOTHAM BOOKS

GOTHAM BOOKS
Published by Penguin Group (USA) Inc.
375 Hudson Street, New York, New York 10014, U.S.A.
Penguin Group (Canada), 90 Eglinton Avenue East, Suite 700, Toronto, Ontario M4P 2Y3,
Canada (a division of Pearson Penguin Canada Inc.) · Penguin Books Ltd, 80 Strand,
London WC2R 0RL, England · Penguin Ireland, 25 St Stephen's Green, Dublin 2, Ireland
(a division of Penguin Books Ltd) · Penguin Group (Australia), 250 Camberwell Road,
Camberwell, Victoria 3124, Australia (a division of Pearson Australia Group Pty Ltd) ·
Penguin Books India Pvt Ltd, 11 Community Centre, Panchsheel Park, New Delhi–110
017, India · Penguin Group (NZ), 67 Apollo Drive, Rosedale, Auckland 0632, New Zealand (a division of Pearson New Zealand Ltd) · Penguin Books (South Africa) (Pty) Ltd,
24 Sturdee Avenue, Rosebank, Johannesburg 2196, South Africa

Penguin Books Ltd, Registered Offices: 80 Strand, London WC2R 0RL, England

Published by Gotham Books, a member of Penguin Group (USA) Inc.

First printing, January 2012
1   3   5   7   9   10   8   6   4   2

Copyright © 2012 by Stephen Davis
Photographs by Peter Simon
All rights reserved

Gotham Books and the skyscraper logo are trademarks of Penguin Group (USA) Inc.

LIBRARY OF CONGRESS CATALOGING-IN-PUBLICATION DATA
Davis, Stephen, 1947–
More room in a broken heart : the true adventures of Carly Simon / Stephen Davis ;
photographs by Peter Simon.
p. cm.
ISBN 978-1-59240-651-7
1. Simon, Carly.   2. Singers—United States—Biography.   I. Simon, Peter,
1947–   II. Title.
ML420.S56296D38 2012
782.42164092—dc23
[B]   2011039561

Printed in the United States of America
Set in Sabon   •   Designed by Elke Sigal

Dedicated to all Carly Simon fans,
past and present.

Contents

Contents

PART II

Contents

PART III

INTRODUCTION

———

$\mathcal{T}$he great American folk music revival began right after the Second World War. Burl Ives from Indiana was on the radio, singing railroad and cowboy songs. Josh White from South Carolina was a sensation with his blues ballads. The Weavers, with tenor Pete Seeger on banjo, toured the nation with the Okie protest songs of Woody Guthrie. In 1957 the Kingston Trio—calypso collegians from San Francisco—transformed the old Appalachian ballad "Tom Dooley" into a national number one hit single, and commercialized so-called "folk music" took off. Coffeehouses sprouted like toadstools. Guitar sales soared. Most of this music was, in retrospect, insipid. But in 1959 a young Boston University coed named Joan Baez started singing Child ballads, barefoot, at Club 47 in Harvard Square, and caused a sensation with her ungodly vocal range and dark choice of repertoire. Lines went around the block. Her album sold tonnage. Folk began to replace jazz as the cultural expression of younger bohemians and intellectuals. In 1960 a twenty-year-old from Minnesota named Robert Zimmerman changed his name to Bob Dylan and took the Greenwich Village folk scene by storm, becoming the enfant terrible of the clubs along Bleecker and MacDougal streets—the Bitter End, the Gaslight, Gerde's Folk City, Café Wha?. Then Baez and Dylan joined forces and became the alpha couple of a movement that mined old American music and new political/protest songs to create a literate alternative to the surf music and pop that preoccupied the enormous postwar generation in the early sixties. The Newport Folk Festival created new stars every summer, and spawned dozens of similar events that drew thousands of college kids.

By 1963 this national phenomenon had gotten its own network television slot. *Hootenanny* was broadcast on Saturday nights, featuring mostly folk singers and groups, but also blues musicians, old-time country singers, and bluegrass pickers. It was must-see TV back then. *Hootenanny* was so popular with its young audience that the program was quickly expanded from a half hour to an hour.

A big problem with the show was that the cream of the folkies— Baez, Dylan, the Kingston Trio, Pete Seeger—never appeared. *Hootenanny*'s stars were mostly from the second tier of folk performers. At the time, we didn't know that the top echelon of folk singers boycotted the show because of its refusal to invite folk godfather Pete Seeger to perform—for political reasons. So instead of the Kingston Trio, *Hootenanny* broadcast the Highwaymen, the Limeliters, and the Chad Mitchell Trio. Carolyn Hester instead of Baez. Theodore Bikel instead of Dylan.

I watched *Hootenanny* anyway. It was still the best music program on TV.

Late January 1964. America was still in a state of shock and disbelief following the bloody public assassination of President Kennedy two months earlier. I was at home watching *Hootenanny* on a cold Saturday night. The show was filmed at a different college each week, and this night it was at a school in Tennessee. The smirking Smothers Brothers, a fake folk comedy act, were the headliners, so I remember being bored, about to change the channel. Then, in glorious black and white, host Jack Linkletter announced, "Ladies and gentlemen—please welcome, the Simon Sisters!"

⟶

Hold on.

Two sisters, brunettes. Matching dresses and Martin guitars. Both beautiful. The higher, Highland-sounding voice comes from the girl on the left. Her taller sister has an earthier, lower alto. They've put a lilting melody to the old nursery rhyme "Winkin', Blinkin' and Nod," and they're singing the stars from the sky. America wakes up, and is then soothed into a restful state by the Simon Sisters' melodious new lullaby.

I was transfixed.

Later in the program, the Simon Sisters returned with a quietly thrilling duet on "Turn! Turn! Turn!," Pete Seeger's popular arrangement of a biblical verse. Again I was glued to the screen as the girls seemed to glow with a cathode-ray halo. Everything about the Simon Sisters, especially their perfect harmonies, drew me in until I was hooked. When they finished, the audience gave them an ovation. They made a little bow, and looked relieved. They had made a stunning national debut, and done it with mesmeric cool. They were talked about in my high school the following Monday.

I went out and bought their album, *The Simon Sisters,* a few days later. Although the record was filed in the Folk section of the record store, I quickly realized that what they were doing wasn't as much folk as it was a collection of art songs. Quite a few tracks were lullabies, soothing music, two young mothers gently crooning to their restive children. I tried to find out as much as I could about the girls, which wasn't much. Lucy was the pretty soprano. Her taller sister was called Carly Simon. I remember thinking I'd never heard the name Carly before.

Right after this, in February 1964, the Beatles arrived in America—as if in response to an occult summons to lift the grieving nation's spirits. They were a smash on Ed Sullivan's Sunday night variety show, and the rest is history. Folk music was deported to Squaresville when Bob Dylan plugged in his electric guitar at the Newport Folk Festival the following year. Many Village folkies left for Los Angeles and turned into rock-and-roll stars. As far as I could tell, the Simon Sisters disappeared from the waning folk scene that was left behind.

In 1967, I was going to college in Boston. One of my colleagues on the student newspaper was a photographer named Peter Simon. We became friends and shared a lot of experiences during that politically turbulent year, as the Vietnam War heated up and the civil rights movement was moving from nonviolent protest into action and militancy. It was an exciting time.

In November we were on holiday with our families, who lived in New York. Peter invited me to his family's house in the Riverdale section of the Bronx. The house was an imposing Georgian-style mansion on a large property in that wealthy neighborhood. Peter introduced me to his mother, Andrea Simon, the widow of the founder of Simon and Schuster, the great New York publishing house. Andrea was beautiful, in her late fifties then, and loved hanging out with Peter's friends, asking about what was going on in their lives and what they thought of current events. She was active in several organizations involved in mental health and civil rights, and "the Simon House" was the scene of regular parties and concerts benefiting her various causes.

We were talking in Andrea's sunroom when a tall girl walked in and sat down. She was very pretty, a little chubby, and very sexy, in a tight white sweater and black hip-hugging trousers. She was shy, this girl. She made only the most fleeting eye contact before lowering her intense gaze. Peter said, "This is my sister Carly." I recognized her immediately: Carly Simon, one of the Simon Sisters. I was taken aback.

"Your sisters are . . . *the Simon Sisters?*" I managed. They laughed at me.

"I saw you on *Hootenanny*!" I blurted. Carly said that a lot of people had seen that show.

Over cups of tea, Carly told me that the Simon Sisters had stopped performing the year before, and that she was trying to write her own songs and get back into the music business. Right now she was trying to break into the jingle industry, supplying themes and ditties for marketing products. I told her my father was in advertising, and asked if I could hear something. So she played a tape of a song called "Summer Is a Wishing Well" for me.

I totally loved it. "Wishing Well" could have been a Top Forty hit record for the Lovin' Spoonful, the Mamas and the Papas, or Strawberry Alarm Clock. It had a sweet little melody and a sighing, double-tracked chorus, Carly singing with herself as if her sister Lucy were there.

From that day on I've followed Carly's career, first as a fan, then as a journalist. I watched her struggle with career and family issues until she launched her run for the rainbow in 1970 with her first solo album. The next year I reviewed her triumphant second album for *Rolling Stone*. I went to those early concerts where she opened for star-quality singer-songwriters such as Cat Stevens and Kris Krist-offerson as she honed her own songwriting skills. I was one of the first people to hear (in Carly's bathroom) the early mixes of "You're So Vain," which Carly had brought back from London, with Mick Jagger's uncredited—and unmistakable—backing vocal on the choruses. The single spent three weeks at number one. The album spent five weeks at the top. Suddenly Carly Simon was one of the booming music industry's most talented and glamorous artists.

Then I watched her try to walk away from it—or at least get it under control. She had married James Taylor, one of the alpha singer-songwriters, in late 1972, and for almost ten years they lived in a celebrity marriage and fame continuum whose ups and downs Carly would chronicle in her heroic run of hit singles and bestselling albums in the seventies.

I didn't see as much of Carly in those years, because she and James were reclusive—he was a heroin addict throughout their marriage—and she had retired from performing to raise their two children, Sally and Ben. But I stayed in touch, and parsed the lyrics of her latest albums to see what was going on, because Carly has always used the stuff of her life to inform the lyrics of her songs. After her marriage was over and as her children were growing up, Carly went back to work, and has been working ever since. Her output has been prodigious—thirty albums at this writing, not to mention the Oscar-winning film scores, an opera, and five books. She's still working as I write. She recently told me that she would like to retire, but she can't—yet. Legions of people depend on her generosity.

During those years, those decades, I've kept watch—sometimes with amazement. It has been a special experience for me to see how the shy ingenue—my friend's sister—matured into one of music's most influential and beloved singer-songwriters, one who was even inducted into the exclusive Songwriters Hall of Fame. (George Gershwin—who was friends with Carly's parents in the 1930s—move over.) I sometimes played a minor role here and there: writing about Carly, interviewing her for a special program on the cable channel VH-1, writing the booklet notes for her 2004 release, *Reflections: Carly Simon's Greatest Hits.*

What has always drawn me to Carly's music was an acute and critical (and self-critical) intelligence, and an almost therapeutic ability to conjure empathy and compassion via the popular ballad. And it's not just me and her other fans who feel this way. Carly's masterpiece "Let the River Run" has become a bipartisan national anthem, used by the government to calm the nation after September 11, 2001, and later to inspire hope and action during Barack Obama's own run for the rainbow in 2008.

Carly Simon has had a life and career that need to be documented while most of the dramatis personae are still around. Carly's story is a page-turner—one of ambition overcoming severe neuroses, of continuing survival of the many battles that life makes us fight: stage fright, addiction, marriages; loss of loved ones, serial heartbreak, death by cancer; corporate incompetence, corruption, and greed; the sense, at a certain age, that time is closing in.

One of the things I do is work with rock stars on their memoirs, and for many years I've been trying to work with Carly in this way, but she has always held back. Someday she will probably write her own story, but until then, this book hopes to be a record of the true adventures of Carly Simon, in her time. This version must recommend itself as "unauthorized," although Carly—generous in spirit—has occasionally helped me with matters of description and accuracy. Despite her jealously guarded wish for privacy, if you have her e-mail address, she's a sucker for provocation, and will probably reply.

The epochal era of the rock star is winding down now. Most of the gods and goddesses have been celebrated and elegized, but not all. If you, like me, feel that you've been touched by her sun, Carly Simon's music will live on, as long as it remains in the keeping of those who understand its value, its deeper meaning, and the transcendental distinction of her wonderful songs.

A few months after I met Carly, I accompanied her mother and brother to the island of Martha's Vineyard, off the coast of Cape Cod, where her family had spent many summers of her childhood. Andrea Simon wanted to buy a house on the island, and Peter and I kept her company while she was shown various properties. This was early June 1968.

One day we were swimming at a spectacular beach called Zack's Cliffs, then owned by the Hornblower family. Peter was trying to tune in a New York Mets baseball game on his portable radio when we heard a bulletin that Robert Kennedy had been assassinated in Los Angeles while running for president. Suddenly a beautiful day turned into something else.

That night we were all exhausted, and Peter went to bed early. Andrea and I stayed up, talking about what had happened that day.

We were smoking, taking cigarettes from her pack of Kools on the kitchen table.

"Andy," I said, "I thought only black people smoke Kools."

Carly's mother looked at me and laughed.

"Why, dahling," she said with a laugh, "don't you know?—I *am* black."

I asked her to explain, and for the next hour or so Andrea Simon told me a story, a fantastic tale, about her mysterious grandmother, and the king of Spain.

Part

I

LADY OF SPAIN

———

*I*n the time of King Alfonso XII, in the 1870s, a young Moroccan girl was working in one of the palaces in Madrid when a member of the royal family got her with child. No one would say who the father was. The king's own legitimacy was often questioned, since his mother, Isabella II, had reputedly been profligate with her guardsmen before she was driven into exile.

As often happened in cases where the royal family required discretion, the young maid was spirited out of the realm, in her case to Cuba, Spain's thriving colonial possession across the Atlantic. There she gave birth to a daughter, and disappeared from history. The little girl was put up for adoption at a Catholic orphanage. Only the name her mother had called her, Chebe, and her nameless mother's registered identity, "a Moor," were left as clues as to whose child she was. ("Chebe" is very close to *cheba,* an endearing term for a young girl in Moroccan Arabic.) But the nuns gossiped that the little Moorish maid had indeed told them who the baby's father was. The Mother

Superior in Havana let it be known that the Sisters had something really special for the right family seeking to adopt a child.

In any event, this possibly royal child was adopted in Cuba by a family called Del Rio and taken by steamer to New Orleans. Her name was now officially Elma Maria Del Rio, but somehow, inexplicably, the name Chebe stayed with her. Around the turn of the twentieth century, she grew into a beautiful young woman with curls around a cherubic face. By the time she was sixteen, she could speak five languages, not all that unusual in polyglot New Orleans. Before she was twenty she was married (or married off, thinks her eldest granddaughter) to a man from Philadelphia named Heinemann, who took her to live in that city's leafy suburb Germantown.

Chebe, as she was still called, then produced two sons, Fred and Peter. In 1909 her daughter, Andrea, was born. The family, nominally Catholic, lived with little money in a state of shabby gentility, and then was abandoned by Mr. Heinemann when Andrea was three years old. Genteel poverty followed, but Chebe insisted on certain standards, and while sometimes there wasn't enough food on the table, they always had tickets to the opera and properly stylish clothes to wear. Sheebie was extremely secretive about herself, and where she came from. She told her children about the connection to a royal person of Spain, glamorizing her origins, but would never say anything more, possibly because that was all she'd learned, or could remember. (One family legend has her born in Valencia, Spain. In this telling, a maid was ordered to throw her off the ship carrying her and her mother to Cuba. The maid refused, or hid the child, and then presented her to the Cuban nuns.) When Andrea and her brothers begged for more information, Chebe would only smile and tell them, "When I die, you will know *nothing* about me. But . . . *nothing*!"

Andrea Heinemann was a star from the beginning. Like her mother, she was petite, dark-skinned, with long curly brown hair and deep brown eyes. She had a sensational figure, was a natural athlete, and sang with a trilling soprano that enlivened many a night spent passing sheet music around the piano. Andrea left junior high school at fourteen to support her mother, working first at John Wanamaker's opulent department store. Then, around 1930, having learned that her drunken husband could be found, literally, in the gutter, Chebe relocated to New York with her three children. Andrea quickly found work as a sales clerk at B. Altman, the great department store on Fifth Avenue. She rode the streetcar to work every day, and by the time the Great Depression began to shut down the American economy, she was the sole means of support for her mother, her brothers, and a boyfriend.

Andrea was also a face in New York's night life, a girl-about-town, popular in both bohemian circles in Greenwich Village and post-debutante society on the Upper East Side. She had an unusual style, pairing her mother's elegant velvet dresses with saddle shoes and no makeup. She was so pretty, so funny, so intelligent, and sang like a lark ascending. She was sexy, the life of the party, great at games and outdoor sports, fun at the beach, and everyone loved her.

Still, things got bad for Andrea and her family in 1933, as the Great Depression kicked in. The country was in a terrible slump, and the new president, Franklin Roosevelt—Andrea knew his playboy son Jimmy—was driving economic reforms that would change the country. Andrea's hours at B. Altman got cut back. Through some musical friends, she took a job at H. Ditson and Company, the old music store on Thirty-fourth Street, off Fifth Avenue. There she waited on many of the great figures of Broadway and popular music, especially the hot young composer George Gershwin, a regular customer.

"I liked working there," she remembered, "selling sheet music and records and just talking about music. The only problem was that I was standing and walking, all day, and my feet hurt all the time. I think I weighed about ninety pounds."

Then one day, on her lunch hour, Andrea bumped into a friend named Jack Goodman, who was a young editor at Simon and

Schuster, the famous publishing company. Jack asked Andrea how she was, and she told him that her feet were aching.

"Jack then mentioned there was an opening at his company for a switchboard operator, with experience preferred. I said, 'Oh Jack— *anything* to sit down.' I told him I had no experience at operating a switchboard, but that I was absolutely brilliant at connecting with people. He suggested I come over that very afternoon and he would arrange an interview.

"I couldn't go to Simon and Schuster in my casual work clothes, so I went to B. Altman and borrowed something smart from a rack the store kept for employees who might need to change clothes. I went over to S&S, and told them that I was a *telephoniste* par excellence. Jack Goodman put in a good word, and the next day they told me I'd gotten the job."

That summer, Andrea started working at S&S, commuting to its Fifty-seventh Street offices via the Third Avenue elevated train. She learned the spaghetti cords of the switchboard system quickly, and soon was a popular and crucial employee. Jack Goodman introduced her to colleagues who, over time, became publishing legends, such as S&S co-founder Max Schuster and the marketing genius Nina Bourne, who was then secretary to the firm's other cofounder, Richard Simon.

Mr. Simon, Andrea noticed, wasn't around the office as much as Mr. Schuster. He was always out meeting people, having long lunches with his authors, handling the social side of the business, while Mr. Schuster minded the shop. Judging by the large number of calls from young ladies that she directed to Mr. Simon's office, Andrea inferred that the thirty-four-year-old publishing mogul was a serious ladies' man-about-town. One day she put through a call to Mr. Simon from Mr. Gershwin, and discovered the two men were good friends.

She finally met Dick Simon when the tall, balding, charismatic publisher came striding down the hall one day and suddenly stopped by her switchboard. Andrea flashed her incandescent smile. He looked down at her for a second and said, "Hello, little woman."

She said, "Hello, big man."

"He was six foot four inches, you know," Andrea recalled forty years later. "And right off the bat, when I saw Dick—*the minute I looked at him*—I knew that there was going to be something between Simon and me. And, God—was he handsome! Devastatingly handsome. Absolutely . . . beautiful. What is it, about those tall men?"

The Pianist

———

"Actually," says Carly, "my father wanted to be a pianist more than he wanted to be a publisher." This was from one of her earliest press interviews, in 1971. "It was just one of those flukes. His father was a businessman who said, 'Now, sonny, you've got to be into business too.' So my father started a publishing company with a friend of his from college, Max Schuster, but they weren't sure what they wanted to publish. They rented an office on West Fifty-seventh Street in New York, just one little room. Anyway, the story goes that they went out to lunch on the first day and had to hang a sign on the door that said Simon & Schuster, and they just decided, 'What the hell? Books!' So they were book publishers from then on. I don't know how true it is, but that's the story they told me."

Dick Simon was born Richard L. Simon in New York City in 1899. His father, Leo, was a prosperous merchant who imported rare feathers and silk ribbons to adorn the lavish hats that fashionable ladies wore in Edwardian times. The family lived in a town house on the Upper West Side. Dick's mother, Anna, had three other sons and a daughter, and all five children were given liberal private educations—the family was Jewish but secular and assimilated; spiritual guidance was provided via the New York Society for Ethical Culture—and were exposed to the music of the era's greatest concert halls. All the Simon brothers, except Dick, would have distinguished professional careers in some area of music. George Simon would be a talented drummer and jazz writer. Henry Simon was a musicologist and opera expert. Alfred Simon became a programmer on radio station WQXR. Their first cousin, Robert Simon, was the first music critic at the fledgling *New Yorker* magazine. But, then, Dick was the most talented musician in the family.

He took to the piano and its classical literature with great passion and an incredible facility. He practiced every chance he could. He would go into raptures just talking about Beethoven and Wagner. Already tall by the time he was sixteen, with powerful hands and long fingers, he enjoyed a physical mastery of the mighty Steinway piano in the Simon living room, and constantly practiced the most difficult works of the German composers—Brahms, Schubert, Schumann. He would go into a trancelike state and play Chopin's piano music for five hours at a time. Dick had ideas about serious piano studies in a proper conservatory. He was naturally charismatic, with ferocious energy and a serious, instinctive understanding of the piano repertoire. His teachers told him he could easily enjoy a professional career, but his father insisted he attend Columbia College instead. There he became expert in bridge, gin rummy, and other card games. He also developed into a talented amateur photographer.

His mother died when Dick was eighteen, and it changed his life in many ways. In her final illness she had been taken care of by a Swiss woman named Josephine Hutsmacher, who had become a dear family friend. After his wife died, Leo Simon asked her to stay on and look after the family. Aunt Jo, as she was called, took Anna's place at the age of about thirty-six, but not in Leo Simon's bed. The bed she shared was Dick's, as the attractive and intelligent immigrant spinster and the grieving younger man became lovers not long after Anna's death. This intense relationship—Dick and Aunt Jo—would last through the whole of Richard Simon's too-brief lifetime. At one point he asked her to marry him, and was turned down by the warm and loving but very practical woman.

In 1922, with a fresh degree from Columbia College, Dick Simon again contemplated studying to become a concert pianist, but again he followed his father's advice: this time that he get a job and support himself. The job he landed was with the Aeolian Piano Company, where he quickly became one of the firm's star salesmen by dazzling potential customers in the showroom on Forty-second Street with rippling impromptus by Chopin and Liszt. He was au fait with all the latest music—Debussy, Ravel, Satie, George Gershwin. Dick Simon could make a piano flutter like the wings of a moth or chime like bells in a cathedral. He was that good.

One day in 1923 he paid a sales call on an acquaintance, to try to sell him a piano. This was Max Schuster, whom he'd known at college. Schuster was about Dick's age and had an interest in trade journals and stationery stores in Harlem and the Bronx. Simon and Schuster bonded over a new biography of Beethoven that Schuster had on his desk. Over several meetings the ambitious young men decided to go into publishing together, with Dick as the idea man and marketer and Max as the editorial presence. They raised eight thousand dollars from family and friends and opened the firm of Simon and Schuster on West Fifty-seventh Street in Midtown Manhattan in late 1924.

Their very first product took off. At the time, in the Roaring Twenties, there was a craze for crossword puzzles, which appeared in the daily and Sunday newspapers. Dick had an aunt who was addicted to the puzzles; she often complained that she had to wait a whole day before the next puzzle appeared. Dick's idea was to commission 50 new crossword puzzles and bundle them into a book, with a yellow pencil attached. Within a year S&S had sold 370,000 puzzle books and the young firm was a phenomenon in the staid world of publishing.

Dick Simon was brimming with ideas, a razzle-dazzle marketer. He advertised his new books, individually, in newspapers and magazines. This was unheard of then, since books were expected to succeed by positive reviews, bookseller recommendations, and word of mouth. He wanted to put popular books between soft covers and sell them cheaply. He wanted to get his products out of stodgy bookstores and into populist dime stores. He persuaded the bridge expert Charles H. Coren to share his secrets, and the book *Contract Bridge for Beginners* sold 997,000 copies in the first year. He published Dale Carnegie's *How to Win Friends and Influence People,* which became a bible for salesmen and sold in the millions, for decades. Seeking to enter the juvenile market, Dick partnered with an obscure Wisconsin company, Western Publishing, and came up with Little Golden Books. S&S published popular novels such as James Hilton's *Lost Horizon,* and Will and Ariel Durant's multivolume histories of philosophy, big books that were ordered by every public library in America. Robert Ripley's highly popular *Believe It or Not!* was a major bestseller. Albert Einstein and Leon Trotsky were both signed up by Dick. Simon and Schuster is generally credited with pioneering the sales techniques of the modern publishing industry. When twenty-four-year-old Andrea Heinemann arrived at the company's switchboard in 1933, S&S was the hottest mainstream publisher in New York, and Dick Simon was already a wealthy and influential man.

MRS. SIMON AND SCHUSTER

$\mathcal{A}$ndrea Heinemann, working the telephones at Simon and Schuster in 1933, began dating one of the firm's writers. Neil Vanderbilt, author of *Farewell to Fifth Avenue,* was actually Cornelius Vanderbilt IV, the charming heir to one of America's greatest fortunes. At the same time, Andrea was enjoying a flirtation with her boss, Dick Simon, who often looked into the switchboard/reception area to see how she was getting along.

Andrea remembered: "Neil would pick me up in his chauffeured Duesenberg, and we'd go to the Plaza Hotel, or the Ritz, the Biltmore—anywhere we could have dinner and dance. Neil was a great dancer and very attractive. He wasn't my type at all, but at least I was eating well. These were hard times, you know, so eating out was a big attraction. The first time I requested a doggie bag for my untouched prime rib supper at the Waldorf Astoria Hotel, Neil was so mortified that I thought he would drop under the table."

"I didn't know you had a dog," he stammered.

"Oh yes," she lied. "I have three." She was thinking of her two brothers and her boyfriend, Ernest.

In the spring of 1934, Neil invited Andrea to the Kentucky Derby, where Vanderbilt horses were in the running.

"When Neil asked me to the Derby, I felt I had to ask Mr. Simon if Simon and Schuster had a company policy about employees dating the writers."

Dick Simon looked at her. "Why do you ask?" She told him.

"As of now, yes, there is a policy."

"After that, I couldn't get rid of him." It was embarrassing at the office. Instead of huddling with Schuster in the Inner Sanctum, the conference room between their offices, Simon was loitering around the switchboard. *Let's go have lunch. There's Gershwin music at Carnegie Hall tonight. Let's go to a show.*

"Finally I conceded. He took me to Longchamps for dinner, and laughed when I asked for a doggie bag. He wasn't embarrassed at all, unlike poor Neil."

She loved being around him. There were many more dinner dates. "He was charming, fun, delightful to be with. He took me to so many concerts, mostly piano recitals, and then we would go to his apartment in Greenwich Village and he would play the same music as the pianist at Carnegie Hall—only better. And I just loved to look at him. I loved to sing, and we'd perform together in his apartment—German lieder, show tunes. I'd sing and he would play. Cole Porter, you know? 'Night and Day.' He was just an incredible pianist, and could have been a major artist if he'd been encouraged to.

"So now, when his girlfriends called the office, I would say I was sorry but Mr. Simon is tied up. He's in conference. He isn't in today. I threw the message slips away, and wondered if they asked him why he hadn't called them back."

There was also a downside to Dick. He was easily distracted, and she could see he sometimes lost interest when she spoke. His nervous tics included tapping piano fingerboard exercises on the table during dinner. There was his unusual relationship with the Simon family's former governess, "Auntie Jo," one that was hard for Andrea to figure out. He intimated that he had gotten one of his girlfriends pregnant, and that she was having his child. (An illegitimate son was indeed born in 1935.)

It took Dick Simon a year to propose to Andrea. It came on a June evening in 1934, after they had driven out to Long Beach in Dick's snazzy Ford coupe. At the end of the day, he drove her back to her family's flat under the Ninth Avenue El.

"He got out and opened my door, put his hands on my waist, and lifted me up onto the running board. He looked up at me—the first time he'd ever looked *up* to me. He said, 'Let's get married.' My knees turned to water. I thought about fainting.

"I said, 'I think we better do a little talking.' He said, 'We talk all the time.' So I threw myself against him and kissed him until I really did think I would faint."

Dick and Andrea went back to Dick's apartment on West Eleventh Street and made love for the first time. Afterward, as Andrea was drifting off to sleep in Dick's bed, she could hear him in the other room expertly playing a gentle piano nocturne by Claude Debussy.

"The next day, I told my supervisor he should forget about my request for a raise—I was getting eighteen dollars a week—because I no longer worked for Simon and Schuster. 'From now on,' I told him, 'I just work for Simon.' "

Henry Luce's *Time* magazine was cutting-edge journalism in Depression-era America. In the July 30, 1934, issue's "Milestones" section, *Time* noted that former president Herbert Hoover's secretary was engaged; that the Episcopal bishop of Montana had drowned in a creek; that a prominent yachtsman had hanged himself; that a five-time U.S. women's golf champion had given birth in Philadelphia; and, somewhat snidely, this: "Engaged: Richard Leo Simon, 34, Manhattan publisher (Simon & Schuster: cross word puzzles; *The*

Story of Philosophy; *Trader Horn*); and Andrea Heinemann, his office telephone operator."

Dick Simon's surviving notes and love letters to his intended bride over the next few months indicate that he was deeply in love with her, but the honeymoon didn't go well. Dick took Andrea to Hawaii, but he told her he felt ill. He was very conflicted and guilty about his abiding love for Auntie Jo, and sent an almost daily stream of cables to his older mistress from the islands. The marriage, according to Andrea, was not consummated on the honeymoon. The unhappy couple returned to New York, confused and emotionally exhausted, but both were determined to make the marriage work. Dick Simon plunged into his business. Andrea jokingly introduced herself to people as "Mrs. Simon and Schuster," which annoyed Max Schuster's much older (and very proper) wife.

SUMMERTIME

——

*O*ne day in early 1935 the telephone rang in Dick Simon's apartment at 245 West Eleventh Street. George Gershwin was on the line, elated, he said, because he had finished the score of what he'd been calling his new folk opera. He told Dick that he was coming over to play some of it, to see what he and Andrea thought of this new music.

George Gershwin, at thirty-seven, a year older than Dick, was the most important composer working in America then. It was a particularly fruitful era, as the other New York composers and lyricists of what has come to be called the Great American Songbook—Irving Berlin, Cole Porter, Jerome Kern, Richard Rodgers—were also at the top of their form. (Duke Ellington was uptown in Harlem, having his own epiphanies.) In an era that has been compared to Renaissance England or the Athens of Pericles, the popular song flourished with the twentieth century's new electric technologies. Radio, the microphone, vinyl recordings, and talking pictures ensured that singing itself would be more vibrant, less operatic, jazzier, even bluesy. But George Gershwin's music transcended American popular song and his Tin Pan Alley origins. The great orchestral works of his (and the century's) twenties—the *Concerto in F, Rhapsody in Blue, An American in Paris*—were among the first to infuse blues and jazz styles into the orchestral repertoire. At the same time, a new Gershwin musical comedy seemed to surface almost every season on Broadway, all must-see shows of the day: *Lady Be Good, Funny Face, Show Girl, Girl Crazy, Oh, Kay!* Gershwin's Manhattan apartment was Jazz Central for all the hot songwriters. Dick Simon was accepted in this elite circle as a musician and even a peer. He idolized Gershwin, who returned the admiration by asking for Dick's opinion of his newest music.

When George Gershwin arrived at the Simons' apartment, he put the handwritten score for *Porgy and Bess* on the piano, sat down, and played most of the new songs and themes of his opera about the trials and tribulations of the colored folk on Catfish Row. Andrea and Dick listened, in awe, to the composer playing "It Ain't Necessarily So," "My Man's Gone Now," "I Loves You, Porgy," and the sublime "Summertime." Gershwin, normally reserved, seemed elated as he played, and this was matched by the growing excitement of his tiny audience, the first (astonished) people to hear this avant-garde, inspiring opera based on American blues and spirituals.

Gershwin thanked his friends for the praise and then asked a favor. Here are the lyrics for "Summertime." Would Andrea mind singing them, with Dick playing piano? This way, Gershwin could hear the song for the first time with fresh ears. This was daunting, but Andrea said she'd give it a try. Dick ran through the piano arrangement once, and then Andrea began to sing.

It didn't work. "Summertime" has melodic curves that soar over operatic octaves, and Andrea wasn't much of a sight reader. Then she went off-key, and Dick banged the keyboard. "No darling," he scolded her, peevish. "Not like *that*. Like . . . *this*." He played the passage again, but Andrea couldn't get it right. It was the first time that Dick had ever expressed disappointment in her. She felt humiliated, but Gershwin consoled her, and told them he hadn't realized that "Summertime" might be the most difficult thing to sing he had ever written.

Two years later, in 1937, Gershwin died of a heart attack in Hollywood, not even forty years old. Dick and Andrea were as shocked as everyone at the loss of an indispensable American musical genius. An inscribed photograph of Gershwin reposed in a silver frame was in every Simon family living room in which Carly grew up.

Andrea Simon's first child, born in 1937, was named Joanna by her father, after his two mothers, Anna and Auntie Jo. (This name wasn't Andrea's first choice.) "Joey" was the first grandchild in the family, and was much doted on and fussed over until 1940, when a second daughter, Lucy, was born. World War II began for America in late 1941, and a third daughter, Carly Elizabeth Simon, was born toward its conclusion. Carly was named after Carly Wharton, the wife of one of Dick's colleagues. During the war years, Andrea left the children with nannies while serving five days a week as a uniformed driver for senior military officers in New York. She later said that her preoccupied husband never learned of this job, and would have disapproved. She would arrive home before he did, change from uniform to house dress, and tell Dick the children had run her ragged all day.

In 1944, Dick and Max sold Simon and Schuster to the mercantile tycoon Marshall Field III, who owned the *Chicago Sun-Times,* with the proviso that both men stay on to run the successful company. This sale made Dick Simon a millionaire, and the family's situation now changed with this new wealth. First Dick bought an entire apartment building, at 130 West Eleventh Street, where he installed his growing family and those of his brothers and sister, now Mrs. Seligman. Andrea's two brothers, Peter and Fred, also had flats, and both Chebe and Auntie Jo lived there, as did other Simon friends and retainers. Then Dick bought a large sporting estate in rural Stamford, Connecticut, about an hour's drive north. The sixty-four-acre property featured a colonnaded mansion on Newfield Avenue, conveniently near the Merritt Parkway; a large swimming pool and a tennis court; mature orchards and playing fields where the dogs could run; a gentleman's barn and cottages that Dick rented to favored S&S authors in the summertime. Andrea remade the Stamford estate into a home/resort/summer camp, with comfortable guest accommodation, and for the next fifteen years the Stamford house was a playground where Dick and Andrea's children gamboled in the idyllic landscape and where Dick entertained celebrity authors such as Albert Einstein and Pearl Buck, star-quality professional athletes (Jackie Robinson; tennis hero Don Budge), famous academics (historian Louis Untermeyer was thought to be adequate in left field in family softball games), and musical friends from Broadway and the arts. A weekend invitation to the Simons' house in Connecticut was a coveted prize in the New York of the late forties and early fifties. Andrea and a staff of cooks, nannies, housekeepers, gardeners, and chauffeurs pulled all this together, whatever was needed. "Publishing is very social," she later recalled. "My husband, as they used to say, was a guest in his own house." Dick's intensely competitive card games, fueled with tobacco and gin and tonics, went late into the summer nights while the children slept upstairs. This was mostly bridge, and a variation of bridge called Fornication (also known as Oh Hell!), because the winner usually ended up screwing his opponents. Bandleader Benny Goodman, the King of Swing, was a regular at Dick's card table during those years.

"Our family had a house in Stamford," Carly said much later. "The house had a large barn, a play barn with a stage, and we used to put on plays, most often musical productions. We rehearsed, had my mother's old ball gowns and mantillas for costumes, lots and lots of hair and makeup. That's really the way we got into music, my sisters and I. We put on ballets, all kinds of plays. And my older sister [Joey] wanted to be an actress, but she wasn't sure if she wanted to be that, or a ballet dancer, or an opera singer. So one night at dinner, some famous writer asked Joey, who was maybe 12, which she wanted to be—actress, dancer, opera star—and she earnestly asked back, 'Which one has more maids?'

"This brought the house down. Someone told Joey that opera singers had the most maids. Joey began to study opera."

Carly Simon's earliest memories are of these two family homes, the cozy brick building, smelling of home cooking, in the West Village; and the imposing but relaxed country house in Stamford. Unlike her two older sisters, Carly was an insecure baby, who then became a crying toddler who could find consolation only in the arms of the family's housekeeper, Allie Brennan, who would rock crying Carly to bed when the child woke up, frightened by her troubled dreams.

BEHIND CLOSED DOORS

$\mathcal{G}$reenwich Village in the late 1940s: cobblestone streets, old red-brick buildings, leafy streets in September. The Richard Simons have the first television in the communal apartment building. The black-and-white screen is the size of a toaster. The kids watch *Howdy Doody* in the evenings. The adults watch Dodger games from Brooklyn and Arturo Toscanini conducting the NBC Symphony Orchestra. Carly follows her sisters to the City and Country School, a progressive private school favored by the neighborhood's well-off bohemians and socialists. Carly is a head taller than the tallest boy, and this makes her self-conscious and nervous. In kindergarten her music teacher is Pete Seeger, who is earning a modest living teaching kids after being blacklisted from show business for his erstwhile membership in the American Communist Party. "He taught us all the old Lefty songs," Carly recalls. " 'This Land Is Your Land.' Woody Guthrie's songs. 'Big Rock Candy Mountain.' He played his guitar or his banjo, and we kids were just enthralled."

It was a relief to her when her brother was born, because she was no longer the youngest in the family. Now the spotlight was directed elsewhere, yet Carly remained an awkward shadow of her two older sisters. She took ballet lessons when she was four, from Lucy's teacher, but it didn't work. "Actually, they kicked me out, because I stuck my tongue out to the side of my mouth, quite innocently and quirkily, while learning first, second, third, and especially fourth positions." She entered the musical life of the family when she sang in Uncle Henry's choir in their building at 133 West Eleventh Street. Henry Simon was the musical editor of Simon and Schuster and an authority on the history of the Metropolitan Opera. He took it upon himself to organize the Simon family into singing weekly rehearsals of classical pieces on Sunday afternoons. (The building's Italian super was the lead tenor.) But Carly couldn't keep a straight face during the rehearsals. She was always goofing off, cracking up Lucy and their cousins. This drove Henry Simon crazy. "This would be a *good* choir," he would fume, "if it weren't for those annoying Simon sisters."

Sunday evenings often featured family musicals. The girls would sing show tunes, accompanied by Dick. Joanna displayed the fruit of her vocal lessons. Uncle George Simon was a drummer who had helped organize the Glen Miller Orchestra and was a prominent jazz critic. Andrea's brother Peter Dean managed cabaret acts—Peggy Lee was an early client—and played a mean ukulele. He teamed up with his brother Fred, called Dutch, to entertain with funny songs and jazzy rhythms. The whole building on West Eleventh Street was a music box, almost every Sunday.

Carly: "Being the youngest girl, I always felt I had to perform in order to get any love at all in my family. I had two older sisters who were both very beautiful and very talented and very much the apples of my father's eye. And, I suppose, my mother's eye, too. I remember all this, from very early on. It is who I am today. When I was four years old and Peter had just been born, Lucy was seven and very angelically shy. Lucy was incredible even then—very attractively innocent and reticent. Hard to get. And Joey, our older sister: ten years old, very sophisticated, good makeup already—a budding actress and singer. Friends of my parents—some of them famous— would come over and ask Joey to sing.

"I remember that baby Peter had a nurse who came to the family just after he was born. Her name was Helen Gaspard and she was introduced to the rest of the family, to the three girls in order of age. Joey came first and, in a very dignified voice, greeted her with, 'How do you do?' And Lucy also said, 'How do you do?' And I thought, *My God! Here are my two sisters, and they seem to have taken up the whole road. You know? These girls have got all the corners filled. What do I do to be . . . different from them?* So I jumped up on the coffee table. I'd just been taken to see *The Jolson Story* at the movies. I jumped on the coffee table, spread out my arms, and said to her: 'HI!'

"Looking back at this, I obviously felt I had to be different—in a performing sense. The pressure was somehow put on me—at the age of four—to stand out in my own way. Not just to be normal, or to be whatever I felt like being. I had to choose a role early on. That was what my family obviously wanted from me."

It was also around the age of four when Carly began to have serious fears in the night. She would come out of her room, after being put to bed, shaking in terror at the dark. It took tremendous energy to calm her and convince her she wouldn't die during the night. A Scots nanny hired by Andrea made the situation even worse. "This woman put stuffed animals under my bed," Carly recalls. "She told me they would come to life and bite me if I got out of bed one more time."

One night when Carly was eight, she had a high fever. Her mother was sitting with her, pressing a cool cloth to her forehead. In her delirium Carly told her mother she could see tiny panda bears crawling up the floral wallpaper in her bedroom. "My darling," Andrea soothed, "you have such an *imagination*." This was the first time Carly heard that word.

In 1950—the year the Weavers were hot on the radio with the Israeli folk song "Tzena Tzena Tzena," which spent thirteen weeks at number one and was a big jam in the Simon household—Andrea Simon told her husband that she wanted to raise their children in a greener environment. This was fine with him, because he'd just received his umpteenth traffic ticket for parking in front of his building. Dick Simon quickly bought a large brick house in the Fieldston section of Riverdale, a suburban enclave in the northern Bronx. The Steinway piano and the large portrait of Brahms were moved into the new house's spacious living room. Dick added a library wing to the right of the dining room and built a state-of-the-art darkroom for his photographic hobby. Carly and her teddy bear were moved into the smallest of the six upstairs bedrooms, her bed and bureau tucked under low eaves. This is where she tried to fall asleep as her restless father poured out his pianism in the evenings, downstairs, sometimes for hours at a time.

In this era, Richard Simon was becoming somewhat abstracted from his family. There were difficulties at Simon and Schuster, where he felt shunted aside by younger editors and was no longer the boss. His emotional life was complicated by his feelings for Auntie Jo and a general estrangement from Andrea after Peter was born. (Andrea, years later: "I think he thought I was too black.")

Ever the dutiful son-in-law, and whatever else, Dick now installed Chebe and Auntie Jo in a comfortable apartment of their own on the Upper West Side. The old girls liked to watch TV in the evenings, in their bathrobes.

When he moved his family to Riverdale, Dick Simon would arrive home in the evening and retire to his library, to unwind behind closed doors. Andrea had strict instructions that he not be disturbed until he emerged from his smoke-filled lair. He would have his supper, and then play the piano after Joanna's vocal exercises were complete. He often gathered the children to listen as he read favorite poems aloud. Sometimes the verses, especially those of Walt Whitman, would make Dick Simon mist over.

THE ARTFUL DODGER

———

*C*arly Simon remembers her childhood with very mixed emotions, because she was only barely comfortable in her own skin. "I was the little girl in the back of the line in first grade, kind of hiding because I'm so tall." Carly's clothes didn't really fit her, having been inherited from her older sisters, the hems let way out so she could wear them. She was very shy in school because she stuttered when under pressure. "I was scared of answering questions in class, of giving a speech, or reading a poem."

When Carly was nine she told her mother that she didn't think her father cared for her. "By the time I came along, I think the novelty had worn off for my father—the third girl child, you know? And also, around then there was some turmoil in his work, and he wasn't able or willing to be close to me. So I sincerely felt he didn't love me." Andrea assured her this wasn't so, but Carly didn't believe her. Dick Simon was distracted and distant from her; she could feel it. Family members say that Dick had indeed wanted a boy and was disappointed in a third daughter. Her father's evident preference for her sister Lucy made his seeming rejection even more difficult. But Carly was determined somehow to find a way into Dick Simon's heart.

"My oldest sister, Joey, was always very sophisticated. She was born that way and allowed to be that way—very poised and theatrical. She did her own makeup from age ten. Lucy was another way: shy, angelic, sweet and soft, and adorable. I remember thinking to myself, literally thinking this . . . that I had to make a conscious decision to decide who I had to be in this family.

"Well, okay. The ingénue's role had been filled by Lucy. The sophisticate's role had been taken by Joey. So I chose my role. The comedian had not been filled yet."

Andrea encouraged Carly in this. "I think my mother knew, early on, that I wasn't terribly interesting to my father. She used to give me little tips on how to win him. She'd tell me, 'Go into his room, darling, and make a funny face.' So I developed a repertoire of faces. I did cartwheels. I made jokey noises. And sometimes it worked. He would react. He'd laugh. He'd tell me I was funny. So I felt that this was the way I could win my father over to me. You can see this in most of the photos he took of me. I'm grinning, being a goofball, showing the gaps in my teeth. I'm playing the clown to get his attention because I had to compete for it with my sisters."

Carly began piano lessons when she was eight. But even this was fraught with difficulties when her father was around. "He was an incredible pianist, but this was only well known to his friends. A famous musician like Arthur Rubinstein would come to our house and ask my father to play Chopin so he could study his technique.

"I started to learn to play, but then I developed a phobia about the piano. If my father was around when I was practicing, he'd say, 'No darling, you play it like *this*,' and I would have to get up and he would sit down, and then he'd forget I was practicing and he'd play for an hour. After a year of this, when I was nine, I had to stop taking lessons."

Carly stayed away from the piano until she wrote the melody to

"That's the Way I Always Heard It Should Be" on the piano, fifteen years later.

What finally cemented the bond between Carly and her father, at least for a couple of years in the early fifties, was their shared love of the Brooklyn Dodgers. And the Simons weren't ordinary baseball fans. Dick's friendships with the Dodgers' management and players ensured that when he took Carly to home games at Ebbets Field, they often sat in the Dodgers' dugout.

Dick Simon had long been a Dodgers fan, and this ardor increased after the team broke the color barrier by signing the brilliant short-stop Jackie Robinson in 1947. Robinson was a great athlete and a ferocious competitor, whose youthful zeal matured into righteous fury when he was subjected to racist slurs, obviously deliberate bean balls, and gratuitous spikings for being the first black player in base-ball's major leagues. By 1952, Robinson was one of the most famous sports figures in America, having helped the Dodgers win the National League pennant in 1949, and having opened the gates to other black talent, including Duke Snider and Roy Campanella on his own team.

Dick Simon wanted Simon and Schuster to publish Robinson's biography, and approached him through the Dodgers. Jackie brought his wife to Stamford for the weekend, and Andrea Simon bonded with Rachel Robinson immediately. Soon the Robinsons and their children, Jackie Jr., Sharon, and David, were regular guests on New-field Avenue, for them a safe haven from the glare of sports celebrity and the occasional threats on Jackie's life.

In the spring of 1952, Dick Simon started bringing Carly along with him to Dodgers home games. Joey and Lucy weren't interested in baseball, and Peter was too young, so Carly got the job of accom-panying her father by default. She was thrilled by this, and by the buzz of being a guest of the Brooklyn Dodgers and a special friend of Jackie Robinson. She learned to mark her scorecard like her dad, and memorized the batting averages of superstars such as Pee Wee Reese and Gil Hodges. On the way to Brooklyn, Carly would quiz her father on baseball statistics. She became a Dodger team mascot, with her own little uniform. Phil Rizzuto would see her and say, "Hi, Carly." So did Don Newcombe.

The Dodgers had narrowly lost the pennant to the rival New York Giants in 1951, so the new season was an exciting time to be a Dodger fan—and there was ecstasy in Brooklyn, and in Riverdale, when the Dodgers won the pennant that year. This immigrant-looking team of Italians and blacks mirrored its polyglot borough of Brooklyn perfectly, especially in 1952, when it went down to defeat by the arch-imperialist New York Yankees, the Bronx Bombers, in the World Series.

"Wait Till Next Year" was the unofficial team slogan.

The Brooklyn Dodgers won the pennant in 1953 as well, and again Dick Simon and his daughter were on hand for many home games. Carly sat on Pee Wee Reese's lap in the Dodger dugout. Father and daughter were growing closer now, and had nicknames for each other. He was Baldy; Carly was Scarlet, or Carlotta. But now that she had partly won over her father, Carly began to lose interest in him. Away from the cocoon of Ebbets Field, Dick would often shrink into himself again. Carly would soon turn for solace to her funny uncles, her mother's brothers, especially irrepressible Peter Dean, who began to take on a more fatherly role for Andrea's youngest children, Carly and Peter.

"My father could be very difficult," Carly said later. "He could be very proper and aristocratic, and then he would burp at the table. He definitely felt that he was terribly, terribly special, and that his children were terribly, terribly special too. He had that complete disregard of reality that all true narcissists have. And this, combined with his strengths, is what made him such a powerful influence on me. He was a very dynamic man, especially when he was younger. People who knew him really loved him, and loved to talk about him. Every day of my life, I still wish I'd known him better."

IDYLLS OF STAMFORD

*T*he Simon estate in Stamford, set in the lush Connecticut countryside, was a childhood paradise for Carly and her siblings, especially during the summertime. "We were the children of the orchard," she recalled, years later. "There was one summer when I spent the whole time up in the fruit trees in our orchard, near the play barn, beyond the huge copper beech. The apple trees were Cortland and McIntosh varieties. There were also two large cherry trees whose bark was rougher on my skin than the apple trees, and so much harder to climb. But, once scaled, the cherry prizes were more thrilling than even the tartest Mac.

"Part of the fun was to savor a sweet, dark purple cherry and then aim the pit at a target below, most often my little brother, Peter, but either of my sisters would do as well. We lived in those trees: me and Joey and Lucy, and Jeanie and Mary Seligman, my cousins. Peter couldn't climb yet, so he ran around below us in his blue corduroy shorts, calling to us to drop him a cherry, please, or just singing or babbling to himself, the only little boy of our tribe."

In those days, the early fifties, Andrea Simon would organize theme summers for the children. One year would be cooking, with a live-in chef. Another would be sewing, with a seamstress. Another would be painting, with an artist in residence. Andrea herself served as a singing teacher. A typical Simon dinner often ended with musical rounds—"Row, row, row your boat," etc.—with family and guests trying to complete the round without goofing up.

"That summer I lived in the trees," Carly recalls, "was the summer of Helen Gaspard. She took care of Peter and was also our in-house playwright and director of the productions we put on for guests in our barn. We learned the lines for *Little Women* sitting in the trees, calling down cues to each other and filling ourselves with fruit. Jeanie and I always had the lesser parts, but we were still young enough to believe Joey when she assured us that even though we only had a line or two, they were pivotal lines, and without them there would be no plot. In the play *The Monkey's Paw,* I merely had to knock on the door. And this was OK because I stuttered . . . could hardly speak. And it was humiliating for me, when people supplied the word I was blocked on, or finished my sentences for me. I didn't even have names for those fears.

"Joey bossed me around a lot. Her technique was to get her way by flattering me. She would always lead me to believe that I was the true star of the show. During the curtain calls, the audience—who were obviously in on the little joke—applauded as if I were Katharine Hepburn. So I definitely grew up with a . . . distorted view of fame."

Carly: "Looking back, I think my childhood was somewhat Chekhovian." This refers to the heartbreaking family dramas of the Russian author Anton Chekhov. "I've seen myself described as the outsider in my family, the black sheep, the ugly duckling. I remember that our extended family played a kind of reverse hide-and-seek game at our house in Connecticut. [This was called Sardines.] The players fanned out over the grounds, and joined each other in hiding until everyone was packed in. The last one out, still searching for the others, was 'it,' and lost the game. And that was always me: the awkward, stuttering child, wandering around alone, at the end of the game—not getting it."

Albert Einstein came to lunch at the mansion in Stamford with its imposing colonnaded verandah. This was a big deal, and there was much housecleaning and preparation. Enormous meals emerged from the kitchen run by Sula, a black cook from the islands, who delivered lobster rolls and peach Melbas to the family and their guests at the swimming pool, barefoot and balancing dishes on her head. Eleanor Roosevelt came for cocktails. The tennis champion Don Budge gave the girls lessons on the family court. Star novelists such as Irwin Shaw lounged by the pool. There were the frequent distinguished guests known as "the Two Bernards"—Baruch and Berenson. Composer Arthur Schwartz, who wrote "Alone Together," and his wife had their own room and came to Stamford almost every weekend. ("They were my parents' closest friends," Carly said.) The Oscar Hammersteins were frequents guests as well, and the girls once rehearsed and performed "A Real Nice Clambake" for the famous songwriter.

Carly: "My mother would say, 'Richard Rodgers and Oscar Hammerstein are coming for dinner tonight. They wrote *South Pacific* and blah blah blah.' After dinner they would sit down at my father's piano and play the score for *Showboat*. I'd enjoy this, but I didn't really understand yet about fame."

There was always a family ball game going on. Sometimes Jackie Robinson would pitch, when he wasn't otherwise occupied in Brooklyn. A typical game on a humid afternoon in August 1954 might have Jackie Jr. playing second base. John Crosby, the television columnist for the *New York Herald Tribune,* is on first. (Crosby rents one of several cottages on the estate.) Don Budge at short. Peter Simon, aged seven, on third. Louis Untermeyer is in center field. Another outfielder is Jonathan Schwartz, age fifteen, who has lived with the Simons in the summer after his mother's early death. (Jonno, as he's known, has a mad crush on Lucy, but then everyone does.) Kim Rosen—Peter's best friend, who lives next door to the Simons on Grosvenor Avenue in Riverdale—is in right field.

The batter, in a floral bathing suit, is Carly Simon, about eleven. She's holding a tennis racket because the game is softball, but with a tennis ball and racket. The pitcher is Carly's uncle Peter Dean. He delivers a softy to her, underhanded.

"Carly tags one," Jonno later wrote. "Her run is a gawky lope around the bases. She is speaking or singing or something as she is running. She has homered, which is easy to do. Breathless and congratulated, she flops down on the grass, kind of sitting, her long legs stretched out before her. She is singing: '*Maybe I'm right, and maybe I'm wrong / And maybe I'm weak and maybe I'm strong / But nevertheless—I'm in love with you.*'"

Jonno would later describe the Simon women: "Andrea was a legitimate sensualist. . . . Joanna was a chanteuse wearing lots of makeup, disguised as an adolescent. Lucy was spectacularly beautiful with almond eyes, sweeping through the apple orchards at age 13 or 14 with a sexual majesty. Carly was wonderfully gawky, with a stutter."

The Simon manse was, for many of its habitués, a hothouse of secrets, deceptions, and estrogen.

Jackie and Rachel Robinson began to feel comfortable in Stamford, and they got the idea of buying a piece of property there and building a home. Rachel saw an advertisement in the *Stamford Advocate* for some land on Cascade Avenue, and made an appointment to see it. But when the real estate agent saw that she was a black woman, Rachel was brusquely informed that the property had been taken off the market.

So Andrea started to go around the town with Rachel and various realtors, and was soon given to understand that Jackie Robinson may have broken the color line in professional baseball, but it was going to be much harder for him to do it in the Connecticut commuter towns of Fairfield County. Houses went off the market as soon as the two women walked in. The Cascade Avenue land had a For Sale sign, but when Andrea called, resolved to act as a straw buyer for the Robinsons, she was told it had already been sold.

Andrea was furious at this blatant racism. "My mother became an endless civil rights worker," Carly says. "And she became very devoted to the cause of integrating Stamford. Up till then, black families couldn't live there, and the truth of it was brushed under the carpet." Andrea enlisted her husband in this crusade. Dick had just been interviewed by Edward R. Murrow for CBS television, and was very much a national figure. "And so my mother and father went to the community leaders—the rabbis, ministers, priests, politicians— and told them, 'This is a potentially very embarrassing situation we've come to, here in Stamford. We're in 1954, and we can't get a piece of property for Jackie Robinson and his family? What kind of town is this? Do you want picket lines in front of your real estate agencies?'"

The Simons started dropping names—Connecticut senator Abe Ribicoff, President Eisenhower, *The New York Times*—and the local realtors soon got the message. Carly: "And so little by little, my parents wore them down, and [the Robinsons] bought the property on Cascade Avenue. My parents invited the Robinsons to live in our Stamford house while they were building theirs, and they ended up staying with us for several months. I got to drive to Ebbets Field with Jackie for Dodger home games. It was one of the most incredible periods for our family. Jackie taught me so much about sports. He was the most incredible tennis player—no one knows this—and could even hold his own with Don Budge. Anyway, it was Jackie Robinson who really taught me how to play.

"This whole situation really energized my mother. From then on, our family was to be associated with the civil rights movement." (The Simons were dues-paying members of the National Association for the Advancement of Colored People, the NAACP, the leading civil rights organization of the era.) "It gave my mother the spiritual resolve to have these civil rights rallies, benefits, and protests on our lawn, especially in Riverdale. [Peter Simon: "We referred to these events as 'Mum's Negro Rallies.'"] One day, my sisters and I were recruited to sing 'Happy Birthday' to a visiting black preacher from the South named Martin Luther King. This was before he was famous, but he was still an incredible presence, and he came to our house."

THE RONNIE MATERIAL

---

*D*uring this period, Carly's mother was carrying on a secret love affair with her son's much younger tutor and companion. When her daughters found out, Joanna Simon says, their world turned upside down.

It had started in 1953. Andrea Simon was worried that her depressed and preoccupied husband's lack of interest in his son, combined with Peter's being raised in a smothering, all-female household, would inevitably lead to the boy's homosexuality. Someone suggested a college man be hired as a part-time companion and tutor for Peter. Andrea placed an advertisement in the Columbia University newspaper.

The ad was answered by Ronnie Klinzing, a twenty-year-old scholarship student from Pittsburgh. Ronnie was tall, handsome, athletic, virile. Andrea hired him as soon as he walked in the door. He was also talented, with theatrical ambitions, and fit right in to the family's musical life. Ronnie could sing. He was also witty, charming, and something of a flirt. He was engaged to be a sort of camp counselor for Peter, teaching him sports and other manly arts. Ronnie lived with the Simons on weekends and in the summer, a vigorous presence in sharp contrast to Dick Simon's general state of depression and withdrawal. Without meaning to, Ronnie triggered an intense sexual competition between his employer and her daughters. Carly and her cousin Jeanie went through his underwear drawer shortly after he moved in. Once, Ronnie caught them snapping his jockstraps at each other, and the girls were properly mortified. Ronnie, a good sport, just laughed about it.

It was Joanna who discovered the affair. She thinks it started about six months after Ronnie joined the family. "From the time their relationship started, until it became common knowledge, was about a year or two." When the children returned from their summer camps to the Stamford house, Joey noticed that some carpentry had been done in the third-floor bathroom. Behind a cupboard, a passage had been cut through to the closet in her mother's bedroom. Ronnie's room was on the other side of the bathroom. Joey, then seventeen, quickly figured it out.

She didn't know what to do. She told Lucy, who wanted to pretend that they didn't know what was going on. But strong-willed Joey was furious at her mother, and felt ashamed for her father. Some time went by. The girls didn't tell Carly, who was in her own world, or Peter, who was too young.

Eventually Joanna confronted her mother, and was astonished when Andrea didn't deny anything. Instead she explained that she'd fallen deeply in love with this man who was twenty-four years younger than she. Joanna recalled, "She told me, 'Your father doesn't give me the support I need with Peter.' That was her justification." Joey insisted that Ronnie be let go, but Andrea refused. "She claimed that Ronnie's presence was necessary so that Peter would not turn out to be homosexual. She said that if Ronnie left, she would go to pieces, and the whole family would fall apart."

Ronnie Klinzing stayed in the picture, to the astonishment of the older girls. "It ruined our lives," Joanna said, bluntly, matter-of-factly, fifty years later. "I wondered about my father. Did he know? Of course he had to." Dick Simon had his own relationship with Auntie Jo. Some thought he must have colluded with his wife's passionate affair with the younger man. "At the time, my guess was that my father was unable to do anything about Ronnie," Joey says. "The whole thing was so painful for me; it was something I didn't want to admit. Later, Lucy and I have both wished we had gotten together as a family and started life anew—without our mother."

For a year or two in the mid-fifties, the Simon family maintained its outward composure. They dressed for supper, and one wasn't allowed to say "shut up" at the table. Joanna continued her voice lessons and sat in the family box at the Metropolitan Opera. Lucy rode the subway to the famous Manny's music store on Forty-eighth Street and bought a Martin guitar. She sat on her bed and practiced every night, with worshipful Carly watching every move. The girls still sang along with the radio as they washed and put away the dishes after supper. Allie Brennan's lemon meringue pie remained a perennial family favorite. Dick Simon played the piano and still read poetry to the children some evenings. During this period, he discovered and published Sloan Wilson's quintessential adman novel, *The Man in the Grey Flannel Suit*, which was a huge success for S&S and became a Hollywood movie starring Gregory Peck.

But this façade of success belied the tension and hurt that hung over the family. It got worse when Ronnie was around, and he was around a lot. Andrea's attention shifted from her needy family to her young lover. They spent a lot of time away from the house with Peter. Carly was left to herself, the odd child out. This emotional withdrawal affected her, and she began to display some alarming symptoms: night terrors, agoraphobia, a worsening stammer, and a painful constriction in her throat that their baffled family doctor described as a "worry lump." Carly hated Ronnie, and she wasn't sure why. She wondered if she hated her mother, too.

"Our family used music to get through this and other rough periods," Peter Simon remembers. "The musicales and jam sessions continued on the weekends and holidays. Our fabulous uncle Peter Dean gave Carly and me as much attention as he could, but it was never enough. I was too young to know what was going on, but I know Carly really suffered: first from our father's rejection and preference for Lucy, and second from our mother's emotional abandonment."

Carly finally learned about Andrea and Ronnie in 1955, when Ronnie was drafted into the U.S. Army and sent to Europe. That summer, Andrea sailed to France to be near him, telling her family that she was on the verge of a nervous breakdown and needed to get away awhile. Auntie Jo was brought in to look after the family, much to the consternation of Carly and Peter, as Auntie Jo was somewhat strict. Once, she took a hairbrush to Peter's backside, something he never forgot.

While his wife was away, Dick Simon suffered a massive heart attack, one that almost killed him.

Andrea didn't come home right away, remaining in Europe while her husband recovered. Her sisters told Carly why. Carly was shocked.

"They said she was madly in love with him," she recalls. "They talked about my father and Auntie Jo, that this was our mother's revenge. I was a child in denial. Even though I saw it in front of me, I couldn't bear to believe it's true. . . . Looking back, I see now that we lived in an atmosphere of erotica. The sexual haze was so thick you could cut it. The whole thing gave me a very good sense of smell, and a sensitivity to peoples' secrets."

For the next fifty-plus years, the Simon sisters (and their various psychotherapists) referred to all this as "the Ronnie material."

When Andrea Simon finally returned home, she found the family in a terrible state. Joey, eighteen, was openly contemptuous. Lucy, fifteen, was cool to her. Carly's stammer had reached the point where she could hardly speak. So Andrea plunged back in. When Carly stumbled over a word, Andrea encouraged her to sing it instead, which sometimes helped. The "worry lump" made it hard to swallow, and Carly had lost weight. She had become obsessed with her sexuality and had made up pet names for her female parts. She loved keeping (and not keeping) secrets, and told anyone who asked that she wanted to be a spy when she grew up, and indeed eavesdropped on Joey and her dates, crawling behind and under the living room furniture to see what Joey was up to. Carly often tried to peek at Lucy while she was dressing to see her developing bust, which Lucy was shy about revealing. ("I was completely in awe of my sister's breasts," Carly said later.)

One morning, Carly freaked out at the breakfast table. She was eating Cheerios and telling her mother about the air-raid drills at school and her fears of airplanes and bombs. Then she had a panic attack. "I ran upstairs and started whirling around the bathroom. I wanted my mother to call the ambulance because I thought I was going to die. My mother somehow subdued me and got me into bed. I think I must have cried it out."

Andrea took Carly to the pediatrician, and Carly overheard her mother telling him, "Carly is often hysterical"; she later looked up the word in the dictionary. The doctor wanted Carly to be evaluated by a psychologist, and this led Andrea to send Carly to twice-weekly sessions with New York psychiatrist Edith Entenmann. By then, Carly was in the sixth grade at Fieldston, a private school in Riverdale. On Tuesdays and Thursdays, Carly was excused early from class to go to the doctor. She felt shame at this, and indeed was somewhat stigmatized. Teachers told her fellow pupils that Carly was "complicated."

"Ronnie," Carly told her therapist, "is the most horrible person in the world." When she couldn't think of anything to say, she made up dream stories to tell. The worry lump came back. She would start to gag before leaving for school in the morning, terrified that the teachers would call on her to speak. Andrea wanted desperately to help Carly, but then she would completely withdraw when Carly complained about Ronnie.

"My mother was best in her role as a mother when you really needed her. She wanted desperately to be needed." Carly would call from school crying because she was unable to recite a poem or give a report. "My mother would tell me, 'Carly, you are an artistic soul, and artistic people have nervous problems. We can conquer this.' It was a terrible situation. I needed her the most, but he took up her time and most of her emotional energy."

Dick Simon was a different man after his heart attack. He seemed frail, and barely played the piano. The evening readings of Whitman, Tennyson, and Shakespeare's sonnets became infrequent. Carly was terrified her father was going to die. A friend told her to make a wish and knock on wood, so she started praying to God and knocking on wood five hundred times, every night. This went on a long time—"my private magic."

Carly: "I remember one night, I was really tired, and I went to sleep after only 132 knocks. He didn't die then, so it reduced itself to 200 knocks, every night, for *years*."

ALL SHOOK UP

———

*I*n 1956, Carly started the seventh grade and, helped by her mother and others, including a speech therapist, began to learn to speak. "Up until then," Carly told an interviewer, "I had a very serious stutter from about the age of six. I was in agony in school because I knew the answers to the questions they asked, but I couldn't say anything because I was scared. My whole face would become distorted as I tried to get the words out. Sometimes kids laughed, and imitated me. It was a harrowing experience.

"I would be at the dining room table with my family. I'd want to say, 'Please pass me the water,' but I wouldn't be able to. So what happened next is that my mother told me, or taught me, to speak in a rhythm. If I stammered, she'd say, 'Just slap your thigh, like Uncle Pete—you know, scat-sing—and add the please-please-pass-the-water, baby, please-pass-the-water-right-now, *yeah—please-pass-the-water-right-now!*' "

This worked.

"So she taught me to add a little syncopation to it, something maybe about this from our genetic make-up, and so I learned to speak with a very bizarre sense of rhythm that my teachers could never quite figure out. But, at least, I started to be able to function in school like a normal person."

Carly got her period for the first time on a midsummer June evening when she was thirteen. In celebration, Andrea, ever the romantic, took Carly and her cousin Jeanie up to the roof of the Stamford house and opened a bottle of champagne. They clinked their glasses and drank a toast to the moon, the stars, and Carly Simon's brand-new womanhood.

Carly still didn't feel right. She struggled with a persistent case of acne that lasted into her early twenties. The way people reacted to her made her think she was ugly. "People would come to the house and say, 'Oh Lucy! You've gotten so beautiful.' And, 'Joey—you look so elegant.' And then they'd turned to me and say, 'Hi Carly.' I took that to mean I wasn't even in the ballgame."

Her family kept trying to reassure Carly. They told her she was very pretty, and that her father loved her very much. She still had an awful feeling about herself. This was validated for her, years later, when novelist Sloan Wilson published a memoir that described the Simon family as very glamorous—except for ugly duckling Carly (who had since become a huge star). "There it was—the horrible truth—finally confirmed," she said sadly. She added that there's still a carry-over from those days. "Even now," she said recently, "I don't want people to concentrate on my looks, because I don't think they'll like what they see."

In the summer of 1956, Dick Simon was in Florida recuperating from his heart attack. Andrea took the family for a holiday on Martha's Vineyard, the old whaling island off Cape Cod, Massachusetts. Dick and Andrea had been renting old farmhouses and beach cottages on the Vineyard since the forties, usually in the westerly "up-island" town of Chilmark. Electricity was primitive and sporadic back then, and ice blocks were delivered to the houses twice a week so the fish and produce wouldn't spoil.

In those days some of the Vineyard's more remote beaches (all privately owned) allowed nude bathing. Dick Simon's photo archive from their early days on the Vineyard has entire rolls of his gorgeous young wife splashing naked in the waves off empty beaches such as Windy Gates, Quansoo, and Zack's Cliffs.

The island community then consisted of farmers and fishermen, and a summer colony of theater people (Katharine Cornell), writers (Lillian Hellman, Dashiell Hammett, Max Eastman), movie stars (James Cagney), photographers (Alfred Eisenstadt), and artists. There was a sizable contingent from the publishing world, and the families that owned *The New York Times* and *The Washington Post* had private estates. Up-island, the legendary Missouri painter Thomas Hart Benton presided over a folkloric musical scene that included talented locals and successful professionals such as Burl Ives, who all got together for Saturday hootenannies at the Chilmark Community Center.

Another large family that summered in Chilmark in those years was that of Dr. Isaac Taylor, who taught medicine in North Carolina. Like the Simon family, the Taylors were very musical, and their five children were likewise exposed to the Vineyard's music scene in that fertile period.

That summer on the Vineyard, teenage Lucy Simon was taught a few guitar chords by Davey Gude, a future sixties jug band member. When the family returned home later on, Lucy started putting some of the music she'd learned on the Vineyard to good use.

Autumn 1956. The Simon family is back in Riverdale after the long summer. Joey has gone off to college at exclusive Sarah Lawrence, a few miles north, in Bronxville. The family watches Elvis Presley—all shook up—gyrate on Ed Sullivan's Sunday night variety show. Rock-and-roll radio beams in with Elvis, Chuck Berry, Little

Richard, and Fats Domino over WINS, 1010 on the dial. The Simons like Harry Belafonte's breakthrough album *Calypso*, the first LP to sell a million copies, a collection of old Jamaican *mento* songs energized by a trained actor who'd studied with Marlon Brando at the famous Actors Studio. Belafonte's mannered, sold-out concerts coincided with the burgeoning civil rights movement, empowering a new generation of black performers—Josh White, Odetta, Leon Bibb—who dedicated themselves to the changes that had to come for still-segregated America's salvation from the legacy of slavery.

Lucy Simon, meanwhile, had a poetry assignment at the Fieldston School. At the age of sixteen, she had plenty of her own issues. Some were similar to her sister Carly's. "I had some problems putting things together at school," she says. "Today it might be called dyslexia. It was very hard for me to memorize anything, especially poetry, which was terrible for me, because my father and I were close and he loved to hear poems recited, especially in the evening. There was this assignment when I had to memorize and recite a poem of my choosing, and I chose Eugene Field's nursery rhyme, 'Wynken, Blynken, and Nod.' It was a favorite of my father's, but I had an impossible time getting it right. It might have been my mother who suggested that I sing it instead. So I put the rhymes to a melody with the guitar chords I knew, and turned it into a song. I wrote out the melody, sitting on my bed, and I distinctly remember Carly sitting cross-legged on the floor of my bedroom, watching me intently as I sang the poem for the first time.

"So now I had this song, and instead of reciting it like the others, I got up in front of the class with my guitar and sang it. The other kids liked it and clapped, and the teacher gave me a good grade. So that's really where the Simon Sisters started out."

September 1956. Dick Simon rejoined his family at home in Riverdale. The Dodgers won the National League Pennant, and were beaten by the Yankees in the World Series. Publishing tycoon Marshall Field III died, and Simon and Schuster was bought back from

Field's estate by Max Schuster and other partners in a deal that did not include Dick Simon. Historians of the American publishing industry who have scrutinized this dirty deal guess that S&S executives excluded the cofounder of the firm because he was profoundly demoralized by both ill health and a much-diminished role in the company. Max Schuster's attorney later claimed (in 1989) that Dick Simon himself chose not to buy in, and so the company's executives went ahead without him.

Even somewhat debilitated, Dick continued to publish important and successful books, such as Henri Cartier-Bresson's *The Decisive Moment* and Philippe Halsman's *The Jump Book,* which caught celebrities such as Marilyn Monroe (and Dick Simon) in midair. But at home Dick, at the age of fifty-seven, was a semi-invalid who worried that his career was over.

"My husband was full of anxieties, all his life," Andrea Simon said later. "He suffered a great deal from them. He worried a lot, largely about his business. It took a lot out of him."

Frank Sinatra's brilliant, disconsolate *Wee Small Hours* album was huge on the Simon household's turntables. (Carly used to listen to it, lying facedown on her bed, several times in a row.) Lucy played her guitar in her bedroom along to records by their old teacher Pete Seeger, sometimes recorded by brother Peter on the family's new wire recorder. Carly Simon's earliest recordings date from this period. And now Carly wanted her own guitar.

Dick Simon had another heart attack in 1957, but one less serious than the first. In the evenings, he sat in his bedroom quietly smoking. Then he had a minor stroke that left him unable to sleep. At night the family could hear him moving restlessly around the house in his bathrobe, turning off lights, before closing his bedroom door. Carly kept knocking on the bedpost and praying to God that her father wouldn't die before he learned to love her.

High School Musical

───

$\mathcal{I}$n 1957 the Brooklyn Dodgers moved to Los Angeles. The Simon family took this very hard.

Carly Simon started high school, having left Fieldston, along with her younger brother, for the more traditional Riverdale Country School. This large private academy was at the time split into separate schools for boys and girls, so Carly was thrown into an unfamiliar, mostly female milieu. There were some social tremors at first, as she found it difficult to fit in with her new classmates, was considered too tall for the "social" private dancing classes, and pointedly wasn't invited to a couple of parties. There were murmurs of anti-Semitism, even though the Simons weren't really Jewish. Andrea used her considerable diplomatic skills to smooth this over. Carly soon made friends and began to fit into Riverdale's preppy, late-fifties scene, using her comedienne's skills to make people like her—for example, by laughing so hard in the lunchroom that her mouthful of milk would spritz through her prominent teeth and spray across the room, making everyone else laugh as well.

By then, as fourteen turned to fifteen, the disparaging terms *gawky* and *awkward* and *gangly* weren't being used to describe Carly Simon anymore. She was developing curves, ironing her hair, allowing her madcap sense of humor to win friends and influence people. She made the cheerleader squad in her sophomore year. One of her first dates, in 1957, was with a tall and very popular Riverdale boy, a couple of years older, named Chevy Chase. Carly remembered: "I was invited to 'the hop,' our school dance. Chevy was two years above me, and I was surprised that he asked me. I wore a red bouffant dress, and he came to collect me in a pin-striped suit that was slightly too short. He had a corsage for me, and was a perfect gentleman, telling me jokes, and making me laugh all night. After our night of dancing, he took me home and we sat in the kitchen with the dogs, waiting for the evening to end. He made me laugh by offering a biscuit to one of our dogs, and then eating it himself instead."

Carly: "I was a typical cheerleader, a very rah-rah high school girl, out to be the most popular. It was a very Ivy League trip. . . . But, in matters of both substance and style, I followed my sister Lucy. I emulated her life. I wanted to *be* her. I lived Lucy's life all during high school. In fact, I have such a pure recall of the details of Lucy's life that it still amazes her. I studied every detail. I copied her style, to the letter. I wore tight skirts and tight sweaters. When she wore her hair with a dip over her eyes like Veronica Lake did, I did too.

"Basically, I *was* Lucy for a number of years. Then, when I was in the tenth grade, she went off to Bennington College, and she became a beatnik. Lucy had her ears pierced. Black leotards. She started wearing peasant blouses and blue jeans that were slightly cut off and frazzled at the edges. She grew her hair long and played the guitar. So, immediately, I became a beatnik too. I started a trend at my school: ethnic clothes and long braids down the back. Other girls started copying my look, and I seemed to be an innovator, but in reality I was still following Lucy.

"The big change in my life happened when Lucy left Bennington and went to nursing school at Cornell. I somehow couldn't see myself as a nurse. She had changed a lot in that phase, and I grew to love her even more, but not identify with her as much. At that point, finally, I became much more myself than ever."

Carly has said that her mother had her fitted for a contraceptive diaphragm when she was fifteen, which, if accurate, certainly says something about teenage Carly in the generally repressive sexual atmosphere of the time. It also speaks volumes about the eroticized atmosphere of the Simon household, in which Andrea was living more or less openly with Ronnie. Birth control was extremely avant-garde, and made Carly something of a sexual pioneer at her school, where rumors of heavy petting and "going all the way" could stain a girl's reputation. But Carly Simon could give her classmates (if they had something going with a boyfriend) the name of the doctor who had fitted her diaphragm. Certainly Andrea Simon's notion of preventing pregnancy, instead of ignoring the risk, was a decade ahead of its time, and also spoke to the sexual aspects of her own life.

The Simon family's animals were a big part of Carly's childhood. Carly's Scottish terrier, Laurie Brown, was very dear to her and inspired an early dog ditty, "Lorelei Brown." Lucy's dog, a terrier called Bascomb, suffered from seizures and inspired Lucy's caring and maternal instincts. (The family accused Lucy of spoiling Bascomb.) Peter had a mutt called Besty, because her owner thought she was the best dog. Prowling the house were a variety of cats, including Guarder, Slinky, and Magellan. The comforting presence of these and other pets was one of the touchstones of Carly's somewhat fraught adolescence.

Odetta Holmes, Carly Simon's idol, had released her first album, *The Tin Angel*, in 1954. A stolid black Alabama native (born in 1930) with a big guitar sound and a burnished female baritone voice, Odetta sang an almost operatic mix of blues songs, southern ballads, and old spirituals with the moral authority of an African American priestess. By 1958 she was a favorite in the Greenwich Village coffeehouses and folk clubs, and would soon be opening for superstar Harry Belafonte, and then headlining on the lucrative college concert circuit along with the Kingston Trio. (Bob Dylan later wrote that Odetta inspired him, in 1958, to switch from rock and roll to folk music.) Carly studied Odetta's 1957 album, *At the Gate of Horn,* and realized that her own deep singing voice matched Odetta's almost perfectly. This was a major inspiration, and Carly spent many nights sitting on her bed, the door closed, singing along to her idol's hypnotic recordings. Andrea Simon said later that she used to eavesdrop outside Carly's bedroom, tearful with joy as Carly sang along to Odetta's records—in perfect harmony. (Carly's high school yearbook for her senior year described her as "Riverdale's answer to Odetta.")

Carly: "I remember, in those days, Lucy sitting on her bed with her guitar. She had a turntable on her bureau with an LP playing. It might've been Pete Seeger. It might have been Harry Belafonte. She was trying to imitate what the sounds were. She taught me the C-chord and the other two chords she knew—she was excited to share them with me—and then we switched the guitar back and forth . . . until I was finally on the subway down to Manny's on 48th Street, with thirty five dollars, to buy a guitar of my own. We were young and malleable, and willing to get our fingers calloused and dirty."

Carly loved the way she and Lucy sounded when they sang together. She thought there was something ineffable in Lucy's sweet soprano voice, a pitch and a sound that she described as "Scottish"— an ethereal presence that perfectly balanced the deeper tones of her own contralto. Carly had always loved to sing with her sisters, espe- cially the three-part choir arrangements for standards such as "Ave Maria" that Joey was bringing home from her college's music library. But there was *something* about the way she and Lucy sounded, alone, that moved Carly deeply. "The sheer *excitement* when we blended our voices—it just thrilled me," Carly said later on.

In 1959, Carly began taking guitar lessons at the Manhattan School of Music. She was also one of the best singers in her school, and a soloist in the chorus of the musical that Riverdale put on every spring. That year, it was George and Ira Gershwin's 1930 *Girl Crazy*, featuring "I Got Rhythm" and "Embraceable You." Soon she began dating the show's male lead, senior Tim Ratner, a tall and handsome high school hero type. One day Carly brought Tim over to the house and casually showed him the photo portrait of George Gershwin—inscribed to her parents—in its silver frame in the Simons' living room. (When Andrea Simon got a load of this new boyfriend, and the gleam in Carly's eye, was probably when she hauled her daughter to the doctor for that diaphragm.) Soon Tim and Carly were *the* campus sweethearts of '59, two star-quality kids strolling hand in hand, evidently in love with each other. They sang show tunes, sang doo-wop, Danny and the Juniors, the Contours, "Get a Job." Late at night, on "study dates," they locked themselves in the Simons' book-stuffed attic and stayed up until two in the morning, snuggling, listening to Frank Sinatra mournfully croon "In the Wee Small Hours of the Morning."

Having fallen in love at sixteen, Carly found that her stammer had almost disappeared.

In the summer of 1959, Tim often visited Carly in Stamford. He saw the whole scene: the increasingly dysfunctional father, the highly organized (but preoccupied) mother, the glorious older sisters, the funny twelve-year-old kid brother who published a mimeographed family newsletter, the *Quaker Muffet Press*. It seemed to Tim that Carly's mother had a much younger boyfriend living on the property, which generated chagrin in his girlfriend, who didn't want to talk about her family, as if she were ashamed or embarrassed by them. At summer's end, Tim went off to Dartmouth. Carly, still in high school, wrote to him often, but eventually met someone else.

~⁓

The venerable Newport Folk Festival in the summer of 1959 was chugging along with its earnest mixture of topical songs, blues, bluegrass, and clog dancing when star folkie Bob Gibson brought out a pretty, dark-haired, barefoot eighteen-year-old singer to join him on a few ballads. The daughter of an academic who taught in Cambridge, Massachusetts, she specialized in old Appalachian songs and sang in a clarion soprano that made the Rhode Island festival's microphones and speakers somewhat redundant. This was the national debut of Joan Baez.

She had been singing, semi-regularly, at the Club 47 coffeehouse in Harvard Square, drawing an adoring crowd of students, Boston bohemians, and folk music fans. They queued down the street for blocks when local hero Joanie was on the bill. Her voice was described as angelic, and authentic. Joan Baez's early career, after an enraptured reception by the folkies and beatniks at Newport '59, would, in days to come, have a major impact on the careers of the two beautiful Simon Sisters.

A DEATH IN THE FAMILY

———

Carly Simon was in the audience when Harry Belafonte played at Carnegie Hall in April 1959. This was a double treat for her, because her idol Odetta opened the concert, earning a standing ovation from Belafonte's audience. These were the days when the civil rights movement began to heat up, with sit-ins and voter registration drives, especially in the South, with activists trying to change America from a segregated society to one that respected the equal rights of all its citizens. Harry Belafonte epitomized the new American Negro, deeply committed to the struggle against racial discrimination. His hyper-theatrical presentation of gentle calypsos and robust protest songs aimed to carry his (mostly white) audience beyond the confines of the venerable auditorium and into a communal spirit of a national struggle for change.

Performing in his trademark V-cut silk shirt and tight black trousers, Belafonte divided the program into three acts: "Moods of the American Negro" (work songs and spirituals), "In the Caribbean" ("Day-O" exploded the house, followed by "Jamaica Farewell"), and

"Around the World," in which Belafonte sang in Hebrew, Creole, and Spanish. The *New York Herald Tribune* wrote, "Not even the presence of a small, rarely used orchestra or some garish lighting were able to deflect the instant rapport between [Belafonte] and his audience."

Carly: "I was a huge fan of his, and we used to go to Carnegie Hall whenever he was there. He was the first performer I ever saw who changed his shirt between songs. His neck was always open two or three buttons deep, and I thought he was very, very sexy. 'Jamaica Farewell' and 'Day-O' were my favorite songs. Harry made a big impression on me from the time I was twelve or thirteen." (The subsequent recording, *Belafonte at Carnegie Hall*, was the first concert LP to be released in stereo, and immediately broke the sales records of *Calypso*, of three years earlier.)

Autumn 1959. One morning Peter Simon was dressing for the seventh grade when his father told him to forget about school and come to work with him instead. Richard Simon informed Peter that, from now on, he would be running Simon and Schuster. "I just looked at my father," Peter remembered. "He didn't look well, and I was worried. I said something like 'Well, Dad, I would certainly like to work for you some day, but I really think I should get to school.'" Dick stared at his son for a minute, saying nothing, swaying slightly. Andrea Simon came in and told Peter to go to school. Dick Simon took to his bed.

He never returned to Simon and Schuster. He suffered a series of jolts to his heart and another stroke. He lived in his bathrobe. Much of the time he was silent, and seemed to suffer from catatonia. Sometime after Christmas, Andrea couldn't take it anymore and sent him away to live in Stamford and be cared for by Aunt Jo. Later Dick Simon's business partners formally separated him from the company in a complicated deal, aided by colleagues who (the family feels) took advantage of his enfeebled condition. At the age of sixty, Richard Simon found his illustrious career as a legendary American publisher tragically over.

Carly was a junior at Riverdale as 1960 dawned, with change in the air. The Eisenhower years were over, and the political high ground was being claimed by the handsome young senator from Massachusetts, Jack Kennedy, who offered the country a new vigor and even a trace of glamour. Kennedy's candidacy was espoused by the Simon family to the extent that Carly started calling her brother "P.T. Boat" after Senator Kennedy's famous wartime torpedo-carrying attack ship.

Young men were constant visitors to the imposing house on Grosvenor Avenue, especially when Lucy Simon was at home. One of her would-be suitors was an MIT student named Paul Sapounakis, who, one day in the spring of 1960, brought along his friend Nick Delbanco, a Harvard freshman and aspiring writer. "And you," Paul told Nick, "can date the younger sister."

Nick Delbanco was from an old European Jewish family that had gotten out of Germany in time. Born in London, raised near Carly (in Westchester County), he was a young writer whose obvious talent was recognized early. He was already a fiction star at Harvard, his work appearing in the university's literary publications. He was shorter than Carly, but handsome, funny, intense, knowledgeable, opinionated, sexy, passionate, older, and Ivy League—everything a girl could want.

Soon Nick was a regular visitor. In March 1960 there was a party at Stamford to which he was invited. Dinner was served, and then the evening's entertainment unfolded. Richard Simon, the august founder of the country's greatest publishing house, was seated in an armchair, in pajamas and robe, alert but silent, his hands folded in his lap. Yet, Nick said, "He was still a magisterial presence in his own home. There was a definite aura there, even at that stage of his life." The family then performed around the grand piano in the parlor, and there had obviously been rehearsals. The three Simon sisters offered show tunes, folk songs, arias, and Lucy's song "Winkin', Blinkin' and Nod," in various combinations, in an informal family revue. Carly expertly channeled Odetta on the folk ballad "John Henry." She sang "Danny Boy" with the soul of a wistful Celtic bride. Uncle Peter Dean, strumming his ukulele, would crack the party up with ribald double entendres and extreme, eye-popping, cheek-bulging gurning. Peter Simon darted about documenting everything with his camera and flashbulbs. Observing the silent, invalided Richard Simon, a legend of the publishing industry, watching his beautiful daughters sing, Nick Delbanco felt that a courageous family was doing its best to carry on in the face of impending disaster.

As for Carly, Nick got to know her on school vacations that spring. "She had the remnants of a stammer, and a forthright anxiety. She said that her family left her feeling insecure, unloved, and that her comic antics were a ploy to gain attention." All she really wanted was for her beloved father to smile at her. Nicky wanted to be more than friends with Carly, but she was wary, preoccupied with high school and family issues, and kept him at a distance—for a while.

The first time Nick saw Carly sing in public was early in the summer of 1960. Ronnie Klinzing had landed the male lead—"the Alfred Drake role"—in a Pocono resort summer stock production of *Kiss Me, Kate*. Joey Simon was Kate, and her sister Carly somehow conquered considerable stage fright and came out and sang a song. The production was *way* off Broadway, but the young cast did their best, and Carly Simon had made her public debut, in the verdant hills of eastern Pennsylvania.

Dick Simon spent the summer at his estate in Stamford, often sleepless, in the care of his oldest friend, Aunt Jo. On the night of July 31, as the cicadas buzzed their mating song through the fruit trees in his orchards, he had a third and final heart attack and died at the age of sixty-one.

Andrea Simon woke Carly the next morning with the devastating news, then drove away with Ronnie to collect Peter at his summer camp in New England to bring him home for the funeral. Carly was left alone in the house. She made it, numbly, to the bathroom, feeling sick. All the knocking on wood, for years, had come down to this. Her prayers had been in vain, and she felt abandoned by God. Carly decided to put on a proper show of mourning—"arrange my attitude," she later said. In truth, she had been anticipating this awful moment for a long time. She later said she felt envious when her sister Lucy came home prostrate with grief. Lucy had called her father in Connecticut to say good night only a few hours before he died.

Lucy later said that her grief for her father was tempered by her sense that her love and respect for him had been completely reciprocated. "My relationship with him was stable, and I felt very loved by him. . . . But Carly's relationship with him was never totally established. His death made it impossible for her to complete this, and that's where her anguish came from." Years later Lucy would say that this unresolved bond between Carly and her father would play itself out in *all* her younger sister's relationships with men.

Dick Simon's funeral was horrible, an ordeal for everyone, a vale of tears. Nick Delbanco showed up at the funeral, offering Carly a solid shoulder to cry on. "That's the first time she took me seriously," Nick remembered. "It was a very dark and complicated time for her." Soon Nick and Carly were secreting themselves in the Simons' attic. "That was the beginning of a real intimacy between us," he says.

Andrea Simon sold the valuable Stamford estate as soon as she could, to an exclusive, all-white private school that she insisted must integrate, as a condition of the sale.

Peter Simon remembers that he and Carly mostly felt numb when their father died, and that his death really hit home when Andrea sold the Stamford house. "Neither of us could believe we were going to lose our country house in Connecticut. It was paradise, lost. We both cried and cried. That's when it really sank in, to me and Carly at least, that our father had died."

CARLY CARES

———

$\mathcal{F}$ifty years after her father died, Carly revealed that she had lost some of her fortune, reportedly some millions of dollars, to a fraudulent financial adviser. This was front-page news during the spring of 2010, with the media invariably describing Carly as the heir to the Simon and Schuster fortune. The old family firm had changed hands several times since 1960, and was by 2010 a multibillion-dollar media empire. Carly, it was generally assumed, was very wealthy because she had inherited her father's vast fortune.

Carly took pains to deny that she was any kind of heiress. She issued a statement to the press: "The Simon family, the sisters and my brother and myself, are *not* the heirs to the Simon & Schuster fortune, because my father sold the publishing company years before he died. And so a lot of people get this wrong." Any money that had been lost by her financial adviser, she explained, had been earned by her during her forty-year career. She pointed out that while of course she did receive some income from her father's estate, the amount wasn't exactly enriching. Carly told reporters that there had never been substantial trust funds for the Simon children, and that she received a small allowance from her mother until she was twenty-one. (Peter Simon estimates that he and his sisters each received legacies of about $80,000.)

So Richard Simon's untimely death had serious financial consequences for his family. No longer would they live in the lap of luxury. Inherently frugal, Andrea Simon was careful with money and toned down the Simon lifestyle almost immediately. The chauffeur, cooks, and other staff were let go. The lavish parties and country house weekends were over. With the Stamford estate sold, the Simons retreated to the comfortable Riverdale house and tried to get over the shock of losing the head of the family. And it wasn't the only shock they received. Many of the obituaries emphasized Dick Simon's precipitous decline at the expense of his considerable achievements. Bennett Cerf, the founder of rival publisher Random House, who had benefited from Dick's friendship in the early days of his company, wrote a melancholy appreciation in the literary magazine *Saturday Review* that the family found embarrassing. Cerf opined that Richard Simon's spirit had been broken by time and progress, and by the corporatization of publishing, once exclusively a family enterprise. He ended his eulogy: "Simon spent many of his last days huddled in a heavy topcoat in an overheated room, pulling down the shades and locking the doors. He had hit upon this method of shutting out death. It was the ingenious stratagem of a sorely troubled mind—but alas, it didn't work."

Andrea wanted to sue, but was talked out of it. "We were outraged," Joanna said, "because it wasn't really true. It was just Bennett twisting the knife because he was jealous of my father from their Columbia days. My father got all the girls and was much more popular." And Simon and Schuster was a more successful company than Random House.

Carly began her senior year at Riverdale in September 1960. Nicky Delbanco went back to Cambridge, and during that academic year Carly visited him as often as she could, lugging her guitar case on the slow train to Boston, sometimes sneaking in a forbidden night in Nick's rooms in Harvard Yard. "Carly was still shy around people back then," Nick recalls, "but she was utterly transformed when she played her guitar." He remembers her being very identified with Odetta, and belting out Odetta's signature "I don't wanna be no other womaaaan" at odd intervals, when in high spirits, which was more often than not, because Carly was truly goofy and uninhibited if she liked you.

Carly: "Meanwhile, Lucy was seriously pretending to be Joan Baez, and she had the soprano for it; and Joey was auditioning for professional operas, so in our family we had an Odetta, a Joan Baez, and an Elisabeth Schwarzkopf. . . . Odetta was my idol and I wanted to sing like her. I listened to Joan Baez's records, and it didn't seem possible that I could ever sound like her. Then, when I was a senior in high school, I heard Judy Collins." This was the first album, *A Maid of Constant Sorrow,* released by the folk label Elektra Records, on which the sexier, twenty-two-year-old, Colorado-bred Collins challenged national sensation Joan Baez, barefoot darling of the Northeast's Ivy League universities, for the throne of folk queen. "When you think you're a singer yourself," Carly continued, "the people who influence you are the people you sound like, people you can imitate; and Judy Collins, I thought I could sound like."

With her boyfriend out of town, Carly had fewer distractions, and she got good grades. She spent hours miming to the radio in her bedroom mirror, swiveling her hips, wagging her finger to the female soul groups coming out of Philadelphia and Detroit. She fiddled with her hair, her look, experimenting with corsets, lift-up bras, and other devices, feeling that most of the time she looked like "a deformed zoo character."

But, if she had wanted them, Carly could have had more dates than Audrey Hepburn. Still, she stayed true to brilliant writer Nicky

Delbanco, to whom she looked—somewhat down—as a sort of protector.

In the spring of 1961, Carly was accepted to Sarah Lawrence, where Joey had gone to college. (By then, Lucy Simon had left Bennington to enroll at Cornell University's nursing school.) The Riverdale yearbook noted that Carly Simon was rarely to be seen without her guitar. Next to her smiling, toothy yearbook photo was the encomium: "There are always crowds around Carly: admiring younger girls, distressed seniors, and bewitched lads. They know that she is sincere, that her emotions are free, and that she can feel and appreciate more deeply than many. Carly cares."

During the summer of 1961, Carly toured Europe with cousin Jeanie Seligman, chaperoned by Jeanie's parents. Nicky was hitching around the continent on his own, and met up with Carly in Paris and Rome, where they threw the prescribed three coins in the Fontana di Trevi.

Andrea Simon drove Carly to Sarah Lawrence in nearby Bronxville in September 1961. The prestigious all-girl college was located on a beautiful campus of quads and venerable buildings, and Carly immediately felt at home and at the same time thrilled to be away from her contentious real home. "I loved being a little college girl," she said later. "I really loved my school, and I loved dormitory life. (I didn't love the gym uniform, however.) I didn't really want to sing, even when I was singing with my sister. I thought I could be married to a poetry professor at a small New England college. I'd serve espresso in little cups around an old farmhouse table where the napkins never matched. That was kind of life I was looking forward to."

At the same time, Sarah Lawrence was academically rigorous, and the students were both highly motivated and competitive. Carly worked hard, especially on her language courses; she wanted to speak better French and Italian because she and Nicky were planning to live in Europe someday. It was her freshman language classes that actually caused Carly to write the first "songs" of her career.

"When I got to college, I was still stammering, feeling a little outclassed by all the budding divas among the Sarah Lawrence girls. And the only way I could remember the poetry we had to recite was to set it to music. This was after my mother had taught me to speak with rhythm. So I started adding my own melodies to these French and Italian poems with a little jazzy syncopation to them. I'd sing these in class—*Il pleure dans mon coeur / Comme il pleut sur la ville*—that was the first one that got the melodic treatment. My classmates were entertained by my singing, and annoyed, some furious, that I was able to do it. I was lucky because I wasn't really the scholarly type, and the other students were far superior in just about everything—other than the singing of romantic Italian verse."

AMBITION AND THE DYLAN ENERGY

---

*A*ndrea Simon made it very clear to her children that she expected them to follow in the footsteps of their father, in terms of having a successful career. For Andrea, ambition was a virtue to be pursued, achievement an imperative goal. She told her talented children that their father would have expected them to make their own way on the strengths of their considerable abilities. Andrea often quoted her Philadelphia hero Benjamin Franklin's pithy maxims to make her point. (There was a huge bust of Franklin in the living room at Riverdale.)

In 1962, Joanna Simon made her debut at the New York City Opera in *The Marriage of Figaro,* and received glowing reviews.

Peter Simon inherited his father's cameras and darkroom, and was ardently encouraged by his mother in pursuing a career in photography.

Lucy Simon was playing guitar and furiously working on songs. She was ambitious for a music career, and saw an opening between the mainstream folk stars: ethereal Joan Baez and earthy Judy Collins on the one hand, and newer performers such as Judy Henske and Carolyn Hester on the other. Lucy's notion was to bring together original songs, lullabies, and traditional ballads in a gentle manner that tended more toward art song than folk music. She found her own soprano too unearthly and mannered for the sound she wanted to capture. But when she got her younger sister to sing with her, Lucy heard in their combined voices—hers tempered by Carly's dusky, burnished contralto—exactly the tone she wanted to put forth in her songs. Even to ambitious Lucy, it was obvious that the Simon Sisters had a better chance at success than the shy and reticent Lucy going out and performing alone.

"I loved the way we sounded when we sang together at family gatherings," says Carly, "but I didn't want to make it my career. . . . The problem was that I didn't have the same ambition that was engrained into my sisters and my brother. I was happy at school. I didn't like singing in front of strangers. I didn't want to be in the limelight. Why would I? It wasn't something I craved, or even needed."

Carly had started her second year at Sarah Lawrence in 1962. "Early on, I became attracted to capes, I think because I had a romantic nature. I'd always wanted to be a spy, so I fit in perfectly at Sarah Lawrence, where everyone wore capes and had pierced ears and was artsy. . . . There was a French singer, Françoise Hardy. *She* was the one. I used to gaze at her pictures in the magazines, and try to dress like her.

"But all the girls at school I idolized were funkier and more bohemian, you know? Hope Cooke became the queen of a Himalayan country. I wanted to be a *bohemian*—that was the life that appealed to me. I knew by then I wasn't going to make the grade as a scholar. And I wasn't going to fit in with the [post-debutante] WASPy enclave, although I . . . kind of . . . *wanted to*. I always associated the WASPy girls with perfectly straight hair. They could whip their heads around a fraction, and make a subtle, but *enormous* gesture. . . . Even their gym uniforms looked great on them. But I was a lankier sort, with frizzy hair. And their socks *never* slid down, but mine always did."

Sometime that year, 1962, Carly and Nick saw François Truffaut's new film, *Jules and Jim,* at the Brattle Theatre in Cambridge. This movie, now a classic of the French nouvelle vague, made an indelible impression upon Carly, who had already recognized something in herself: that the love of just one man might never be quite enough for her. Later, she went to see *Jules and Jim* again, and then again. Jeanne Moreau played Catherine, torn between her husband, Jules (Oskar Werner), and her lover, Jim. In the end Catherine kills herself and Jim in front of Jules in a desperate attempt at reconciling her conflicting emotions. The rhapsodic soundtrack music by Georges Delerue only made the film's tragic ending feel worse.

Carly Simon was deeply affected by this, as were audiences throughout the Western world. "That film, *Jules and Jim,*" she said later (and this is crucial), "absolutely ensured that, for the rest of my life, I would *always* be part of a romantic triangle."

Meanwhile, folk music was going nationwide. Commercial groups such as the Chad Mitchell Trio outsold rock-and-roll records. In 1962, *Time* magazine put Joan Baez on its cover as a symbol of a new generation that used music to validate the national heritage while protesting social injustice, especially the cause of civil rights. The outspoken twenty-two-year-old Baez created a stir by dismissing folk music's stylized practitioners (Theo Bikel, Oscar Brand) as hopelessly passé and calling Harry Belafonte "Harry Bela-phony" for his overly dramatized calypsos—music that was now irrelevant to the new group of young troubadours taking over the Greenwich Village folk clubs. Chief among these was a recent arrival from Minnesota who styled himself "Bob Dylan."

His real name was Robert Zimmerman, and he'd arrived in New York a year earlier, in 1961. He was a disciple of iconic dust bowl bard Woody Guthrie, then living in a hospital in New Jersey with an incurable degenerative disease. He visited Guthrie, received his blessing, and began to play the folk clubs—Gerde's Folk City, the Gaslight, the Village Gate. He was an immediate sensation, at the age of twenty-one, for his intense verbal delivery, his jazz-inflected harmonica solos, and his passionate guitar playing. He attracted the attention of *New York Times* critic Robert Shelton, who pronounced him the next big thing—an enormous boost for Dylan's career. First regarded as a folky harmonica virtuoso, he played on a Harry Belafonte recording session, then on another for Carolyn Hester. The legendary producer John Hammond signed him to Columbia Records, not long after Robert Zimmerman legally changed his name to Bob Dylan (in August 1962) and signed a management contact with Albert Grossman, who also managed Peter, Paul and Mary and other stars of folk.

Carly and Lucy both bought the nervy, haunted, shivering album *Bob Dylan* when it was released in late 1962. The record sold only about five thousand copies, but (as they joke about the Velvet Underground) everyone who bought it would later start a band of their own. By early 1963, "Bobby," as he was then known, was the elusive avatar of the East Coast folk music scene, appearing in Cambridge, New Haven, and Philadelphia as well as the Village. Within months, Dylan would become the protégé, then the lover, of Joan Baez, who over the next year would introduce the "difficult" young singer to her entranced, sold-out audiences as she toured the college concert circuit singing ballads, civil rights anthems, "Blowin' in the Wind," and other visionary songs of this curly-headed genius from the North Country of Minnesota.

This was the beginning of the singer-songwriter movement, a new era when the most talented vocalists began to write their own songs, instead of relying on the talents of others. This protean era, the artistic flowering of the postwar generation, would produce a crowd of musical geniuses, and eventually inspire the career of one of the best singer-songwriters of them all.

The Simon Sisters

———

$\mathcal{I}$n the spring of 1963 the young President Kennedy was being criticized for not doing enough to help the struggle for civil rights. Andrea Simon, ever the activist, was holding benefit parties for groups such as the Congress of Racial Equality (CORE) and the Student Nonviolent Coordinating Committee (SNCC) at her big brick house in Riverdale, and she often asked her daughters to sing for her well-heeled guests. At one of these events Lucy Simon rehearsed some songs with Carly, and the girls got an enthusiastic reception. Afterward, they were taken aside by their uncle Peter Dean. He was now a well-known talent agent who had been important to the early careers of singers Dinah Shore and Peggy Lee, and he understood the attractions and pitfalls of show business. Until then he had never been keen on promoting the enthusiasms and aspirations of his sister's children, but now he heard something in Lucy and Carly that made him think again.

"You know," he told his nieces, "you girls sound terrific together.

I think you could actually have an act." Uncle Pete pledged to Lucy that he would help her if she wanted to make a stab at his business.

This encouragement made Lucy Simon determined to get into the game. And she was determined to drag her charismatic but shy younger sister, kicking and screaming, along with her.

"I was so lucky to have Lucy to inspire me," Carly said later. "We were raised together, you know, so we spoke alike, and therefore we phrased alike. This is so important in singing. Although Lucy is a high soprano, and I'm practically a baritone, we pronounced words the same, and this had an effect on the people who heard us. A big part of blending, really, is the pronunciation of words. . . . It's actually very hard to get the words of a song to sync up so they *blend* in a harmonious way. That blend was what Lucy and I had together and, I have to say, it often sounded really great, even to us, the Simon Sisters, whose levels of self-esteem were never at what you could call a fever pitch."

March 1963. Folk music's dominance reached its American apogee with the ABC-TV series *Hootenanny,* broadcast nationally on Saturday nights. Each segment was filmed at a different college, with four acts delivering their songs at a breakneck pace until the show's second season, when *Hootenanny* was extended to an hour. The show was controversial from its inception because ABC had blacklisted folk godfather Pete Seeger due to his left-wing politics, which engendered an ironclad boycott by Dylan; Baez; Peter, Paul and Mary; and the Kingston Trio—all the folk stars who really interested the masses. *Hootenanny* made do with the commercial folk echelon: Ian and Sylvia, Johnny Cash, Doc Watson, the interracial Tarriers, the Limeliters, the Smothers Brothers, the Clancy Brothers and Tommy Makem, Judy Collins, the Brothers Four, the New Christy Minstrels. The Chad Mitchell Trio managed to get a few quasi-protest songs on the show, such as "The John Birch Society," a parody of the shadowy right-wing political lobby, a song banned from many radio stations. Pete Seeger was later invited on the show, but only if he signed a loyalty oath to the United States, and of course he refused. The boy-cott grew, so *Hootenanny* started featuring comedians—Bill Cosby, Woody Allen, and Vaughn Meader, who did a dead-on imperson-ation of Jack Kennedy.

"We liked the Tarriers," Carly remembered, "and we used to hang out with them because they were so funny. Marshall Brickman was in the group. [Brickman later co-wrote the Woody Allen films *Annie Hall* and *Manhattan*.] So was [actor] Alan Arkin."

Lucy Simon wanted to sing "Winkin', Blinkin' and Nod" on *Hootenanny*. Soon she would get her wish.

May 1963. When Carly finished her second year at Sarah Law-rence, she was press-ganged into the Simon Sisters by Lucy, who had been working on new versions of old songs. Lucy had "Winkin', Blinkin' and Nod," as it was now called, and arrangements for an assortment of traditional ballads and lullabies: "Delia," a woman shot by her man; the spiritual "The Water Is Wide"; the old Scots ballad "Will You Go, Laddie?" Pete Seeger's "Turn! Turn! Turn!" sounded incredible when Lucy and Carly sang it. So did Bob Dylan's civil rights anthem "Blowin' in the Wind."

This song had appeared, also in May 1963, on Dylan's second album, *The Freewheelin' Bob Dylan,* and was quickly received as an emergency telegram from the postwar generation. Dylan's first album had been a rehash of old folk forms, but *Freewheelin'* boasted eleven original songs informed by the civil rights struggle and a fear of nuclear war inspired by the terrifying Cuban Missile Crisis of Octo-ber 1962. "Blowin' in the Wind," "Masters of War," "Girl from the North Country," "A Hard Rain's A-Gonna Fall" (to the ancient tune of "Lord Randall"), and "Don't Think Twice, It's All Right" changed the soul and spirit of the postwar American generation that summer, and established the twenty-two-year-old Dylan as the avatar of a new kind of performer, the singer-songwriter, an American balladeer who wrote his own material—sometimes romantic, sometimes topical—and performed with an authenticity shaped by influence and contact

MORE ROOM IN A BROKEN HEART

with the older, venerable ones who sang of the dust bowl and the grapes of wrath.

Peter, Paul and Mary released their version of "Blowin' in the Wind" as a single, and the record spent the summer of 1963 at the top of the charts. Lucy and Carly translated Dylan's song into French as "Ecoute Dans Le Vent," and it became an audience favorite.

So now the Simon Sisters were a high-end folk act, a savvy combo of the sensual and the intellectual, hard-wired for the college concert circuit.

Carly: "We got the name of a dressmaker on Lexington Avenue and had some matching dresses made. I had stage fright and didn't really want to be a singer, but I did it for my sister. I trusted her judgment, so I did whatever she said, almost no questions asked. That was the beginning of the Simon Sisters."

Lucy: "I was still in nursing school at Cornell, and Carly was at Sarah Lawrence, so at first it was just something to do on our summer vacations. We packed our things—the matching outfits—and our guitars—maybe six chords between us—and took the bus to Provincetown, at the tip of Cape Cod. We didn't have much money, so we rented a room with a double bed in a boarding house on the edge of town. We proceeded to audition at all the local clubs, but got turned down by everyone. Finally we were hired to sing at The Moors, a pub whose resident folk singer had just been sent to Viet Nam. The Moors was way at the other end of Provincetown from where we were staying. So we started hitch-hiking to work in our matching dresses and peasant blouses [plus cross-gartered sandals from Greece, very fashion-forward]. Even with our guitar cases, it was sometimes hard for us to get rides. We taunted those who blew by us: 'Ha ha, you idiots, we'll see you at The Moors!' "

The sensational Simon Sisters caught on at the Moors. Their sexy mix of ballads and lullabies contained authentic human heartbreak and astounding close harmony, the kind that only blood relatives can achieve when they sing, *ensemble*. Soon the place was filled with eager young men early in the evening, waiting for the girls to go on. Lucy's soprano was enthralling. Carly tried to lay back, a presence more muted and deferential, but her singing could be much more assertive, as if to make up for Lucy's natural reticence.

"At The Moors, we realized we were ready," Carly later wrote. "We had hope, harmony, and expectations."

A New York talent agent, someone Lucy knew named Charlie Close, caught the Simon Sisters' act in Provincetown. He worked with Harold Leventhal, who managed a stable of folkie godfathers that included the Weavers and Pete Seeger. Uncle Peter looked at the contracts and made sure the girls weren't getting screwed, financially at least. So now the Simon Sisters had serious management, and their career began in earnest.

As the summer of 1963 went on, Carly spent time with Nick Delbanco at an old fishing camp he rented in Chilmark, on Martha's Vineyard. The dilapidated shack was on a hilltop and looked out over Menemsha Pond and the hills, toward remote Gay Head. Carly told Nicky about the Simon Sisters' big adventure, and Nicky, very ambitious himself, seemed both proud of her and slightly envious of her budding career. He had an idea for his first novel, he told Carly, and he was going to Europe in the fall to research and write it. An old farmhouse in the South of France was being made available through a friend of the family for Nick to write in. Nick wanted Carly to come with him, keep him company while he wrote; she could use the time to write songs on her own. Nick made the romantic Riviera sojourn sound like the lost days of Scott and Zelda Fitzgerald. Carly told Nick that France was very tempting, but right now she was still in college and committed to this project with her somewhat driven sister, to whom the success of the Simon Sisters seemed to mean the world.

Carly's grandmother Chebe died that summer, a real blow. Andrea Simon was renting puppeteer Bil Baird's house on the Vineyard when she got the news. She collected Carly from Nicky's house and together they drove down to New York for the funeral, crying the whole way.

August 1963. Harold Leventhal booked the Simon Sisters into the Bitter End, the brick-walled folk club on Bleecker Street in Greenwich Village. It was late summer, and only tourists were around, but the famous folkie venue still sold out almost every night. The sisters performed four sets a night in cable-knit sweaters, white pedal pushers, and flat shoes, their hair ironed straight, their lipstick matching. Soon the Simon Sisters were the Bitter End's resident opening act, working two and three weeks straight, supporting established folk stars and rising young comedians—Bill Cosby, Dick Cavett, Joan Rivers, even the outlaw satirist Lenny Bruce. One night, backstage at the Gaslight, the basement folk club on MacDougal Street, after Woody Allen's Brooklyn intellectual shtick had really bombed before an out-of-town audience, Lucy and Carly eavesdropped as Woody's veteran manager coached him in timing and intonation, especially his use of hard consonants to make his points. And so the Simon Sisters were exposed to the bare bones of the New York cabaret world in the autumn of 1963. On several occasions, Andrea and Ronnie came to the Village to cheer the girls on. Nicky Delbanco came, too, as did Peter Dean. Peter Simon shot a dozen or so rolls of film with his father's Leica camera.

Meanwhile, Carly was still trying to go to college. "We were playing the Bitter End and the Gaslight, opening for various soon-to-be-famous people. Afterward, we had to catch the last trains from Penn Station, very late at night, back to our schools. These were fancy schools, quiet campuses. The dorm mothers frowned on my late night arrivals—several times my mother had to intervene—and the professors thought even less of my overdue papers."

Something had to give. Carly's college days were numbered.

WINKIN', BLINKIN' AND NOD

$\mathcal{B}$y the late summer of 1963, Lucy Simon felt that the Simon Sisters were ready to record. Their management agreed that the two girls had enough songs, both "trad." and original. Charlie Close started bringing record people to the Bitter End to hear the Sisters, who were quickly signed to a two-album deal by Dave Kapp, owner of Kapp Records. Kapp also signed the Chad Mitchell Trio around then (via Harry Belafonte's production company) and had a current pop/R&B hit with "Our Day Will Come," by Ruby and the Romantics, a song that Carly really loved. In "Winkin'," Kapp heard a potential hit single that sounded like the same kind of sweet lullaby that had put "Puff, the Magic Dragon" on the charts a year earlier for Peter, Paul and Mary.

In mid-October 1963, Carly and Lucy went into the studio with thirteen songs. The sessions were produced by Charlie Close, with arrangements credited to Stuart Scharf. The girls were accompanied by two additional guitarists, a cellist, and bassist Bill Lee. Lee was a Brooklyn jazz musician who moonlighted with folk music's elite, especially in concert settings. (He was also the father of future film director Spike Lee.) Over the course of ten days this ensemble recorded thirteen tracks:

"So Glad I'm Here" is a Peter, Paul and Mary–style freedom song, a greeting song that the Sisters would soon use to open their sets. "Breton Lullaby," an ancient air adapted by Lucy, is a folkloric performance backlit by a dusky cello. "Delia" is an old Appalachian ballad with a jazzy bass line; the girls trade verses of this old song that had been popularized by the Kingston Trio and then done by almost everyone else on the folk circuit. The old Scots song "Will You Go, Laddie, Go" is sung a cappella with celestial harmonies; the Byrds would later record it as "Wild Mountain Thyme." Carly's lead vocal on "Chicken Road" sounds a slightly funky note, somewhat removed from the Sisters' refined, chamber-folk stylings. The album's first side ends with another Child ballad, "Once I Had a True Love," sung by Lucy at her most feminine, and wistful.

Side 2: "Wind Spiritual," with dueling guitars and terrific harmonies; "Winkin'" is taken up-tempo, two minutes of radio-friendly fairy-tale twinkling; "A La Claire Fontaine" is another French song in the Sisters' repertoire; "Rise Up," written by Lucy and Carly, has a bluesy civil rights feel. "Lorca Lullaby" features classical Spanish guitar and is a sad paean to the poet murdered by fascists in the Spanish Civil War. "Waley, Waley (The Water Is Wide)" is sung by Lucy in her virginal soprano, with cello accompaniment. The final song is a saucy flamenco, "Sano Duso," arranged by Carly and Stuart Scharf.

Having cut an album, the Simon Sisters went back to work, playing the folk circuit. They listened to their tapes and asked each other why they were so good at singing lullabies. (Eventually, over three albums, lullabies would equal a third of the Sisters' recorded output.) "I am convinced," Carly wrote in 2006, "that Lucy and I have a natural ability to exude that time of the evening when lulling can quiet even the heaviest of hearts. Something in our natures and history must have needed it ourselves, and so we passed it down . . .

"I have never put this analysis into words before, but I think Lucy and I offered this to the listener . . . Even when we were unsophisticated and unsure of who we would be eventually, as musicians and as people, we knew we wanted to reassure and comfort and hold the babies of the world in our voices."

The Simon Sisters' first album would not be released for another six months. A few weeks after it was recorded, President Kennedy was assassinated in Dallas, Texas. At her mother's house that awful weekend, Carly watched as the veiled, deeply shocked Jacqueline Kennedy and the late president's brothers followed the hearse to the cemetery. Carly's mother, distraught, said that she had a gnawing feeling that life in America would never be the same again.

Instead of returning to Sarah Lawrence after the winter break, Carly notified the college that she was withdrawing, and ran off to Europe to be with Nicky Delbanco. This was a rebellion against her family and the Simon Sisters, but Carly felt she needed to get away from both.

She flew to Milan in January 1964. There she hooked up with Nick, who had a book contract with the Philadelphia publisher J.P. Lippincott. He had been working on his novel in London and Greece since September. They went shopping, and Carly bought a Phillips reel-to-reel tape recorder so she could work on songwriting. Nick bought an Alfa Romeo sports car and an Olivetti typewriter so he could work on his book. They then drove to a tiny village called Opio, near Grasse, the perfume capital of France, where a romantic rustic cottage awaited their arrival.

Nick: "My father's oldest friend had been the architect for the renovation for an old estate, of which we occupied the gatehouse. It was rather a classy joint. [Actor] Dirk Bogarde lived just behind. Julia Child had a house across the way. My father asked his friend, his friend asked the old lady who owned the estate, and presto—the children move in."

Their sojourn in Grasse was supposed to be idyllic, but it didn't quite work out that way for Carly. It was still winter, even in the South of France. The fragrant lavender plantations around Grasse had been harvested and were lying fallow, waiting for spring. The swimming pool was empty except for leaves. The old house was primitive and barely heated, with water drawn from a well. And Carly felt terrible from the beginning with various ailments, including guilt at abandoning her studies, night-time panic attacks, grief over the loss of her grandmother, and a reaction to the antibiotics she was taking, as she later told an interviewer, because Nicky had given her a sexually transmitted disease when they were together in Milan.

("I was baffled when I read about this," Nick Delbanco said recently, "since I definitely did *not* have a venereal disease in Europe, whatever Carly might have fantasized. In fact, I remained wholly faithful to her during the months I was working in London—full of a romantic notion of fidelity and lasting love. So she either contracted an infection from someone else or imagined it entirely. Over and out.")

Carly found the adjustment to life in France somewhat jarring. She changed her style and look to resemble the popular French singer Françoise Hardy, whose picture was in all the magazines. This was so effective that when they went into the Riviera towns—Nice and Cannes—young people would sometimes ask Carly for her autograph. Gradually she and Nick fell into a routine. "We'd get up in the morning," Nick said, "and I'd go off to one of the rooms and type, type, type. Fine, or at least I thought. But Carly was very unhappy, even aggrieved. She wasn't sleeping well, and would shake and tremble violently, and ask me to hold her until she fell asleep again."

Carly: "At least I started to write songs when I was living in France. At first I was sending little tapes of letters home to my family, then I began writing melodies to my own words. I was living with a novelist, in the sweetest little cottage looking over terraces of olive

groves and mimosa trees coming in the windows, and he often contributed lyrics. Other times I would take a local poem and put that
to music. It was the first period in my life that I set everything else
aside and really tried to write songs."

After several months in France, Carly had written four songs.
"Nick chopped wood," Carly later recalled. "I started writing songs.
We drank local wine from Grasse that I'm sure they made with perfume. A village couple, Jacques and Odette, looked after us. I learned
to say 'garlic' in French and I made suppers almost every night copying
recipes from my engagement/calendar book. This was tricky because
the oven had no thermometer. I had to watch, and guess. There was
no hot water and every bath had to be filled with ten pans of water
heated on the wood stove. Nicky chopped more wood. We felt very
groovy and entitled to be living on the cheap."

In February, Carly and Nick drove to Barcelona. "Carly cried the
whole time," Nick said. "I asked her why she was so upset, and she
went through the whole thing about Chebe being Spanish and she much
missed Chebe so much, and so on."

Today Carly sometimes ties her fragile emotionality in this period
to the birth control pill she was taking, Enovid. This early contraceptive pill injected a high daily dose of estrogen into the system, with
often unpredictable results for the young women who took it.

The young couple drove back to France. Nick kept typing, and
Carly read Stendhal's *The Red and the Black* and tried to get a tan
by the empty pool. She wondered what she was doing there. The night
tremors got worse, then really horrible. Odette brought Carly breakfast in bed when she felt ill. Carly got through to her mother on a
neighbor's telephone and told Andrea that she thought she was having a nervous breakdown. ("The first of many," Carly would later
write.) Andrea told Carly to come home as soon as possible and get
some help. Nicky was heartbroken, but nothing would sway Carly
from going home. He took photographs of Carly standing in front
of their house looking downward, contemplative. He drove Carly to

the airport at Nice. "It was a very hard time," he remembered, "and I was sorry to see her go. After she decamped, I went back to Greece and continued to work on my novel."

On the long TWA 707 flight from Paris to New York, Carly spotted Dionne Warwick sitting in first class. Warwick was one of the great pop singers of the era, whose collaborations with songwriters Burt Bacharach and Hal David had produced huge hit records such as "Walk on By" and "Anyone Who Had a Heart." Summoning up her courage, Carly introduced herself to Warwick as a budding songwriter, and asked if she would listen to some demo tapes she was working on. Warwick said sure, and scribbled her address on a menu. Carly duly sent Dionne Warwick a tape of the four songs she'd written in France, and was disappointed never to hear back from her.

Hootenanny Saturday Night

‾‾‾

*C*arly returned to New York in April 1964, and the night-time shaking stopped. She began four years of costly psychoanalysis that would wipe out most of her inheritance. Partly for financial reasons, she resolved to re-form the Simon Sisters. "My sister was very irritated with me," Carly said later, "and rightly so, because while I was gone they couldn't promote the records or do anything. I was very torn, because I never got into the Simon Sisters the way Lucy did. But when I came back to the United States, Lucy and I started taking our songwriting seriously again."

Lucy and Carly went back to work at the Bitter End and the other folk clubs in the Northeast. They had low expectations for their career in the wake of the Beatles' arrival in America the previous winter, which had sounded the death knell of the folk revival. "We were clueless, and really naïve," Lucy says. "We didn't think we amounted to very much." Carly thought they looked uncool—"like Tweedle Dum and Tweedle Dee"—in their matching stage outfits.

As if the Beatles' advent weren't enough, the March 1964 release of the album *Getz/Gilberto* set off a national bossa nova craze when "The Girl from Ipanema," with Astrud Gilberto's soft vocals, became the coolest song on the radio in America. Stan Getz had already popularized the new Brazilian wave with his *Jazz Samba* album, and now his collaboration with Joao Gilberto and Antonio Carlos Jobim was the newest sound in popular music. Carly Simon was irresistibly drawn to the new Brazilian sound, an influence that would resonate throughout her career.

The Simon Sisters opened for the legendary comedian Lenny Bruce at the Gaslight in New York in April 1964. Dave Kapp told them he was finally going to release their first album, now that Carly had returned. This time around, the Simon Sisters found stage fright easier to manage. Lucy recalled that "our stage fright now worked in a funny way, because backstage Carly would be literally shaking in her boots and I was calm. Once onstage, under the lights, I'd get scared and Carly would be completely cool."

The Simon Sisters, a monaural LP, was released in late April 1964, along with a 45 rpm single version of "Winkin', Blinkin and Nod." Album notes were supplied by Lee Hays of the Weavers, who noted that the Sisters were gutsy to try to break into the male-dominated folk scene. On the first day of sales, Lucy and Carly went to the Doubleday bookstore on Fifth Avenue to buy their album, and were shocked to find it had sold out. As they were leaving, they over-heard the sales clerk say, "Yeah, their relatives have been coming in all day."

But "Winkin', Blinkin' and Nod," a catchy single, ravishingly sung, got on the radio in both New York and Boston and entered *Billboard* magazine's Hot 100 chart at number seventy-three on April 25, 1964. The girls and their family were thrilled to hear the song broadcast on WMCA and WMGM in New York. Their booking agent now got more offers for them to perform; the record company exercised its option to cut a second Simon Sisters album; and the producers of *Hootenanny* offered them a slot on America's premier music program of the day. This was big—national TV exposure during prime time on Saturday night, coast to coast—and the Simon Sisters were properly terrified.

They of course knew about the boycott of *Hootenanny*. Pete Seeger had been their kindergarten music teacher at the City and Country School, and they were loath to appear on the program, but their management and record label insisted. In late May 1964 they arrived at the University of Tennessee in Knoxville, where they would appear on a filmed *Hootenanny* bill headlined by the Smothers Brothers, supported by the Carter Family and the Cumberland Trio. The show's stage manager, the future impresario Fred Weintraub, wanted the sisters to appear in cheerleader outfits, which they refused to do. They rehearsed their two numbers—"Winkin'" and (cheekily) Pete Seeger's "Turn! Turn! Turn!"—and nervously waited their turn to sing.

Carly: "Before our set, Lucy and I were both numb and shaking. Different parts of our anatomies shook and were numb. Lucy's voice shook. My hands and knees shook, which made it hard to play the guitar or assume a graceful pose. We were so stiff, like scared mannequins, like young clenched fists with mouths and vocal chords."

But after being introduced by the leering Tom and Dick Smothers, the Simon Sisters performed beautifully in their demure matching dresses and low heels, both girls strumming their Martin guitars. After their segment was filmed, the director told them they'd been sensational. Lucy remembered that, afterward, a smirking, fidgety Dickie Smothers sidled up to her and said, "You girls are *sisters,* and Tom and I are *brothers,* and maybe we could kind of team up, and maybe do something together sometime." Lucy said that would be great, but Dickie interrupted. "Actually, I meant something . . . um . . . *sexual.*" But that didn't happen.

The Simon Sisters pretty much stole the show when *Hootenanny* aired later that summer. The girls sang like lusty virgins and looked angelic, with a black-and-white, cathode-ray TV aura. Carly's mellow, burnished harmonies descanted Lucy's Highlands soprano perfectly. They were so purely musical that everyone who saw the program, and knew anything at all about music, noticed and remembered them. (One of these viewers was Jac Holzman, the boss of Elektra Records, which, along with Vanguard Records, was the premier folk label in America. Holzman had loved "Winkin'" when he'd heard it on Jonathan Schwartz's radio show in New York, and now that he saw the Simon Sisters on television, he filed away their indelible image for possible future fruition.)

The Simon Sisters recorded their second album, *Cuddlebug,* in late June 1964. Production values were higher this time, with members of Count Basie's orchestra playing on some of the sessions. The title track (cowritten by Alan Arkin of The Tarriers) is a sort of ironic bossa nova about a security blanket. "If You Go Down to the Water" is one of the songs Carly worked on in France with help from Nicky Delbanco. It has a gospel feel, with some tricky shifting tempi. "Turn! Turn! Turn!" is a lovely rendition of Pete Seeger's adaptation of verses from the Book of Ecclesiastes (and follows Judy Collins's version from the year before). "Ecoute Dans Le Vent" is "Blowin' in the Wind" in French. "Hold Back the Branches" is pure art song (with an oboe solo), translated from the Spanish poet Lope de Vega and sung by Carly.

The rest of the album is filled out with traditional material: "Motherless Child" follows the a cappella version sung by Ronnie Gilbert of the Weavers. "Dink's Song" has a sultry lead vocal by Carly, while "No One to Tell My Troubles To" has a strong lead by Lucy. She also sings "If I Had a Ribbon Bow" in her sweetest solo voice. "My Fisherman, My Laddie O!" is an old Scottish ballad credited to the blacklisted screenwriter Waldo Salt. "Feuilles-Oh" is another of Lucy's translations, this one from the song "Leaves," by Lee Hays. The album concludes with a new song by Carly, "Pale Horse and Rider," in a country-and-western arrangement that is almost proto-folk rock. The sisters were told that their new album would be released in the autumn of 1964.

Nick Delbanco came back to New York around then, his novel almost finished. He took Carly to one of the inexpensive French restaurants along West Forty-ninth Street, and they shared a celebratory bottle of wine from the Grasse region where they had lived. That night, for the first time since she returned home, Carly suffered the strange body tremors that had plagued her in France. She talked this over with her psychiatrist.

"It wasn't difficult to put two and two together, and realize it was due to an allergy to the wine," Carly later said. "There can be a lot of things that will spur a person into analysis, and for that reason I often distrust that a lot of my anxiety symptoms are purely psychosomatic. I learned to look for chemical, including hormonal, reasons why I may be feeling out of sorts, terribly depressed, or vaguely suicidal."

Around this time, the Simon Sisters were forced to cancel a few engagements because Carly had a sore throat. Out came her tonsils, and Carly stopped singing for a month.

CARLY AND THE VANDELLAS

$\mathcal{S}$ummer 1964. Carly is dancing and singing in front of the mirror on the landing of her mother's house in Riverdale while her brother photographs her pretending to be Martha Reeves of Martha and the Vandellas. Carly admires Martha's glacial cool on *American Bandstand* and would love to be her. Carly is moving to "Dancing in the Street," a big jam on the radio in that summer of civil rights marches and voter registration drives in the segregated American South. Progress is in the air, predicted by Bob Dylan, the protean young prophet singing "the times, they are a-changin'." President Johnson improbably gets the Civil Rights Act passed by Congress, and Martin Luther King Jr. will shortly receive the Nobel Peace Prize for his nonviolent crusade against racial discrimination in America. Motown groups— the Supremes, the Temptations, the Four Tops—are in the vanguard of this movement. "Dancing in the Street" is the summer's anthem, a call to arms, an invitation across the nation. The song is a bridge between peoples, defusing the tensions of a nation struggling with its past and its present.

Carly Simon digs Martha Reeves, big time. She'd even settle for being a Vandella.

When Carly's throat healed, the sisters moved to Martha's Vineyard, where they played several times at the Mooncusser coffeehouse. The year-old venue presented mostly Boston-based folkies (Tom Rush, the Jim Kweskin Jug Band, the Charles River Valley Boys) and some New York singers affiliated with Elektra Records (Carolyn Hester, Mark Spoelstra, Judy Collins). Carly was living again with Nicky, who was driving a truck for Poole's Fish in Menemsha. That little fishing village had a seasonal general store called Seward's that had famously been on the cover of *The Saturday Evening Post*. One day Carly was buying a soda at Seward's when her path on the store's porch was blocked by a bunch of kids whom she vaguely recognized from the Vineyard music scene. One of them, a tall boy known to her as a good guitar player, was sixteen-year-old Jamie Taylor. Carly had seen him play at the Mooncusser's hootenanny nights. "I heard a lot about James on the Vineyard in those days," Carly said later, "although he was referred to as Jamie Taylor." James and his crowd were younger than Carly and Lucy, so there was no interaction between them other than sideways glances, but Carly later remembered this particular Menemsha sighting in precise detail.

In August the Simon Sisters moved to the Berkshire hills in western Massachusetts for a two-week residency at the Music Inn, a hip summer resort in the rolling hills near Lenox that featured mainstream folk acts and jazz groups. Brooklyn-born Randy Weston was the resident bop pianist. The Simon Sisters were assigned to the venue's smaller tavern/nightspot, the Potting Shed, where they would play seven nights a week for a fortnight. All went well—the sultry sisters attracted a rowdy crowd of young single men nightly—until Odetta came to headline at the main room, the Music Barn.

The girls were living in the staff dormitory, sharing a row of beds with the cooks, waitresses, and cleaners. Since they didn't start to sing until ten o'clock, they were able to hear some of the talent passing through: Ornette Coleman, Dave Brubeck, Pete Seeger, Judy Collins. Carly remembers the excitement in the dorm when Odetta was due to perform:

"We were—all of us in the dorm on Friday night before her show—so nervous and excited to have her in our midst. I knew by heart every song she'd recorded. I was famous in my high school for singing like her; they even put that in my senior yearbook. There was a buzz in our dorm about almost every act coming to the Music Barn, but I especially remember the buzz about the beautiful, regal, brilliant favorite singer of mine."

Carly and Lucy attended Odetta's concert at eight on Saturday night. Odetta came out with her big Dreadnought guitar, accompanied by Bill Lee on upright bass. Carly went into trance from the first booming note. "I remember being visited by things other than from this world. I remember believing how—someday—I might be as self-assured, and have my voice ring out in a real concert hall. I just loved this woman on stage." Yet reality intruded on Carly's reverie. "It was also hard to think that we would be singing shortly after Odetta, Lucy and I, in our matching peasant blouses and with our Scottish folk songs."

Odetta's concert ended at 9:30, leaving just enough time for the sisters to brush their hair, change into their stage clothes, and run over to the jam-packed Potting Shed, five minutes late for their first set. They unpacked their guitars and tried to catch their breath as they heard their introduction: "Ladies and gentlemen, and now . . . the angelic voices of the Simon Sisters!"

The girls got onstage to a warm welcome and tore into "Winkin'." This got major applause, as it did every night. Carly: "Then I looked at the table closest to the stage. The room was heavy and warm with summer and smoke. Single men were whistling at us from the bar in the back. I looked at the front table again . . . Odetta! My god! She was there. How did she get there? Why? Oh God . . . Oh no . . . Oh, I'm blacking out. Lucy! I'm not kidding, I'm . . ."

Carly came to after a minute. Someone was taking her pulse. Someone else was taking her picture. "But Odetta was looking down on me and fanning me with a menu. She was asking me if I was alright. I felt so embarrassed being so weak in front of her. I got up so fast, and the energy of simple embarrassment lifted me onto the stage.

In Carly's account of the incident, the Sisters performed their eight songs and Carly sang without fear. "It was perfect. It was a night like no other. I couldn't even talk afterward."

Lucy has a different memory. "The only time Carly *really* lost it was when we were booked into the Potting Shed in Lenox. We came onstage and were preparing to sing, and we looked down and Odetta was at a front table. Carly completely froze, and then she walked off. I did the set by myself. I think Carly came back and was able to do the encore—just."

Cuddlebug was released in September and flopped. The Simon Sisters were depicted, according to Carly, "in dreadful pink sweaters and matching pink makeup." No one bought this passé look, or the album either. The competition (from Motown and the British Invasion bands) to get on the radio that month was murderous. "Dancing in the Street" was number one, Manfred Mann's "Doo Wah Diddy" was number 2, and the sisters didn't stand a chance.

In early September the Simon Sisters were appearing at one of the coffeehouses on Yonge Street in Toronto. They were staying at the same semi-besieged hotel as the Beatles, who were playing for the first time in Canada. One of the Beatles' entourage offered them tickets to the September 7 concert at Maple Leaf Gardens, the city's hockey arena. The girls, at their first ever rock concert, were shocked at the lack of decorum.

Carly: "I think it was Dusty Springfield who opened for them. Everyone was being extremely rude and standing on their chairs and screaming. 'WE WANT THE BEATLES!' Well, great ladies of the theatre that we were, my sister and I looked annoyingly on those people. It only later I realized that the whole point of the concert is the electrical charge, and not to make contact with that is absurd."

Then the sisters' career stalled. There was talk of teaming up with the three talented Chapin brothers—Harry, Tom, and Steve (sons of a Big Band drummer)—to form a pop group like the New Christy Minstrels or the Serendipity Singers, to be called Brothers and Sisters, but nothing came of it. This was in the middle of the presidential election, Johnson versus Goldwater, which featured TV ads of mushroom clouds and the first American "advisers" in Vietnam.

Carly and the rest of her family voted for Lyndon Johnson.

Then Carly broke up with Nicky.

Carly [speaking in a 1972 interview]: "My first boyfriend, whom I was with for six years and I was very in love with, was a little bit threatened by my going into the music business. I remember him saying to me that when I was on stage and he was looking at me, he hated the fact that everyone else was also looking at me. I also think he was worried that I would meet somebody else out on the road, or I would be glamorized, or caught up in the whole glamorousness of the business, and that I wouldn't be satisfied by a simple life anymore. In fact, that's why we finally broke up.

"I don't know why, but I've always had these men that I allowed to tyrannize me, or scare me out of a professional life. 'Now Carly, you know that isn't going to make you *happy*. It'll *ruin* you.' That kind of thing. . . . We finally broke up because I went into analysis and I realized that I wasn't satisfied by being tyrannized. It's not fair to say that he tyrannized me, but I realized that my will was being thwarted by giving in to him, all the time."

Nicholas Delbanco's first novel, *The Martlet's Tale,* was published two years later, to enthusiastic reviews. The author's photograph was taken by Peter Simon, and the novel was dedicated to his sister, Carly.

SWINGING LONDON

———

$\mathcal{S}$ummer 1965. The Rolling Stones' pop art masterpiece "Satisfaction" (whose main riff is an inversion of "Dancing in the Street") is the number one song in America. The Simon Sisters have some possible gigs in England, so Carly leaves for London to follow a charming British shoe salesman with whom she's been infatuated in New York. Things don't work out with the shoe guy, so instead she falls, quite madly, in love with the Simon Sisters' potential English booking agent, the notorious London rake Willie Donaldson.

Willie was thirty but looked forty with his thinning hair and baggy suits. He was a popular, semisuccessful figure in London's entertainment world, centered in Soho. He'd gone to a good public school, then to Cambridge, and then gravitated to the theater; he'd been one of the producers of the brilliant review *Beyond the Fringe*, which had launched the careers of Dudley Moore, Jonathan Miller, and Alan Bennett in London's West End before migrating to a long run in New York. Willie had also been involved in bringing Bob Dylan to England for the first time, in 1964 (and can be seen in the background of the documentary *Don't Look Back,* which documented Dylan's 1965 UK tour). Willie was tall, blond, charming, and utterly hilarious. Long divorced, he was well-bred, but raffish and louche, unburdened by any great reputation for financial probity, and when he met Carly he was about to be dumped by his girlfriend, the actress Sarah Miles, who specialized in slatternly roles in noir British films such as *The Servant.* But Willie Donaldson's most recent productions had flopped in London, and when Carly came into his life he was on something of a downward spiral. Anyone who knew Willie would have told Carly to stay away, far away, but she fell for him.

She first contacted him at his office at the Players and Writers Agency. Her diary noted that on July 14 she visited him at Sarah Miles's apartment on Hasker Street. Carly herself was living in a small flat on Wilton Street for ten shillings a week, rolling her drying hair over beer cans so it would be straight like the actress Julie Christie's. She was attracted to Willie immediately, as he had many of the physical attributes of her father, including the thinning hair and slightly stooped bearing. Having broken up with Nicky and lost interest in the shoe salesman, as she noted on July 20, "I feel very close to Willie, even if he does call me 'Simon's Sister.'"

Carly was flattered that Willie seemed interested in her. He was the funniest man she'd ever met. "We were instantly attracted to one another's wit, Willie's being far more everything than mine, but me being a great audience for him." Her diary for July 26 mentioned that Sarah Miles had kicked him out of her house and that he had moved into 6 Wilton Street, across from where Carly was staying. Diary entry from the end of July: "Willie has the body of an old man. What is it that I want? *Oh Carly—watch out!*"

By early August, Carly and Willie Donaldson were glued to each other. On the night of August 3 they roamed the streets of Mayfair and Soho in an all-night walk as Willie showed Carly around. With the summer sun rising over leafy St. James Park, Willie confessed to

Carly that something in him was very damaged, but he felt that her love was helping him recover. Carly loved this. Nick had always been her protector, but now she felt she could heal Willie's psychic wounds with her love, and this meant a lot to her. Willie was big on nicknames. He started calling Carly his "little frog footman," for reasons she never quite understood. Then he asked her point-blank, half in jest, if she would marry him, and Carly immediately said yes, she would.

Carly was, as Donaldson later wrote, "the answer to any sane man's prayers: funny, quick, erotic, extravagantly talented." He was as besotted with her perfume as she was with his.

The affair, for Carly, was naked and sexual. Donaldson had been the lover of innumerable actresses, starlets, and harlots, and was very experienced. Carly has described him as being very tender with her, and adorable in every sense. "It's pretty amazing that an affair can be so intense as to . . . *halt me*—in that way," she told Willie's British biographer many years later. "We had a wonderful sex life, although, like me, he was shy about the way he looked, and didn't want to be seen in the light." Willie took Carly on a nostalgic visit to Cambridge, where they viewed his old rooms at the university. "He was very sentimental about this," Carly recalled.

Willie wanted to launch the Simon Sisters in England, so Carly called Lucy in New York and told her about him, saying that he would pay her airfare to London; but Carly actually paid Lucy's way, just to get her to London so her older sister could see what was going on between her and Willie. He took the two sisters to tea at Fortnum & Mason, and Carly was startled to realize she became almost insanely jealous every time Willie even looked at Lucy. The girls moved into lodgings in Cadogan Square, a grand old house Willie dubbed Toad Hall, as in (when putting the girls into a taxi): "Take the Simon Sisters to Toad Hall!" He then arranged London auditions for them at Take One, and at the Rehearsal Room, above the Royal Court Theatre in Sloane Square.

Lucy indeed saw that Carly was really in love with this suave, swinging Englishman. Lucy: "Willie was charming, elegant, intelligent, and best of all he was able to make Carly relax. He really brought out her humor. They were talking very seriously about marriage, which surprised me quite a bit at the time. I wasn't sure what to make of it."

At the end of August 1965, Lucy heard there was work for the Simon Sisters at home, and the girls booked passage for New York on the ocean liner S.S. *United States*. After a river of tears, Carly left England under the firm impression that she was going to wind up her life in America, return to London, and be married as the second Mrs. William Donaldson. Once aboard the ship, she opened a telegram that read, "LITTLE FROG FOOTMAN COME BACK SOON."

Sailing from Southampton, the girls noticed actor Sean Connery boarding the ship on his way to another film role as James Bond, agent 007. After they checked into their stateroom, Carly sent a note to Connery, who read it on the massage table. Ten minutes later he knocked on their door, his hair still unctuous from massage oil. For the next few days, Carly says, James Bond gently pestered the sisters for sex. "He tried to persuade Lucy and me to do things we'd never even heard of." But on their last night at sea, Carly decided that if Sean called, she would visit him in his deluxe penthouse suite, putting aside her troth to Willie for one memorable night. But she was in the bathroom when the phone rang, and Lucy answered it instead.

Asked what happened next, Lucy allowed only that she'd had a "fascinating" supper with Mr. Connery that evening.

Carly arrived at her mother's house in Riverdale on September 8, 1965, and announced her marriage plans. Andrea Simon was taken aback. Other family members were worried for her. Then Willie's letters started arriving, and Carly read aloud his amusing declarations of love for her, and her family began to understand why she found this older man so dazzling. Carly wrote to him every day, expressing her thrilled anticipation of their forthcoming marriage. She wrote a couple of new songs inspired by Willie: "You're the One" and "The Best Thing."

Then Willie's letters stopped. Carly was shocked at first. She tried phoning him, but he was never in, never returned her calls. She became frantic, then devastated as she realized the truth. On October 24 a letter arrived from Willie. Sarah Miles had taken him back; with deep regret, he informed Carly, the marriage was off.

Carly was crushed. "It was terrible," Peter Simon remembers. "My sister couldn't stop crying, really blubbering, almost deranged. Then she started to stammer again and we knew she was seriously bereft."

Carly has admitted that she never really got over her affair with Willie Donaldson. She said much later that it still made her sad that she could never seem to get back to that sense of herself that Willie fell for, and found so attractive. Carly Simon would love other men, but perhaps none with the ferocity of what she felt for Willie.

As for Willie, he went on the skids soon after dumping Carly. Sarah Miles left him, in turn, for the screenwriter Robert Bolt, whom she later married. Homeless, Willie found work as a pimp and moved into a brothel. Then he spent a decade addicted to cocaine. He turned his hand to writing, churning out comic novels, essays, and newspaper columns. When he died in 2005, the London *Daily Telegraph* hailed him as "a pimp, crack fiend, sex addict, and a comic genius."

In his memoirs, Willie Donaldson wrote about his affair with Carly in the summer of 1965:

> [One evening] Carly quite embarrassed me. She took a bath and then stretched out on the bed with nothing on. "What do you think?" she said. She looked magnificent, in fact, but I felt more uncomfortable. She'd slipped embarrassingly out of character. . . . This was a woman I loved and respected, a

woman I was going to marry. No doubt I climbed into bed and turned away, thought about tall silent women prowling the stage with nothing on. Carly had confused herself for a moment with a Helmut Newton woman, a woman whose business it was to do this sort of thing, to pose and mock you at a distance, to wear thigh boots and stand in the corner if I told her to.

Carly Simon says that this and most of the other details concerning her in Willie Donaldson's various writings are fiction, because they never happened.

THE FEMALE BOB DYLAN

*M*eanwhile, in Woodstock, Bob Dylan was burned out.

This was 1966, late winter, early spring. The previous year, flying on speed, Dylan released the two albums that signified his radical turn to electric rock and roll. *Bringing It All Back Home* had "Gates of Eden," "Maggie's Farm," and "Mr. Tambourine Man," which basically invented the new genre of folk-rock. A few months later came *Highway 61 Revisited,* which had "Like a Rolling Stone" and "Desolation Row." In 1966, Dylan went to Nashville and cut the fourteen songs about to be released on his epochal double album *Blonde on Blonde.* He toured constantly with his band, the Hawks, telling his managers to keep them on the road; he needed the money.

But Dylan's management team was worried. To Albert Grossman and John Court, the principals of Grosscourt Productions, it was obvious that their star client was burning out and had to crash, sooner or later. If Dylan stopped touring, a big money flow would dry up. It was John Court, apparently, who had the notion that they had to find a female Bob Dylan. If Dylan crapped out, or retired awhile, the female Bob Dylan could go out on the road with the Hawks, singing Dylan's songs, and maybe it could be a blast and at least there would be a revenue stream. Court said that he'd heard about a girl who might just fill the bill.

It took Carly Simon a long time—well into 1966—to get over being jilted by Willie Donaldson. She told friends that it had been a fantastic romance; she had been ready to marry this man. "I got a terrible Dear John letter from him," she told an interviewer much later. "That was my first hard lesson in love, and . . . the first cut is the deepest."

Yet once she regained some form of psychic normalcy, with the help of her therapist, Carly picked up her guitar and began to write again. Carly: "It wasn't until my first real—I mean, *real*—heartbreak, that I began writing the kind of songs that, to this day, I find the most gratifying. The ones that . . . allowed me to see things in the third person, almost like reportage. That insight about writing was the only beneficial effect that heartbreak ever had on me."

Then Lucy closed down the Simon Sisters. She'd started dating her psychiatrist, David Levine. Lucy: "I saw that, as the Simon Sisters, our moment was past. We weren't selling records or making much money. I wanted to have children and be married. I thought: this is all I've wanted to do all my life, *and I want no interference*. Carly, anyway, was the more talented performer, and it was clear that she would go on in the business, and be successful."

Carly: "My sister was tired of my nerves, and got married."

So now Carly was on her own. She needed a place to live, and moved into the rear bedroom of her sister Joey's apartment at 400 East Fifty-fifth Street in Manhattan. Joey was still bossy toward her youngest sister, and Carly was often prohibited use of the flat when Joey was entertaining menfriends such as TV panelist Henry Morgan, musician Zubin Mehta, or ballet star Edward Villella. Carly suffered, mostly in silence.

Then she got a call from John Court, who had (maybe) heard of her from Willie Donaldson. Court invited her to meet his partner, Albert Grossman—Bob Dylan's manager!—to discuss her career. Carly was incredibly excited and felt her first break as a solo singer might be imminent.

At the time, Albert Grossman was the most important talent manager in the music business. He was forty-ish, corpulent, rumpled, with long gray hair falling below his shoulders and wire-rimmed granny glasses that made him look like Ben Franklin. Grossman was a tough guy, having emerged from the Chicago folk club scene, and had immediate entrée to all the important record companies. Carly met with him at the Grosscourt offices on Twenty-third Street. Carly later wrote about this period:

"Once Lucy was married, I got involved with Albert Grossman. Without my dear sister's protection, I was a sitting duck. He offered me his body in exchange for worldly success [which Carly found strange, because Grossman was famously married to glamorous Sally Grossman, who lounged in a red trouser suit on the iconic cover of *Bringing It All Back Home*]. Sadly, his body was not the kind you would easily sell yourself for."

Grossman sized Carly up, listened to her demo tapes, and told her she was a hard sell, that he wasn't sure what to do with her. She told him about her stage fright and said that her ambition was to write songs and record them, but not to perform in public. He told her flat out that she was a spoiled rich girl with an entitled attitude.

Then he told her about the female Bob Dylan idea. "Albert said, 'You should get Bob to write a song for you.' I said that would be great. He said, 'I'll get Bob to come over here and meet with you, and you'll go into the studio with his guys. Let me make some calls and see if I can get Columbia [Dylan's record label] to pay for the sessions.' "

Carly said okay to this, but felt uneasy. "I thought I was being exploited with this female Dylan thing. These people hadn't even heard me sing, it was mostly on the basis of my looks. They thought if I sang Dylan songs I would make it as a female Dylan. In my mind, it didn't really follow, but I went along at first."

Carly met with Bob Dylan a few days later, on July 28, 1966. This was almost beyond belief for her. *Blonde on Blonde* was the hottest album in America. The radio blasted out the album's first single, "Rainy Day Women #12 and 35," and its clarion call to anarchy "Everybody must get stoned." It was like taking a meeting with Jesus.

It didn't go that well. Dylan hid behind his sunglasses and didn't make eye contact. He was disheveled, and his hands shook. Carly: "We went into a little cubicle in Albert's office, and Bob took out an old song and added some new lyrics. I tried to question him, but he was really out of it—very, very wasted . . . talking incoherently, saying a lot about God and Jesus, and how I had to go down to Nashville."

Dylan went on: "Hey . . . you know, . . . oh . . . you . . . Nashville! . . . the *players*, man . . . are just . . . you gotta . . . just . . . just believe me . . . *believe me!*" Dylan stretched out his arms, crucified, repeating "Believe me" over and over. Carly: "It was an odd experience."

But Bob Dylan, prodded by management, had indeed written some new lyrics, tailored to Carly, for a female version of "Baby, Let Me Follow You Down," which he had performed on his debut album, saying that it had been taught to him by singer Eric Von Schmidt "in the green pastures of Harvard University." Dylan handed Carly the lyric sheet and left without a farewell. He was driven back to Woodstock, the upstate New York village where he'd found refuge near Grossman's country home, and a few days later broke some bones in his neck when he crashed his motorcycle into a tree.

Just as Grossman had feared, Bob Dylan retired to recover from his accident and his speedy life since 1963. Dylan would not be touring that autumn (and Dylan wouldn't tour for another eight years, when he again went out with the Hawks, who had rebranded themselves in 1968 as the Band). Now Grosscourt Productions needed their female Bob Dylan more than ever.

"So Bob disappeared for a while," Carly said, "freeing up Robbie Robertson and all the people in his band. So I went up to Woodstock and started working with Robbie on a daily basis"—hammering out an arrangement for the new "Baby, Let Me Follow You Down." Carly Simon was about to record a song with America's hottest working band, Bob Dylan's band, the Hawks. The producer supervising the session was Bob Johnston, a portly middle-aged Nashville veteran who had worked on *Blonde on Blonde*. Almost at the last minute Carly was teamed with singer Richie Havens, another Grosscourt client, and this ensemble lit into a full-throated version of "Baby" that chimed much like the Byrds' hit single version of "Mr. Tambourine Man." The Carly/Havens pairing also echoed the sound of Sonny and Cher, another huge folk-rock act that covered Mr. Dylan's songs.

The session was stressful. Carly was "singing out," giving the lyric a lusty, full-throated delivery. Carly: "But Albert kept coming into the studio and directing me. I felt like just a piece of meat, actually." Grossman wanted Carly to slavishly imitate Dylan's distinctive, breathy/nasal intonation of the song's lyrics. Carly gently told Grossman that impressions weren't really her thing. "It was really meat city, because they made me feel like a sex object, not like a musician at all."

They also recorded a forgettable song, cowritten by Bob Johnston and Wes Farrell, called "Goodbye Lovin' Man"—"a song they'd never heard me sing until I got into the studio. It was, 'Let's make a B-side quick.' But the musicians were incredible, super-studded; star-studded: Paul Butterfield, Mike Bloomfield, Levon Helm. I think Al Kooper was there. And I had a major crush on Robbie Robertson." Richie Havens sang backup.

But later, after the musicians had packed their instruments and gone home, Bob Johnston told Carly where it was at. She expressed hope that the sessions had gone well, and Johnston told her that if she were *real nice* to him—and to Carly the implication was unmistakably sexual—he'd make damn sure she got a hit record out of it. He was blatant about it, asking, "What time you want me to come over?"

Carly was shocked. "I'm just not . . ."—she stammered—". . . not that desperate." Badly shaken, she walked out. Carly: "It was such a typical Hollywood-type casting couch routine that I was amazed to hear it actually come out of someone's mouth."

"I went home and sobbed," she later said, and resolved to quit the music business. "If I'd been a hungry girl from Spanish Harlem, I would have had the same sense of shame, but if I didn't have my family to fall back on [financially], desperation might have actually led me to sleep with him. I don't know." It was a terrible letdown for her.

Carly told Grossman the female Dylan thing wasn't for her, and her record was shelved, Columbia having passed on releasing it. Then Grossman thought he could sell an act called Carly and the Deacon, the "Deacon" being Richie Havens. Carly liked the idea, and thought it could work with the right songs. Havens had real energy and talent, but Carly and the Deacon never got into the studio.

"Albert said to me, 'On a one-to-ten scale, as a woman, you're a nine . . . But you've had it too easy, you haven't suffered enough, you don't know what working for a living is like." Carly thought this was stupid, but didn't bother arguing with him, "as if you'd had to have ridden freight trains, or sold your body, to have soul." There was no arguing with Albert Grossman anyway.

Meanwhile, Carly was having a major flirtation with incipient rock star Robbie Robertson (who was actually about to marry his beautiful Canadian girlfriend). Robertson was tall, dark, charismatic, extremely hip, and played guitar with Bob Dylan. For a time, Carly thought Robbie might be her rebound from Willie. They had some furtive lunches together in the Village—Robbie was very cynical about the music business and told Carly point-blank that it wasn't for pussies—but the dates never came to anything serious.

The Woodstock adventure had been a hassle for Carly, a bummer. "I was terribly disappointed," she said a few years later. "I let myself get brought down a lot, thinking that they didn't like me, that I wasn't worth much. Al Grossman had led me to believe I was hot shit, but they thought they could just . . . *mold* me into whatever they wanted. I tried it, out of desperation, because I so wanted to be wanted by these people. But I was *not* ready to be molded by anyone else."

INDIAN HILL

So now Carly Simon retired. She gained weight. Peter Simon, her brother: "We were quite close in this era, the late sixties. She had tried to go solo, and project herself, alone, in order to gain attention from the record companies and the public, and it wasn't working. Carly became very down on herself, and very negative about her chances of making it. These were some difficult years—between 1967 and 1970—when she was bouncing around New York, on the fringes of the music business, mainly writing and recording commercials and jingles, and just in general feeling very depressed about her career."

"During that time," Carly has said, "I worked as an overweight secretary for a production company. I pretended to type while extending my lunch hours to drown my sense of failure in puff pastry and pudding." An executive, Len Friedlander, whose wife was a childhood friend of Carly's, assigned her to one of his company's TV programs, *From the Bitter End*. She was in charge of the green room, taking care of the talent. She made tea for Peter, Paul and Mary. She looked after Richie Havens, who was breaking through with a brilliant album, *Mixed Bag.* She met sixteen-year-old Janis Ian, whose interracial love song, "Society's Child," was a national hit record. "I took care of the Chad Mitchell Trio, the Staple Singers, many others, and didn't try to sell them my songs. I was happy to be around this incredible group of performers, getting them cough drops." One day, Motown star Marvin Gaye came in to lip-sync his latest record.

"In the case of Marvin Gaye, I went into his dressing room to ask if he wanted something to drink, and he said, 'Can you please stick out your tongue for a minute?' So I stuck out my tongue, and he grabbed it with his mouth . . . I couldn't release my tongue for a while, because he was sucking so hard—an experience never to be forgotten. I was so naïve, really; essentially puritanical like my father, so I was confused by Marvin's behavior."

Meanwhile, sensational sounds were beaming in from California. The Doors, from L.A., were dominant with "Light My Fire." Jimi Hendrix, a new guitar warlock out of London, literally was on fire. The San Francisco bands—the Dead, the Jefferson Airplane, Big Brother—were changing popular music. Jefferson Airplane's Grace Slick and Janis Joplin of Big Brother and the Holding Company were proving that women could more than hold their own fronting a modern rock band. Carly found this encouraging.

Her sister Lucy married Dr. David Levine in March 1967. It was a low-key wedding, held in the sunroom at Riverdale, with only family present. After the ceremony, the Simon sisters repaired to Joanna's apartment on East Fifty-fifth Street and opened some champagne, without their mother.

For Carly, her sister's marriage coincided with an onset of fears and phobias. She could hardly explain it to her therapist, but she knew she felt weird, as if she'd lost her best friend and protector. She kept telling herself that she didn't want to be "in show business," but that she was somehow, irresistibly, perhaps fatally, attracted to its dangers. Her image of herself was as a songwriter who recorded her own music, but not a performer who put herself on the line, every night, for her audience. That was more stress than she could imagine.

Summer 1967. Carly wanted out of the city, and took a job teaching guitar at Indian Hill, an upscale arts camp near Stockbridge, Massachusetts. Emanuel Ax ran the chorus. Andrew Bergman did drama. Carly loved the piney woods of the camp, and spent the summer walking around barefoot. Her campers, boys and girls, totally adored her. One was Ellen Epstein:

"I was fifteen years old, from New Rochelle, when I went to camp and Carly Simon was my counselor. She took me under her wing, taught me a lot about the guitar—it was totally thrilling. She was this totally attractive and sparkling presence, and everyone wanted to be around her. She molded the camp rock-and-roll band—Lust 4 Five—around her music [including a young piano player named Billy Mernit]. She was always working on new songs, especially one called 'Secret Saucy Thoughts of Suzy.' We spent that summer working on my solo showcase for the talent show, an arrangement of 'The Water Is Wide' that Carly wrote for me to sing. I loved Carly so much that when camp was over my parents engaged Carly to give me private guitar lessons that branched into things like wardrobe and even cooking. Carly Simon could make a mean chicken fricassee. Then she fixed me up with her brother, who became my boyfriend, and so we were like family in those days."

Indian Hills's star counselor arrived a few days late. His name was Jacob Brackman, and he taught writing to the more literate campers. A 1965 Harvard graduate, he was an ambitious young film critic who contributed to *Esquire* and other hip periodicals. He also was just about to publish a major article in *Playboy* on the insurgent underground press. Jake Brackman was coolness personified, and at first he proved resistant to Carly's charms. Jake had a girlfriend, and Carly was in the midst of a flirtation with one of her young music campers. But gradually Carly won Jake over: not with sex, but with her humor and wit. For Carly, it was an incredible blessing that she was *not* physically attracted to tall, handsome, charming Jake Brackman. She loved Jake for his mind; she knew his talent and sensibility might be able to supply lyrics for the melodies that were coursing through her musical soul. She was able to confide to Jake in a way that previously had been only for her lovers. Carly and Jake formed an unshakable bond at Indian Hill during the summer of 1967, a meeting of the minds that would be crucial for both their careers in years to come.

Jake Brackman was a big hit in Riverdale when Carly brought him home in September. Her mother liked him, and he fit right into the Simon family circle. Lucy: "I think that Jake reminded Carly of Willie Donaldson—someone smart, witty, very sophisticated. We knew at once that they could make a great team someday." Beginning that autumn, Carly started hanging out with Jake and his hip friends. Jake was an aspiring screenwriter, and in his apartment she met the young director Terry Malick, actor Jack Nicholson, the brilliant Czech émigré director Milos Forman, and other up-and-coming people in the arts. In Jake's pot-smoke-filled living room she played her guitar for Jerry Brandt, a young promoter (married to actress Janet Margolin) whose interests spanned New York's teenage nightlife and Andy Warhol's avant-garde extravaganza Exploding Plastic Inevitable. Brandt was interested in Carly, and told her to write some new songs and make a demo recording. Maybe they could do something together, someday.

PLAY WITH ME

———

$\mathcal{A}$fter camp, in the autumn of 1967, Carly worked at *Newsweek* magazine as an editorial assistant. She also began a career in the jingle business, writing pithy commercial ditties to order. She contracted with an agency whose clients included cosmetic firms, candy companies, car dealerships, and some banks in rural New England. Some of the most talented musicians in New York worked in these Midtown Manhattan jingle factories, churning out commercial music for hire. In the jingle studios, Carly worked among famous stars such as Ron Carter, who played bass with Miles Davis; and singer-songwriter Jake Holmes, whose songs, such as "I'm Confused," would be appropriated by Led Zeppelin. In this period, Carly wrote and recorded jingles for Chevrolet, J.C. Penney department stores, and a New Hampshire bank, among other clients. This was an education for her, a stark look at music as a "commodity"—something to be written, recorded, broadcast, and then thrown away. Carly: "The good side of the jingle experience was that it gave me a discipline I'd never had before. It put my head on a totally different plane, having to think about tomato ketchup for a week. The bad side was having to find music for things like fabric softeners. My I.Q. took quite a dip in that era."

As 1968 dawned, Carly kept working on her own material. One of the jingles evolved into a new song, "Summer Is a Wishing Well." Another, called "Play with Me," impressed her friends, so Carly cut a demo, produced by John McClure. Carly: "I was writing songs and sending them to people I admired in hope that I could make some money from the publishing. My mother had a strict attitude toward allowances—none. I sent my songs to Dionne Warwick, whom I'd met; her collaborator Burt Bacharach; Cass Elliot [of the Mamas and the Papas]; and Judy Collins, one of my heroes. I never heard from any of them until years later, but never anything about my songs." A tape of "Play with Me" was also sent to record producer Jerry Ragovoy, who had the best ears for new talent in the music industry. He heard a typical Simon Sisters lullaby, offset by coy sex kitten lyrics, and it just didn't work for him.

He asked Carly to stop by the office. He told her he loved her voice, "but I just don't know who you are—musically. A country singer? A folk singer? A jazz singer? A rock-and-roll singer? I don't know what I could do with you."

Carly crossed her long, miniskirted legs, and said, "Jerry—isn't that kind of exciting?"

Ragovoy passed.

"My high hopes for this song were . . . *dashed*," Carly said later.

Indeed, in this era, Carly's new music had outrageous competition. Joni Mitchell's album *Song to a Seagull* featured gems such as "Night in the City" and "Cactus Tree." Laura Nyro's album *Eli and the Thirteenth Confession* was a staple of the new "progressive rock" FM radio (in stereo sound) format. Carly's disc jockey friend Jonathan Schwartz was playing both Mitchell and Nyro in heavy rotation on New York's premier radio station, WNEW-FM. Judy Collins was at the top of her game, featuring the songs of Leonard Cohen on her new album, even charting with a hit record of "Who Knows Where the Times Goes?" Carly could only hope, somehow, to break through the heavy new female talent that seemed to be blocking her path. At the same time, she enrolled for a term at the Juilliard School of Music in New York, to learn how to annotate the intriguing new melodies she was hearing in her head.

In this period, she began dating Milos Forman, whose film *Closely Watched Trains* had established him as a star of the New Wave of European directors. "He put me in his movie *Taking Off,* starring Buck Henry. The film was about a series of people doing auditions, and I was only one of them. I was appalled when I saw it, because I looked so goony, and so gawky. Oh, God! I suspect I had a certain energy that he liked, but it wasn't a big part at all."

This was after the 1967 "Summer of Love," and like most young people, Carly threw herself into the river of so-called free love that energized the American sixties—now seen as a historic two-decade window of sexual promiscuity that occurred between the advent of the birth control pill and the scourge of AIDS. Carly climbed through this window along with the rest of her generation; the mores of the day were almost such that it was poor manners not to go to bed on the first date. "I still had a hard time sleeping alone," Carly recalled, "so I never did. There was no reason to. . . . I always had these constant, random thoughts about sex when I was in my twenties, thoughts that made you want to get into bed with just about anyone." Andrea Simon sagely advised Carly that she should be in love with every man she slept with; the result was that Carly convinced herself that she really was in love with all of them.

In the spring of 1968, Carly contributed a song she'd written to a private foundation project that matched local rock groups with the classical music community. A band called Elephant's Memory was chosen to play her song at Carnegie Hall. Like many new bands, they were integrating jazzy horns into the basic rock band mix, a wave that was sweeping the music scene at that point. At first there was a rapport between Carly and the band, and they asked her to be their singer without an audition. Carly signed some papers, and the new-look Elephant's Memory played some gigs around New York, sometimes opening for Al Kooper's new horn-based group, Blood, Sweat and Tears. Carly was joined onstage by a male vocalist for a few shows, but then he got fired. "I hated the gigs," Carly later wrote. "We played clubs where they smoked dope and cigarettes at the same time. I couldn't hear myself and I kept losing my voice." After a few weeks the band—most of them living in the poverty hole of the Lower East Side—began to resent Carly's uptown polish and attitude. They thought she was spoiled and uptight. She didn't want to rehearse in their grungy, slumlike studio. They told her that if she wanted to be in the band she had to get off her fat ass and help them haul their speakers. (Carly: "I did have a fat ass, by the way.") Tensions finally blew up at the club Wheels, when the band was rehearsing for the night's gig. The seven musicians verbally beat Carly up, and she went home and let the band go on without her that night. That was effectively the end of Carly Simon as a band singer. (A few years later, Elephant's Memory worked with John Lennon when the former Beatle moved to New York. They also tried, without success, to sue Carly for songwriting royalties after she had hit records in the 1970s.)

Midway through 1968, Carly quit her jobs and renewed her crusade to get back into the music business. She asked her brother for a loan, to build a war chest for a signing campaign to land a recording contract, but Peter Simon turned her down, very reluctantly. "It wasn't like I was rolling in money," he says. "Neither my sisters nor I had that much to spare." Carly's mother loaned her some money instead. That's when she met Dan Armstrong.

Armstrong was the premier electric guitar merchant in New York. His shop, Dan Armstrong Guitars, on West Forty-eighth Street, featured the choicest vintage Telecasters and Gibson SGs, and was *the* one-stop repair shop in the city. Eric Clapton jammed with Danny in the back room when he was in town. Danny kept the store open late for Jimi Hendrix, who liked to come in around midnight. As a luthier, a maker of guitars, Dan was the hottest guy in the business. In that year, 1968, he designed a new line of bass guitars for the Ampeg corporation of New Jersey; these were luminous instruments built from clear, see-through Plexiglas; guitars that soon became famous for their excellent electronics, interchangeable pickups, and an arsenal of long, sustained notes reverberating through the unusual plastic bodies. Soon Jack Bruce of Cream was using a Dan Armstrong bass guitar, and was soon followed by every other rock bassist who could get his hands on one of Danny's prized instruments.

Dan Armstrong was ten years older than Carly, was breaking up with his wife, and was the father of four children. He had long hair and a bushy mustache that reminded Carly of Clark Gable as Rhett Butler. "He was such a *comely* guy, when I first met him in his guitar shop." Carly had brought her Martin guitar in for some repairs. He knew her as the singer from Elephant's Memory, but she identified herself as a Juilliard student.

Over time, Carly got to know Armstrong as a keen musician, totally arrogant, highly opinionated, and a bit of a Neanderthal, with arms too long for his body. But there was a real spark between them, and Carly and Danny went at it like a pair of tigers, making love in cars and outdoors, most memorably under the arches of Central Park's bridges. He dared her to make love with him in a taxi, and she went for it. Her family liked him but thought he was too far beneath Carly, socially—which was true. He also didn't think much of her music (except her singing), told her she would be much happier if she forgot about a music career, and generally played her chronic low self-esteem like a violin.

"Danny was a real trip," Peter Simon says. "He was basically a good guy, and I liked him in part because he had, by far, the best marijuana in New York; in fact, the best I'd ever had up to that point. That summer of '68, for me, will always be 'The Summer of Danny's Pot.' My girlfriend Ellen and I double-dated with him and Carly a few times, and the thing I always noticed was that Danny could have treated Carly with a little more respect. He was a guy who had to be the god of his household, always had to have the upper hand in everything." With a less-than-supportive boyfriend, Carly often leaned on Peter that year, sometimes asking him to accompany her to stressful auditions and jingle recording sessions.

Her affair with Dan Armstrong lasted almost two years, some of it spent in his squalid apartment above his guitar shop after he moved it to LaGuardia Place in Greenwich Village. She was miserable through most of it, her ambition thwarted, her boyfriend an egocentric blockhead with zero interest in seeing Carly Simon succeed.

FEAR OF FLYING

———

*I*n 1969, Lucy Simon was pregnant with her first child and music was pouring out of her in a torrent of quarter notes. She was setting poems to these melodies, using words by William Blake, Edward Lear, Lewis Carroll, Christina Rossetti, and Longfellow, among others. Lucy was offered a recording deal with the Columbia Children's Record Library. Thus were the Simon Sisters reborn, temporarily, in 1969.

Carly and Lucy cut eleven songs with arranger/conductor Sam Brown early in the year. "Winkin', Blinkin' and Nod" reemerges in a folksy banjo arrangement and leads off the album. The rest of the songs continue in the Sisters' chamber-lullaby vein and are mostly vehicles for Lucy's maturing soprano. Carly is heard best on "The Lobster Quadrille," and especially as a solo presence on "A Red, Red Rose," set to the verses of Robert Burns. (Dan Armstrong was at the "Rose" session and suddenly realized he'd been wrong about Carly. Her soft, dusky phrasing caught up with him, and he finally got it—that his girlfriend could be an important star someday.) The new album would be released later in the year as *The Simon Sisters Sing The Lobster Quadrille and Other Songs for Children.*

One night Carly and Danny walked into Joanna's darkened apartment. Suddenly the lights came on and Joey's boyfriend, ballet star Edward Villella, began leaping around the living room wearing only a tiny sock over his privates. This turned out to be a "ball warmer" Carly had knitted for Danny; she'd persuaded Villella to model it for him as a kind of cosmic giggle.

It was around this period that Carly borrowed some money from her mother and rented her first place alone, a sunny one-bedroom flat on East Thirty-fifth Street, not far from the new Murray Hill digs of her now-inseparable friend and cowriter Jake Brackman. Andrea Simon drove in from Riverdale, scoured the apartment, put fresh paper in the kitchen drawers, and changed the locks. Carly Simon now had her own home, at last. Dan Armstrong was getting the uneasy feeling that his days in Carly's life might be numbered.

Lucy had her baby, a girl named Julie, in June 1969. Carly was overcome with mixed emotions as she stared at her niece through the thick window of the maternity ward. She decided to write a song called "Julie Through the Glass," about how much this moment had moved her. She felt so confused. On the one hand was a desire for a family and the stability that Lucy had with her husband. On the other was her yearning for artistic recognition and a career. Meanwhile, her louche boyfriend was dealing kilos of marijuana out of her apartment, and he already had a bunch of kids. Carly began easing away from Danny that summer, when man walked on the moon for the first time. She now spent more time collaborating with Jake, trying to get something going with a new melody she was working on.

She had notated the song, as she had learned at Juilliard. The melody had grown out of a freelance job, writing background music for a television documentary, *Who Killed Lake Erie?* She liked the song, but was completely blocked on the lyrics. She gave Jake a demo tape that had her singing la-la's instead of words. He thought of the stories Carly had told him about her childhood, and began working with images that had stayed with him: her ailing father smoking in the dark, ignoring her. Her preoccupied mother reading magazines but not forgetting to say good night. Jake and Carly spent hours on her sofa trading lines and lyrics back and forth, deep in the throes of an intensely experienced collaboration. Jake was trying to write for Carly, as he later put it, "like a playwright writing for an actress," using her biography as a springboard for the lyrics that would define her forthcoming career.

Meanwhile, Carly had another new song, "Rains in My Heart," which she and Lucy sang on Dick Cavett's TV talk show after they'd performed "Winkin' " to promote their new record. The sisters wore matching gold dresses, Carly's offset by a pair of sexy black tights. (She also had a sore on her chin that layers of TV makeup couldn't hide.) Carly took the lead vocal as Lucy descanted behind her, but the new song was tuneless and sad, not the kind of song to make any impact in the hot summer of '69.

Carly and Danny didn't make it to the Woodstock Festival in August. She saw the pictures of naked mud-smeared kids massed at a farm upstate, and decided that it wasn't for her. Around then, she agreed to become the public face of a fast-food fried chicken company that Jake and some friends were trying to launch, but this opportunity never materialized.

Late 1969. There was a much-anticipated total eclipse of the sun in the Northeast. It was considered a special cosmic event. Carly's younger brother and his friends were repairing to the tip of Cape Cod to experience near totality. Some of Jake's friends were talking about chartering a plane to fly to Nova Scotia, where the observer would achieve total totality.

Carly stayed in New York, in part because she had started to see a new therapist, someone she thought could really help her find her way. The immediate symptom was Carly's morbid fear of flying. She simply could not get on an airplane without acute panic attacks. She then explained that she felt blocked and constrained in almost every area of her life. The therapist told her he thought he could help her look at things in different ways, and that with sufficient treatment he knew she could move forward. This is what Carly desperately needed to hear, and she saw Dr. Willard Galen, on and off, for the next seventeen years.

Early in 1970, Jake Brackman got Carly together with Jerry Brandt, who was moving into managing talent. Carly played some of her new music for Brandt, who was especially interested in "That's the Way I Always Heard It Should Be." This song had a pretty tune and lyrics, by Jake, that expressed a young woman's frustrations with the limited opportunities for her generation of women—highly educated and ambitious, yet expected to naturally fall into the socially correct roles of wives and mothers. The chorus went, "But you say it's time we moved in together / And raised a family of our own, you and me / Well, that's the way I always heard it should be / You want to marry me—we'll marry." It was obvious that this song could reverberate within the emerging movement for women's rights—"women's liberation"—and be a commercial hit as well. Brandt told Carly he was completely sure he could get her a record deal. He said he would love to manage her, and those magic words: "I'll put up money for you to do a demo."

Carly signed up with Jerry Brandt's management company, and he funded a five-song demo tape produced by musician David Bromberg, a sort of protégée of Bob Dylan's. Brandt took the tape to Clive Davis at Columbia Records, who was selling millions of Janis Joplin and Sly Stone records and was looking for the next big thing. Later in the day, Brandt told Carly that Clive had listened to the tape and then thrown it across the room, asking Brandt, "What the hell do I want with a Jewish girl from New York?"

Jerry Brandt's next try was Jac Holzman, who'd founded Elektra

Records, the country's premier folk music label, twenty years earlier. Elektra's roster was eclectic, from ur-folkies such as Jean Ritchie and Josh White to blues shouters such as Koerner, Ray and Glover. Elektra was big on songwriters—Phil Ochs, Tom Rush, Tim Buckley. The label had branched out to rock with the Paul Butterfield Blues Band, and then the Doors, whose mega-selling albums had changed Elektra from a small label to a corporation. The queen of Elektra was Judy Collins. Carly was thrilled that she might be in such lofty company.

"From the time I was in high school, all the records I liked were on Elektra. It was such an appealing label. They had artists I liked— Theo Bikel, Judy Henske singing 'Wade in the Water.' I loved her. And the Butterfield Band. And Judy Collins, who I admired so much. I emulated her, copied her songs. That she was on Elektra meant a lot to me. Plus Elektra had Nonesuch [the label's classical music division], and I had a big library of Nonesuch albums. So this was great for me. Elektra had good taste, and seemed to have real values. And I'd heard that Jac Holzman was terrific, a good person."

Jac Holzman: "Jerry Brandt, who was sidelining into management, brought me a tape and said, 'Look, I think this girl is rather unusual. Her name is Carly Simon.' I asked if she was one of the Simon Sisters, because one of my favorite songs was a little lullaby called 'Winkin', Blinkin' and Nod.' " Holzman explained that he was taking his son Adam to Japan to visit Expo '70 in Osaka, and that he would listen to the tape over there. "So I'm staying near Lake Hakone in a little inn with paper walls, sleeping on a futon; it's four in the morning, and I haven't adjusted to the time difference, so I slip on the Carly Simon tape and listen through headphones." Jac Holzman loved what he heard. "So there I was in the Japanese countryside, no phone at the inn. I don't even know how to dial a phone in this country. And I am going to lose this artist! A few days later, back in Tokyo, I call Jerry and tell him I love the tape and definitely want to work with Carly."

Around this time, Danny Armstrong rang the bell at Carly's

apartment on Thirty-fifth Street. The door was opened by a younger guy, only half dressed—actually Kim Rosen, her brother's best friend, with whom Carly was having an affair. Sorry, Kim said, Carly wasn't home. Dan went back to his place and left some messages with Carly's answering service, but his calls were not returned.

When Jac Holzman returned to New York, he played Carly Simon's tape for his A&R staff. No one liked it. Carly: "Even though his whole staff had vetoed signing me, Jac was willing to override them. I was signed to Electra Records in 1970."

"I'd begun therapy," she said later, "because I was stuck. I wouldn't fly. I was in love with a man who was degrading, and demoralizing my entire existence, but I felt I'd die if I left him. Then I went into therapy with the genius man of all time. He just moved me so fast from A to B to C . . . Got me out of living with Joey, where I was so aware of her as the all-powerful big sister, where I was stuck in the same family role I'd been in my whole life, where it was better to be defeated than to be successful. I moved out. I broke up with the creep, got a band together, got a recording contract, even started to fly! It was the most acceleratedly productive period . . . *of my life*."

Part

—

I I

—

A GIRL CALLED ELEKTRA

———

Sometime in the spring of 1970, Carly Simon hailed a taxi to the Gulf and Western tower at 15 Columbus Circle. She rode the elevator to near the top of the building and walked into the outer office of Elektra Records and told the receptionist that she had an appointment with the company's president, Jac Holzman. She was told to take a seat and that Mr. Holzman would see her shortly.

She was a bit on edge because the meeting was about who would produce her album for Elektra, and it was crucial to find the right person to help choose the songs, hire the studio, find the musicians, and often arrange the actual music, and supervise the recording and mixing sessions. Carly had only met Holzman when she signed the Elektra contract; this would be their first working meeting. Suddenly she felt a slight sensation, as if the floor were moving under her feet. She quickly suppressed a panic attack. Then she felt it again. Was it dizziness, vertigo?

She stood up and must have looked alarmed; the receptionist told her not to worry, because the Gulf and Western building was so tall that its upper floors actually swayed when the wind blew hard across Central Park.

Elektra Records had been founded in 1950 in the back room of Jac Holzman's folk music record shop in the Village and had since come a long way, having sold millions of albums by the label's rock bands, especially the Doors. As Carly was joining the company in 1970, it was being transformed from a successful indie label into a division of corporate entertainment. This happened when the three top independent labels in the recording industry—Elektra, Atlantic, and Warner/Reprise—were purchased by the Kinney National Company, a parking lot giant run by mogul Steve Ross. Kinney retained the services of the label's founders (Holzman, Ahmet Ertegun, Mo Ostin) and merged them into a conglomerate called WEA to compete with industry titans EMI, Columbia, and RCA. The sale of the company allowed Elektra to expand further into rock while retaining its folkish allure and its Nonesuch label, one of the first to explore what came to be called world music. Jac Holzman, who'd started as a hi-fi nut, was building a state-of-the-art recording studio for his company in West Hollywood, which he now suggested Carly might use for her first album.

Carly had other ideas and wanted to talk about them. She found Holzman sympathetic, if somewhat remote. He spoke in carefully composed sentences. He had what she called "leadership quality." He was tall, straight, impersonal, intense. She told people he was like a machine, but with a fluid, imaginative style. He was a doctor's son, raised in Manhattan. His social geography was similar to hers.

At first Holzman told Carly he thought she was an interpretive singer, not a writer. He gave her albums by Elektra singer-songwriters—Jeff Buckley, Paul Siebel—and said he thought she could cover their songs. He also mentioned Tim Hardin and Donovan. Carly replied that she was interested in writing and presenting her own material, and songs she was working on with Jake Brackman. She mentioned Carole King, a writer more than a performer, as a model for what she wanted to do. She told Holzman that she saw herself as a singer who recorded her songs, not as an interpreter. "If I did that kind of record," she said later, "I'd have to go out and promote it, but I was too scared of getting on stage. I *hated* to do that. But I hadn't really discussed this with Jac or with Jerry Brandt. I almost hadn't discussed it with myself. It was just more panic."

Then Carly told Holzman that she hated to fly, and she wanted to record there in New York.

The next item was finding a producer, and Holzman surprised Carly by suggesting she meet with Eddie Kramer, one of the top recording engineers in the business. Originally from South Africa, Kramer had distinguished himself in London working with Jimi Hendrix, Led Zeppelin, and Joe Cocker. He was currently designing a million-dollar recording studio for Hendrix in the Village, which Holzman suggested as a possible studio for Carly when the facility opened in June 1970. Kramer, Holzman told her, might be a good fit for her as well. Later, Carly said she was relieved the meeting had gone so well; she wanted to feel she had a home at Elektra, a company named after a princess who killed her father.

Carly auditioned for Eddie Kramer at Jake Brackman's apartment in Murray Hill. Kramer had heard a cassette of her demo tape and hadn't been impressed, but had been persuaded that she was talented and that the label would back her up. It was worth a shot. Kramer, a long-haired London rocker, was dressed in a leather jacket, a dirty silk scarf, shades, bell-bottom trousers, and scuffed Chelsea boots. Carly played him some things she was working on, and again he was less than awed—until she played "That's the Way I Always Heard It Should Be."

By then, this collaboration between Carly and Jake had evolved into a song of sadness and low expectations, but the lyrics were acutely personal. Carly acted out the song's differing voices. The singer introduces her dysfunctional family, and then despairs of hateful suburbia and its conflicts. She's under pressure to be married, but she's a rebel, sneering at societal norms and sexual imprisonment. The passion in her wants to triumph, but by the third verse, she's a caged bird living for her husband. The song ends in resignation and a woman's stifled sense of self, as Carly sings, "We'll marry," in a regressed, little-girl voice that has forgotten the brazen alto of the verses and chorus.

Kramer sensed that this song—an ironic take on "women's lib"—would resonate with young women, and he told her he wanted to work with her. She also played him another new song, called "Dan, My Fling." Again, this was Jake writing the musical of Carly's life in the form of a lusty ballad about breaking up with Dan Armstrong, and it was clear it could be a big production, possibly with orchestration, the whole deal. Kramer told Holzman he wanted to do the record, and quickly made a deal with Jerry Brandt to produce Carly, under the supervision of Jac Holzman, at Electric Lady Studios. This was the team that would make the *Carly Simon* album later in the year.

ELECTRIC LADY

———

*C*arly now began a somewhat frantic search for songs. She kept working with Jake Brackman on ideas. She kept trying to get Jac Holzman to accept her as a writer. "He liked my voice," she said, "but he didn't want to give me the gift of my own songs. But I kept inserting my own songs into the various demos until he finally said, 'Wow—who wrote that one?'"

Carly was listening carefully, nearly every day, to *Sweet Baby James,* James Taylor's second album, a heartbroken, visionary sequence of new songs released by Warner Bros. Records in February 1970. Her brother, Peter, played it for her first, and she wasn't sure what she felt. Then she became obsessed with Taylor's addictive lullabies and grieving blues. Some of these new songs were indeed stunning. "Sweet Baby James" was a frosty winter lullaby, very melancholy, with a crying steel guitar. "Fire and Rain" was about mental turmoil, and death and loss by suicide. James's voice had an endearing Carolina twang that especially touched the hearts of his female listeners, and his guitar playing as heard on *Sweet Baby James* was extremely masterful for someone who was twenty-one when he made this record. Carole King, a hero of Carly's, played piano on "Steamroller Blues," which at least showed that this melancholy prophet had a sense of humor. But even a song called "Sunny Skies" was disconsolate, because the singer was so alone in his remote, existential world.

Sweet Baby James was eventually summed up by the song "Country Road," which describes taking to the highway and disappearing into the land. All over America young people, exhausted by opposition to war and the psychic turmoil of the sixties, were leaving the cities for communal living in the woods. It was the same with young musicians. The music of the Band and Neil Young constituted this movement's anthems up to that time. Now hippie communes from Maine to California took up James Taylor like magic mushrooms. The album got to number three on *Billboard* magazine's chart and sold around three million copies. The "Fire and Rain" single also rose to number three, an almost apocalyptic song that managed to sound soulful and important on AM car radios and the FM dial.

(There was also a critical backlash against Taylor, whom some regarded as a prophet of disengagement, a singer whose self-absorbed navel-gazing distracted his listeners from the epochal cultural energies of the previous few years. A Boston deejay dubbed him "the White Zombie" for his stoned or wooden demeanor in concert. His supporters countered that Taylor's deeply felt songs concerning his mental state and drug use constituted a sort of unprecedented heroic candor. Both sides were probably right.)

Carly was hooked on Taylor's album. "It actually took me three or four listenings, to get into *Sweet Baby James,*" she remembered, "and then there was *nothing* else—almost no other record—I could play. Everything else around that theme kind of . . . paled."

Around this time Carly took to the highway, heading north to Vermont, where Peter Simon and some friends had bought an old farm on two hundred acres of rolling pasture, with beaver ponds and birch trees. It was down the road from Total Loss Farm, a hard-scrabble artistic commune led by the young radical editor Ray Mungo. Peter and his friends, including Kim Rosen, established Tree Frog Farm as a more upscale, Woodstockian commune that emphasized country pursuits, serious gardening (mostly in the nude), and working with animals. Music was big. James Taylor vied with Joni Mitchell, Crosby, Stills and Nash, and the Rolling Stones as the most played artist. Carly came up to the farm a few times to get away from New York and discover whether country life could do anything for her. Eventually the lure of her career always drew her back to Manhattan after a few days of fresh air.

In this era, over the course of several months in 1970, Carly was part of an intense sexual roundelay that left her spiritually exhausted and emotionally spent. This involved the production of a movie Jake Brackman had written, *The King of Marvin Gardens,* the story of two struggling brothers in a gritty, slumlike Atlantic City. The filming brought a crew of glamorous Hollywood types to New York, including actors Jack Nicholson and Bruce Dern. The film's director was Bob Rafelson, who had worked on *The Monkees* TV show and was involved with several moderate-budget collaborations with Nicholson. Now the parties at Jake Brackman's place grew more interesting, and Carly was seen with Jack Nicholson, the hottest star in Hollywood after his star turn in *Easy Rider* the year before. But Nicholson had a famous girlfriend back in L.A. He gave Carly's number to his friend Warren Beatty when the actor arrived in town. Carly grew "close" to Beatty, as she put it, for a brief period of time. When Warren returned to the West Coast, she began seeing Bob Rafelson, who needed consolation because he wasn't getting much from the actors, who felt the script was too bleak. The filming complete, Carly went to Jamaica on holiday with Rafelson's brother, Don. They stayed at an almost deserted resort on the island's north coast. Carly wrote to her brother that it rained almost every day.

As this cycle of relationships petered out, Carly began working on her album. Her emotions were raw and bruised, as revealed in her letters from this period. She felt she had been passed around this group of powerful and attractive men for a couple of months ("treated like a piece of meat," as she later described it); some of this experience transcended contemporary mores and accepted sexual behavior, and evoked in Carly a sense of embarrassment. The artistic ideas generated by the feelings were too recent to be transformed into songs for her current album, but they would have an explosive impact for her music a couple of years in the future.

Summer 1970. Joni Mitchell is writing *Blue*. Carole King is writing *Tapestry*. Carly begins recording in the new underground Electric Lady Studios at 52 West Eighth Street. Jimi Hendrix, who lives nearby, has sunk his fortune into this first studio owned by a rock star, and likes to look in when he's not on the road. The vibe of the place is brilliant, and it is booked solid for months. (The space used to be the club Generation, where Jimi liked to jam until late. The reception area now displays a mural of a pixie girl at the controls of a spaceship.) Eddie Kramer basically built the facility from the sound-boards up, and has complete run of the three recording rooms. In fact, he is also producing a band called Zephyr, in studio B, while working with Carly in studio A.

Carly brought in her songs. These were "That's the Way I Always Heard It Should Be," "Dan, My Fling," and some other material she later described as only half-prepared.

"Not all the songs had arrangements," she said later. "A lot of them were head arrangements—just get in the studio with a bunch of people and figure it out. Eddie Kramer knew all the musicians. I made some input, but I didn't know too much about what I was doing."

She brought in *Sweet Baby James* and told Kramer she wanted the drums to sound like James's drummer, Russ Kunkel, on this or that track. She said she wanted the piano to sound like the guy on Judy Collins's record. Sometimes it felt as if she weren't being listened to. "I felt intimidated every time I opened my mouth," she said in 1972. "The producer also seemed intimidated by my mouth opening, so there wasn't a very good feeling in the studio."

At least Kramer had enlisted some cool musicians to play on the record. Paul Griffin had played piano on all the great Bob Dylan albums and would also work on the orchestrations for Carly's record. Jeff Baxter was a hot session guitarist. Ditto Tony Levin and Jerry Jemmot on bass. Carly brought in David Bromberg and Jimmy Ryan to play guitar on various tracks.

Jac Holzman went to some of the early sessions, and things seemed to be getting on. Then he went to Europe, and Kramer had a freer hand with things such as drum sounds and orchestrations. Carly rebelled, then stopped showing up. She called Holzman, but he was out of town. His brother Keith Holzman, a competent executive, ran over to Electric Lady and mediated between Carly and Kramer, eventually getting the sessions back on track. In fact, they got so on track that the members of Zephyr noticed that they were getting the short end of the stick because Eddie Kramer was now working only with Carly. Then they noticed that Carly and Eddie left the studio together, and returned together the next day. Zephyr assumed that Carly was having her way with Eddie Kramer, "not the most macho of men," as Zephyr's lead guitarist put it later.

The main problem between Carly and her producer had been the drum sound. Carly, writing in 2011: "We were recording 'That's the Way' at Electric Lady and I wanted to have big drums on it. Everyone disputed and disagreed. They said it was such a ballad, and they said no drums belonged on the song. But I had become addicted to the way Russ Kunkel played on 'Sweet Baby James' and especially

'Country Road.' I begged Eddie Kramer to have a drummer on the session who could hit hard. So he hired Jimmy Johnson and waited to see what the hell I meant.

"I heard the chorus with a very strong entrance and primarily tom-toms going through the entire chorus, instead of a steady snare and bass drum backbeat. I started to literally conduct the strokes of Jimmy, gesturing what I wanted from him, most likely to his utter chagrin and that of all the other drummers I have worked with since. But my Leonard Bernstein soul flowed through me as I vaulted my hair in front of my thrusting arms. I wondered what the drummer thought of this. He must have been on the verge of leaving. Who did I think I was? Where did this chutzpah come from? Can I put that on Chebe? Uncle Peter? Certainly not my father's side of the family. Jimmy Johnson was amused. All I wanted was to be able to be brought aloft both spiritually and viscerally by the sound of the variously tuned toms.

"Eddie ended up liking it and I gave him his way on something I had been extremely opposed to: doubling my voice. I thought it was a low-class idea. I don't know what I associated it with, but it was definitely a no-no. But Eddie had his way, as I'd had with that thrilling drum part and sound. Anyway, I was amazed to find myself, at the beginning of my career, displaying an astonishing amount of direction in the face of a producer right out of the studio with Mad Dogs and Englishmen.

("[Drummer] Andy Newmark was to suffer on the next few albums, not to mention Rick Marotta and all the wonders in between and later on. I can't think of a drummer I haven't thought about sleeping with, but that's not for publication.")

Carly was invited to Electric Lady Studios' official opening party on August 26, 1970, some three months after it had opened for business. Jimi Hendrix was a splendid host, as Carly noted when she saw him repeatedly escort select guests into the studio lavatory. (Carly: "I just thought, 'Gee, he's in the bathroom with his friends.' I was quite naïve, and I did not understand drugs.") The event was star-quality: Jim Morrison dropped in briefly. Yoko Ono. Some freaks from the Warhol entourage huddled in the corner. Janis Joplin came by. Johnny Winter. Mick Fleetwood. Al Kooper. Carly felt excited to be currently recording in the coolest studio in the world. Later that night, she and Kramer went to the rock club Steve Paul's The Scene, where Jimi Hendrix jammed with Johnny Winter's band until dawn. Paul McCartney was there with his new girlfriend, Linda Eastman, a New York photographer whom Carly had known for years. This is where she first heard the sad news that the Beatles were breaking up.

THAT'S THE WAY I ALWAYS
HEARD IT SHOULD BE

———

𝒯hen, three weeks later, Jimi Hendrix died suddenly in London. This caused shock and grief at Electric Lady. Early info was hazy. Jimi had been in England to play at the Isle of Wight and some other gigs. He was hanging out with a German woman, and popped some pills to turn off the adrenaline and get some rest. On the night of September 18 he choked to death. There was immediate and serious speculation that he had been murdered. He had been trying to fire his manager. To some people—those in the know—Hendrix had been worth more dead than alive.

Eddie Kramer now fell apart and required extensive hand-holding and consolation. Carly's sessions grew desultory as Kramer turned his total attention to a quick mix of unreleased Hendrix tracks (with Mitch Mitchell) that became the posthumous *Cry of Love* album. Carly then broke off with Kramer, and he stopped coming to the studio for her sessions.

Jac Holzman came by Electric Lady and found Carly almost alone in the studio. She had the basic tracks for her album, which now needed to be mixed. She tearfully stammered to Jac that she didn't want to sing in public, that she suffered from severe stage fright, and reminded him that she was deathly afraid to get on a plane. When he reported this at a staff meeting, his people told him they hadn't wanted to sign Carly Simon in the first place. "Jac thought he'd discovered the female Mick Jagger," one Elektra executive said, "and then she told him she didn't want to perform. Jac was just going nuts. There was a lot of *I-told-you-so* over this."

Holzman deputized his brother Keith to oversee the mixing of the album so it could be released as scheduled, early in 1971. He assigned troubleshooting Elektra executive Steve Harris to soothe Carly and win her over to performing and promoting her record. Harris had been able to "handle" the volatile Jim Morrison from time to time, and now he would babysit Carly and try to bring her along as a responsible and committed Elektra artist.

Harris recalled: "I met Carly before she finished the album. [Comedian] David Steinberg was friends with her, and he took me over to her apartment, a lovely flat on Thirty-fifth Street, just off Lexington Avenue. When I walked in, there was something about [Carly] I couldn't put my finger on. Sometimes she looked attractive, other times she didn't. We started talking about the record. I hadn't heard it. She asked me, 'Would you like to hear one of the songs?' She picked up her guitar and sang 'That's the Way I Always Heard It Should Be.' When she started to sing, her whole face changed, and her whole manner shifted. She became absolutely beautiful, and I thought, *If anything happens to this record, and if we can get her out and working in front of an audience, this is going to be just killer, and she is going to be a major star.*"

Eddie Kramer was urged to return to the studio to help Carly. Then, she recalled, "Eddie and I had a serious falling out, and by October [1970] I was mixing the album by myself."

Then Janis Joplin died of a heroin overdose.

Jac Holzman visited Electric Lady toward the end of November to review the mixed, and sequenced, tapes of Carly's songs. "That's the Way" now had its drum sound—the "weeping tom-tom" fills popularized by Ringo Starr, Levon Helm, and Russ Kunkel. The piano and strings were lyrical and subtle, giving a sense of mystery to Carly's ironic take on contemporary women's "issues." Holzman hadn't heard the song before. It wasn't part of the original demo tape he had listened to in Japan. Now he quickly realized he'd heard the first honest song about contemporary middle-class female angst—and it had to be the album's first single release.

"Alone" came next, a breaking-up song with a country music flavor spiced by a pedal steel guitar. Then "One More Time," a foray into country-rock, Southern California style. "The Best Thing" spoke to a woman's regret over losing a fabulous London lover—Willie Donaldson?—in a serpentine arrangement that evolved into art song, with an echoing female chorale. Hard rock ended the album's first side, with Mark Klingman's "Just a Sinner," a confessional rock song with metallic guitars and an anvil chorus.

"Dan, My Fling" (written by Jake Brackman and Fred Gardner) opened side two as the second big production number after "That's the Way." It was presented as a lusty gospel piano ballad whose thwarted yearning is tempered with a sense of humor, since it was hard to sing "Dan, my fling is all flung out" with a straight face. Carly's "Another Door" sounded like the Simon Sisters, a philosophical song about spiritual confusion and seeking enlightenment. Then came "Reunion," cowritten with Eddie Kramer and Billy Mernit, who had been one of Carly's campers at Indian Hill. Beautifully sung, with cello and harpsichord accompaniment, the song described an incomplete family circle and wrong turns on the highways of existence—a wistful, bittersweet performance that could have been on an earlier Joni Mitchell record.

The mood was lifted by "Rolling Down the Hills," a romping hippie jingle with deft harmonica playing. The album ended with "The Love's Still Growing," written by Buzzy Linhart, a New York singer-songwriter, a friend of Hendrix's, and a respected figure on the local music scene. The track was the album's final Big Statement, echoing with muted psychedelia, Earth Day–era lyric clichés, and washes of string music.

When the listening session was finished, there was quiet in the room. Carly thought the record sounded like a glorified demo, but when she looked over at Jac Holzman, he was smiling. Elektra's boss actually loved the record, and he told her so. Holzman later wrote, "The album was different from anything else I'd been hearing, and that buoyed me. The songs were sophisticated and openhearted, a rare combination. Some of the lyrics reminded me of Stephen Sondheim, with their keen sense of the cross-currents of life and the human condition." He thought that, even with a rock-style backing, the polish and breeding of her background came through to him, loud and clear, and this was something she needed never to lose.

Jac told Carly he thought "That's the Way" had to be the first single. "We didn't know that it was going to be the single," Carly said, speaking of her and Jake, "but Jac did. I thought it was really important that a song and a singer really match up. If the singer and the song are closely interwoven in personality and essence, then it has a chance of catching on. So I was thrilled when Jac picked 'That's the Way I Always Heard It Should Be,' because that song meant so much to me. Back then, I could hardly even describe why, but Jac was really able to see it. I felt it was a smart choice, because it would be introducing me to a public that wasn't aware of me, with a song that was unusual, that wasn't the typical single of the day. Jac Holzman took a chance on it."

Carly was pleased when the Elektra boss approved the final mix of *Carly Simon*. She was immensely relieved that she had pulled this off. "I wasn't really prepared for it. I'd had no experience in a modern recording studio, and my producer had barely produced a record before." Now the main work on the record was complete, with only the jacket photographs to be taken and the album sleeve to be designed.

Everything would be great, Carly thought, as long as they didn't make her go on the road to promote the record. At the time, this was her biggest worry.

So Carly took her tapes up to Riverdale and played the record for her mother. Andrea loved the music beyond belief, but had trouble expressing her admiration to her daughter. Carly's brother, Peter, was visiting from the farm in Vermont, and he, an immense music maven and fan, was bowled over. "Our whole family was in a kind of ecstasy about how good this record sounded. Uncle Peter Dean said it was the best debut album he'd ever heard. It was an incredible time for us." Andrea Simon did tell Carly how proud her father would have been of her singing, and especially her songwriting.

Around this time Carly was seeing a friend of Peter's, a blond, funny British academic named David Silver. "I had been teaching in Boston," Silver remembered, "where I also had a TV series on public television. But my marriage was going south, and I wanted to move to New York. I called Peter Simon, and he said, 'Come meet my sister, she'll make you feel better.' So I showed up at the big house in Riverdale, where Andrea Simon was holding a benefit cocktail party for Robert Morgenthau, the Manhattan district attorney. I got there, and Carly and Peter were sitting on the front steps. She was wearing a tight-fitting blue-knit jumpsuit—the sexiest woman I'd ever met in my life. After a while we went upstairs to listen to Carly's record. I never did get to the cocktail party that was raging downstairs."

David was totally in love. "One day I went over to Carly's apartment on East Thirty-fifth Street. Sunny place, chintz-covered sofas, fresh flowers. We were having tea when Dan Armstrong came over with one of his new guitars. He tried to vibe me out of the picture, but, hey—*I'm* the boyfriend now. We ended up jamming for three hours. He wasn't such a bad guy actually."

A few days later, Peter Simon drove back to Vermont, ferrying Carly and David and Peter's enormous yellow Labrador retriever, Cosmos, in his blue Volvo station wagon. Carly brought along a wardrobe of dresses, the idea being that Peter, now a professional photographer, would produce the photo for the jacket of *Carly Simon*. Carly had already done a photo session with Joel Brodsky, who often worked with Elektra's artists, but Jac Holzman and the label's art director wanted an image that was more intimate, more feminine.

Peter recalled: "We set up a little photo studio in the living room of our two-hundred-year-old farmhouse in Guildford, Vermont. We hung an embroidered cloth as a backdrop behind an antique loveseat we had. Carly tried a lot of poses, with different dresses and shawls and wraps on this bench, but we weren't really satisfied until Catherine Marriott, who was part of our communal family, went upstairs to fetch a dress she thought might work." This was a long, pinkish, almost prairie-looking dress with lovely lace embroidery of flowers and vines. A few months earlier, Catherine had worn the dress to a county fair in Colorado, where she happened to be snapped by the legendary photographer Henri Cartier-Bresson, an image that much later became an iconic postcard image of the master's. "So Carly put on Cate's dress, and accented it with a yellow knitted shawl, and suddenly we had our picture. I shot a roll of this dress, and the one they picked has the shawl off her shoulder and her legs tucked in front of her with her knees far apart. But I never thought it was provocative. It seemed to me that Carly was saying. 'Here I am, and I want you to get to know me.'"

SETTING YOURSELF ON FIRE

———

So now it's 1971 and Elektra is getting ready to release "That's the Way," and the label—famous in the industry for promotional prowess—starts to give Carly a media surge. She tells a reporter from London's *Record Mirror* that she wants artistic satisfaction more than she wants fame. The reporter tells his readers that Carly—constantly cracking jokes—is the funniest person he's ever met. She tells the *Chicago Sun-Times* that she doesn't really care about "making it" in the music industry; that she just wants people to really like her songs. She attends Elektra's first national sales convention in Palm Springs, California, on January 11. Elektra wanted to impress its parent company, Warner Communications, with its roster of talent, and so Jim Morrison and the Doors made a rare appearance, as well as new signings Carly Simon and Harry Chapin. Barbra Streisand currently has a number one album with *Stoney End,* produced by Richard Perry, someone Jac Holzman thinks would work well with Carly. But she seems determined to get the guy who produced the Cat Stevens records.

Then, fortunately, Carly's manager left town. Jerry Brandt, unburdened by any great reputation for taste, relocated to Los Angeles, giving up his management clients. It felt like another abandonment to Carly, and could have been a disaster for her career had she not almost immediately hired Arlyne Rothberg to manage her. Rothberg was a well-known New York talent manager who mostly represented comedians and actors. Her client David Steinberg persuaded her, at first against her better judgment, to take Carly on. She had met Carly a few years earlier, when Steinberg was doing stand-up comedy at the Village Gate. Arlyne had remembered Carly's endless stockinged legs and her sultry, seductive way of laughing. So Arlyne became a trusted and loyal friend to Carly, as well as her business manager. Arlyne saw Carly through the next thirteen years of her occasionally tumultuous life.

Now there was a serious buzz about Carly. Elektra was whispering to its pet media outlets in New York and Los Angeles that she was going to be a big star. Carly slipped Simon family friend Jonathan Schwartz an early acetate disc, and Jonno started playing the album mix of "That's the Way" on WNEW-FM, even before the single was officially released on February 15. The station was a major arbiter of taste in New York during the rock era, and telephone response to Carly's song from its listeners was already impressive.

Rolling Stone's first article on Carly appeared in its February 4 issue. It was written by Elliott Blinder, one of her brother's communal farm friends (and the husband of the woman whose dress Carly wears on the cover of her album). Blinder asked about Carly's privileged upbringing.

Carly: "All backgrounds are inescapable, and mine somehow has been frowned upon in the music business." She described her experience with Albert Grossman, who'd told her that she hadn't suffered enough (as if he had any idea). "It's the old cliché, again: poor little rich girl, she doesn't have any soul. She wasn't in a chain gang in Alabama, or in a concentration camp. She can't have any soul, if she grew up in a nice house in Riverdale—no matter *what* your parents did, that you saw them doing. [!]

"I still have ambivalent feelings about success, though. I obviously want my talents to be recognized by people other than the dear friends sitting around my living room. But on the other hand, I've seen what stardom can do to people—paranoia, hard drugs, mental hospitals. My main problem now (well, I don't know if this should be getting out) is that I *don't* want to travel. I'm *scared to death* of flying. I have *horrible* stage fright, and I am *terrified* of eating out-of-town tuna sandwiches, so I really don't think I can discuss becoming a star intelligently."

Carly bought a copy of *Time* magazine, dated March 1, 1971, because James Taylor was on the cover. *Time* was a major barometer of mainstream American culture, and a cover story was a huge deal. The story—"James Taylor: One Man's Family of Rock"—announced that the loud, clamorous rock music of the sixties was passé. "Over the last year, a far gentler variety of rock sound has begun to soothe the land." Danny Kortchmar, who played guitar in Taylor's band, was memorably quoted: "After you set your guitar on fire, what do you have left? Set fire to yourself? It had to go the other way." The era of seventies soft rock had officially begun.

Time proclaimed James Taylor one of the major pop innovators of 1971, his music an intimate mixture of Carolina lyricism and personal expression. Plus he'd sold 1.6 million albums. Plus he'd just finished starring in a "New Hollywood" movie. His twenty-seven-city national concert tour had sold out. "Lean and hard (6 ft. 3 in., 155 lbs.), often mustachioed, always with hair breaking at his shoulders, Taylor projects a blend of Heathcliffian inner fire with a melancholy sorrows-of-young-Werther look that can strike to the female heart—at any age."

The article went on to provide the anguished outlines of Taylor's private life. "Drugs, underachievement, the failure of will, alienation, the doorway to suicide, the struggle back to life—James Taylor has been there himself." The Taylor family's unhappy story of dysfunction, alcoholism, and mental illness was made public, as was James's ongoing romance with alpha songstress Joni Mitchell. *Time* noted that three of Taylor's siblings had recording contracts, and mused about whether a dynasty was incipient. Taylor, readers were informed, was building a house on Martha's Vineyard, where most of the family now lived. "It may just be," James was quoted, "that we can't find anything more comfortable than the time we all had there, as a family. Or maybe it was something that was never there, that we miss, and are still trying to put together."

Around this time, Jac Holzman got a call from his wife in California. She'd been driving on the freeway when "That's the Way" came on the radio, and she reported that she'd been so moved by the song's emotions that she had to pull off the road. Holzman didn't usually get that kind of passionate feedback from his wife, and he took it as a sign that the song could really move people. Elektra's promotional people were ordered to push the single. By the time Carly returned from a winter vacation in Jamaica, "That's the Way" was in the Top Thirty.

Steve Harris was on the phone every day, promoting the record, and he knew that in order to go Top Ten, he needed Carly in front of an audience in a major radio market. The previous summer, an unknown singer from London called Elton John had played two nights at the Troubadour in Los Angeles and, overnight, became a one-man music industry with his Band-like songs about Americana and country comforts.

Harris recalled: "I was pushing Carly. I called up Doug Weston, the owner of the Troub: 'Who've you got coming in?' He reads me off about nine weeks' worth of bookings, and when he got to Cat Stevens I said, '*That's* the show, Doug. I want that show.'"

Harris rang up Carly: "Carly! Carly—we're going to play the

Troubadour! You're opening the show for Cat Stevens starting April sixth!" He told her about Elton John breaking big after playing there. The same thing could happen with her. But Carly was upset: "I was completely flustered, because it never occurred to me that this record was going to take off. I tried to tell them I really couldn't do it, that I didn't really want to be a performer. But they wouldn't accept this. They thought I was just being difficult. Eventually, I got the word from Jac, through my manager, Arlyne: 'Carly, you can't *not* promote this record.'"

Steve Harris went over to Carly's flat. She said, "I can't go out there. I'm afraid to fly."

"So am I," he said.

She said, "I haven't got a drummer."

He said he'd get her the best drummer in L.A.

She said, "I have to have an operation."

What kind?

"A minor one."

"She put all these roadblocks in the way," Harris remembered. He told her they would fly, together, loaded on valium and whiskey, and that he would hold her hand and look after her. She seemed to agree. Later that evening, she called him at home and said, "I can't do this job without a drummer."

Whom did she have in mind?

"Somebody who sounds like Russ Kunkel"—who was, Carly knew, on the road playing in James Taylor's band, and thus unavailable.

Harris rang up Kunkel: "Russell, what are you doing April sixth through the twelfth?"

"Nothing. James isn't working."

"Great. Carly Simon."

"Five hundred bucks."

Harris called Carly. "I got you someone who sounds exactly like Russ Kunkel."

Joanna, Carly, and Lucy Simon singing around the piano in their family's Greenwich Village apartment, circa 1951.

Richard Simon, around age fifty.

The Simon family at their front door in Riverdale: Richard, Joanna, Andrea, Lucy, Carly, and Peter, circa 1953.

Carly with her doll,
taken by her father in
Stamford, Connecticut.

Carly's sixth grade
yearbook photo.

With Nicholas
Delbanco on the lawn
in Riverdale, circa 1961.

The Simon Sisters, circa 1964.

The Simon Sisters—Lucy on left, Carly on right—in 1963.

Hailing a taxi to Electric
Lady Studios in 1970.

The *Anticipation* cover, taken
in Regent's Park, London, 1971.

Cat Stevens with Carly at Carly's London flat while recording *Anticipation* in 1971.

Carly and Kris Kristofferson at the Bitter End in 1971.

The Carly Simon Band at the Boston Music Hall in 1972. From left: Drummer Andy Newmark, manager Arlyne Rothberg, Elektra Records' Steve Harris, Carly, guitarist Jimmy Ryan, pianist Paul Glanz.

Carly ascending the
back staircase in
Riverdale in 1973.

James and Carly at their wedding
in Manhattan in 1972.

James and Carly right after they
got married, with their matching
robes in their New York apartment.

James and pregnant
Carly on their way to
the Hit Factory in 1973.

James and Carly, probably
in a studio setting.

Carly pregnant
with Sally at the Hit
Factory. Producer
Richard Perry is at the
far right, James next to
Carly, studio engineer
in the middle, in 1973.

Carly pregnant in the studio.

Carly did some of her best singing in the studio while expecting.

Carly and Ben on the Vineyard, circa 1979.

"Oh . . . who?"

"Russ Kunkel."

Carly screamed down the line. Then she recovered and told Harris that he'd won. "I guess I really have to do this, don't I?"

So Carly gave in. She called guitarist Jimmy Ryan ("We have *Russ Kunkel*?") and pianist Paul Glanz, and rehearsed her songs in her apartment for a month. This was the beginning of the Carly Simon Band. She tried to work out her crippling fears with her therapist, and in interviews. "What frightens me [about performing]," she said, "has nothing to do with the actual singing and playing. It's got to do with the expectation, the focus [on me], the feeling of being trapped. It's like claustrophobia, or a phobia of having to stay in one place. I feel pinned down by the lights. I can't make eye contact with the audience. My adrenaline starts rushing, and all I can think of is, *I gotta get out of here, or I'm going to die.*"

Early in April 1971, Steve Harris picked up Carly and her favorite guitar in a black limo and they drove out to the airport. "So we flew," Carly recalled, "first class, Steve and me, on valium—five milligrams for me, forty for Steve. He really was scared to fly, and wanted to just float through the ordeal. And it was very exciting, but I tried not to think about it, because it really was . . . very scary."

THE TROUBADOUR

—

Carly had never been to Los Angeles, and remembers it was
exciting just being driven to the Continental Hyatt House on Sunset
Boulevard in West Hollywood. "It was so un-East Coast, and so
dramatically far away. It was just thrilling. I started thinking, *Well,
I don't have to be scared, this is a foreign land; these people won't
even speak the same language.*"

Steve Harris was happily married, so he and Carly were just
friends and colleagues. They shared a sense of humor, and goofed on
the tacky hotel's platform-mounted beds and plush red wallpaper.
They went to the rooftop pool and ordered drinks. Carly tried to get
some sun. "This was my first time on the West Coast, and I wanted
everything the West Coast had. I wanted it all, including a tan. But
being April, it was cold, and I couldn't really work up any color to
my New York pallor."

Harris had with him an advance copy of *Rolling Stone* magazine's review of *Carly Simon*. Written by Timothy Crouse (the son
of Broadway composer Russell Crouse), the review positioned Carly

as a poetic champion of middle-class Americana: "Carly writes songs dedicated to the proposition that the rich, the well-born and the college-educated often find themselves in the highest dues-paying brackets. Some of her songs sound like Updike or Salinger short stories set to music."

The next day, Carly and Harris went over to the Troubadour on Santa Monica Boulevard and she had a rehearsal with Russ Kunkel: tall, clear-eyed, big heart, and big smile. He was one of the best rock drummers in the country. Carly: "He was like a demigod to me, because I was already in love with James Taylor—from a distance— and in love with that whole sound. So I was in awe of Russ, amazed to be rehearsing with him." Carly was so taken with Russ that she happened to be sitting in his lap, seductively teasing his long, thinning hair, when his singer wife, Leah Kunkel—sister to Cass Elliot of the Mamas and the Papas—walked into the club. Carly was out of Russ's lap like a flash.

Carly was beset with conflicting emotions. She didn't know how she was going to get through with preparing and delivering the six songs required of an opening act. She kept telling herself, *It's only six songs.* Yet she was fascinated by her new role as a musician in a group. "I had such a wonderful band, and it all started then. I loved Jimmy Ryan so much. Russ was basically the first drummer I ever played with. The guys were so great that I started to love being around musicians, their sensibilities. This was my first *real* band experience. It was *heavy.* I *loved* it. That's something I've never lost."

Elektra was going whole hog. Cat Stevens was on A&M Records, and label bosses Herb Alpert and Jerry Moss had invited a starry Hollywood guest list to check out their new English minstrel, hoping Stevens could replicate Elton John's triumph from the previous summer. Opening acts usually don't have much technical clout, so Jac Holzman flew in to supervise the sound check personally. (Steve Harris: "I wanted him there in case there were any technical problems. Jac found romance rewiring machines as well as music and the artists.") Holzman decreed that the club had an adequate sound system, but he still ordered Elektra's best studio microphones sent over for Carly to use. He was relieved that Carly showed no fear during the sound check. She seemed to him like a real pro.

"We went back to the Hyatt House," Carly recalled, "and ordered room service, the first time I'd ever had room service, 'poor little rich kid' that I was. I had a steak and French fries. (I was eating meat in those days.) Russ stayed with us, and we watched some boxing matches in my room with Steve and Jimmy." Russ had just played on Joni Mitchell's new album, *Blue*, along with James Taylor, who sang on some of the tracks. Russ talked about his experience with Scientology, and Carly was impressed with his very "clear" persona. Again, she said, "I found hanging out with men who were musicians or in charge of my career to be kind of heady—a new experience, the first sign of life from me that there was going to be something about it that I really liked.

"That evening was the opening, my first opening night—*ever*. The guys left around five o'clock, so I could get ready. Steve Harris said he would pick me up at seven."

When Harris arrived, Carly was shaking, undergoing a massive anxiety attack. "She was trembling like a kitten; she couldn't focus, she was stuttering. She could hardly speak. She said it was an old problem, from her childhood." But she was dressed to kill, in a flowing dress and cool boots, her hair long and shag-cut in the rock star style of the day. Carly trembled all the way to the club, shook while tuning up in the dressing room, hardly made eye contact with the band, who knew what was up but tried to be cool about it. Carly asked how many people were out front, and was told the place was sold out. Cat Stevens was a huge draw, with his heathery singing voice and sweet little songs that could be sung in a twee English nursery. Leon Russell was out front. So was Randy Newman. And Joni Mitchell with James Taylor in tow. Jack Nicholson. Carole King was a maybe. Elektra's publicists had placed a rose on every table, with a note: "Love from Carly and Elektra." She thought that was a nice touch.

Carly was in a state. She asked Steve if she could go down and talk to the audience, kind of make friends. "No, you can't." Could they go for a walk? "Yes, we can." Harris walked the quaking Carly down the stairs, past the Elektra staff waiting to support her, and out the front door. Carly looked so upset that some thought she was leaving for good. They returned through the back door. Carly told Harris: "After the show, if Jac Holzman comes backstage and tells me how wonderful I am . . . I'll know I failed. I'll know he's faking. I don't want to hear that, Steve. 'Carly, you were just fabulous.' Don't let him come back and say that to me."

And then it was a walk out into the colored lights and: "Ladies and gentlemen, please give a warm Troubadour welcome to Elektra recording artist Carly Simon."

Applause. Carly sat down at the piano, nodded to the band, and went into the first song. The studio microphone produced a vocal tone that someone described as "aqua-luna—moonlight on the water." Later, Carly told an interviewer what happened next: "I only had to do my six songs. I found myself singing and playing the piano, but the microphone kept slipping away as I was singing into it. It kept veering off to the left, and I'd follow it and, still playing the piano, swing it back in front of me like a typewriter and start again, and then it would go further and further to the left, and the audience was watching me do this. No stage manager, no Doug Weston, no Steve Harris or anybody came up and tightened the mike. . . . But this preoccupied me so much that it preoccupied me right out of the fear, because I was too concerned with the mechanics of this microphone slipping. It was actually a wonderful thing, a little angel to distract me so I wouldn't be afraid.

"So I did six songs, and 'That's the Way I Always Heard It Should Be' was the encore. The band was great. That's what happened."

There was long applause, and flowers in the dressing room. Jac

Holzman came back and, of course, said, "Carly, you were *wonder-ful*, and we're behind you one hundred percent!" She looked— daggers—at Steve Harris, who headed downstairs to handle the press. When he ran back upstairs to the crowded, smoky dressing room, James Taylor was sitting on the floor talking to Carly. His little sister, Kate Taylor, a beauty of twenty-one, was sitting next to him. James was wearing an old suit jacket over wide-whale corduroy trousers held up by suspenders, very rural-looking, his hair hanging below his shoulders. James had come to say hello to his drummer, and explained to Carly that the reason he wasn't working that week was because he was helping sister Kate with an album she was mak- ing for Cotillion Records. Russ had told James that he was working with this new girl singer called Carly Simon and that he should come by the Troubadour to see the show.

James was very shy, and mostly kept his eyes averted, but he surprised Carly by reminding her that they had previously met on Martha's Vineyard a couple of summers before. "We passed once in the driveway of my mother's house," he told her. "Your brother and you were going to talk to my brother Livingston about a job you were going to do together. I passed you, and said hello. And Peter said hi and introduced me to you. And then I left."

Steve Harris looked on. Carly and James were locked into each other, amid the bustle of the room. James was telling her about the house he was building on Martha's Vineyard, while his girlfriend Joni Mitchell was downstairs listening to Cat Stevens sing "Peace Train."

"They were having this fabulous conversation," Steve said. "I can see the sparks are flying." Meanwhile, there was a noisy bunch of young kids from the first show, and they're calling to Carly from the alley behind the club. So Carly took her guitar and opened the win- dow and played another song to them from the fire escape. Then Joni Mitchell arrived to drag James away, and the moment was over.

Steve: "At that point, I guess, Carly was feeling no pain. She looked over at the musicians and said, 'Well, guys, we've got a second show to do.'"

The Carly Simon Band persevered for the three-night stand, two sets a night. Two girls, Hilary and Molly, teenage fans from the first show, started coming around with brownies and other stuff for the sweaty band while they hung out between shows, and the guys were pleased to have (platonic) groupies of their own. Carly also had a few L.A. dates (mostly lunch) with the successful physician/novelist Michael Crichton, whom she dubbed "Big Boy" because he was six foot four.

But there was a strong undercurrent now, a premonition Carly had after talking with James Taylor at the Troubadour. "I had this strange, prescient, almost eerie feeling that we were going to be together. Every time I saw a picture of him, even before I met him, I'd think: *That's my husband.* I'd see a picture of him with another woman, and I'd get upset. I've never had that with anybody else. It wasn't good or bad, but somehow, I saw it coming."

Still, Carly was also enraptured by Cat Stevens. She watched his fervently performed sets several times, and became enchanted by his beautiful songs: "Moon Shadow," "Wild World," "Morning Has Broken," "Into White." "Wild World" was a hit single, and Stevens was huge on American radio. His presentation was wispy, almost feminine, light as air. When he asked Carly for her phone number in New York, she gave it to him in total anticipation.

Carly Simon's Troubadour shows were a smashing success. She was in instant demand for interviews and Hollywood dinner parties. She cajoled the press with humor and intelligence, charming reporters and radio deejays with jokes and offhand remarks. Photographers clambered for her, this new, sexy young woman of the seventies. The radio was playing album cuts as if they were singles. Magazines began to do spreads on Carly's look, her songs, describing hers as a new female energy for the coming decade. Pop music critic Robert Hilburn praised her in the *Los Angeles Times*: "Carly Simon is one of those individualistic singer-writers that one immediately associates with such artists as Randy Newman, Laura Nyro, and Joni Mitchell." Carly did a session with photographer Jack Robinson for *Vogue,* all long dresses and cross-gartered sandals, which left dents in her legs. "I dressed real hippie," she said recently. "Still do. I wore Indian skirts, or jeans, Indian tops, long earrings, open-toe high heels. I still have clothes from those days, and I still wear them.

"I was the new girl in town," she said. "And you can only be the new girl in town once. I never remembered being so popular in my life as then. . . . It was like a swarm of bees. People invited me to their house. Men fell in love with me that wouldn't have looked at me twice before. Songs were written about me, people at the dressing room door, flowers, drugs offered . . . I *really* felt it at Elektra. Everybody's rooting for you, everyone's plugging for you in a way that they never will again."

Now Arlyne Rothberg began to take some serious phone calls. Country music star Kris Kristofferson had seen Carly play and he wanted her to open for him at the Bitter End in May. She was invited to open for Cat Stevens at Carnegie Hall in June. Carly's career now took off.

Carly recalled this era with great affection: "You know, there are certain periods in your life when a lot of events come together and they influence the rest of your life. The year I met Jake Brackman was very important to me. And April 6, 1971, was a confluence of a lot of people and energies—Cat Stevens, meeting James, the success at the Troub—those three nights changed my life."

"That's the Way I Always Heard It Should Be" was number twenty-five on the charts when Carly played the Troubadour. Sales continued to build over the new several weeks, and eventually the single would get to number ten with a bullet.

SILVER-TONGUED DEVIL

---

*M*ay 1971. Carly opens for Kris Kristofferson at the Bitter End, an old haunt from the days of the Simon Sisters. To Carly, Kristofferson is something else. A thirty-five-year-old former Rhodes Scholar, army helicopter pilot, and, later, a sex symbol and movie star, Kristofferson writes what *Time* magazine called "bluntly sexual protest songs that have made him the most controversial songwriter-singer of the day." He wrote "Me and Bobby McGee" for his girl pal Janis Joplin, who had a national hit record with the song after she died of a heroin overdose in 1970, a month after Jimi Hendrix. Other songs included "Sunday Morning Coming Down" and "Help Me Make It Through the Night." Tall, bearded, and craggy, Kris performed in a sexy chamois suit, leather soft as butter. He was going around the country promoting his new album, *The Silver Tongued Devil and I,* and he was weary and really hitting the bottle. The first night, he called Carly back to the stage after his regular set and they sang together, to the delight of the packed Bitter End. It was Local Girl meets New Nashville, big time—a sensation. The next night, they went back to his suite at the Gramercy Park Hotel and he played a new song, inspired by Carly: "I've Got to Have You."

Carly took him home another night. Kris was pretty drunk. He looked around the place: chintz-covered sofas, good furniture, flowers, and shawls. He kept repeating, "Carly, . . . you have . . . the most . . . beautiful . . . the most beautiful . . . *kitchen*." She was telling him her life story when she noticed he had passed out. She kept calling her manager, asking what to do. Arlyne told her to let him sleep it off.

Another night, Kris brought Bob Dylan over to Carly's place. She wasn't surprised that Dylan couldn't recall their business meeting of five years earlier, in Albert Grossman's office. Then major league songwriters John Prine and Steve Goodman turned up. Everyone got drunk. After Dylan left, Carly's guitar got passed around, as the four songwriters tried out some new things on one another. Carly turned on her Wollensak tape machine and made a clear recording of that "magical evening with the four of us" on East Thirty-fifth Street.

"My relationship with [Kris] was kinda stormy," Carly said a few years later. "It lasted around six months, with like a five-month hiatus within that time. We were hot for each other, but he made me feel insecure. I always felt I could be booted out at any moment. But it probably turned out more songs than any other relationship I'd had to that time."

⌒

June 1971. Carole King's *Tapestry*, an album about love and motherhood, is number one, chased to the top by James Taylor's *Mudslide Slim and the Blue Horizon*. "That's the Way I Heard It Should Be" is number six on Chicago's WLS Hit Parade. (The Rolling Stones' "Brown Sugar" is number one.) Carly is working on her second album, urging Elektra to hire Paul Samwell-Smith to produce it in London. Samwell-Smith had made the two recent Cat Stevens albums, *Tea for the Tillerman* and *Teaser and the Firecat*. Carly wanted his intimate sound and gentle sensibility on her record as well.

Samwell-Smith turned Elektra down. He hadn't liked the orchestrations on *Carly Simon,* and he was busy producing the soundtrack to the film *Harold and Maude,* with music by Cat Stevens (destined to become a cult classic). Carly told Elektra to keep trying. She *had* to have Paul Samwell-Smith.

She was writing prolifically now, turning out some serious new songs. "I loved music, and I didn't want to confine myself to one type of song," she said. But she also realized she was working in a crowded marketplace. "You had to have a kind of signature, to have something that you're recognized as being. So when I started to write songs, this singer-songwriter personality emerged." Now her writing solidified into the narrative form that Carly continued to deploy for the rest of her career. The songs would almost always tell stories, usually in four verses, with the bridge before the final chorus, "like the ballads I used to sing that reach a climax around the fourth stanza." Carly's twist on this was an ironic turnaround in the last verse, indicating the real deal going down when all the facts are finally on the table and all pretense is useless.

Carly also started seeing her therapist again, after a long break. She needed to get to the issues behind her stage fright. "He helped me to understand why I was like that," she said, "but there was still this utter bewilderment, when I came face-to-face with it. Once onstage, I forgot everything I'd learned." She was determined somehow to come to grips with her fears, no matter what it took. And when she wanted something in those days, she usually got it.

Cat Stevens called Carly when he arrived in New York. She would soon be opening some important concerts for him in Boston and New York. She invited him to her apartment, and then was very nervous that the adorable minstrel was on his way, so she picked up her guitar, sat down on her bed, and wrote "Anticipation"—the complete song—in fifteen minutes. "I was so excited that day, waiting for Cat

Stevens," she recalled. "I was excited, aglow, a-glimmer, and trying to get myself to calm down."

Cat Stevens duly arrived with his guitar, accepted a cup of tea, and he and Carly began to sing together. Steven Georgiou was twenty-three years old, a hirsute Byronic poet with more than a touch of Mediterranean romance from his Anglo-Greek heritage. He had been a teen idol in England, then an art student, but had reinvented himself as a songwriter in the mold of the late, brilliant Nick Drake, whose whispered ballads had been stilled by an overdose of antidepressants the year before. Cat Stevens was a modern English troubadour. Some found his music and presentation overly precious and cloying, but girls loved it and were buying his records in mass quantities. The songs on *Tillerman* and the forthcoming *Firecat* completely enchanted Carly, and by the end of the evening, the anticipation she had felt at the budding friendship was on its way to consummation.

The chorus to "Anticipation"—"These are the good old days"—was an indication of the growing confidence and assurance Carly felt. After years, decades, of struggle, maybe the tide was turning in her favor. She now knew, with a killer instinct, that this year, and the next, were going to be those she would remember for the rest of her life, as the time of her life.

Carly Simon and her band—Jimmy Ryan and Paul Glanz, joined by drummer Andy Newmark—opened Cat Stevens's show at Boston's sold-out Symphony Hall in the middle of June. Their six songs went down well, and the opening notes of "That's the Way" drew scattered applause. A few nights later, in New York, Carly would open for Cat in venerable Carnegie Hall on West Fifty-seventh Street. When she arrived backstage, there was a telegram waiting for her. It was from her sister Lucy, and it read: "SEE YOU AT THE MOORS."

Carly—"a little stiff, but only around the edges"—did a backstage interview with Patricia Kennealy, the editor of *Jazz & Pop* magazine, and admitted to severe nervousness about playing Carnegie Hall. "I like to be able to see the audience," Carly said. "In clubs like the Troubadour and the Bitter End, I could see them, and sing to their faces and their reactions. This [big hall] is *so* different—a big black nothing, with red lights, and it makes a lot of noise, and you can't see it."

The enormity of this concert was compounded by the presence of Paul Samwell-Smith, whom Elektra had flown in from London with the idea that if he saw Carly perform, he could be persuaded to produce her new album. He was a rock star himself, having founded the Yardbirds, a band that had replaced the Rolling Stones in London's mid-sixties club land, and gone on to start the rock movement with their long, jamming raves. Tall and handsome, with impeccable manners, Samwell-Smith greeted Carly before the show and accepted her ardent appreciation for his production work on Cat Stevens's records. Immediately after the concert, impressed by what he had heard, and deeply felt, he signed on to produce Carly's next album at Trident Studios in London later that summer.

Carly and her band took the stage at Carnegie Hall on an early summer Saturday night. The audience, described as "the Westchester– North Jersey axis" (read: suburban), was surprisingly well mannered and attentive. Carly looked ultra-svelte in a long brown dress, green suede boots, and a peasant shawl tied around her hips. With her shag-cut hair and overbite, she looked fabulous and every inch the next big rock star. The band sounded great. Jimmy Ryan played tasty guitar fills and doubled on a transparent Dan Armstrong bass. They played six songs, including the brand-new "Anticipation," to an audience who was aware of Carly and responsive. Three songs in, Carly stepped up to the microphone and said, "You know, there's nothing to be afraid of, in Carnegie Hall." There was laughter. Some people applauded, including her mother and sisters, in the third row.

Jazz & Pop: "She takes to the piano for her airplay hit, 'That's The Way I've Always Heard It Should Be.' She plays authoritative piano and exuberant, though uncomplicated, guitar. Watching her sing, head back, eyes closed, reveals the joy of the feeling of the song. The weight, of course, is the voice—clear, balanced and astonishingly strong. Not all her songs measure up, but Carly Simon could sing a shopping list and make it sound good."

STICKY FINGERS

———

*L*ate June 1971. Joni Mitchell's epochal *Blue* album was out, giving Carole King and James Taylor (Joni's now-ex-boyfriend) a run for their money. Joni, Carole, and James Taylor—the alpha singer-songwriters—were now Carly Simon's competition, and she found this daunting. The Rolling Stones were, as usual, dominating the rock scene with their new *Sticky Fingers* album. Designed by Andy Warhol, the Stones' album jacket featured a pair of jeans with a real fly-front metal zipper that fans could pull down, as if they were undressing Mick Jagger for a blowjob. The band's new logo was a crimson lapping tongue. The new-look Rolling Stones were running very hot, augmented with a ballsy horn section led by the big and blustery Texan saxophonist Bobby Keys. Carly listened to *Sticky Fingers* with care, and read that the lovely strings on "Sway" and "Moonlight Mile" had been arranged by Paul Buckmaster. Buckmaster's orchestrations were unusually subtle, and ultramusical, and Carly wanted to get him involved in her new album when she got to London.

Carly wanted Mick Jagger as well. She had loved the Rolling Stones for years, and Jagger was now the major personality of the entire rock movement. If she could somehow entice him to her recording sessions in London, she felt she could get him to sing on her record, something that Jagger had never done outside his own band. Getting Mick to sing would be an incredible coup, and Carly imagined she could pull it off. She had the idea that she could meet Mick if she interviewed him for a magazine. The reviews of her Carnegie Hall concert noted how much she looked like Jagger: the cheekbones, the overbite, the haircut. Jagger was famously narcissistic; maybe he would be attracted to someone who looked a lot like him. He had just married his pregnant twenty-one-year-old Nicaraguan girlfriend, Bianca Pérez, but Carly would not let that minor detail stand in her way.

Cat Stevens returned to England. He promised Carly he would sing on her record. Traveling with Kris Kristofferson, Carly flew to Washington, abjectly terrified of the plane crashing. On the flight back to New York, Kris became annoyed by her cringing and bluntly told her to cool it. Soon after that, he said good-bye and flew west to California. She flew east, to England. Carly and Kris's affair had come to an end, but both had gotten some good songs out of it.

⁓

July 1971. James Taylor's version of Carole King's "You've Got a Friend" was the number one record in America. Jac Holzman called Carly and invited her to a farewell dinner before she and her band left to record in London. They arranged to meet on the evening of July 4. Carly: "Jac was supposed to pick me up at the Algonquin Hotel [on West Forty-fourth Street], where I was having cocktails with [photographer] Peter Beard. But I had some kind of anxiety attack and had fainted, and was brought up to Peter's room. A doctor came in and looked at me, and said I was okay. Jac appeared and took over. We went to a Japanese restaurant on Forty-eighth Street. I was absorbed in my own story, and went on and on about it. And eventually he said, 'Well, I've had a bad day too,' and he told me that Jim Morrison had died the day before, in Paris. He cried. I was totally shocked.

"He was very emotional, trying to keep it together. I'd have been crumpled, and having a fit. But Jac's emotional expression took a very different path from mine. He didn't cancel our dinner. He stayed in control. But as much as anyone can imagine Jac Holzman losing it, or being out of control—he really was very upset—running back and forth to the telephone."

Holzman later wrote that sharing the news of Jim Morrison's death with Carly Simon really lightened his load. No one knew about it yet, and he thought that he could count on her discretion. But when she got back to her apartment, Carly called Jonathan Schwartz, who was working at WNEW-FM. A few hours later, Holzman got a call from Alison Steele ("The Nightbird"), who did the evening shift at Schwartz's station. Holzman: "Somehow, Alison had gotten my unlisted home phone number. She asked me point-blank if Jim was dead. I told her the truth, and asked her to play 'Riders on the Storm.'"

By mid-July 1971, Carly and her band were in London and working on her record. They were staying in a rented house in Camden Town and commuting to Trident Studios, down a narrow alley at 17 St. Anne's Court in Soho. Trident had been one of the first English studios to feature Dolby sound technology and an 8-track mixing desk. The Beatles recorded "Hey Jude" there, and sent most of their Apple artists (including James Taylor) to Trident. The Stones loved the place. Singer Harry Nilsson had just finished a record there. A new rock star called David Bowie was coming in next. Between recording sessions, the musicians who worked there liked to nip over to the nearby pub, the Ship, for a pint of English ale.

Carly and Paul Samwell-Smith clicked immediately. Slender and intense, he had just left his wife, and so, fairly quickly, his and Carly's professional relationship took on an intimacy of its own. The sessions went well from the beginning, because this time, Carly wasn't intimidated by her producer. He was sympathetic toward her, and his vulnerability gave her confidence. "He found a quality in me, a kind of fragility," she remembered (wistfully) a few years later, "that has not been tapped since."

Carly had brought in a good collection of new songs. "Anticipation" was hopeful about an impending love affair. Paul began it as an acoustic ballad, then brought in drums (later augmented by Jim Keltner) and finished it as a rock song with its electric coda: "And stay right here 'cause *these* are the good old days." It was Carly's tribute to her moment, but it also resonated with many listeners wondering what the new decade—the seventies—would mean to their lives.

Like "Anticipation," Carly's "Legend in Your Own Time" was written in part about Cat Stevens, although she has said that other factors played in.

Carly: "I was in the passport office, waiting to get one. It was a long line, on a hot day. I was on my way to London to make *Anticipation*. The guy in front of me was reading an article about [the late country music star] Hank Williams. The headline said, 'A Legend in His Own Time.' And, somehow, the story of Hank combined in my mind with what would happen to me if I ever became a 'legend.' Then I thought of the singer-songwriter stars with whom I was smitten, alone in their hotel rooms after a night onstage, with all the love that had been directed toward them that evening. Then I caught the echo of a room service cart coming down the hall with a piece of burnt toast and an overcooked egg and a pot of cold coffee.

"I thought of the hours before the 'man on the road, the legend' gets the room service, and of all the connections he can't make in the parties after the show; in the bar after the parties after the show; with the girl he brings to his room who may still be asleep as the cart gets closer to his hotel room with the non-breakfast. How sad—and sadder—for the contrast of what the love onstage had been, and what it had felt like." Ambition and loneliness often go hand in hand, the song says, with guitars and bongos and close, double-tracked harmonies on the fugitive choruses.

"Our First Day Together" and "The Girl You Think You See" were story songs, the former a folkish ballad, almost an homage to Joni Mitchell; the latter, a funny bit of Broadway-inflected soft rock. The album's first side would conclude with "Summer's Coming Around Again," a pretty bossa nova—the boy from Ipanema—that had been kicking around Carly's repertoire for years, resurrected here with a soft arrangement for guitar and piano.

⌒

Now Carly heard that Mick Jagger was in London, and she told her people that she needed to meet him. Through Elektra's London office, she received an invitation to the Rolling Stones Records press party for the rereleased single of "Brown Sugar"/"Bitch," augmented with an extra track, "Let It Rock." Carly attended this affair with the two Pauls—Samwell-Smith and Buckmaster. Introduced briefly to Mick, she importuned him about singing on her record, but he explained that he was preoccupied with making the new Stones album, and then was swept away. Carly was disappointed, but she felt that now she had at least met the Rolling Stones' protean front man.

Trident Studios, Soho: July through September 1971. They worked on "Share the End," with lyrics by Jake, an anthem for an apocalypse. Jake also cowrote "The Garden," a slightly spooky ballad. Carly wrote "Three Days" about her time with Kris Kristofferson: a short-term reverie and a regretful parting. "Julie Through the Glass" was a piano lullaby for Carly's niece, Julie Levine: "And we'll help you to love yourself / 'Cause that's where loving really starts." The album would end with Carly's version of Kris Kristofferson's new "I've Got to Have You," a dark song of sheer desire, with a southern accent and a crying, fuzz-toned guitar solo offset by dramatic drum fills and intimations of romantic pain. These were the tracks that would appear later in 1971 on the album *Anticipation*.

"Making that album gave me the best memories of recording— maybe ever," Carly said later. "The entire album was just me and my band in London. Cat Stevens was the background singer on a lot of the songs, and there were strings on a few songs [arranged by Del Newman], but it was basically the three guys in the band and myself. On the whole it was so sparse, but I loved it."

In September, Elektra flew Carly's brother to London to take the album photographs. Peter Simon found his sister holding hands with Cat Stevens and talking quietly with him in the backyard of the house she was staying in. Peter was a massive Cat Stevens fan, and loved that Cat was hanging around the house and the studio, staying as close to Carly as possible. One afternoon they took a taxi to Hyde Park, where Peter posed his leggy sister in a diaphanous skirt, holding on to the park gates like a lioness shaking her cage. Another sequence showed her running through a leafy glade. Carly also did some press interviews while she was in London. The man from *Record Mirror* was smitten: "She has the kind of dark Latin good looks and attractive sultry features which would have left me a mooning adolescent at sixteen and, as it was, left me a mooning thirty-year-old as we sat on the living room couch of her tasteful rented house in Camden Town."

Carly told writer Keith Altham that working with Paul Samwell-Smith brought out something new in her work. "Paul turned me down at first. He couldn't tell who or what I was from that first album, but then he came to hear me at Carnegie Hall and I reached him through that. I was so jealous of the Cat Stevens albums he produced; they were so clear and exciting.

"On this new album, I'm more naked than I've ever been before. It was embarrassing listening to the playbacks at first, rather like looking at yourself without make-up in the mirror for the first time. Most of the material is just me and my guitar. Paul is keeping it very simple. It has a quirky feeling, but as the album progresses I'm beginning to like it, and that's the secret."

How About Tonight?

$\mathcal{E}$lektra released *Anticipation* in early November 1971, and it was an immediate hit record. Radio had been playing the "Anticipation" single since late October, and the 45 started surging up the sales charts. It stayed on *Billboard* magazine's Top 40 chart for the next three months. The album sold a half million copies in that period and stayed on the charts until mid-1972. Jac Holzman's faith in Carly, despite the doubters on his staff, had been validated. (Carly dedicated the album to Steve Harris, Elektra's star minder, who had held her hand in some of her darkest moments.) Holzman gave some of the credit to the producer, Paul Samwell-Smith. "He made a very caring and lovely record," the label chief later wrote. "He gave the songs a frame of easy intimacy that helped the listeners to welcome them into their lives. *Anticipation* really consolidated Carly's position as a writer-singer of enormous craft, imagination and honesty." Reviews were generally positive and sympathetic. *Rolling Stone* recognized Carly as representative of the new "liberated" woman coming of age in the early seventies, and took her new songs as signifiers of what progressive women were (really) thinking about. Mainstream American magazines—*Vogue, Redbook, Ladies' Home Journal*—said the same thing. (But not everyone bought into this. In New York, the antibourgeois *Village Voice* frigidly dismissed Carly's songs as simply more pop pabulum for the ruling class.)

On the evening of November 9, Carly went to see James Taylor perform at Carnegie Hall. She had heard the rumors that James had been dumped by Joni Mitchell, who had tired of babysitting a high-functioning heroin addict. Carly noted how fervently and vocally James's youngish fans, especially the girls, reacted to the despondency of "Fire and Rain"—calling out to him between songs—and how they were then soothed, rapturously, by the lullaby "Sweet Baby James." This was the first time Carly had seen the essential James Taylor, in full cry. For her, his performance had an endearing, heart-breaking quality that moved her to tears.

Carly knew Nat Weiss, James's attorney. He offered to take her backstage to see James. When she got there, she found him seated, still holding his guitar, amid a throng of well-wishers, including his sister and brothers. When James saw Carly, he quickly stood up and leaned down to accept her kiss. His demeanor changed markedly, brightening up. Band members Danny Kortchmar and Lee Sklar checked out James and Carly interacting with each other. They both had the same thought: *"Mrs. Taylor."* Gradually the dressing room emptied out, until it was just Carly and James and a couple of his brothers. As she got up to leave, she told James that if he ever felt like a home-cooked meal, he should give her a call.

James looked at her and asked, "How about . . . *tonight?*" Everyone else laughed. Carly said she would make him something delicious, and gave him her address. James said he would be over later.

James Taylor arrived at Carly's apartment a couple of hours after that. She made him some eggs and toast. They stayed up most of the night. He made no move as if he wanted to leave. She said she was tired, and was moving to the bedroom, and he could join her. She put on something more comfortable and got into bed. James took out his guitar, sat down on the side of the bed, and started playing to her, as she lay with her hair spread on the pillow in the soft pink light of the lamp. He played and played, beautifully, expertly. It was a predawn serenade, a private recital, bold as love. It was beyond touching, beyond moving—James Taylor playing his heart out to Carly Simon. His head was bent low, and his eyes were closed most of the time. James broke Carly's heart for the second time that night.

A year later, an interviewer asked Carly about that first night with James. "It was great," she replied. "We went back to my place, and then we went into the bathroom and fucked." James denied this, and maintained with a straight face that he and Carly didn't have sexual relations until they were married.

Carly had a gig headlining the Troubadour in Los Angeles beginning November 18. She flew west with Billy Mernit as a traveling companion. As their flight was descending, Billy noticed the reflections of overhead clouds in the cup of coffee on Carly's tray table.

"Look, Carly," he said, "clouds in your coffee."

Carly had sold out the Troubadour. The band was happy that their groupies Hilary and Molly were back with their hash brownies and backrubs. Jake Brackman was in town, doing movie business. Don McLean was opening the shows, about to have a big hit record with "American Pie." The opening night went well. The crowd cheered for "Anticipation," and sang along. There were repeated calls for encores, and Carly was flushed with excitement. Later, in the dressing room, she said she wasn't ready for visitors, but relented when Steve Harris told her that Warren Beatty was waiting on the stairs. He was the biggest star in Hollywood. Carly knew that he was involved with actress Julie Christie, but she also knew that didn't matter. Warren was very complimentary about her performance, and wanted to know where she was staying.

A few hours later, Carly and Jake were in Carly's room at the Chateau Marmont, listening to a tape of her performance, when there was a knock on the door, which Jake answered. It was Warren, back again. Jake left. Carly later told Steve Harris that Warren Beatty had been "very, very persuasive" with her.

Carly flew back to New York after the Troubadour shows and seriously took up with James Taylor. Jake Brackman noted that all Carly's romantic liaisons now ceased to exist. Ex-boyfriends and new flames who called her for dates were told, "I'm with James Taylor now." Then she changed her phone number to an unpublished listing.

James took Carly up to Martha's Vineyard to show her the house he was building. This proved to be an austere, fanciful, extremely vertical bachelor's shack, still under construction, on some forested land James had bought with the money he'd earned from the *Sweet Baby James* album. The carpenters included James's youngest brother, Hugh Taylor; the brilliant local artist Laurie Miller; and Zack Wiesner, who'd been in James's first band, the Flying Machine. The house's ground floor was basically a recording studio with a galley kitchen. The upstairs was the bedroom and a mixing board. There was a wood stove, and electric baseboard heat upstairs, but the house was still cold. Little David, James's German shepherd dog, barely recognized him. The whole scene was very early seventies: communal, rustic, and rudimentary. Carly would wake up in the morning to find the carpenters, roofers, plumbers, electricians, various band members and their girlfriends, plus hangers-on (and delivery men) drinking coffee and having breakfast downstairs. "There were all these people," she recalled, "and they were eating our food, making coffee all the time." It was a serious adjustment, but she did her best to accommodate James's crew. (They called themselves No Jets Construction, after a local campaign to stop commercial jet aircraft flying into the island's primitive, World War II–era airfield.) With his new wealth, James was a leading source of employment for his friends, the island's impoverished young artisans, and Carly decided she had to make the best of her new boyfriend's Vineyard scene.

Carly, speaking ten years later: "James was the kind of person you looked at and wanted to save. We went to live on Martha's Vineyard, where I found two years worth of unopened mail, stacked up to the ceiling. I spent the first six months of our relationship going through it. It was a labor of love. I was determined to get James out of this hole of unopened correspondence. And I remember that the house was filled with hangers-on, all the time."

As for James Taylor, he had fallen hard for Carly Simon. This level of emotion was unusual in his life, and he told friends he was deeply affected by it. He had found someone who would really look after him, something he had always needed. One night, he got into a fight with his sister's boyfriend, who'd been rough with her. James called him out, and it ended badly. James, extremely upset and fairly intoxicated, disappeared into the woods. Carly went out looking for him, calling his name. It started to rain. Eventually she heard him calling back to her, his disembodied voice echoing through the bare trees. "I *love* you, Carly," he cried. "I *love* you, Carly."

On December 18, Carly headlined at the Bitter End. The line to get in ran for a block down freezing Bleecker Street. She was worried because she had a bad cold and a sore throat, but the show had to go on. She climbed on the tiny stage in a high-necked blue dress, crammed in with her band. Her mother was sitting at a table in front. Her brother, Peter, was rushing around with his camera. Her sister Joanna swept in, late, fresh from singing a performance of J. S. Bach's *Mass in B Minor* at Carnegie Hall. Carly called her very pregnant sister, Lucy Simon, up to the stage and together they sang "Winkin', Blinkin' and Nod." This proved a sensation. Down in front, Andrea Simon was pounding the table and shouting for more. The second set was even better than the first.

The next day a reporter asked Carly what she thought her "image" was.

"I don't think I have any one image, but other people seem to think I do. I'm told they see me as a new kind of woman; very strong; very, very liberated, independent, large, forceful, big smile, lots of teeth. . . . But I never think of myself as one person. There are so many different Carly Simons. There's a shy and introverted one, acquiescent, intimidated. Other times, I can be the master of ceremonies, the person bringing everyone else together. Different people bring out different things in me."

Carly had also started to write songs again, the first new material since she had worked on *Anticipation* the previous summer. One was called "God and My Father," with a complex lyric about what had happened to her inner self when Richard Simon died. Carly: "One night I was curled up in bed with this new notebook of pages that hadn't been written on, and I just decided to write and see what came out on paper. The first line I wrote was about hearing God whispering lullabies. I just kept on, not really knowing where I was going. It was a strange sensation."

At the end of the year, Carly was interviewed by the British music paper *Disc and Music Echo*. She told the reporter that she loved working in London and would definitely make her next record there. She repeated that she liked playing in clubs, and hated concert halls, where she couldn't see the audience. She said, "My feelings get very hurt if I'm not liked," so success was very important to her. Asked about her relationship with James Taylor, she allowed, "Let's just say that it's not a professional entanglement."

The year 1971 had been a good one for her, Carly said. "I liked the acclaim [of having a hit record]. It made me feel . . . in *awe* of myself . . . for the first time in my life, really. Now I feel driven to get this feeling—again and again."

Poor Moose

———

$\mathcal{N}$ow it's early in 1972 and Carly Simon is supposed to be writing songs for her third album, but she is distracted by various problems, including finding someone to produce it—Paul Samwell-Smith is otherwise engaged—and someplace to live with her new boyfriend, James Taylor. J.T. has made it clear to her that he needs taking care of, and Carly is sure that she's the woman to do it. It isn't clear if she even knew at the time that James was using heroin. She is sure that her apartment off Lexington is too small, and his house on Martha's Vineyard is still under construction—and will remain a work site for the next thirty years. Carly starts to look around someplace familiar—the Upper East Side of Manhattan, zip code 10022—and after a few weeks she finds a place in the East Sixties that will do for the two lovers, at least until they get busy and two turns into three.

James Vernon Taylor was born in Boston in 1948. His father was Dr. Isaac Taylor, originally from North Carolina, lately of Harvard and the Harvard Medical School. Dr. Taylor married the beautiful Trudy Woodard, the daughter of a waterman and boatbuilder from the North Shore of Massachusetts. Their first child, Alex, was born in 1946. James came next, followed by brother Livingston, sister Kate, and brother Hugh. In the early 1950s Isaac Taylor moved his young family from Boston to Chapel Hill, North Carolina, where he became instrumental in founding the state university's school of medicine and was a prominent medical educator.

The Taylors of North Carolina were an old mercantile family that went back to Colonial days, blue-blooded American root stock. But recent generations had coped with mental illness and alcoholism, and this extended to James's father. It led to friction between James's parents, and this in turn may have contributed to Dr. Taylor's decision, in 1956, to leave his family for two years to take a post with the U.S. Navy's mission to Antarctica as chief medical officer of the naval base. (In fairness to Ike Taylor, as he was widely and affectionately known, he had spent World War II in Cambridge, getting his education, and had sat out the 1950–53 Korean conflict as well. The navy job may well have been his way of fulfilling a desire to do something for his country.) The upshot was that the Taylor family's father disappeared for two long years, and the five children grew under their mother's sometimes distracted watch.

Trudy Taylor made the best of her lot, as her husband now communicated with her and the children through letters, mostly long delayed. Still, she took her brood on European summer vacations. Music lessons were important: James had four years of cello lessons and played in his school orchestra. Alex played the violin. Kate had piano lessons and took up the Carolina mountain dulcimer. Liv played the banjo. They all sang in home and at church and learned to vocalize in the characteristic Appalachian accent of the Carolina country singers.

Dr. Taylor returned to the family after two years, but things were never the same. Much later, James was quoted to the effect that his father came back but never came home. Rather than reintegrate with the family, he built a beautiful modernist house for them in the

Morgan Creek Road neighborhood and threw himself into his academic work, eventually becoming the respected dean of the University of North Carolina Medical School. His political liberalism and aura of aloofness made him something of an outsider in his community, but it also served him well as a leader and authority figure. Despite his reputation as a two-fisted drinker, everyone knew they could depend on him. The Taylors entertained a lot as part of their academic world, and music was always a feature of this, much as it was in the Simon family in the same era.

Also as in the Simon family, the children's best memories were of family vacations to Martha's Vineyard, where they had many seasonal friends and the blissful pastimes of sailing, fishing, and swimming. Music was a big draw there, and Jamie Taylor and his siblings almost never missed the hootenannies at the Chilmark Community Center when they were on the island.

James Taylor at fourteen was over six feet tall, introverted, shy, and under the baleful influence of his older brother, Alex, who was rambunctious, getting in scrapes, and starting a rock-and-roll band. The Taylors decided to send Jamie to one of the great New England boarding schools, where he could grow in a protected environment. They chose Milton Academy, near Boston. Founded in 1792, Milton was then divided into separate schools for boys and girls. Both of President Kennedy's younger brothers had gone there. James arrived with his cello in September 1962, already very homesick. But he tried to fit in and was given the nickname Moose, because he was the tallest boy in the class. Later that year he got permission from his mother to sell the cello, and bought a guitar instead. "It saved my life," James has said. He taught himself a personal fingering style, still in use fifty years later. By the tenth grade, Moose was one of the popular boys in school. He could play Beatles songs on his guitar after hearing them once. His was a serious, brooding presence. He told his friends he missed North Carolina all the time, and was trying to write a song about it.

The summer he was fifteen, he met and started playing music with a friend on Martha's Vineyard. Danny Kortchmar, or "Kootch," was a little older than James. His family had a summer house in Chilmark, near where the Taylors stayed, and so there were many opportunities for the two boys to put their guitars together and practice. James had a quirky, very moody personality, and Danny could see that he wasn't real happy, but he was already a brilliant guitar player. That year, Danny asked James to play the Chilmark Community Center's annual talent contest with him, which they proceeded to win with a standing ovation.

During his third year at Milton, James had some health problems. Despite being the star musician of the school's weekend coffeehouse, he seemed depressed, missed classes, slept all the time. In 2011 he looked back in an interview: "When I was fifteen, I could hardly live inside my skin. It was like I'd been born on the dark side of the moon." The school decided to send him home for a rest, and he spent the rest of the year recuperating and playing in his delinquent brother's band, the Fabulous Corsairs. Alex was the lead singer, James the lead guitar; they rocked a lot of dances and frat parties in the Chapel Hill area.

He tried again in the autumn of 1965 as the Beatles' new songs blasted on Boston's WMEX and WRKO. But again he lost his way, settling into a deep depression that unnerved his friends and teachers. You couldn't talk to Moose. He just looked down at his shoes and retreated into his guitar for solace. Milton was a famous prep school, and everyone in his class was excited about applying to colleges and universities. James was too depressed to bother, because he knew he wasn't going to college. "It was really just me and my guitar," he remembered about this painful time.

Everyone tried to help. One of the guidance counselors asked James if he could put his feelings into words. James described a process that would start with him not feeling well, which then evolved into insecurity, fears—what he called getting the blues. Then came the inexplicable onset of really black moods, and then despair—very deep. This turned into a profound, almost narcoleptic fatigue. By the time school officials intervened, James was sleeping for twenty-hour stretches. He was removed from his dormitory and placed under closer supervision, in one of the masters' houses. Poor Moose was beloved by many, and his illness was breaking almost every heart at Milton. When he went home for the Christmas break, he resolved not to return to the school. But he could never quite bring himself to tell his parents, who were having trouble with the designated black sheep of the family, Alex.

Jamie went back to Boston in January, but first crossed the river to Cambridge to talk to Stan Sheldon, a teacher who was married to his mother's best friend. He told Sheldon that he was afraid he was going to kill himself if he went back to school. Sheldon took him to a psychiatrist, who declared an emergency. The Taylors were called, and James agreed to a voluntary commitment at McLean Hospital, the famous psychiatric facility in Belmont, Massachusetts, affiliated with Harvard Medical School. James agreed to go if he could bring his guitar with him, and he spent the next nine months, as he later called it, "knocking 'round the zoo."

McLean was basically a luxurious asylum, and very upscale. Detox and rehab were specialties. Famous patients had included Ray Charles, the poet Robert Lowell, and members of the country's great families. James was enrolled in McLean's private academy, the Arlington School, from which he graduated in 1966. (This was the end of his formal education. Both his brother Liv and sister, Kate, would follow him to McLean and the Arlington School. None of the Taylor's five children would attend college.)

At McLean, James underwent daily psychotropic medication. He ate meals with plastic utensils that were counted upon return, and stared out the barred windows while the psychiatrists tried to figure him out. When he was eligible for the draft, he was called for a physical examination by the army, and was literally escorted to the draft board in Cambridge by men in white hospital coats.

He also wrote some songs, including "Knocking 'Round the Zoo."

By September 1966 he felt well enough to check out. He'd had enough. The doctors told him that he was acting "against medical advice," and that he would have to be observed by staff in a locked ward for three days before they could discharge him. So James hid himself and some of his record albums in the back of a friend's van and escaped from McLean, hoping never to return.

He called his friend Danny Kortchmar, who was living in New York with his young wife. "Kootch," he said, "I'm out!"

"Come to New York," Danny said. "Let's start a band!"

APPLE CORPS

———

$\mathcal{W}$hile James Taylor was in the hospital, Danny Kortchmar had been working in a New York band called the King Bees, which became the house band at Arthur, the famous disco in Midtown. When James came to New York with some great new songs— "Knocking 'Round the Zoo," "Carolina in My Mind," the beginnings of "Rainy Day Man"—Danny knew that an incipient rock star had fallen into his lap. He proposed that James become the lead singer of a new group, the James Taylor Band. James declined this honor, and the group was renamed the Flying Machine. Joel O'Brien from the King Bees was recruited on drums. They taught the bass parts of James's songs to their Vineyard friend Zack Wiesner (the son of MIT president Jerome Wiesner, who had been an adviser to the late president Kennedy). The band rehearsed in the basement of the Albert Hotel in the Village, and eventually got a gig replacing the hit-bound Lovin' Spoonful as the house band at the Night Owl Café, an old Village landmark. This resulted in James writing another new song, a rollicking R&B number called "Night Owl," which the band recorded and released as a single that failed to get on the radio.

This lasted about seven months, well into 1967. Then James started using hard drugs. "Joel O'Brien had been doing heroin," Kortchmar said much later, "and then one day I realized that James was, too." This caused a rift in the Flying Machine, and eventually the band disintegrated as James's habit became more acute. But for James, heroin was a miracle; it actually made him feel better. The drug is a potent analgesic painkiller, and for James it became a highly effective medication against acute depression and the suicidal feelings that continued to plague and frighten him. Heroin's narcotic euphoria left him free to function, at least creatively, at a higher level than he had ever dreamed of. The downside, of course, was that heroin addiction is an expensive full-time job. After his band fell apart, James could be seen passed out on the benches of Washington Square Park after scoring another fix of the inexpensive Southeast Asian heroin that was flooding America as the Vietnam War continued. Then he turned his apartment into a crash pad for other junkies and some strippers. "I had fallen in with some people," he said later, "who could have done me some harm. There were warrants out for these two guys, Smack and Bobby, who were staying with me. They were robbing people to get money for dope. I was addicted myself. I was getting desperate. Then I ran out of money, and no one would lend me any."

Strung out, sick, hungry, at the end of his rope, James called his father in Chapel Hill. Isaac Taylor listened to his son. He said, "What's your address? Stay put. I'll be right there." Indeed, Dr. Taylor got in the family station wagon, drove straight to New York, and rescued his son from depravity and almost certain death.

When he felt better, toward the end of 1967, James left for England to seek his fortune there. His model was Jimi Hendrix, who had left New York as an unknown the year before and now was the biggest rock star in the world. James's intention was to busk in the streets, write some new songs, and get discovered.

It worked.

His father's mother had left him a little money, supposed to go to him on his twenty-first birthday. His parents let him have the legacy early—James was only nineteen at the time—which was enough for him to get to London and buy a car. He packed an old acoustic guitar he'd bought in Durham, North Carolina, when he was fourteen and flew to London, staying with friends in Notting Hill and Chelsea and, indeed, singing for money in busy tube stations with an open guitar case for the coins people tossed in. He bought a little Ford Cortina and took off for Formentera, the idyllic Mediterranean island favored by Europe's hippies. He met a girl named Karen and together they took the ferry to neighboring Ibiza, where James wrote "Carolina in My Mind."

James played some of his songs for friends. A young woman who worked for the BBC and knew people in Soho, where London's music and film industry was based, encouraged him to make a demo and shop it around. James's money was running low in early 1968, but for eight pounds (about fifty dollars) he purchased a forty-five-minute block of time in a Soho jingle studio on Greek Street. Playing by himself on a stool, recorded by one microphone, he recorded "Something in the Way She Moves," "Carolina in My Mind," "Rainy Day Man," "Night Owl," and six other songs. A few days later, he collected them pressed on an acetate disc that timed out to forty-five minutes.

Spring 1968. James Taylor called his friend Danny Kootch on a hunch he might have a connection into the London scene, and of course he did. Danny read *Billboard,* which had announced that Peter Asher, late of hit-making British Invasion stars Peter and Gordon, had taken a job with the Beatles' record label, Apple, as a talent scout and A&R executive. Peter and Gordon had a run of fourteen hit singles in America during the previous three years, including a number one in 1964 with "A World Without Love." (Peter and Gordon's hits had all been written by Paul McCartney, whose girlfriend Jane Asher was Peter's sister.) The King Bees had toured with Peter and Gordon as their American backing band—connection made. Danny gave James a number for Peter Asher. Asher picked up the phone. He told James Taylor, "I'm listening to everything."

James: "I went in and played 'Something in the Way She Moves' for Peter Asher. Then Peter played my acetate for Paul and John [Lennon], and suddenly I was on their label. It was my big break. It was like a door opened, and the rest of my life was on the other side."

Paul McCartney: "I heard [James's] demos. Peter played them for me, and I heard his voice and his guitar, and I thought he was great. And then Peter brought him round, and he played live [for Paul and George Harrison at Apple's headquarters on Baker Street], so it was just like: 'WOW! He's great.' And he'd been having troubles. Peter explained that he'd just got clean off drugs and was in a difficult time in his life. But he was playing great, and he had enough songs for an album." George Harrison loved "Something in the Way She Moves" so much that he later stole the title for his song "Something." James Taylor, after only a few months in London, became the first American musician signed to Apple Records. Somewhat in a state of shock, he called his parents in North Carolina and told them that everything was going to be fine because he was working with the Beatles now.

James needed a recording band. Peter Asher took out ads in *Melody Maker* and *New Musical Express*. They were given an attic loft at Apple and held auditions for people who answered the ads. Musicians were hired, and Joel O'Brien came from New York to play the drums. Soon James was drinking codeine cough syrup. Then he was smoking opium. Then he got back on heroin, plentiful in London's music world. Then he was injecting speedballs, a hot combo of heroin and amphetamine. His first album, the brilliant *James Taylor*, was recorded under the influence, at Trident Studios, between July and October 1968, while the Beatles were making their double *White Album*. Paul McCartney played bass on "Carolina." George Harrison and Peter Asher contributed background vocals. These luminaries were "the holy host standing around me" that James sings about on "Carolina in My Mind."

It's not hard to know how he felt. The Beatles were angel-headed hipsters, avatars of their age, and here was James in their midst, at the zenith of their career, sponsored by them at the beginning of his. He would come into the studio as they were finishing for the day, and listen to early versions of "Hey Jude" and "Helter Skelter." He held on to his chair while listening to the spiraling sonic vortex of "Revolution 9."

While James was working at Apple, he was trying to stay afloat mentally, but he was, as he later said, "in disarray." This was some heavy stuff he was living through, in his twentieth year. "I was changing houses every two weeks—high rent, too much noise—while I tried to keep to the recording schedule and fullfill Peter and Paul's faith in me." His girlfriend from New York, Margaret Corey, was staying with him. Her brother Richard, a friend of James's, was around. (Their father was the comedian "Professor" Irwin Corey, a regular on Johnny Carson's *Tonight Show*.) In New York, James had become close to one of their friends, another troubled young soul named Suzanne Schnerr. "I knew Suzanne well in New York," James said later. "She was from Long Island. We used to hang out together and get high." But Susie Schnerr had committed suicide after James moved to London, and his friends let him know about it only once the Apple album was complete. James was very upset that they hadn't told him. "Margaret and Richard and Joel [O'Brien] were all really close to Susie Schnerr. But they were also excited for me having this record deal and making this album, and when Susie killed herself, they decided not to tell me about it until later because they didn't want to shake me up." The day after learning of his friend's death, fighting despair, James wrote the first verse of a new song called "Fire and Rain" in his basement flat on Beaufort Street in Chelsea.

He was using the British equivalent of methadone to combat withdrawal from heroin, but it wasn't working well. His album complete, he flew back to New York in late November 1968, checked into a Manhattan hospital for detoxification, and called his mother. There he wrote the second verse of "Fire and Rain."

Trudy Taylor came to New York. A few days later, mother and son drove to western Massachusetts, where James Taylor signed himself in to the Austen Riggs Center, a private psychiatric hospital in the village of Stockbridge, amid the wintry Berkshire hills. It was there he wrote the third and final verse of "Fire and Rain."

Rain and Fire

———

$\mathcal{A}$pple Records released *James Taylor* in December 1968, about a month after *The Beatles* (aka "The White Album") came out. But James was in rehab in Massachusetts and the album didn't sell. The American release of *James Taylor* in February 1969 barely made the charts. But at least the treatment he was receiving was beginning to work.

Austen Riggs went deeper into a patient's problems than merely "curing" addictive behavior. Using the psychiatric model, therapists probed into patients' lives to discover the underlying emotional problems that caused their self-destructive behavior. In James Taylor's case, he was helped to uncover a sense of rage—inexpressible, non-specific anger—that might have been fueling his urge for oblivion through heroin. He may have been helped in this therapy by the timing of his parents' divorce in 1969. Isaac Taylor's alcoholism had become so acute that Trudy divorced him that year, which sent their five children into varying degrees of grief.

"The idea that I *have* to perform made me angry," James said later. "I had gotten into my music as an act of rebellion, you might say." Now he felt that his "alienated musical soul" had turned into a businessman making a product for a corporation. "And in that way, recording an album might have made me angry. And might have made me turn to drugs to stomach that anger. Obviously, if you can't express it, you'll have to swallow it somehow."

In June 1969, after five months of treatment, James left Austen Riggs drug-free, driving the Massachusetts Turnpike from Stockbridge to Boston, and then to Martha's Vineyard. In July he performed, solo, at the Troubadour in Los Angeles for the first time. Back on the Vineyard that summer, he crashed a stolen motorcycle on a fire road in the island's state forest, breaking both feet and both hands. The rest of the year was spent in plaster casts. In this period, James got to know his brother Alex's baby son, James Richmond Taylor, now two years old—the original sweet baby James.

Meanwhile, in London the Beatles were imploding over acute business problems. Apple was bleeding money, much more than the company took in from sales. As record executives, the Beatles were too preoccupied to manage their label, so the products simply weren't selling. Peter Asher left the company to go out on his own as a record producer and talent manager. He asked James if he could manage him, and James did not hesitate to say yes. Asher then persuaded Paul McCartney to cancel James's contract with Apple so he could move to another label, and Paul convinced the rest of the Beatles that this was the right thing to do.

Peter Asher then approached Warner Bros. Records in Los Angeles in September 1969. They loved the Apple album, and signed James Taylor to the label for forty thousand dollars. When the casts came off his broken limbs, James took up his guitar and erupted into a creative state that produced many of his best songs. "I think I had built up a lot of energy," he recalled, "because as soon as I got out of those casts, I went into Sunset Sound in L.A. and it was just explosive. That album just went so fast."

When James got to Los Angeles, he called Danny Kortchmar, who'd been living there since the Flying Machine broke up. Kootch had joined a rock band called the City, which had an album out. Personnel included drummer Jim Gordon, bassist Charlie Larkey, and Larkey's girlfriend, the former Brill Building songwriter Carole King. As a teenager, she had cowritten some of the biggest hits of the era, such as "Up on the Roof," "One Fine Day," and "Will You Love Me Tomorrow?" Now, at twenty-six, she had left her husband and relocated to North Hollywood's Laurel Canyon neighborhood, prepared to start a new career as a performing artist. She was about to make her first album under her own name, but Danny persuaded her to help him make James Taylor's record first. Peter Asher, who was producing the record for Warner Bros., agreed that Carole King's band would provide backing for James's incredible book of new songs.

These included the material that would make his career, and which, he later ruefully said, he would be forced to sing for the rest of his life: the lullaby "Sweet Baby James"; "Country Road," written in Stockbridge; the jazzy but disconsolate "Sunny Skies"; "Blossom"; "Anywhere Like Heaven"; and others, including a hip rendition of "Oh Susannah," which he used to sing for the late Susie Schnerr. But it was the song partly inspired by her, "Fire and Rain," that would make James Taylor the first major star of the American 1970s.

James in 1972: " 'Fire and Rain' has three verses. The first verse ['Suzanne the plans they made put an end to you'] is about my reactions to the death of a friend. The second verse ['Won't you look down on me, Jesus'] is about my arrival back in this country with a monkey on my back. And there, Jesus is an expression of my desperation in trying to get through the time when my body was aching and my time was at hand—when I *had* to do it. 'Jesus' was to me something you say when you're in pain. I wasn't actually looking for a savior. . . . Which I don't believe in, although he can certainly be a useful vehicle. The third verse of that song ['Sweet dreams and flying machines in pieces on the ground'] refers to my recuperation at Austen Riggs, which lasted about five months."

It is the "There's hours of time on the telephone line / To talk about things to come" lines in the last verse that give the song a message of hope and redemption, that the friendless, self-pitying singer of the album's other songs would somehow pull through to sing again another day.

Sweet Baby James was made in only a few weeks, for about eight thousand dollars. The basic tracks consist of James, Danny on second guitar, and Carole King on piano. Several different bassists were at the session, and the session drummer, Russ Kunkel, from nearby Long Beach, plays with an uncanny sympathy for the mood that James and Peter Asher were trying to get.

Meanwhile, James joined the community of local musicians. That spring in 1970, he participated in the sessions for Carole King's album *Writer.* The core musicians then formed a band called Jo Mama and were signed to Atlantic Records. And James started spending serious time with Joni Mitchell at her Laurel Canyon home, where she was writing her *Blue* album. He played guitar on "California" and several other tracks on her record.

The "Sweet Baby James" single didn't even make the charts when Warner Bros. released it in March 1970. No one played it on the radio. The album stalled at number ninety. Nothing more happened until that summer, when the "Fire and Rain" single took off and hit the Hot 100 on *Billboard*'s chart. It was then that the album took off, and things were never the same for James, or his family, again.

He was in England with Joni Mitchell when this happened, playing concerts on his own, and then supporting her when she played a show broadcast by the BBC. "Fire and Rain" was on the radio in Britain and was being recognized as a major statement from a young master songwriter. The audience was rapturous when Joni brought him onstage. Together they played "California," "For Free," and "The Circle Game," with Joni on piano and dulcimer and James on guitar. They played the world premier of "You Can Close Your Eyes," a lullaby James wrote for Joni early in their relationship. The BBC later reported they had received a record number of requests for tapes of the concert.

When he returned to California, James took a starring role in a Hollywood movie, *Two-Lane Blacktop,* directed by Monte Hellman. It was a modest road movie about a cross-country car race. James was the driver. Beach Boys drummer Dennis Wilson was his mechanic. Dialogue was minimal, plot even more so, but the script had an existentialist drive, and James was interested in how film production worked. People on the set loved his record and kept telling him what a huge star he was going to be. (Neither James nor Dennis Wilson appeared in a Hollywood movie again.)

As *Sweet Baby James* smoldered its way up the sales chart and James's fame spread nationally, the Taylor family, James's siblings, signed recording contracts of their own. Brother Liv signed with Atlantic and released his first album that summer. Sister Kate signed with Cotillion, an Atlantic subsidiary. Even brother Alex got a deal, with the southern label Capricorn Records, and made a pretty good album in Atlanta with local musicians. James now felt in a strange position, as he told friends. With his parents divorced and his father out of the picture, it was like he had become the head of his fiercely loving but troubled family. It was a position he wasn't comfortable being in. When *Rolling Stone* put James on its cover, the headline was "The Taylors." The long family saga revealed that two of James's siblings had also been hospitalized at McLean: Livingston for depression; Kate for hurting herself. No one in the Taylor family was happy with this kind of publicity.

James played guitar on the sessions for Carole King's second album, which was made in five days in January 1971. The band was Danny's group Jo Mama with Russ Kunkel on drums. Songs included

"I Feel the Earth Move," "It's Too Late," "So Far Away," "You've Got a Friend," "Tapestry," and "A Natural Woman." James and Joni Mitchell both sang backup vocals. The album, *Tapestry,* was released a month later and went on to sell twenty-five million copies.

At the same time, James was helping his sister make her first record and trying to finish his third, which was taking a toll on his equipoise. He was also facing a thirty-city concert tour with Carole King, backed by the Jo Mama band. He was under a brutal corporate deadline to finish the sequel to his last album, which was now selling about a million copies a month. He sang "Fire and Rain" and "Sweet Baby James" on Johnny Cash's popular network TV show and became a mainstream American heartthrob overnight. In March he appeared on the cover of *Time* magazine, discussing his problems, including addiction, as well as his music.

He was much more interested in the house his friends were building for him on Martha's Vineyard than he was in making another record. He wished he had a hammer in his hand instead of a guitar. He took up heroin again, felt better, and finished his album. Decades later, looking back in candor, James said that sometimes his addictions had been "of service to me at the time." He was a cult hero now, with people wanting to speak with him after shows. Parents brought their children backstage to meet him. His lyrics were plumbed for meaning, as if he had a secret knowledge and solutions to life's mysteries. He was a physical wreck, but kept going.

His new album, *Mud Slide Slim and the Blue Horizon,* came out in late March. The basic tracks are played by James, Carole King, Russ Kunkel, with Leland Sklar on bass. James appears on the album jacket with his new moustache, looking obviously stoned. The album sold like hotcakes, getting to number two. (*Tapestry* was number one.) James's version of Carole's "You've Got a Friend" was released as a single and became a big radio hit. Carole King and James Taylor were now the bestselling musicians in the country. *Mud Slide* had only a few great songs, but these included Carole's "You've Got a

Friend" and "Long Ago and Far Away," both with Joni and Carole singing backup vocals. "Hey Mister, That's Me Up on the Jukebox" is a candid self-portrait of a young artist at the end of his rope and ready to quit. In the song, echoing mighty "Country Road," he disappears into the land, where carpenters are working on his cabin in the woods (and he even name-checks the building crew). Artist/craftsman Laurie Miller's drawing of James's austere little barn adorned the back of the album jacket.

Mud Slide Slim firmly locked James Taylor, in the imagination of his contemporaries, into the persona of a saintly junkie, a patron saint of druggy anomie. It was an image he had never pursued, but it was commercially successful, and was inspired by who he was and what he was doing. As his legion of fans celebrated the authenticity of his songs and as his celebrity began to unfold, James described "a feeling of aura" around him. In interviews, he described the instant fame that was happening to him as a feeling he called "holiness." He wasn't conventionally religious, but the huge (and unexpected) success, and especially the intense national media attention, made him feel as if a glowing halo were over his head. "What's all this talk about 'holiness' now?" he was asked by Joni Mitchell. He explained that it was a simplistic reaction to fame descending onto him, in an intense manner, in a short amount of time.

That's when James Taylor went to see his drummer playing with a new girl singer at the Troubadour nightclub in Los Angeles on April 6, 1971.

"LOVE FROM CARLY"

———

*T*his happened mostly because Joni Mitchell wanted to see Cat Stevens. And then Russ Kunkel, who'd worked on both their records, said he was playing with Carly Simon on the same bill, and please come on over and say hello after the show. They went with Kate Taylor and were given a good table near the stage. James hadn't heard much about Carly Simon, and he hadn't heard "That's the Way I Always Heard It Should Be," which was already a hit record in April 1971. This was mostly because he never listened to recorded music— no radio, no records, especially his own. His musical world was influenced mostly by the melodies he composed in his head. Kate told him that Carly was one of the Simon Sisters who used to play at the Mooncusser that first summer when James started playing the open-mike evenings there.

At the Troubadour, there was a vase with a crimson rose on their table and a note that read, "Love from Carly."

Backstage, Steve Harris decided not to tell Carly that Joni Mitchell and James Taylor were in the house. Carly came out and nailed her six songs, expertly propelled through her set by Russ's steady rhythms. So Carly was surprised, and very pleased, when Steve told her that James Taylor was on the staircase and wanted to say hello. Carly kissed James and Kate. James sat on the floor as Kate and Carly sat on the little sofa. They compared notes on the Vineyard, how their paths had crossed in summers past. Then Joni sent word up to James that it was time to get in the limo, and the meeting was over. Both Carly and James later said it was a fateful evening.

Then James went back on the road with the band, focused on getting through the tour until the last stop in Chicago. Danny Kortchmar: "People were in awe of him, treating him with kid gloves, whispering around him like he was Montgomery Clift, or a prophet who knew everything. He was being pursued—by every chick, by everybody around—to where it was painful for him. By the time we got to Chicago in '71, he was in bad shape, and we'd wonder if he'd make it to the next show." Joni Mitchell broke up with him.

This tour was not an artistic success. Reviewers described James as sluggish and distant from his audience. After a Boston concert, his brother Livingston upbraided him about seeming uncomfortable at the adulatory applause he was getting.

James: "And he said, 'What the fuck are you doing? These people *love* you. Why can't you *enjoy* it?' He was really angry at me [about] the way I was coming on. And then I read an article by [critic] Jon Landau [who was producing Liv Taylor's second album] in which he assumed that the way I had come on was on purpose, that I actually was in control of it. Whereas, I really had . . . *no control* over it, at all. Sometimes . . . I just don't know how to act."

But James Taylor kept going. He was on the cover of *Rolling Stone*. His single version of "You've Got a Friend" charted at number one in July and stayed at the top for weeks. (It was the only number one record of his career, to date.) *Mud Slide Slim* was certified a gold album, then platinum. His stage patter was subtle, funny, and self-effacing. He usually introduced "Sweet Baby James" by insinuating that he didn't really like children, which made the audiences laugh out loud. Some critics raved about his concerts. By the autumn of 1971, James was the primo male of the American singer-songwriter movement, embodying the popular notion of the singer-songwriters as their generation's shamanic conveyers of sympathy, sincerity, healing, and trust; bardic harpers whose songs told of the times and mirrored the sensibilities of their audience.

He was also running out of dope on the road. James: "This was the fall '71 tour, with just myself [onstage]. I found myself on the road with no drugs and quite a habit. So I went to Richmond. The first gig I had was in Williamsburg, and I was sick for the job. And it went lousy. I ran into a chick I knew from London and she took me to Richmond and we copped there from this guy named Hangdown. He sold me enough to keep me going until I got to Chicago."

In the meantime, James played Carnegie Hall, and then started seeing Carly Simon. He couldn't tell her about his drug habit, for the shame of it, and he resolved to get off dope when the solo tour wound up. "When I got to Chicago, I got in touch with a doctor who was a friend of mine. And he got some methadone for me, somewhat illegally. He figured it was either he'd break the law, or else I would go down. I stayed on the methadone he gave me for almost a month."

As they began seeing more of each other in early 1972, James continued to hide his addiction to heroin from Carly. He was good at secreting his stash and his works: needles, spoons, cotton, lighters. He covered up his absences by pretending to rest, or brood, or just be remote. She didn't understand it, but accepted it as being part of the Taylor's family back story, as had been reported by the national media over the past year of his success.

"It was a harrowing time for me," she said a year later. "In the beginning of our relationship I didn't really understand the extent to which James was addicted, or needed drugs. It just kind of confused me that there was always this . . . wall up between us. And I didn't know exactly what it was, because I was never close to anybody who was really addicted to anything before. There was just this remoteness I was always aware of. I was aware that I couldn't depend on him either. And at the same time, I wanted him to depend on me more, but there just seemed to be this barrier between us that I could not break through."

Eventually James told Carly what was going on. She wanted him to get into treatment and said she would do anything in her power to help him. This is what he wanted to hear. She said she needed to know why he got so remote, so far away from her.

"It was partly drug abuse," James said later. "And it was partly that—instead of communicating what feelings I had—I would get off on a drug instead. My mind was occupied by the drug—even the *idea* of getting off on the drug. The idea of keeping it from Carly was a big part of it. But . . . I still needed her very much."

Carly understood this and resolved to stand by James. The needier he became, the more she accepted it.

It was a struggle. James threw out three different sets of "works" (syringes) in the late winter and spring of 1972, each time swearing to himself that his heroin habit was over. He kept reaching out to Carly for support, but it was hard for her. She loved James but now saw the negative aspects of the personality he was submerging under narcotics. To her, he could be many different people, alternately bright, withdrawn, arrogant, romantic, reckless, depressive, cruel, cutting, tender, brilliant. It bothered her that, before their first meeting, he had never heard any of her songs and seemed completely uninterested in her music and career. Sometimes he seemed childish to her, something he readily admitted. "Being a pop star is a very regressive thing," he said later. "All of a sudden, anything you want to do is allowed. You become a spoiled child when you become a pop star. You really get spoiled, something awful, and it happened to me."

Meanwhile, both Carly and James had albums to write. They were both contractually obligated to the same media conglomerate, and now both had production deadlines to deal with. Sometime around April 1972, James replaced heroin with "methadone maintenance," and began to work on his next album.

Hardworking Carly Simon, meanwhile, was drawing inspiration from her tense, touching, and incredibly exciting romance with superstar James Taylor to write some of the songs that would define her for the rest of her career. The next few months in 1972 would produce some of the premier moments of her life. And then her next hit record would put even her unstable boyfriend's career firmly in the shade.

BEST NEW ARTIST

———

$\mathcal{B}$y early 1972 Jac Holzman thought the singer-songwriter movement was already passé. He noticed that a lot of the good ones really wanted to be in a band and play rock and roll. But Elektra signed Harry Chapin on the strength of his songwriting. The label passed on unsigned Bonnie Raitt because she didn't write her own songs. Holzman talked to Carly about this, because she was looking for a producer for her third album, and Holzman wanted something very different from *Carly Simon* and *Anticipation,* which was still in the Top Ten album chart.

Carly had ideas of her own. She wanted to be produced by Paul Buckmaster, the dashing young British arranger who had worked with the Rolling Stones and Elton John.

She made a two-song demo with Buckmaster in New York, played on by James Taylor and Danny Kortchmar. The highlights of this tape were an earthy version of John Prine's "Angel from Montgomery" and an old song by Carly, "I'm All It Takes to Make You Happy."

She played the tape for Holzman, who was polite but firm. Paul Buckmaster was out. Holzman insisted that Carly's new record be made by mainstream pop producer Richard Perry. He wanted Carly to make a record for the massive rock music audience, not the post-folk singer-songwriter crowd. "I wanted fresh producer meat," he later wrote, "someone born in the studio, with solid arranging skills, a person who would push Carly and not flinch when she pushed back, as I knew she would. My candidate was Richard Perry."

Perry, thirty-two, was one of the most successful producers of pop music. Recent projects had included bestselling albums by Barbra Streisand and singer Harry Nilsson. Carly listened to these records and just didn't get it. She thought they sounded slick, glossy, over-produced. But she also wanted something different this time. "I was tired of the whole self-pitying thing that was going on in many of my songs," she said later. "I didn't like to see myself talking about dis-enchantment as much as I had. [*Anticipation*] was about things that never quite turned out the way I'd wanted them to. Things that were disillusioning. I wanted to wipe out all that melancholia and come up with something more positive, more interesting, subjects that haven't been . . . *delved* into."

She told herself she had to stay positive, because the spotlight was really on her now. "Going into it, I felt a lot of pressure on me, that it had to be good. It's a show business syndrome that you get caught up in; that you must surpass yourself all the time to stay in the ball-game.

"So I went into that album quite frightened of working with somebody that I didn't know. I didn't know if I would get along with him, in part because he's from a different borough [of New York City]. He's from Brooklyn and I'm from the Bronx. I'm not joking about the boroughs. . . . I was against the idea. I thought he was too slick for me. Barbra Streisand—I didn't want to have that kind of sound."

Elektra prevailed. Carly would make *No Secrets* in London, at

Trident Studios, with Richard Perry and the crew of star-quality English musicians who had just worked on Harry Nilsson's album *Nilsson Schmilsson*. Now she just had to write the songs—and get Mick Jagger to sing on her album.

In early January 1972, Carly flew to Los Angeles, and then to Palm Springs for Elektra's sales convention, where she was due to perform for the company. When she arrived she was informed that the airline had lost her luggage, which was never seen again. Missing or stolen were all her jewelry and the American Indian long chamois dress she wore onstage. Carly: "But the thing that killed me was my journal was gone. It was a black leather Gucci notebook with loose-leaf pages. My whole first smell of success, my opening at the Troubadour, that whole year—James Taylor—was all in my journal. It also contained all my lyrics up to that time, all the different versions of all the songs. All gone. I was sick."

Carly went shopping with Steve Harris's wife, Nicole, and found a dress she could perform in. She had to follow Elektra's new signing, Harry Chapin, who knocked 'em dead with his pianism and dynamic songs. Jac Holzman was the master of ceremonies, and he told his staff, "Remember our success last year with Carly Simon. Harry Chapin is this year's Carly Simon."

Carly, before she started her set, leaned into the mike and said, "Harry, if you're this year's Carly Simon, you must have had some very interesting boyfriends over the past twelve months." The whole room laughed at this, and gave Carly a heartfelt ovation when she finished with "Anticipation."

Then Carly and Arlyne decided that Harry should open concerts for Carly later in the month. The first was at Symphony Hall in Boston on February 12. When Carly's audience gave Harry a thunderous ovation at the close of his set, Carly wondered about the wisdom of having a tough act to follow. She went on and played a concert that was criticized by the local press for being nervous and shallow.

February 1972. "Anticipation" is the number four record in

America. Harry Nilsson's bombastic "Without You" (produced by Richard Perry) is number three. Don McLean's "American Pie" is number two. Al Green is on top. Carly flew to Los Angeles to play the Troubadour, this time as the headliner. (Don McLean opened for her.) There, despite the reassuring presence of Warren Beatty at the club, Carly had a weekend-long panic attack. She discounted the pleas of her manager and her record label; these Troubadour shows would be her last public performances for several years.

In March the National Academy of Recording Arts and Sciences (NARAS) announced their annual Grammy Awards. Carly Simon won for Best New Artist. James Taylor won Best Pop Vocal Performance (Male) for "You've Got a Friend," which was also voted Song of the Year. Carole King and her *Tapestry* album won most of the other major awards.

In April, Warren Beatty called Carly in New York and said he was working to get George McGovern the Democratic nomination to run for president against Richard Nixon later in the year. Beatty wanted James Taylor's phone number so he could importune him to play benefit concerts to raise money for McGovern. Carly gave Warren James's number on Martha's Vineyard, where James was working on his house and making his next record. A few weeks later James and Carole King headlined a benefit concert with Barbra Streisand in Hollywood that raised a quarter million dollars for Senator McGovern's campaign. Over the next six months, James and (occasionally) Carly would appear at McGovern benefits in Massachusetts and New York in an effort to get rid of the hated Nixon, whom they regarded as crazy and a crook.

Spring 1972. Carly was writing. She was still working on the song "God and My Father," hoping to make it a big statement on her next album, but she was having trouble getting the right connections within a difficult song about feeling abandoned by God when her father died. "I realized I had my father confused with the Devil, and I was writing things I didn't understand myself. It was as if someone was dictating the verses to me and I was writing it down." At one point she called her manager from the Vineyard and sang the song over the phone. Arlyne Rothberg said that this moved her to tears.

It was easier for Carly to find inspiration in her love for James Taylor, especially when she flew up to visit him on the Vineyard. James was using his considerable new wealth to buy more land on the island, and also in Nova Scotia, where old farms were selling for a song. Carly wrote most of the song "No Secrets" on the Vineyard after a long talk with (a mostly reluctant) James about his previous love life. (Unlike Carly, who tended to stay friendly with former lovers, James wanted nothing to do with his ex-girlfriends.)

Flying back from the Vineyard to New York, Carly wrote "The Right Thing" in the back of an Air New England DC-3 plane in celebration of her affair with James. She had a cassette recorder with her, and by the time the plane landed, she had developed most of the structure of the song. She had recently seen the film *The Last Picture Show,* and "loving you is the right thing to do" came from a line in the film. Carly: "It actually was one of my absolutely undisputed songs about James, written three months into our relationship."

Carly also had strong hopes for a new narrative song, "His Friends Are Fond of Robin," which described in detail someone much like a character in a J. D. Salinger short story. But her most important new song was still in her new journal. It had begun in the old one, the one that was lost, under the title "Bless You, Ben." The lyric was about "an imaginary man who came into my life." But the lyric seemed morose to her. Then the song shifted focus as Carly thought about some of the men she'd been with, and how some of them had treated her. She'd had a line in her notebook for about a year: "You're so vain, you probably think this song is about you." The title of the song now shifted to "Ballad of a Vain Man." It had a killer hook of a chorus, and in her head Carly could hear herself singing on it—with Mick Jagger.

How to get to him? "I got this idea to do an interview with Mick

Jagger. Arlyne mentioned it to an editor at *The New York Times*. He said if Jagger was willing, it would be great. We got in touch with Chris Odell, who worked with the Stones." Mick liked the idea; he had a new album—*Exile on Main Street*—coming out, and said he could use the publicity. Carly: "So last May [1972] I casually went out to L.A. and ended up hanging around waiting for Mick to show up—for five days. When he finally arrived he had been on airplanes for thirteen hours and was exhausted. All we talked about that night was how much we hated flying. It was very strange, that first meeting, because I expected to look so much like him. People were always commenting on the resemblance. I expected to walk into a mirror. But then, I didn't think we looked anything alike.

"Mick was wearing a cotton suit in turquoise, very short white socks, and saddle shoes. And he kept apologizing about how tired he was. And then I had to leave for New York the next morning. I saw him again when I was in L.A. in June, but by then we had become friends and I felt it would be too difficult to write an objective piece."

Carly's career in journalism was now over, but the ploy had produced the desired result. Mick Jagger told Carly Simon that if he survived the Rolling Stones' North American tour that summer, he would try to be in London when she made her record in September.

ON BEAVER POND

$\mathcal{I}$n June 1972, Carly flew to Los Angeles to meet her new producer. Richard Perry was tall, bushy headed, with a long face and a prominent nose. Carly had been romantically involved with both her previous producers, but this was not to be the case with Perry. They met at Elektra's studio on La Cienaga. She sat at a piano and played some of her new songs for him. When she sang out the "you're so vain" chorus, he was ecstatic. Perry knew a hit song when he heard one, and he told Carly that their creative collaboration was going to work really well.

While she was in L.A. Carly met with some movie people who were interested in her. There was buzz in the industry about Carly—successful, single, available, hot, a potential new star. There was talk of her being (type)cast in the film *Fear of Flying*. What no one knew was that Carly's stammer, which could still surface when she was anxious, would keep her from accepting the films that would occasionally be offered to her.

Carly also saw Mick Jagger again, just before the Stones went on tour. He told her that he hoped no one died, as they had the last time the Rolling Stones came through. Mick's wife, Bianca, he said, was jealous and didn't like her husband consorting with Carly. Bianca told her friend Andy Warhol that "the only girlfriend of Mick's she ever got jealous of was Carly Simon, because Carly is intelligent and has the look Mick likes—she looks like Mick and Bianca."

Carly spent the rest of that summer commuting among New York, Martha's Vineyard, and Los Angeles. "Ballad of a Vain Man" was in development. (When Carly musically annotated the song, she titled it "You're So Lame" on the score.) "God and My Father" was now called "Nighttime Songs." She was tinkering with the material constantly, sometimes unsure of herself. James kept telling her to hold back and not give too much of herself away.

That summer there were so many carpenters and craftsmen working on James's property that the couple decided to get away awhile. James acquired a mobile home, and he and Carly and his dog, David, drove around New England for a couple of weeks. While they were staying in the Berkshires, Carly suggested they visit her brother on his communal farm in southern Vermont. James was amenable. Peter Simon: "Somehow James managed to get this huge Winnebago down our mile-long dirt road and into the driveway. They stayed all afternoon, and seemed to really enjoy the quiet of Vermont. I took them up the hill to show them our beaver pond. James needed a cover photo for his next album, so he went back to their motor home and put on a fresh shirt and a tie, which gave him a formal, sort of prep-pie look." Peter asked him what the title of the record was, and he said that he had briefly considered *Farewell to Showbiz* and also *Throw Yourself Away,* but no one liked these titles. Then he chose *One Man Parade,* but changed his mind and was calling the record *One Man Dog.* "So I got him out on the pond with his dog in this aluminum boat we had, and I shot the photo from the shore.

I found the tie to be a little strange, but the photo was also about James's general isolation—a man and his dog against the world. He must have liked it, because it was on the sleeve of *One Man Dog* when it came out later in the year."

Late in August, Carly was back in Los Angeles, staying at the Hotel Bel-Air. "Every time I come to Hollywood," she told an interviewer, "I move up a rung in the hotel game. I don't know how I ended up at the Bel Air, but now that I'm here I don't know where I can go next."

She bridled at another reporter who wanted to know about her love life. "That's all she seemed to want to know about. I was offended by the way she rattled them off. 'And just how long did your affair with *him* last?' So I asked why she wanted to know, and she said, 'Well, that's what the public wants to know about, more than anything.'

"Then I thought, 'Well, what is my private life?' In a sense it is my public life, too. In the last two years [the media] needed a hook on me. It made me more interesting when I was going out with someone famous, but sometimes they made more of things than there actually was, and it embarrassed me to have these things so distorted. What I need to do now is develop a proper self-censorship method, so I don't blurt out the truth all the time." She added that James Taylor was helping her with this.

On a Saturday in early September, Carly flew to London with Arlyne, Jimmy Ryan, and drummer Andy Newmark. Carly and Arlyne checked into the Portobello Hotel, while the two musicians were installed in a nearby flat. Arlyne recalled that Carly was under serious pressure now. "She had two months to finish the album so it could be out for the Christmas rush, and she was working with a producer she'd never worked with before."

The first sessions at Trident Studios began on the following Monday, and were discouraging. Carly and the musicians were jet-lagged, and nothing seemed to go right. Richard Perry came on, Carly thought, like a film director: barking orders, full of high-voltage energy, very opinionated. Carly was frustrated. She didn't want a director; she wanted an interpreter. She tried to call Jac Holzman to complain, but the switchboard at Elektra said he was traveling and couldn't be reached. ("I'd heard there were problems in London," he said later, "but I decided to let them sort them out.")

Carly: "Richard Perry was trying to do the same thing I was, which was calling all the shots. But he had more endurance and perseverance than I had. But when I sang the way he wanted me to, it sounded forced and unnatural. He would realize this and say, 'I'm sorry, go back and sing it the way you feel it.' And that would always end up the right way. Almost all my vocals [on *No Secrets*] are original—I did them when the original track was being laid down. I wasn't thinking about how I was singing them, and they turned out to be the most 'honest' vocals we had."

The problems continued for a few days. Carly was unhappy with what she considered Perry's overuse of orchestration, feeling that it marred the simplicity and sincerity of some of the songs. "I doubted myself, my judgments, an awful lot," she remembered. Her frequent calls to James on the Vineyard left her feeling lonely and confused. James was into musical minimalism, and kept telling Carly to hold back in her music, not let everything come blasting out.

The sessions improved by the second week, as the new songs began to coalesce. Laying down the tracks for songs such as "No Secrets" and "Loving You" was exciting, as Carly could see how Richard Perry was building a cohesive sound that took her music into another level of sonic sophistication. But now it didn't sound slick to her, just up-to-date and "adult contemporary," as the format was known at the time. Perry got some of the best musicians in London to play on the tracks, including Beatle-affiliated bassist Klaus Voormann, American drummers Jim Gordon and Jim Keltner, and Ray Cooper, who played percussion in Elton John's band.

James Taylor came to London during the third week, and Carly was elated. They spent most of their time in Carly's suite, did some sightseeing, and cuddled in Soho's atmospheric pubs. She told Arlyne that James had visited her mother in Riverdale to formally ask Andrea Simon for Carly's hand in marriage. Carly: "I mentioned one morning to James in London that I thought we should get married. And he said, 'Oh well, there's really no reason to get married. We love each other and we've been living together.' Later in the afternoon James said, 'You know, I've been thinking about it. Maybe we should get married.' I said, 'Well, what happened between this morning and this afternoon?' He said, 'This afternoon it was my idea.' "

The issue was left open for the time being. James came to the studio almost every day and played guitar on several tracks, but after he went back to the States, Richard Perry erased the work he had done, so James would only barely appear on Carly's album.

In early October, Carly and Richard Perry began to work on the album's vocal tracks. Perry brought in Harry Nilsson to sing the backup chorus on "You're So Vain," which they all recognized as the album's first single and potential radio grenade. Nilsson had written some of the best songs of his generation ("Without You" was the best known), but he was most famous for singing "Everybody's Talkin' " (written by Fred Neil) from the 1969 film *Midnight Cowboy*. Carly and Nilsson worked hard on "You're So Vain," but the song, with what Carly called its "big intervals," was proving somewhat difficult to sing. After some frustrating first attempts, Richard Perry cut the session short and said they would try a fresh approach the following day.

SON OF A GUN

One evening Carly and Harry Nilsson were working on background vocals for "The Ballad of a Vain Man" at Air Studios in Soho when the phone rang.

Arlyne: "I got a call from the receptionist saying that the Rolling Stones office was on the phone. I thought she meant *Rolling Stone* magazine, but when I picked up the phone, Mick Jagger was on the line, asking for Carly. I was amazed, almost speechless."

Jagger had run into Klaus Voormann, who told him Carly was recording in London.

Carly: "I hadn't seen him in London yet. I was right in the middle of overdubbing the vocals to 'You're So Vain.' I said, 'Mick, you wanna come over and sing vocals on this song?' And he came right up."

Carly was singing with Nilsson when Jagger walked in the studio at eight o'clock in the evening. Richard Perry almost went into shock. Here was the most famous rock star in the world, fresh from a mega-successful U.S. tour, whose face had just been on every magazine cover in America. He was dressed in well-tailored tweed slacks and a collared shirt with a tartan pullover under a sharp single-breasted trench coat. "He was at ease," Arlyne recalled, "very relaxed and calm, nothing like anyone pictured him. He was very fair, with that great ruddy English complexion. He sang with Carly, and then kept coming to the studio almost every night, even when he wasn't dubbing 'You're So Vain.' Some nights he just sat quietly and watched the recording. Others nights he spent time teaching Carly some basic rock-and-roll licks. He told her she was a rock-and-roll singer and she shouldn't be afraid to admit it."

⌒

"'You're So Vain,'" Carly has said, "is about a certain type of man—very into themselves—that I've been affected by, adversely, in the past. A man who's more concerned with his image than with a relationship with me.

"Their career was always more important than mine. There were people who treated me in a way that . . . I felt like a piece of meat. I got knocked about. There's that line: 'You gave up all the things you loved, and one of them was me.' So there is *anger* in the song, the first bitter song I ever wrote. And I *loved* writing it, on my aunt's piano in my old apartment on 35th Street. I was thinking about three or four people—a composite—when I wrote it, and there was an element of vengeance there. And then I loved singing it."

Richard Perry's quest for perfectionism was at its most intense during production of "You're So Vain." The rhythm track had to be great. Perry recorded three different versions with three different drummers. Carly: "It took a hundred takes to get it right. Three drummers rushed to England from L.A. and then back again. Jim Gordon's drum part stayed on the choruses, but Jim Keltner and Andy Newmark's parts are still a little there on the verses. And we've got two pianos on that track. Klaus Voormann was—literally—instrumental. We heard him warming up one day, kind of strumming the bass, and to me, it set the mood of a swaggering, self-indulgent man prancing into a room with his hat and his scarf." This bass guitar figure would provide the intro to the song, over which Carly would whisper, "Son of a gun."

"That song," Carly later wrote, "is really a composite of different people. But Warren loves that people think it's about him because of the apricot scarf." The line about the yacht came from a party at her sister Joey's house when Henry Morgan walked in and someone remarked that he was dressed as a yachtsman. "I didn't know anyone who raced at Saratoga or went to view the total eclipse of the sun," she later said. "I just wanted to portray someone who thought he was ultra-cool. And then later, James actually did fly up to Nova Scotia, but it didn't have anything to do with the lyric of the song."

Carly meanwhile was hanging out with Mick Jagger. She has always denied a romantic relationship with him. They took walks together, had some meals in restaurants. Carly says that this is as far as it went. "Mick and I were acquaintances before London," she later wrote. "Then, when we were doing background vocals, Mick called the studio to become ever so slightly more acquainted. He came over to Air Studios where we were working, and he and Harry Nilsson and I sang on the choruses. Mick listened to the playback and then worked out his part very quickly. Harry then graciously demurred and said he didn't think he should get in the way of some obvious vocal chemistry. (More probably, dear Harry just wanted to get out to go to the pub.) So Mick and I finished it together—fabulously, I thought."

"Yes, Mick and I spent some time together in London," she told an interviewer, "but it was complicated, because there were other men in my life. Mick was so compelling, and flirty, and charismatic, that it's hard not to be taken in by him, but James was my love."

Mick and Carly cut several versions of the "You're So Vain" chorus. Listening to the playback later, she could scarcely believe her ears, because it sounded so great. It was a gas to have his help in the studio. "Mick was very devilish and sexual," she said later, "but he was not so vain. He wasn't worried about how his voice would sound; he didn't ask to listen to it afterwards in the control room. He just had the confidence of a racehorse that had won many races."

Mick Jagger's only stipulation was that he appear uncredited on "The Ballad of a Vain Man," as the song was still called (and would remain so until Carly thought of "You're So Vain" after the record had been mastered).

Later Carly would often be asked if "You're So Vain" was written about Mick Jagger. "It certainly wasn't lyrically about Mick," she wrote a friend. "I'm sure something inspired me. It was usually the Stones or Cat Stevens in those days, if it wasn't James. If there was a single inspiration for that song, it must remain mysteriously shrouded in my robust ego which tells me that I MUST keep a secret. Those who think they know, don't."

Mick kept telling Carly she was a natural rock singer, so she decided to let it rock the night they put the vocals on "Night Owl," which had appeared first on James's Apple album. The instrumental tracks had been recorded at Trident. One night, Mick brought horn player Bobby Keys and pianist Nicky Hopkins—both performed with the Stones on tour—to Air Studios to hear the vocal sessions. Keys, who'd memorably played the sax solo on the Stones' "Brown Sugar," unpacked his horn and played a typically blustery solo. Nicky Hopkins put some of his barrelhouse piano on the track as well.

Carly: "It was about two in the morning and we'd been discussing the vocal backups for 'Night Owl.' Paul and Linda McCartney came by from their own recording session, and we had Doris Troy and Bonnie Bramlett there, too, for the backups. Nicky Hopkins was on piano and Jim Keltner on drums. Klaus, Mick, Paul Buckmaster—they were just sitting around, to be there.

"Then Paul said, 'Can I sing on the vocals, too?' So it started with Bonnie and Doris and myself, and Paul and Linda, and Jimmy Ryan and a few others doing vocals, like eight of us. It was completely crazy, like too many cooks and everyone wanted a part, so I decided to bow out so it would be easier to record. The result was fantastic. Everyone was just grooving. The vibes were so high. It was the highest night I ever spent in a studio, anywhere."

When Carly finally made it back to her hotel, the sun was streaming through the wide French doors that opened into a little garden. Exhausted but still burning with the evening's intensity, she got some sleep, and then frantically wrote another song, "Waited So Long." They recorded it the next morning, just under the studio deadline, and Carly raced to Heathrow airport to catch her plane back to New York. Two days later she flew to Los Angeles with James for the album's final mixing. (James dubbed his "she's no virgin" line into "Waited So Long.") Carly finished the album, literally days before the record would be pressed. And, at the very last minute, she changed the name of the song to "You're So Vain."

The first people in America to hear "You're So Vain" were the guests at a Saturday afternoon tea at Andrea Simon's house in late October 1972. The party was for Joanna Simon's birthday and the launch of Peter Simon's first published photography book, *Moving On, Holding Still*. The listening session was in the Simon family's large upstairs bathroom with its great acoustics, Carly and Peter having managed to synchronize two battery-powered cassette recorders so a few guests could enjoy an exclusive preview in a reasonable facsimile of stereo. Among those crowded into the bathroom were writers from *Rolling Stone* magazine and executives from Elektra and Asylum Records. (These two companies were about to be folded into one, much to the consternation of Carly.) After the first play of "You're So Vain," the Asylum promo guy said, "That backup singer on the chorus sounds *exactly* like Jagger." Carly winked. Someone said, "Carly, you're kidding." She just smiled. "Is he credited on the record?" She replied that he didn't want to be. One of the *Rolling Stone* writers asked her how she got him to sing with her, and she answered, "It was all hormonal," and everybody laughed. Then everyone demanded to hear "You're So Vain" again, and three more times after that. Afterward it was agreed that this was a historic recording, an incredible coup, and the record would be a chart-busting hit.

But James Taylor was conflicted when he heard Mick Jagger's vocals on "You're So Vain," and Carly's version of his own "Night Owl," which now sounded like an outtake from *Exile on Main St.* Mick Jagger had left his scent on Carly's record like a dog on a hydrant. This put James Taylor in a complicated position. Mick Jagger never did this for anyone, and no one who heard "You're So Vain" didn't believe that Carly and Mick had had a sexual relationship. Then, on November 1, 1972, James answered the phone at Carly's apartment.

It was Bianca Jagger, and she was hopping mad. She told James, "You know, my husband and your fiancée are having an affair." James told her he didn't think it was true, and ardently defended Carly's virtue. Bianca told James that they *must* have had an affair because Mick sang on her song and he *never* did this for anyone. Carly, she reasoned, had seduced Mick. She also told James she had found a provocative letter from Carly to Mick, and a letter from Mick to Carly that she had intercepted before it could be mailed.

Carly told her boyfriend that she hadn't been with the other guy, and that she loved only him, which was good enough for Jim. Two days later, on November 3, 1972, Carly Simon and James Taylor were married—in a civil ceremony by a judge, with only their families present, in Carly's snug apartment on East Thirty-fifth Street.

Don't Let Me Be Lonely

Carly Simon's marriage to James Taylor had some of those close to her scratching their heads. The marriage looked great on paper—two of the stars of the American singer-songwriter movement joining creative (and reproductive) forces. But everyone knew also that there were bound to be some serious issues. Carly was older than James, who was openly struggling with the downside of national stardom at the age of twenty-four. Drugs—heroin and cocaine—were part of the burden that Carly took on when she accepted James's heated proposal after Bianca Jagger's upsetting phone call.

"I was afraid of drugs," Carly said of this later, "and extremely naïve about it all. I just didn't know what people were doing in the bathroom with needles and white powder. And [James] was very clever about hiding it. But once I realized that James was addicted, I became terribly afraid—for his *life*. I started realizing he was quite different when he was using, and I could tell when he was using this or that. But being so naïve, I thought that the love I felt for him would help him get better, because it had to. That's how I felt at the time."

Some people close to Carly reflected that the careers of the two stars might be about to diverge, with Carly's star ascending while James's was going down. His (low-key, totally brilliant) album *One Man Dog*—eighteen short songs in thirty-seven minutes—was released in November 1972, but didn't sell as well as his previous records, despite a huge budget and an impressive roster of talent. The single "Don't Let Me Be Lonely" would only reach number four in January 1973. Meanwhile, insiders realized that *No Secrets* and "You're So Vain" were about to propel Carly to the highest levels of their profession. Some worried the effect this might have on the marriage, since James Taylor was known to be quite competitive in his professional life.

Meanwhile, Joni Mitchell had just released *For the Roses,* an entire album about her relationship with James. *For the Roses* was immediately recognized as a pinnacle of the singer-songwriter era, an important and beautiful work of art that would prove to be one of the great albums of the century. The songs dealt frankly with James's heroin addiction and the difficulties and heartbreak of living with it. Some of the lyrics bitterly described James's underdeveloped personality, annoying personal habits, and his continual and often desperate search for drugs. Other songs remembered the beautiful and tender side of him—"while the song that he sang to soothe her to sleep / runs all through her circuits like a heartbeat." If listening to this utterly thrilling new music, explicitly about her troubled young husband, gave Carly Simon any pause, she never mentioned it to anyone.

Andrea Simon, at home in Riverdale, had been expecting the call from Carly saying that there was to be a wedding, but she wasn't expecting to be told the wedding was the next day. On November 3 she arrived at Carly's apartment with as many autumnal chrysanthemums as she could round up for a proper floral display. She asked Carly what she wanted for a wedding present. Carly said that there was a piece of furniture in Riverdale she'd always loved. Andrea was a bit taken aback by this. "But, Carly, darling," she said, "don't you know—that's a *real antique*." The subject was dropped for the time being.

The wedding was in the late afternoon. That evening James was playing a sold-out midnight concert at Radio City Music Hall, in Rockefeller Center. Afterward, Warner Communications, which had both bride and groom under contract, would throw a post-midnight party for James in the Time-Life Building, just across Sixth Avenue.

The guest list was small: Andrea Simon and Carly's sisters, James's mother and siblings, Jake Brackman (semicatatonic, unable to speak for reasons unknown), and the judge. Peter Simon documented the wedding with his camera: his sister barefoot, with flowers in her hair; the groom exceedingly calm in a loose-fitting suit, his long hair recently trimmed. The atmosphere in the apartment was crowded and tense, almost like something was happening under pressure. There weren't many smiles. Afterward the judge who married them told Trudy Taylor, "This was a ceremony of hope."

Halfway through his concert that night at Radio City, James stopped the show. A girl shouted, "We love you, James!"

He said, "Well, I got married this afternoon." There were loud screams and applause. The adoring girls seated down front started yelling, "*Who?* Who did you marry?" James looked down at his shoes and softly answered, "Carly Simon." More screams, more applause. James played his new song "Don't Let Me Be Lonely Tonight."

The party started at three in the morning, in the Time-Life Tower Suite. Guests were delighted that the corporate event had turned into a wedding celebration. James asked Joe Smith, the affable president of Warner Bros. Records, to give the toast. As he raised his glass, Smith later wrote, he noted the contrast between the two families: "with the aristocratic German-Jewish Simon family on one side, and the [hairy-hippie] Taylors from North Carolina, complete with everything but livestock, on the other. I was touched by being asked to give the toast, because James was very vulnerable, and you always wanted to repay that trust with sensitivity."

James Taylor, when asked later about the day he married Carly, played a concert, and partied all night, replied, "Well, it was a . . . full day." Andrea Simon's wedding present to Carly and James was a vintage set of the *Encyclopedia Britannica*. A few days later, Richard Nixon buried George McGovern in the landslide 1972 presidential election. (The only state McGovern carried was James's native Massachusetts.) James was bummed. "I really loved George McGovern," he told an interviewer.

A few days later, Carly and James drove up to Martha's Vineyard, where James stayed on methadone maintenance and continued to saw boards and drive nails in his rustic cabin, which the locals were now calling Woodhenge, or Shingle Mountain, since it looked like a cottage somewhere in Middle Earth. Their real honeymoon would take place later in Hawaii, when Carly accompanied James on his first tour of Japan in early 1973.

A Piece of Ass / A State of Grace

$\mathcal{I}$n November 1972, Elektra Records executives held a listening session for *No Secrets* at their swaying skyscraper offices in New York. "The Right Thing" started the album, with Carly's piano figure and a swaying rock song supported by congas, strings, and luscious backing vocals—the florid template of Carly's "sound" for almost her entire career. Sung with total conviction about choosing a man, the lyrics acknowledge that "the river"—Carly's image for female sexuality—had been running too close to her door, making her "a little too free" with herself. Those days, the song says, are now over. Next came "The Carter Family," a little waltz with verses about missing old friends and lovers, and especially Grandma, whose criticisms were usually wise.

The third track was "You're So Vain." Those in the know smiled at the sales and promotional staff's reaction when Mick Jagger's vocal—mixed way up for maximum effect—blasted out of the speakers. Carly's final yell—"Yeah!"—at the end of the last chorus got an ovation. Steve Harris shouted, "Take that to the bank! You can bet the house!" The album's first side finished with the romantic ballad "His Friends Are More Than Fond of Robin," and then the title track, "No Secrets," another lush rock ballad and a great song about too much information from a lover. Bright shiny strings, swooning cones of sound, and Jim Gordon's subtle drumming added an atmosphere that would make "No Secrets" a staple of Carly's music for years.

The album's second side began with "Embrace Me, You Child," the song about her confusion following her father's early death. "Waited So Long" was a country rocker that Linda Ronstadt could have sung, if she'd wanted to tell her daddy that she was no longer a virgin anymore. (Members of the band Little Feat and its guitarist Lowell George had played on the track in Los Angeles.) The sentimental "It Was So Easy" (cowritten with Jake Brackman) was followed by the full-bore action of "Night Owl" with its sticky, Stones-y energy and *Exile*-style chorus. The album closed quietly with "When You Close Your Eyes" (lyrics written with Billy Mernit), a lullaby for insomniacs, cushioned by Carly's piano and Paul Buckmaster's moonlit orchestral sheen.

High above Columbus Circle: handshakes and backslaps all around. The Doors might be dead, but Elektra was still on fire. Christmas bonuses were safe. It was generally agreed that Mick Jagger—with his participation on "You're So Vain" and "Night Owl"—had bestowed the Rolling Stones' sacred imprimatur on Carly Simon. This could now translate into serious credibility with radio, the press, the retail music industry, and fandom. *No Secrets* was a huge step up from *Anticipation,* and would lead to new worlds for Carly, and then worlds beyond.

Elektra released *No Secrets* in late November 1972, and radio stations started playing "You're So Vain." The cover photograph (by Ed Caraeff) was provocative, starring Carly's braless nipples, a floppy hat, and a fashionable pastel tote bag. Carly's suggestive hands could have been painted by Thomas Lawrence. The album jacket projected

"New Liberated Woman"—in your face. The inner sleeve featured a leg-spread, come-hither bedroom image taken by Peter Simon.

Three weeks later, her manager's secretary phoned Carly at her New York apartment to say the album had earned a gold record for half a million units sold. Two weeks after that, in early January, both *No Secrets* and the single "You're So Vain" were number one on the *Cashbox* and *Billboard* charts, outselling Joni and Linda and Carole and Barbra—and Carly's husband. By early 1973, Carly Simon was the top female singer in America. *No Secrets* remained at number one for five more weeks.

Carly was in Hawaii then, on her honeymoon. Her brother photographed her—bare-breasted, lei-bedecked—with James, on the balcony of their hotel overlooking palm trees and surf riders. This photo appeared on the cover of *Rolling Stone* in January, when the magazine published Stuart Werbin's long interview with the couple, done in New York the previous Thanksgiving and in two subsequent sessions. Werbin had been one of the writers given a private preview of "You're So Vain" in Riverdale the month before. This was also the first interview James had given since the controversial 1971 *Time* cover story, which had embarrassed the Taylor family and turned him firmly against further "revealing" publicity.

Nevertheless, the long published text (headlined "The Honeymooners") was unusually revealing about the newly married couple's passion for each other. James described his feelings for Carly as "religious." Carly described her attachment to James as "addicted." James delivered thoughtful soliloquies on his drug use and his current life on methadone, while Carly reported her general anxiety about married life with a junkie. They discussed their hypothetical children, their difference in ages, and bickered about James's complete (and unapologetic) lack of interest in Carly's music. "But *honey*," James pleaded, "I don't even listen to *my own* music."

James was adamant that he had been damaged by the pressure of corporate deadlines in his musical life, which had once been an escape but was now a job: "Carly and I agree that the best thing for us to do, would be to really get into our *own* selves, in terms of writing music—for ourselves. And trying to *screen out* the point of view that we've been more or less indoctrinated with—doing things for an audience, for record sales. Thinking in terms of singles—that sort of thing."

The interview closed with James's pithy observation about his feelings for his wife: "She's a piece of ass. It bothers me. If she looks at another man, I'll kill her."

Before the couple would sign off on the interview, all references to Martha's Vineyard had to be changed to "Cape Cod." This was because some of the millions who had bought James's albums were getting on the ferry from Woods Hole and then asking the locals where James Taylor lived. Some of them made it down his long country road. The last thing James Taylor needed to be was a tourist attraction.

In a taped interview with her brother later in January, after their return from Japan, Carly confessed that she didn't feel driven to work, even though her record label was already talking about her next record. "*No Secrets* was a new direction for me, an expansion. I still need the approval, the confirmation, but right now, married to James, sometimes I think I'm in the state of grace I've been looking for. So, I'm not as ambitious as I once was."

Would it be harder to write love songs now?

"I hope not. But my marriage has replaced ambition somewhat. It's a different source of satisfaction. I'll write different kinds of love songs now, more for myself than for the public."

James came in the room and watered the plants. Carly asked if he was hungry and said she would make him something delicious.

"I didn't think I would marry until I met James," she continued when he wandered off. "And yes, it's really interesting. We both needed the security of the other person making the commitment, in order to be ourselves. . . . It's been such a relief for me. We were both surprised to find ourselves actually feeling better."

Peter noted that a radio station in Los Angeles had started a contest to guess who "You're So Vain" was about.

"It's my first bitter song," Carly said, "and I really liked writing it. I was thinking about three or four people when I wrote it, so there's an element of vengeance. I love singing it."

What about Mick?

"Mick called the studio. I said come over and sing backup with me and Harry. He got into it, and Harry graciously decided to bow out. Mick's presence added a certain tension to the track that just wasn't quite there before."

Asked if she was thinking about new songs, Carly reiterated that she was exhausted for now. *No Secrets,* she said, was wrenching and incredibly difficult to make. Right then, she added, she and James were just lying low, playing possum, and working mostly at making their marriage work.

HOTCAKES

——

*L*ooking back on this time and her marriage to James Taylor from the distance of the twenty-first century, Carly wrote, "Then started a long run of hits, marriage, motherhood, stability, success and fortune. Not much is ever written about those things."

Carly and James were now beginning their decade of living in a glamorous-celebrity-marriage-and-fame continuum. In these years they would move among New York, Martha's Vineyard, and Los Angeles, where James usually made his albums in the late winter and spring. The summer months were usually spent by Carly on the island with their children, while James went out on the road.

In 1973, the couple moved to a house in a quiet residential block on East Sixty-second Street in New York, where Carly became pregnant in March. The Vineyard house continued as a semipermanent construction project. James and Russ Kunkel built a cabin, which was then merged into part of the house as the ramshackle structure mushroomed (very expensively) over the years with new additions, wings, guest houses, studios, barns, stables, stained glass, skylights, sunrooms, and outbuildings.

Carly enjoyed pregnancy, she told friends. She wanted a quiet life now, a middle-class life like her mother had had. She got rid of the leeches who'd been hanging around the Vineyard house, James's old cronies, and she was hated for it. "You're So Vain" had been the number one record in America for three weeks, but Carly now was semi-retired. This was what she had originally wanted: to be a recording artist who didn't tour or perform much in public. Her husband now needed most of her attention, especially since he had been trying to get off drugs and live a "normal" life after he returned from his Japanese tour an almost completely burnt-out case. While he and Carly were on a brief trip to Europe with friends that summer, James decided it was time to get help. When they returned to New York, he entered a private clinic. Carly, now visibly pregnant, tried to visit him every day.

James's efforts to get off dope put a strain on the early days of the marriage. Carly did not know James when he wasn't on heroin or methadone until she was six months pregnant, and he wasn't easy to live with for the half year in which he was trying to quit. "It was a very hard time. He was very fragile," Carly remembered. "It was like walking on eggshells—he was in a lot of agony. The beginning of our marriage went through a lot of pain." Another strain was the relative lack of sales of number four *One Man Dog* compared to number one *No Secrets*. James denied it at the time, but their different levels of success bothered him. Much later, he admitted, "Yeah, it got to me—sometimes."

Spring 1973. Carly and James were living in New York. One night, they went to see the off-Broadway production of *National Lampoon's Lemmings,* a Woodstock spoof that launched the careers of young comedians John Belushi, Christopher Guest, and Carly's old friend Chevy Chase. They didn't know that James was one of those parodied, along with Bob Dylan, Joan Baez, and others.

Christopher Guest appeared as a depressed and downcast James, singing, "Farewell to New York City, with your streets that flash like strobes / Farewell to Carolina, where I left my frontal lobes."

Later, a mortified Guest recalled, "James Taylor came to the show with Carly Simon. She was laughing, but he wasn't. As a joke, it was a major cheap shot. They came backstage afterward, and I was kind of devastated, because he was such a hero to me. As a satirist, you're not supposed to care about that, but I did."

In the summer of 1973, Carly designed a circular garden at the Vineyard house. Her mother bought a house on top of a hill in nearby Chilmark with a million-mile view of the Atlantic. When James saw this, he told his carpenters to build a tower on his no-view property so he could see the ocean, too. Pregnant, with time on her hands, Carly started talking about building a nightclub on the island that would give local talent the same kind of opportunities that the Simon Sisters had found at the old Mooncusser coffeehouse ten years earlier.

While her husband was trying to stay straight, Carly was working on songs for her next record, scheduled to begin production in September. Many of the lyrics ("Safe and Sound," "Think I'm Gonna Have a Baby") were about the domesticity she was pursuing. (The baby she was carrying jumped inside her when Carly played "Mind on My Man.") She also had the idea for her and James to remake the classic soul song "Mockingbird" as possibly her next single. But while she was supposed to be working on her music, Carly was distracted by the turmoil at her record label. Jac Holzman was leaving, and to Carly it felt like another paternal abandonment.

A few months earlier, Warner Communications had merged Elektra Records with David Geffen's Asylum Records. David Geffen would run Elektra/Asylum Records while Holzman joined Warner as a senior vice president for technical affairs (where he would do pioneering work in developing home video and cable television systems). Carly now felt like "the ugly step-daughter," as she put it, at the new label. She and the newly signed English band Queen were

Elektra's major assets. Asylum had a powerhouse talent roster that included the Eagles, Neil Young, Jackson Browne, and Bob Dylan. Joni Mitchell was Asylum's reigning queen, and Carly realized that her position would always be secondary to Mitchell's at the new company. Elektra's roster was now drastically trimmed, and some of the executives Carly had worked with lost their jobs. Even worse, it got back to Carly that David Geffen had made disparaging remarks about her in staff meetings. So began a series of business-related struggles that Carly later described as "eight months of mayhem" that would come to a head when her next record was released.

Carly made Richard Perry beg for the job of producing *Hotcakes*. She thought he'd been too rough with her in London, had bullied her, and she let him know she was shopping around. Perry took her to lunch at Tavern on the Green, in Central Park, in early June. She let him plead awhile, and said she would think about it. Eventually he got the job. James and Carly flew to Los Angeles in September to begin production, living in a rented house in Malibu and building the new songs at the Producers Workshop in L.A. In October, they returned to New York, and the sessions began at Jerry Ragovoy's Hit Factory, the top Manhattan recording studio, on West Fifty-fourth Street.

From day one, they got word that David Geffen was complaining that Carly's album was too expensive. But they plunged ahead, working with some of the top musicians in New York. James Taylor was sober now, and not a little shaky, but he played his usual deft guitar in the sessions and impressed people with how clear-eyed he looked, for a change. Also noted was the intense, familial closeness between him and Carly, like a firewall of passion around the couple.

And they worked hard on this album. It had to be better than good. Something in Carly's voice had also changed. Her burnished low tones sounded richer and more passionate than ever. (Some fans think Carly's singing on *Hotcakes*, while she was pregnant, was some of the best in her career.) "Safe and Sound" would open the album with a wordy Brackman song about incongruity and a nice Carly chorus. "Mind on My Man" was conga-flavored, with James on acoustic guitar and some great jazz players: bassist Richard Davis and Bucky Pizzarelli. Drummer Jim Keltner gave a Band-like kick to "Think I'm Gonna Have a Baby," with its career ennui, perhaps a not-so-subtle message to David Geffen. James also played on "Older Sister," Carly's piano-based memory of wearing her sisters' handed-down, patched, and rehemmed dresses. (The electric lead guitar on this and other tracks was played in New York by David Spinozza, a musician and arranger whose tasty playing was appreciated by Carly and especially James.) "Just Not True" was almost operatic, an abject love theme sung with James and illumined by Paul Buckmaster's light-classical strings and woodwinds. This was the first time Carly had sung with James on one of her songs, and the studio staff remarked on how incredible they sounded together. The title track, "Hotcakes," was a fragment featuring jazz-rocker Billy Cobham on drums, Howard Johnson on tuba, Bobby Keys on tenor sax, and a couple of horn players, all arranged and conducted by James.

"Misfit" was a total Richard Perry production, L.A. pop more worthy of Streisand or Dory Previn: a heavily orchestrated, hip-to-be-miserable song. Carly and James collaborated on writing "Forever My Love," a hopeful ballad about their marriage. James played on it, with his drummer Russ Kunkel and bassist Klaus Voormann flown in from London for the sessions.

The recording of "Mockingbird" was all-star, and more than captured the spirit of "Night Owl" from *No Secrets*. Dr. John, aka Mac Rebennack, played piano. The Band's Robbie Robertson contributed his chicken-scratch guitar. Bobby Keys played the big baritone sax, but the tenor sax solo was done by Michael Brecker, a young jazz musician beginning to make his name in New York. The rollicking original song, a hit for Inez and Charlie Foxx in 1960, was given additional lyrics by James on the "She's gonna find me some piece of mind" verse. When they listened to the playback at the end of the evening, Carly knew they had her next single and it was going to be a big hit.

Carly's "Grownup" was another memory song, written before her daughter's birth. It was as if her pregnancy were sending her back in time, distilling images and feelings from her sometimes difficult childhood. The album would end with "Haven't Got Time for the Pain," a collaboration with Jake, who wrote the line "Suffering was the only thing made me feel I was alive."

Carly (writing in 2004): "Jake wrote the words of this song after experiencing Arica training, a Sufi tradition modernized by Oscar Ichazo. The song is clearly spiritual and with very little human intervention. I set the words to melody in Malibu, California, during the time just before recording *Hotcakes*, when I was preggers with Sal . . . I must say that it is one of the least interesting songs, to me, that I've ever been a part of. It seems trite in retrospect and the heavenly or devotional aspect of it was Jake's trip and not mine." (But "Pain"— perfect EST-era pop, with Paul Buckmaster's pretty string concerto tacked on to the end—would touch a nerve in Carly's mostly female audience, and become a crucial part of her music. Today, one still hears it played much more than anything on, say, Joni Mitchell's *Court and Spark*.)

Carly and Richard Perry finished *Hotcakes* in late November 1973. Ed Caraeff took the jacket photo of a pregnant Carly in a white room in a cottage at the Beverly Hills Hotel, flashing a big, toothy smile. The interior snapshot, of Carly four months pregnant, was taken in Italy by Vieri Salvadori, who had been with Carly and James in Europe earlier in the year. Elektra Records released *Hotcakes* in January 1974, around the time Carly's first child was born.

MOCKINGBIRD

———

*C*arly gave birth to Sarah Maria Taylor on January 4, 1974, and immediately fell in love with her little girl, known as Sally. Suddenly there was a new light in Carly's life; in her diary she wrote, "*This* is what I'm here for." But she also acutely experienced the changes in her body and mind, postpartum. She told an interviewer, "I definitely went through a period of post-partum depression, and I thought I'd never work again. I didn't want to do anything else but devote myself to raising this child—this miracle. So, out of a sense of utter joy—and utter panic—I sold the song 'Anticipation' for $50,000 for a ketchup commercial. And of course—even though it was well done and funny—I've regretted doing it ever since.

"Of course I did go back to work after Sally was born, but I had problems with subsequent albums because when I was in the studio, my mind wasn't a hundred per cent on my music. I was thinking, 'Oh my god. I want to get home, give Sally her dinner, put her to bed.' It wasn't like before, when I used to spend twelve hours in the studio and that was the point of my day."

Elektra released *Hotcakes* the same week that Sally was born. Radio started playing the funny, rocking "Mockingbird" single, credited to "Carly Simon and James Taylor," which shot up to number five in February 1974. The album faced major competition and made it only to number three, a disappointment for Carly. "I was distraught for a while," she allowed. "I thought this meant that I was slipping." As she had feared, there was even competition within her label, which released Joni Mitchell's *Court and Spark*, and *Planet Waves*, a new album by Bob Dylan and the Band, at the same time as *Hotcakes*. Mitchell's album happened to be brilliant, and Dylan was back on tour with the Band and making history in an enormous burst of media frenzy. *Hotcakes* quickly sold nine hundred thousand copies, but it was hard to get attention amid all the hoopla for Carly's label mates. David Geffen had assured Carly that she was going to have a solo release and it would be promoted individually, but it didn't happen. (Geffen said later that he'd been distracted in this period by his torrid romance with Cher.) Depressed and displeased and feeling overshadowed, Carly told Arlyne Rothberg (herself a new mother) that she wanted to leave Elektra/Asylum and make a fresh start. Arlyne foresaw a lengthy legal war and persuaded Carly to let her renegotiate her contract instead. But the damage had been done. Carly's relationship with her record company was now described by her manager as "a suspicious, careful one, that's a bit like a re-marriage."

While Carly breast-fed Sally in what for her was an ecstasy of maternal satisfaction, and as the Arab oil embargo shook the foundations of the world economy, James began work on his next album, *Walking Man*. He was off methadone now, he said, supported by Carly's love and a serious course of psychotherapy. It was considered too risky for him to record in Los Angeles with Peter Asher and his L.A. community of friends, so he stayed in New York. His album was produced by David Spinozza, employing some of the musicians Carly had used on *Hotcakes*. (Carly's longtime drummer Rick

Marotta comes in here.) Carly sang on five of the album's ten songs, while Linda Ronstadt and Paul and Linda McCartney sang backup on several songs, including "Let It All Fall Down," James's comment on the Watergate scandal that was about to undermine Richard Nixon's presidency. Richard Avedon, then the preeminent photographer in America, took the stark and sober portrait of James that would serve as the album cover. *Walking Man,* downbeat songs by a recovering addict, was finished by April and released in June 1974. Two singles were issued, but neither made the sales charts. No airplay, either. The album reached only number thirteen. There was no gold record hanging on the manager's wall.

Early that summer, James took Carly and Sally and his band on a month-long tour that crossed the entire country. Many of the concerts had sold out in minutes, and James's young fans paid rapt attention to his performances and collectively swooned when he played "Sweet Baby James" and (especially) "Fire and Rain." After breast-feeding baby Sal backstage, Carly joined James for a surprise encore of "Mockingbird." Almost every night, she waited in the wings to go on, quaking with stage fright, muttering, "I can't do this . . . I can't go on." James's audiences would let out a big roar the minute Russ Kunkel started pounding out the song's familiar rhythm, and then an even louder din when Carly, barefoot and really beautiful, took the stage with her own microphone and danced around her husband with her signature gawky choreography. She did twenty "Mocking-birds" on the road that summer of '74 and helped establish Simon and Taylor as a major live draw. Concert promoters kept asking for a Carly Simon tour, but Arlyne Rothberg said that Carly was still so fearful about performing that she would have felt like Judy Garland's manager if she had pushed Carly onstage before she was ready.

Meanwhile, "I Haven't Got Time for the Pain" was released as a single. It played as an anthem on the "adult contemporary" radio format and garnered decent sales as well, reaching number fourteen that summer. President Nixon resigned in disgrace in August, much to the delight of James Taylor.

Fall 1974. Carly was trying to write songs, but it was hard. Her mind was often elsewhere. She was doing all the parenting. James was no father figure, plus he was also trying to write an album, trying to stay off dope, and, anyway—as he often told his audiences—he wasn't crazy about children. He was still almost completely indifferent to Carly's music (and to everyone else's), and this didn't do a lot for Carly's confidence. "James was often silently critical about my music," Carly recalled. "But he often made it clear that he admired me, and I was proud when I'd catch him humming one of my songs. As for the children, he was supportive when it was convenient for him to be. That sounds like a cruel thing to say, but then, I don't think men have the same kind of instincts and feelings about children that women do."

The title track of *Walking Man* was about James's often absent father, and also about James's visceral dislike of November, when New England grew colder and leafless. So, in late November 1974, the Simon-Taylor family flew to Los Angeles, where Carly would work on *Playing Possum* and James would record his *Gorilla* album. They rented a comfortable house in Beverly Hills for the winter (at four thousand dollars per month) and Carly leased a Mercedes convertible to get around. That Christmas, she and James were to be found caroling along Santa Monica Boulevard in West Hollywood, along with Joni Mitchell, Linda Ronstadt, and other friends.

SLAVE

———

$\mathcal{N}$ow it's late March 1975 and the Vietnam War is almost over. Everyone is talking about Patricia Hearst, the newspaper heiress kidnapped by crazy radicals. Led Zeppelin is playing sold-out shows in Los Angeles, and the Rolling Stones are about to tour America. Disco music is all the rage. There's a new high-camp singing sensation from New York called Bette Midler, and Linda Ronstadt is at the top of her game. Bob Dylan's *Blood on the Tracks* is a big hit. The best band in L.A. is Little Feat. The best band in America is the Meters, from New Orleans. People are talking about this new thing from Jamaica, reggae music, and about Bob Marley and the Wailers.

Carly Simon is still in Los Angeles, having just finished her new album, *Playing Possum*. When a reporter catches up with her, she is in an erotic art gallery in Beverly Hills trying to buy a present for her producer, Richard Perry, with whom she had spent the past three months battling over almost every aspect of the album.

Carly knew she hadn't done her best work, but she made it clear to everyone that she found motherhood very distracting, and she just wasn't up to actually living in the studio, the way she used to. The biggest battle was over the choice of her next single. Carly wanted a new song, called "Slave," an anthemic, embarrassing de-affirmation of everything the women's movement of the seventies stood for. The lyrics expressed total devotion for her love, a "burning, yearning" desire for voluntary servitude, and an expression of sexual hunger and longing that was unusual, even for a Carly Simon song. And there was, indeed, a feeling of hypersexual torch carrying in many of Carly's new songs. Sally was weaned now, and Carly had gotten her body back. She described the spirit of the new music as a "renewal of the lust." She said the new songs such as "Slave" and "Waterfall" (about the female orgasm), and even "After the Storm," were about regaining the woman she was when she first fell in love.

But nobody else "got" "Slave." The lyrics were banal and cringe-worthy. Carly's manager hated the song, and so did her label, which preferred the dance-floor-ready "Attitude Dancing," with Jake Brackman's proto-New Age lyrics. In the end, the company said that issuing "Slave" as a single was career suicide, and Carly was overruled. Most people didn't even want "Slave" on the album, despite James's star turn on guitar.

Carly had worked on the record at Sound Lab Studios and Sunset Sound. Richard Perry was using cocaine, so the atmosphere was weird. The sessions were star-studded, with James on lots of guitar, Ringo Starr on drums, and input from Dr. John and Carole King, among others. Cocaine (lots of it) was their drug of choice. (Carly tried cocaine a few times with James, but she was already so adrenalized making this record that she didn't think it did much for her.)

At the gallery, Carly chose a sexy portrait of a woman not unlike herself, with long flowing hair, as Perry's present. As the print was rolled into its carrying tube, Carly told the gallerina that she loved art, but that her husband wouldn't let her have any pictures in the house. "He doesn't like anything up on the walls," Carly said.

Carly and the reporter had lunch at Mr. Chow's in Beverly Hills.

Carly liked the famous restaurant's hybrid Chinese/Italian cuisine. She whispered, "They give you very small portions here, and charge you a lot." On the verge of a steak-and-grapefruit diet, she ordered egg noodles and white wine. The new album was sexy, she averred. "My body began to assume its former shape. There was this sort of, 'Oh, my god. Here's *this body* again,' and I sort of got . . . *turned on* by it." She talked about her problems with David Geffen and noted that her new contract with her label remained unsigned. She talked about "Slave" being rejected as a single. "The song says, 'I'm just another woman, raised to be a slave.' And they'll say, 'How *dare* she do that, she's supposed to be a liberated woman, and here's she's talking about being a *slave*?'"

Asked about James Taylor's fathering skills, Carly smiled and said, "He's a great . . . *appreciator*." But she allowed that, once in a while, he got up early to take care of his daughter. She mentioned that she had joined James in the studio and sung on a new version of the old Marvin Gaye song "How Sweet It Is," which looked to be James Taylor's next single.

The stage fright was still there. But she said she was thinking about trying to play small places in the autumn. "My idea would be to perform under an assumed name—'Fraulein Himmel'—at a small club where nobody knew me and I could sing my ass off, just sing great in a situation like that. Nobody expected anything of me, nobody came in loving me, or wanting me to fail. . . . Last year, on tour with James, the crowd was so excited, there was this kind of *roar* when I stepped onstage [for "Mockingbird"], and it was precisely *that* exhilaration that frightens the hell out of me."

The reporter recounts the current rumors about Carly in Hollywood: that she has been offered several roles opposite Robert Redford; that she has been approached to star in a remake of *A Star Is Born* with either James Taylor or Kris Kristofferson; that she turned down *Fear of Flying*; that she can't act. "All true," she said, laughing. She said she was thinking of writing a screenplay with Jake Brackman in which she could play a part. "But you know, to be frank, I would feel guilty, because there are so many really fine actresses. I think I'd feel that I would be cheating someone out of a part."

After lunch, Carly did a little window shopping on Rodeo Drive. She slipped into a boutique to try on an outfit by Chloe; "I Haven't Got Time for the Pain" was playing on the shop's sound system. She passed on the expensive dress, but paid for a $135 salmon-hued Christian Aujard blouse with her credit card. The reporter than followed Carly's Benz convertible back to the house she was sharing with James, Sally, and an au pair. As they pulled into the driveway, James was leaving for the studio. "Goodbye, Himmel," Carly called to him. "See you tonight, Himmel," James replied. She watched his car vanish down the drive and said, "He goes away forever, every day."

Carly gave a birthday party for James around that time at their rented house in Coldwater Canyon, but it didn't go well. There was already some friction between the two because Carly's brother, Peter, was in town, working on a book for publisher Alfred A. Knopf about Carly's career (and also taking pictures of Led Zeppelin, part of their entourage). James complained to Carly that Peter was hanging around too much, and that more privacy was required. Carly also suspected that James was using drugs at the studio, because much of the time after he came home from there, he was such a cipher—sitting, staring, out of it. James denied using, and said he was merely exhausted at the end of the evening. They got through the birthday party, but when the last guest had driven off, they engaged in such a terrible row—said to have been about Joni Mitchell—that the baby woke up and started crying. Carly was so upset that she fled the house and checked into a hotel for the rest of the night.

Carly's most recent album cover, *Hotcakes,* had featured her as a demure, pregnant princess of pop. This time the art director wanted something racy. Norman Seeff was a photographer who specialized in jellied, soft-focus, black-and-white portraits. Carly liked him, liked the fine California wine in his studio, liked the hip dance music he was blasting. Off came her clothes, revealing the famous little black lingerie and the high black boots. "I had bought a number of different changes of clothes and I was wearing that black chemise under a dress. When I took off the dress, someone said, 'Let's do a couple in this [chemise].' They had to go out and get some darker stockings because my skin looked too white next to the black chemise. It wasn't anything planned, like I wanted to appeal to the S&M crowd." Soon Carly was on her knees, hooting and posturing, her mouth in a sexy moue. Snap, snap: a famous—and soon to be notorious—album jacket.

There was a new presence in the studio while Carly made her record. This was Andrew Gold, a talented musician and songwriter admired by Richard Perry and signed to Asylum. (He was the son of Marni Nixon, the great singer famous for overdubbing vocals for movie stars in film musicals.) In his early twenties, he was a major player in the L.A.-dominated pop rock of the seventies. He'd helped arrange Linda Ronstadt's 1974 breakout album, *Heart Like a Wheel,* and was also working with James, Maria Muldaur, and Jackson Browne. Gold played on many of Carly's tracks and contributed to the glossy, polished sound that Richard Perry was after. Much later Gold described a memorable day at Sunset Sound in Los Angeles: "I was playing drums on Carly Simon's *Playing Possum* album, the one with her wearing a negligee on the cover. And she had just come back from that photo session. We were working and it wasn't really happening, so then Carly came in, and she'd had a couple of drinks. She wasn't drunk, just feeling kind of gay, in the old version of the word. She had this big fur coat on, and she said, 'I think I'll give them some inspiration.' So she came in the studio and stripped off the fur coat and started dancing around in this shimmering little negligee. She was hilarious, and it *was* an inspiration."

"After the Storm" opens *Playing Possum,* a piano ballad with a jazzy feel and lush orchestration. Carly wrote it after that fierce fight with James, and the subsequent reconciliation, shortly after they arrived in California. "Love out in the Street" follows, Carly's sexual predator persona singing rapturously with Rita Coolidge (now Mrs. Kristofferson) and Clydie King. James Taylor puts some beautiful acoustic guitar on "Look Me in the Eyes," another cry, from deep in the singer's heart, for more intimacy, more passion, more love.

Dr. John plays like Professor Longhair on his song "More and More," while Ringo Starr lays down a funky shuffle and Steely Dan guitarist Jeff Baxter rips off some tasty licks. Carly sings the lyrics very soul-style, perhaps in tribute to her longtime idol Martha Reeves. This is followed by "Slave," written with Jake. It only made it onto *Playing Possum* because Carly had a fit and threatened to walk out if it was left off. She anticipated a backlash from people who would take the abject lyrics at face value. But people did have the feelings expressed in the song. They were authentic. "The thing that I feel is, that it is *true*," Carly has said. "I *do* feel sometimes a victim of my own enslavement, but I'm angry about it in the song. It's *damn it, sometimes I actually still feel like a slave.* That's what the sentiment [in the song] is."

Much of the drumming on *Possum* is played by Carly's regular drummer Andy Newmark, but Jim Gordon plays on "Attitude Dancing," with lyrics by Jake. (Willie Weeks plays bass on many of the tracks.) Carly later wrote: "It was about our enjoying the thought of all those early dances—the hully gully, the locomotion, the mashed potato—being danced at the same time: a creative mélange of self-expression." Carole King and an uncredited James Taylor sing in the chorus. Elektra executives liked the disco-tinged song, figuring it could be a hit on the dance floor.

Carly multitracks her vocals, echoing the days of the Simon Sisters, on Billy Mernit's "Sons of Summer," while he plays piano on his arty song. This is followed by "Waterfall," one of Carly's greatest compositions. James's rhythm section—Russ Kunkel and bassist Lee Sklar—came over from James's sessions. James sings with Carly on the chorus and wails a full-throated, wordless vocal solo in the bridge. (The high spirits and love in the song are almost unmatched in Carly's music.) Carly's "Are You Ticklish" is old-fashioned and corny. *Playing Possum* finishes with its title song, a portrait based loosely on her brother's old friend Ray Mungo, who was a fire-breathing radical editor in the sixties but was now the owner of a bookstore "with patches on his sleeves." "Playing possum" is an old expression for hiding out and keeping a low profile, something that Carly wanted for herself, so there was a lot of sympathy for the character. In this song, James again sings his ass off with Carly, as the orchestra comes up and star-crossed *Playing Possum* fades to black.

There was one more battle before the album could be released. The sexy picture of Carly on her knees wasn't her first choice. Her bottom showed, and the scene had a sort of louche, bondage/discipline allure. "It looks like I'm . . . *fired up*, in some vaguely sensual way," she said. "I liked a more ordinary, mundane shot of my teeth."

But the sexy picture stayed. The teeth were bared on the inner sleeve. "I guess it *is* pretty sexy," she allowed. "If it wasn't me, I'd probably be turned on."

In an interview a little later, she related showing off for the camera to her childhood feelings toward her father. "I felt that clowning for him was the way I could win his love. Sometimes, with other photographers, the memory of that comes back."

WHERE'S CARLY?

Playing Possum was released in late April 1975. By June the album had reached number ten, its highest chart position. "Attitude Dancing" didn't hit with the disco deejays, and got only to twenty-one. Elektra next tried the brilliant "Waterfall," which stalled at seventy-eight. Dr. John's song "More and More" made it only to ninety-two. Then there was the minor furor over the risqué album cover.

The nationwide Sears department store chain banned the album from its shelves, which cost dearly in sales. Her mother hated it and told her so. There were even hassles for Carly in the street. She would be shopping in Saks Fifth Avenue or Bergdorf Goodman and well-dressed matrons would come up and, usually with a gloved hand on Carly's sleeve, gently reproach her for appearing half naked on her album cover. (No one remembered that Joni Mitchell had posed naked for *For the Roses*.) A woman in Bloomingdales told Carly the photo was disgusting. For the first time in years, the only Carly Simon songs on the radio were oldies.

Carly, speaking much later: "You know, when I released *Playing Possum*, it was a flop. 'Waterfall' only made it to the bottom of the charts, and I was 'over' in my own mind. Then there was much stir over the cover. More self-loathing was mine. I didn't understand my failure but I got over it fast, though. I was always going on to another song, because I *had* to. The piano was always there, and there were guitars everywhere.

"But now, today, when I listen to 'After the Storm' and 'Look Me in the Eyes' and those other songs. I'm very impressed with the musicality. I was really practicing then. I worked very hard. In those days I was—always and only—very interested in stunning James with my music. I mean, to get a reaction from him, and that was hard to do. It was good to have a competitive relationship in many ways. It just makes you better. James wrote some of his best songs during that time. He would never admit it, but he was competing with me, in a good way." James's best song—"Another Grey Morning"—was written around that time.

Rolling Stone called Carly's music "shrink couch rock," but a jiving Carly was on the cover in May, and the magazine ran a long and very positive profile of her by Ben Fong-Torres. Another interviewer asked about the song "After the Storm," which opens the album on a subdued note, more smooth jazz than pop or rock. Carly replied, "I wrote 'heat's up, tea's brewed, clothes strewn around the room . . .' when I woke up one morning at 242 East Sixty-second Street, our home for four years, when Sally was sleeping beside me in the bassinet. James and I had had a terrible fight the night before that ended up in just a huge love. That's where those feelings came from." She went on to say that when *Possum* came out, she'd gotten a call from Jack Nitzsche, the great arranger who'd worked with Phil Spector and the Stones. "He said he was angry with me for the ridiculous chord changes on 'After the Storm.' He didn't think a woman should be capable of that sort of creativity. It was very Beach Boys influenced, I think, even though not consciously."

Asked about the sexy photo: "It was generally thought to be risqué and tasteless. I was a new mother! What could I be thinking?"

Carly's husband, meanwhile, was riding high and back on top. Where *Possum* had flopped, James's new album, *Gorilla,* released in May 1975, started selling half a million and going gold. Carly sings with James on the album's two Top Five singles, "Mexico" and the great Marvin Gaye standard "How Sweet It Is," and on the lullaby "Sarah Maria." David Crosby and Graham Nash also sing on an album mostly played by L.A.-based jazz musicians. The song "Gorilla" was (also) inspired by a row with Carly in New York, while James was trying to cure himself of drug addiction. James stormed out of the house and walked up the street to Central Park to try to cool off. He went into the monkey house—"knocking around the zoo"—and started looking at a mountain gorilla. The ape stared back at JT. *This,* he pondered, *is probably how Carly sees me.*

In the summer of 1975, with James's music on the radio all the time, Carly stayed on the Vineyard while he and the band went on the road. He changed his act, tried to lighten up and tell some jokes, and play more rhythm and blues, which he did well with a great band. He tried to stay sober, but it was hard. And his young, mostly female audiences kept shouting, "Where's *Carly*?" and calling out for "Mockingbird." James would tell them that Carly was at home with the baby, and there were often loud groans of crowd disappointment that Mrs. Taylor wouldn't appear in the encores as she had the year before.

James's success that year came as a relief for Carly. She told close women friends such as Rose Styron and Libby Titus that she was more comfortable when James was more successful than she. It put less stress on the marriage and left him free to write, which he often did while playing his guitar, sitting in a spare wooden corner by the fireplace in the house on Martha's Vineyard. (Just then, James was working on two new songs: "Shower the People" and "A Junkie's Lament," a graphic description of drug withdrawal.)

Carly also told friends that she wanted another child.

Carly didn't appear on *Lucy Simon,* her sister's first solo album, released by RCA Records later that year, with Lucy's songs and (heavenly) voice backed by top New York jazz musicians. The music was arty and didn't fit the commercial formats of the day, and so was something of a misfire. The most gripping song is "My Father Died," a stricken-sounding threnody for Dick Simon that tells the story of how he passed away in his sleep, suffering no pain, after calling Lucy and arranging to meet. It is very sad, and Carly wept every time she heard it.

The rest of 1975 Carly spent writing new material for her next album, and readying herself to work in California with a new producer, Ted Templeman, best known for his hit records with the Doobie Brothers. Carly was uneasy about this. Her manager later remembered, "*Every minute* of her career was drama."

In November, Elektra put out *The Best of Carly Simon,* her first compilation, her greatest hits. This comprises six Top Ten singles, two lesser hits ("Attitude Dancing" and "Legend in Your Own Time"), and two album tracks, "Night Owl" and "We Have No Secrets." Released for the Christmas market, the album reached number seventeen and then sold for decades in the multimillions because Carly would not release another greatest-hits album for twenty years.

Late in the year, the Simon-Taylor family returned to California on its annual winter migration to record new albums. They settled into a sprawling compound on Rockingham Drive in suburban Brentwood, a few blocks from Sunset Boulevard. Carly started working on her new album, *Another Passenger,* at Sunset Sound, about a half hour away in Los Angeles, while James worked on his, *In the Pocket,* at Warner Bros.' studio in North Hollywood. Their sessions were lucrative for the local musicians, the best of whom spent the next three months shuttling between the husband's studio and that of his wife.

Meanwhile, when she wasn't working, Carly was learning to seriously shop. "Up until then," she recalled," I had an inordinate sense of guilt about buying clothes. There was embarrassment and shame at having more than my sisters—or having James think I was 'superficial.' Even at Hollywood parties I was still the barefoot, second-hand clothes, unmade-up frizzy-haired gypsy girl. Not until 1975 did Libby Titus, Betsy Asher, and I start having lunch in Beverly Hills and discovering Maxfield, and buying Chloe and Armani, then dipping into Tiffany and buying sterling silver bracelets. We'd meet at the Beverly Hills Hotel and have Ramos gin fizzes and then go on the town, our Mercedes in tandem, and play dress-up. I was buying clothes and still feeling guilty about spending money that I'd actually earned myself. The guilt continued."

ANOTHER PASSENGER

———

$\mathcal{T}$ed Templeman, thirty-two, a staff producer at Warner Bros. Records, was friendly, young, blond, professional, methodical. He was not snorting Peru, at least not in the studio. There wasn't much drama with him. He had helped the Doobie Brothers, who had started as a stoner/biker band, to national prominence. He arranged for Little Feat and the Doobie Brothers to play on Carly's record. He didn't hear an obvious hit single in any of the songs Carly had brought with her to California, but he didn't care. He liked her music and told her he would find something good for her. He then brought the Doobie's lead singer, Michael McDonald, into Carly's orbit, and this would later result in one of her best songs.

Carly was now competing for audience with the resurgent Fleetwood Mac, the English blues band that had moved to California and hired two locals, guitarist Lindsey Buckingham and his dervish girlfriend, Stevie Nicks. Their debut album with this lineup had ruled the charts in 1975 and helped usher in the soft rock era (described in the sales charts as adult contemporary). Their new album, *Rumors*, would soon spawn many hit singles and emerge as one of the bestselling records in history.

Carly spent the first three months of 1976 working on her material with Ted Templeman and some of the best musicians in the country. Five of the album's twelve tracks were written by Carly alone. Her favorite was "Fairweather Father," a pretty samba about a husband who doesn't do diapers. The wife is desperate. Her husband is a prick who ignores her and her child. James sang on "Father," along with Jackson Browne. (Jazz master Victor Feldman, who famously turned down Miles Davis's offer to join his band—Herbie Hancock got the job instead—contributed the chiming marimba to the track.) Carly always said that James was *not* the fair-weather father of the song, but of course no one believed her.

"Cow Town" is a narrative about a real French woman (Simone Swan, the mother of Carly's friend François de Menil) who married into a wealthy Texan family and was now living large on the range. De Menil had told Carly about her over lunch in exchange for a decent steak and a song written about him. (He also took her shopping.) The song could have been a Broadway showstopper, with its lusty chorus and with Little Feat providing the drive. (The real Simone threatened to sue Carly when the record came out, but was talked out of it. Carly: "She wanted to sue me over 'Cow Town,' until our mutual lawyer talked her down.") Carly's love for Brazilian music is again reflected in "He Likes to Roll," with lyrics about a woman chasing a man she already owns. The track features some of the best singing on the album, with the Brazilian guitarist Laurindo Almeida contributing some tasty guitar fills. Vic Feldman adds more pastel marimba to Carly's palette, and Bud Shank warbles on a pretty flute. One of the most difficult tracks to record was "In Times When My Head," a song that was very important to Carly. It is a piano ballad with a confessional tone, what Carly described as "internal, difficult feelings," a confidential message to the listener about a marriage with infidelity on both sides. There's another man in the lyric, the "boy in the backwoods." (What was this?) Jim Keltner plays drums, and Klaus Voormann reappears on bass. The chorus is sung by Carly with Linda Ronstadt, Leah Kunkel, and Carly's current best friend, Libby Titus.

Libby, then in her late twenties, was a year or so younger than Carly. She had a powerfully seductive affect and became an important influence on Carly, who called her friend "Leeby." They had met when Libby was living with Levon Helm and their daughter, Amy, who was two years older than Sally Taylor. Libby had grown up in Woodstock, the beautiful daughter of a Russian immigrant. Her milieu was Catskills bohemia, with entrée into the exclusive worlds of Bob Dylan, the Band, and Carly's old nemesis, Albert Grossman. Libby had sloe eyes, an alabaster complexion, a head of black curls, and a lively intelligence. She'd had a son with the heir to the Helena Rubinstein cosmetic fortune when she was twenty. She left him and became close to Eric Clapton and other rock heroes. Libby had a pretty singing voice, very fragile, and she was also a talented songster, having cowritten "Love Has No Pride," a hit record for Bonnie Raitt. Carly loved the ultrasophisticated Libby Titus so much that she wrote about her; "Libby" was the first eponymous song about a real person Carly had ever recorded. The lyrics describe a fantasy journey to Paris with Libby, complete with schmaltzy, cod Française accordions. The song assumes an intimate, sisterly friendship, with Carly confessing to Libby that she is "another passenger, guilty of your crimes." (Insiders whispered that the song was also something of an apology for an incident that occurred the previous April [1975], when Carly and James double-dated with Libby and Levon. They were driving back from dinner, with Levon at the wheel and the girls in the backseat. They'd all had good wine. According to Libby, Carly leaned into her and, referring to Levon, whispered that he wasn't good enough for her. But Levon heard Carly's remark. He was mad as hell, and reportedly broke up with Libby Titus the next day.)

Three songs on *Another Passenger* have lyrics by Jake Brackman, again writing in the Carly Simon persona, as he saw it. "Half a Chance" opens the album, "packing your bags in a trance," with smooth jazz, a sax solo, strings, and some passionate singing on the choruses. "Riverboat Gambler" is a piano ballad that pleads for access to a tight-hearted lover, someone like Carly's remote and preoccupied husband. Those feelings evolve into the conflict of "Darkness 'Til Dawn" (cowritten by Van Dyke Parks). Listeners experience more marital discord here, more quarreling all night, more of Carly thinking (hard) about a lover from another era (often Dan Armstrong). Lucy Simon sings harmony on the track with her little sister.

Carly also cowrote two songs with Zack Wiesner, one of James's best friends from the days of the Flying Machine. (Zack lived next door on the Vineyard, on land given to him by James for a song.) "Dishonest Modesty" is Carly fronting Little Feat, with Dr. John on rhythm guitar. (Rebennack was now keeping company full time with Libby Titus.) Carly's brother-in-law Alex Taylor sings with her on the chorus. The song has critical lyrics about a selfish friend with authenticity issues. (Carly commented, with candor, much later: "It was a mean-spirited, nasty song and I was clearly jealous of the person. There is no need to reveal anyone, as the aspiration was not kind and the song is just not that good.") Zack's other contribution is the lullaby "Be with Me." It is light, simple, and very pretty. James plays guitar and Carly sings. They eventually used it to close the album.

Two tracks came through Ted Templeman. "One Love Stand" is a Little Feat song, a generic L.A. shuffle that makes Carly sound like Bonnie Raitt. Michael McDonald's "It Keeps You Runnin'" had already been a hit for the Doobie Brothers. Now Ted Templeman reframed it around a full-throated, almost operatic performance from

Carly. Her version of "Runnin'" has great energy, and would be everyone's choice for the album's first single.

Another Passenger was finished in March 1976, around the time Carly became pregnant with her second child. The jacket pictures, taken in New York by star photographer Mary Ellen Mark, Carly's longtime friend, were muted and demure. Carly dedicated the album to her husband. *Passenger* was released in June 1976, at the same time as *In the Pocket*, James Taylor's last studio album for Warner Bros. Records. So, not for the first time, Carly and James went head-to-head in the commercial marketplace. (Some observers criticized the couple's management for allowing these simultaneous releases to happen, the theory being that fans of both Carly and James might have limited resources to spend, and so would be forced to choose one over the other.) Neither album scored big. With no concerts to help promote it, *Passenger* got to only number twenty-nine, and the "It Keeps You Runnin'" single topped out at number forty-six. A *Rolling Stone* critic wrote that *Another Passenger* was Carly's best record and added that she "conveys the monied angst of the leisured classes with moving conviction, something no one else has ever done."

"Never before have so many women fueled the creative impulses of pop music," opined the *Saturday Review*. "Of those currently in the top echelon—Carole King, Joni Mitchell, Dory Previn, Carly Simon and Phoebe Snow—Ms. Simon is the most slickly facile, and surely the most accessible to a broad audience."

James's *In the Pocket* climbed to number sixteen, his lowest-charting record since his first album. But his wonderful single "Shower the People" (with Carly's prominent backing vocals) got to number twenty-two on the pop charts that summer, and was a number one adult contemporary hit by September.

Spring 1976. The hottest show on American television was now *Saturday Night,* broadcast live from NBC studios in New York. The cast of young comedians—John Belushi, Dan Aykroyd, Gilda Radner, and especially Carly's former prom date Chevy Chase—were all on the cutting edge of current satire: very sharp, keen, and funny as hell. Every week, *Saturday Night* showcased a musical guest. The show's producer, at Chevy's urging, invited Carly to play a couple of songs during one of the last broadcasts of the program's first season.

Carly, pregnant, told her manager she couldn't do it. She could not appear on live television, coast to coast. It would be too much stress for her, and she was afraid she would miscarry and lose the child. There was a lot of back-and-forth. Elektra was screaming that *Another Passenger* wasn't selling and needed this enormous publicity boost. Someone suggested that Carly be allowed to tape her two segments. NBC said that *SNL* was, famously, a *live* broadcast. But Carly was adamant, and she won. On the May 8, 1976, show, a frizzy-headed Carly was introduced by host Madeline Kahn and played "Half a Chance" with the house band. The second segment, "You're So Vain," was introduced by Chevy, who mentioned that he and Carly went out together when they were kids. He explained that Carly had taped her songs about an hour before the show, the first time a performer hadn't played live on the show. He then joined Carly's backup singers, banging a cowbell and sporting a conspicuously apricot scarf around his neck, as if he were the lucky/unlucky guy sung about in "You're So Vain."

THE SPY WHO LOVED ME

―――――

Now it's the hot summer of 1976. Jimmy Carter, the former Georgia governor, is running for president. Stevie Wonder's *Songs in the Key of Life* is the album of the moment. (Stevie played a classic harmonica solo on James's "Don't Be Sad," on *In the Pocket*.) British rock star Peter Frampton owns the airwaves, but James's churchy, hymnlike "Shower the People" is everywhere, too. In late July, *New York* magazine sends a writer to Martha's Vineyard to profile Carly, who picks her up at the island's airport. Carly is visibly pregnant, her long, voluptuous mane of brunette frizz blowing in the wind as she guns her blue Mercedes convertible back to the house off Lambert's Cove Road. Carly is deeply tanned "to a handsome red-brown." She wears a faded blue cotton jersey over red linen pants, and always goes barefoot. She tells the reporter that she has canceled her yoga class and the riding lessons scheduled for that day, and offers a quick tour of the sixty-five-acre property.

"It's a very domestic scene," Carly says. "We're into our garden and the things we're planting." The house is covered in Cape Cod gray clapboard and boasts a forty-five-foot tower. The windows are cheerfully trimmed in bright yellows and pinks. They walk into James's old house, "originally an Appalachian shack," Carly says. Today it serves as guest quarters. The cabin James and Russ Kunkel built is now an attached music room and studio. James basically designed the rest of the house, which was built in sections. Sally's room was finished only a few days before she was born. Her live-in babysitter stays in another cabin, which is soon to become the care-taker's house. Return visitors often found that bathrooms could disappear and be reconstituted elsewhere.

There's a large open room with polished wooden floors, almost empty except for a large dining table by the windows. It's a nice place to sit and look out the windows at chickadees and canary-colored goldfinches nibbling at seed. Sally's toys are scattered around. The summer sun is flooding the rooms with light. With the lumber joints and trusses showing, the rooms have an airy feel, very open. The walls are almost bare, except for a few family photographs and some drawings by James's friend Laurie Miller.

The place is surprisingly modest and understated. The master bedroom is upstairs. James's tarnished silver christening cup is in Sally's bathroom. Carly says she now needs a room of her own to write in, and she is going to build a "shack" of her own after the new baby comes. (She's hoping for a boy this time. She and James have a name picked out, but Carly said it might be bad luck to reveal it.) The bedroom is Carly's lair. It's a white boudoir with a quilt-covered double bed placed before billowing white curtains. On Carly's (left) side of the bed is a corner bookcase with a white touch-tone telephone, an old Rolodex card file, silver-framed family snapshots, and a modern stainless-steel lamp. (This is where she talks to friends in the evening, chatting on the phone as the children sleep in their beds.)

A cleaning girl, a young island friend, is polishing the toaster oven in the kitchen. Carly says she loves to cook, chop vegetables, experiment with the herbs they grow. James comes in and is introduced. He asks Carly if he can go fishing. He tells Carly to only buy sunflower seeds for the bird feeders, because it attracts a higher-quality bird. He has a fading, yin-yang-looking tattoo on his left shoulder.

The tour continues outdoors. Two carpenters are working on something garden-related, and the "rock man" is rebuilding one of the old sheep farm's ancient stone walls. An archery target is set up at the end of the pasture, where James likes to practice. The tower looms over everything. "James always wanted a tower," Carly says, sighing.

Back in the house, the island girl is picking up Sally's toys, mostly *Sesame Street* puppets. The writer asks Carly if she is working and is told not really. The last time she was in a recording studio was a few weeks earlier, when she and James sang backup on a Livingston Taylor track. James is observed inspecting shrubs recently planted around the house. He's in a stained and faded T-shirt and dirty shorts. Carly whispers, "Sexiest legs in the world." James enters with a book, *Conifers for Your Garden,* and the planting of spruces is earnestly discussed. James is "immediately appealing, surprisingly friendly. He is a shy, gentle man, who, Carly says later, 'watches television violence—all the time.'"

Lunch is served: salad, melon, iced tea. The sun is high and hot. Birdsong fills the air. The oak leaves flutter in the breeze. James is fixing the garden hose. "The Taylors have an easy intimacy. The grounds are large enough for them to be alone-but-together, and when they pass, James calling from the guesthouse porch and Carly answering from the house, it's an easy 'Hiya, sweetie.'" The writer wonders if this happy couple is putting on a performance for her. Carly confides that James's highly publicized heroin addiction is totally over. (But, she tells friends, she still rifles his pockets to make sure.)

Carly frets because she hasn't planted the marigolds yet. James wanders around with a beer. A plumber arrives, provoking a long discussion about where to put the toilet in the guesthouse. "James and Carly are used to having people work for them and have found just the right combination of graciousness and command."

James tells Carly to leave the toilet placement to him. The baby-sitter has taken James's Audi, so Carly and the writer drive off to town in the Mercedes, with Carly singing along to the Spinners tape in the dashboard. Asked about her famous stage fright, Carly lists all the remedies she has tried: psychotherapy, yoga, transcendental meditation, EST, hypnosis, biofeedback, drugs, more yoga, acupuncture. She speaks "longingly" of being able to perform in her husband's concerts. "My secret pipe dream," she muses, "is James and me and the children, traveling around together in a much less high-powered scene, maybe a motor home, playing shows and then moving on." She mentions that James owns a 350-acre farm in Nova Scotia that she's never even seen.

Later in the day, Carly drops the writer back at the airport. She would have asked her to stay the night, but the William Styron family—their best friends on the Vineyard—have recently arrived on the island, and Carly is having them over for a barbecue, a campfire, and games—badminton, volleyball—for the children. Novelist Bill Styron is a depressive, hard-drinking Virginian, so he and James get along. (Carly: "They were both Southerners, and talked of southern things, mainly biscuits and ham."). Rose Styron—a lovely poetess, independently wealthy—is one of Carly's closest friends. The kids are beautiful. At evening's end, James will be persuaded to produce his Martin D-18 guitar and sing something. The Styrons' oldest daughter is named Susannah, so "Oh Susannah" often gets a workout when the two families socialize.

In the autumn of 1976, James Taylor and his band were still on tour. Carly moved their growing family into an enormous rented apartment at 135 Central Park West. The twelve-room flat occupied the building's entire sixth floor, overlooking Central Park. When the Macy's department store's annual Thanksgiving Day Parade proceeded down the avenue in November, the giant balloons were so close to their windows that Sally Taylor wanted to offer milk and cookies to Kermit the Frog and Mickey Mouse. The actress Mia Farrow (who had been married at twenty to Frank Sinatra but was now single) also lived in the building. Carly and Farrow became so close that Carly agreed to stand as godmother to Farrow's son Moses. "I wanted to *be* Carly," Farrow later told a biographer. "I would see her walking down West 72nd Street, smiling, with a big bunch of flowers, and her coat brushing the sidewalk—that woman can *stride*—and I knew all was well with the world. Even though she was riddled with phobias and she was always running herself down, she was also fearless—in love and in life. . . . Carly was like a warrior, and the most loyal person I know. . . . I've spent my whole life around celebrities, and I've never known a celebrity less likely to get any safety and comfort from her success. It's like she's nine years old sometimes. . . . She is the most romantic, and the most *indiscreet* person I know."

Now, and for the next three years, the magazine writers all began their profiles the same way: "Carly throws open the front door of a luxurious, enormous Central Park West apartment, extends a hand and draws me in. She's a glamorous creature, tall, grinning, turquoise silk pants, bare feet, a corona of fluffy hair. Magnetism, charisma, and sex . . . 'Kome eento my drawing roum,' she says, affecting a playful Middle European accent, and drifting over to plop down on a brown velvet couch overlooking the landscape of the park." She kept telling the interviewers that James's problems with heroin were safely in the past.

Around that time James switched record labels. Warner Bros. was slow to pick up his expiring contract, so he signed with Columbia instead. Warner Bros. released *James Taylor's Greatest Hits* for the Christmas market, and the record took off, selling over a million units by early 1977. James couldn't get permission from the Beatles' dysfunctional Apple Corp. to include "Something in the Way She

Moves" and "Carolina in My Mind," so he recut the songs in Los Angeles with his rhythm section and session players in October. A live "Steamroller Blues" was from his 1975 tour. *Greatest Hits* got to only number twenty-three in *Billboard,* but the album became a fan favorite, stayed in the charts for years, and sold in the multimillions.

Late in the year Carly took a call from her manager, who was excited about a new opportunity. The new James Bond movie, *The Spy Who Loved Me,* was in production in England. But John Barry, who usually wrote the scores for the Bond series, was in tax exile and unable to work in Britain. So the producers had hired Marvin Hamlisch, a New Yorker who had won Oscars for his music for such Hollywood blockbusters as *The Sting* and *The Way We Were,* and for several Woody Allen comedies. Hamlisch and his girlfriend, Carole Bayer Sager, had written a new song for the film called "Nobody Does It Better," and they wanted Carly to sing it on the movie's soundtrack. Arlyne Rothberg told Hamlisch that Carly would definitely do it, and then called Carly.

Hamlisch telephoned Carly on a snowy day in early December and was invited to the apartment. Carly: "I was so knocked out, that they had offered me this, that it almost didn't matter what the song sounded like. It had been a lifelong dream on mine to sing a song for a movie. When Marvin came over to the apartment to play it for me, I thought he was the tax accountant I had made a date with for that day, only later on. I was in the kitchen making tea when Marvin sat down at our piano and played that wonderful, cascading opening to the song. This was some accountant! And yes, even songwriters can wear stiffly starched shirts, dark suits, and have their hair combed straight across their foreheads."

Carly sang "Nobody Does It Better" for the first time from the sheet music Hamlisch had brought with him. Hamlisch told her it was a perfect fit. She told him that she wanted Richard Perry to produce her vocal track when she and her husband came to Los

Angeles after the baby was born, sometime in January. James would be working on his next album, and the James Bond project would distract her from the rigors of new motherhood. She told Hamlisch that she used to mime movie songs in front of her mirror. "So often, what you do in the mirror as a small person comes to fruition. And I also had fantasies about being a spy. So I really wanted to do this. I even owned several trench coats, and I had a pocket flashlight that doubled as a moisturizer."

As the year ended, Carly attended the wedding of her older sister Johanna, who married Gerald Walker, an editor at *The New York Times*. Carly was in the last month of her pregnancy. She was worried about her husband, who was hanging out with some of the brilliant, drug-addled comedians in the *Saturday Night Live* cast. No good could come of this, Carly knew, but there was nothing she could do except settle in and wait for the baby to come. Between Christmas and the New Year, they were on Martha's Vineyard. There was a comfortable chair by the fireplace, and James would sit there for hours, playing the guitar, working on songs. There was something new that he was trying out, a song that Carly really loved, that James was calling "Secret O' Life."

THINGS WE SAID TODAY

———

*J*anuary 1977. Carly put a heavy fur coat over her white maternity gown and went to a party at the Dakota, the Gothic pile of an apartment house only a few doors away from her own building. Also present were Dakota residents John Lennon and Yoko Ono. They both made a fuss over the very pregnant Carly. Yoko kissed her, and John wished her good luck.

Carly gave birth to her son, Ben Taylor, on January 22. James Taylor was in the birthing room, timing the contractions and making up little stories for each one. Carly was in labor for about six hours, and the delivery was natural. At first everything went well, but when they got Ben home, it seemed the baby never stopped crying. The only way Carly could comfort the child was to pick him up and put him to her breast. This went on for weeks, and started to drive James Taylor crazy. Ben cried more than he slept. They were all in a state. The doctors noticed that the baby's temperature was always slightly elevated, but they didn't understand why. The pediatrician diagnosed a sleeping disorder, but no one seemed to know what to do about it. The parents were exhausted.

Carly, her sisters, and their mother appeared on the cover of the February 1977 issue of *Ms.* magazine, the New York media industry's outlet for commercial feminism. The article, "The Extraordinary Simon Women," traced the outlines of the Simon family's history while revealing none of its secrets. By now, Carly's responses to the usual questions about her approach to feminism were almost generic: "I'd been educated in a way that didn't have much space for women's opportunities, except marriage." Et cetera.

~~~~~

March 1977. The Rolling Stones were famously in Toronto, trying to keep Keith Richards out of jail after he was arrested for heroin possession. Then the Canadian prime minister's wife—and this triggered worldwide headlines—ran off with Stones guitarist Ronnie Wood. Mick Jagger arrived in New York and left multiple phone messages with the Taylor family's answering service, which annoyed James, who had never been completely convinced by his wife's denials of any amorous adventure with Mick.

Bob Dylan was being divorced. Fleetwood Mac's *Rumors* album was the hottest record in the land. Once again Carly and James took the children and the nanny to California, staying in a Bel Air house owned by music mogul Lou Adler. Carly worked with Richard Perry on "Nobody Does It Better," giving the vocal a loving, buttery texture that perfectly caught the sly double entendre of the lyrics. They brought in old friend Paul Buckmaster, who helped with orchestrations. Carly also contributed to James's first album for Columbia, cowriting part of the great sailing song "Terra Nova," and supplying a heart-stopping Highland vocal drone in the ballad's coda. (This was the only writing credit she received on one of her husband's records.)

While in Los Angeles, Carly also worked on Libby Titus's first solo album. Paul Simon and Robbie Robertson were also producing tracks for Libby. Carly sang on two: "Darkness 'Til Dawn" and "Can This Be Our Love Affair?"

James Taylor later told friends that he was "still doing drugs" when he and Peter Asher made the *JT* album, but the drugs must have been helping, because he was burning up the studio and making his best album in years. "Secret O' Life" and a cover of Otis Blackwell's "Handy Man" would both be hit singles. "Another Grey Morning" and "There We Are" are both beautiful and less-than-idyllic sketches of a contemporary marriage that had its variable moods and malaise. "Terra Nova" is an ultimate traveling song, visionary and deeply emotional. These songs portrayed a seemingly unfiltered James Taylor for the first time in years, and would resonate with his audience when the album was released in June 1977.

The month before that, Carly was persuaded to play two nights at the Other End, formerly the Bitter End, her old haunt on Bleecker Street. The small club was filled with record people, the press, Carly's family, and a few celebrities, including Warren Beatty, Diane Keaton, and Art Garfunkel. On the second night, Elektra's Steve Harris was sitting in the club's back booth with Alyne Rothberg and Diane Keaton. As Carly started to sing, Mick Jagger slid into the booth with them. Keaton was so flustered by Mick's sudden presence that she called him "Mike" for the rest of the evening.

Two different female critics panned Carly's shows in the downtown weekly *Village Voice,* both on socioeconomic grounds. One described her as impossibly culturally privileged. Regarding her romantic songs, the other described Carly as "too sleek and well-adjusted to be a credible victim." For arch-feminists in the crumbling New York of 1977, Carly was too preoccupied "with that old, demeaning dance of courtly love" to be taken seriously. New York in the squalid seventies was no place for an old-fashioned romantic like Carly Simon.

Columbia released *JT* in June. James's new album sold two

million units by the end of the year. His singing with Linda Ronstadt and Graham Nash (and Leah Kunkel) transformed "Handy Man" into an Appalachian soft blues song that got on the radio all that summer and climbed to number four. (James would win a Best Pop Vocal Grammy Award for "Handy Man" the following year.) The philosophical "Secret O' Life" established James as a national junkie savant, dispensing quiet teachings and aperçus like a secular American guru. James and the band went out on the road for the summer. Carly was worried about him. But then, she was worried about a lot of things. Baby Ben still wasn't sleeping. She had a permanent foreboding, she told friends, and a lingering feeling that something was wrong.

Then she had her own hit record that summer. United Artists Records released "Nobody Does It Better" in July and it proved to be Carly's biggest hit since "You're So Vain" of four years earlier. The single, awash in strings and flourishes of brass, was number two for three weeks on the Hot 100 and number one on the adult contemporary chart. Many fans thought Carly wrote the song, but Marvin Hamlisch and Carole Bayer Sager received the Academy Award nomination for Best Song.

Carly went to the gala premiere of *The Spy Who Loved Me* in New York. She recalled, "There was a huge blackout in the Northeast the day of the screening. As Roger Moore was drifting to earth with that famous Union Jack parachute, he started falling more slowly, and my voice in the soundtrack got lower and lower, and then there was nothing. No Roger. No me. No lights in the theater."

Peter Simon married his girlfriend, Ronnie Susan Goldman, on Martha's Vineyard that summer. Carly attended the ceremony, conducted by Peter's spiritual adviser, Baba Ram Dass, formerly Professor Richard Alpert of the Harvard psychology department. The wedding reception was held at Andrea Simon's house, Highmark, with its infinity view of the sea. The wedding ensemble was led by

John Hall, the lead guitarist of the rock band Orleans. Hall came over to Carly's house to rehearse the day before, and she showed him some clever wedding lyrics—at Ram Dass's slight expense—she wanted to insert into "Chapel of Love." She also fronted the band doing the Beatles' "Things We Said Today," which sounded great in the open summer twilight as bride, groom, and guru danced barefoot, holding hands.

At some point Peter asked Ram Dass to speak with Carly. Kindly and heavily bearded, the guru had a calmness about him that Peter thought might appeal to Carly, who was living a somewhat frazzled existence then. "Be here now" was Ram Dass's mantra, describing a way of living that emphasized presence of mind and an absence of anxiety over events that were beyond an individual's control.

Carly liked him, and told him her troubles. She said that her image of herself wasn't clear, and that this bothered her. She spoke about her marriage, and the competitiveness between her and her husband. She told him that she had this feeling that something was not all right. Carly recalls, "He was immensely alert and a great listener. He made me believe that I was all right, but not full of illusions about myself. I said I thought that our feelings of competitiveness were a good thing. He said that wasn't an illusion. He agreed with me that I was earthbound, and unready to assume my mystical duties. The main thing he told me that was I was all right. I need confirmation of this every couple of weeks."

Later that summer James was home from the road, and he and Carly went to the old Jungle Beach in Chilmark with some houseguests and friends. There was a strong undertow that day, so no one was in the water. James was quiet, mostly listening to the conversation on the hot and sunny day. When some clouds moved in, the sea picked up and James went in for a swim. He swam straight out to sea with long, easy strokes. Soon he was a quarter mile out, and barely visible. By the time a series of combers began to crash on the beach, he had disappeared. Carly grew alarmed. She walked down to the water. Her husband wasn't in sight. She came back to their blanket with tears on her cheeks. Why did he need to be so reckless and frighten her? Someone was suggesting they try to get help when James could be seen walking back to them from way to the east, where the inexorable current had carried him.

Why'd You Tell Me This?

⎯

*J*ames Taylor hated November in the Northeast. Its shorter days and colder nights reminded him of his traumatic prep school days, which is why for the past few years he and his wife and children decamped to sunny southern California, where he could make his records without the rigors of what later came to be called seasonal affective disorder.

But in 1977, Carly Simon didn't want to go to California, and James wasn't about to go without her, so during the winter of 1977/ 78, the family stayed home. The plan was that she would record her next album in New York, with a new producer. Sometime in the spring, they would return to California, where James would cut the follow-up to the bestselling *JT* album.

So in November 1977, Carly began work on *Boys in the Trees* with producer Arif Mardin. He was one of Atlantic Records' Turkish mafia, close to the label's cofounders Ahmet and Nesuhi Ertegun. He was a consummate New York record man—suave, savvy, sophisticated—and he had worked with major stars from Aretha

Franklin to Diana Ross to Bette Midler. His specialty was lush orchestration that could propel a diva into a sonic cloudscape beyond her usual comfort zone. Elektra executives thought he would supply Carly with a more grown-up sound with which to cross over from the rock market to a broader commercial appeal.

Arif Mardin didn't hear a hit single in the new material Carly brought to the early recording sessions at legendary Atlantic Studios (Ray Charles et al.) on Broadway and A&R Studios in Midtown. But in December, providence intervened, under pressure, in the form of Carly's last producer, who sent her a tape of a new song by the Doobie Brothers' singer Mike McDonald. Carly: "Teddy Templeman sent me a tape, a 'la-la-la-la-la' tape to what is now the melody of 'You Belong to Me,' and I had to fill in the spaces—within minutes!— because the Doobies were in the studio and seriously about to record the song. It didn't have *any* words, except the very, very important ones: 'You belong to me.'

"So the rest of the lyrics, on my version, was a direct-to-the-gut response to his 'you belong to me' start. I put myself into the position of a woman whose man is being attractively waylaid by another woman. I wrote the lyrics in the kind of short time that panic elicits— panic that someone else will steal your job. Teddy gave [the lyrics] to the group and they recorded it on the spot. Several months later, I recorded it too, and it became my first [self-written] hit in a while.

"I always found it odd that during all those months Michael [McDonald] and I never spoke. It was all done through middlemen: the producers. Although when my version went Top Ten, Mike McDonald very graciously sent me a plant.

"I know for sure that my audience used to think the song was about James—but no, not really. In fact, later on, I was shopping at Tiffany's on Fifth Avenue. A man came up to me and said, 'James Taylor—that *rat*. How could he have *done* that to you?' This was overheard by a woman, who joined in and said, 'Yes, Carly, you *have* to fight back. Get him *out* of your life, be *strong*.'

"This was always a problem for me in those days. I so often had to reassure those that really care about me that 'It's only a song' and that I operate under poetic license all the time. Then of course there are those times when I take *no* poetic license—songs like 'Anticipation' and 'Like a River'—and there are those that are very reporter-esque and utterly true to fact. I found this to be the most satisfying thing about being a songwriter, or any kind of fiction writer: that you can so easily disguise or mislead. I could be lying to you now . . . but I'm not."

Carly was recording in New York City for the first time since she'd made her first album at Electric Lady in 1970. Carly: "I now met many of the musicians I would play with for years to come: [drummer] Steve Gadd, [bassist] Richard Tee, [keyboardist] Hugh McCracken, [multi-instrumentalist] Mike Mainieri, [arranger/guitarist] David Spinozza—to mention some of those spectacular New York chaps." The rhythm section of Steve Gadd and Richard Tee was the nucleus of the performing band Stuff, which recorded for Warner Bros. and played clubs while mostly doing daily service in Manhattan's busy recording studios. Various permutations of these above players would now record and perform with Carly over the next decade, identifiably her "middle period," from 1978 to 1988.

But in many instances the guiding spirit of *Boys in the Trees* was James Taylor. Sticking close to his wife, and spending some serious time with her in the studio, he produced, arranged, sang, and played on most of the album's tracks. He's first heard on "You Belong to Me," as a vocalist, riding the rail between soft rock and soft jazz, a locus now owned mostly by Fleetwood Mac. James plays expert-level guitar on the title song, a haunting (and very memory-driven) acoustic ballad/art song about a risible girl's adolescence. The album's fulcrum is a duet between Carly and James on "Devoted to You," the old Everly Brothers standard from 1958. James did the vocal arrangement and plays guitar on Carly's cod calypso "De Bat," based on a true-life incident on Martha's Vineyard.

"Tranquillo (Melt My Heart)" was Arif Mardin's attempt to land Carly on the dance floor in the au courant disco world of *Saturday Night Fever*, John Travolta, and the Bee Gees. The lyrics are mostly about their son, baby Ben Taylor, who was still crying all the time (and still no one quite knew why). The lyric wondered, "Can't stay up and won't go to sleep / What does it mean?"

"He was just a very noisy, crying baby," Carly remembered, "and I started calling him 'Tranquillo' as a nickname, thinking that I would magically imbue him with that characteristic. And he cried all the harder, and of course I was . . . Well, I always picked him up whenever he cried. He would quiet down and I would kind of sing this song to him."

James Taylor wrote (but doesn't play on) "One Man Woman," on which Carly is expertly backed by the Stuff players, augmented by Michael Brecker, whose soulful saxophone solos were deployed by both Carly and James on their records. Other tracks on *Boys/Trees* include the operatic "Haunting," with both of Carly's sisters on backing vocals; "In a Small Moment," a guilty moment closely observed; "Back Down to Earth" (with John Hall on guitar); and "For Old Time's Sake," sentimentally cowritten with Jake Brackman—for old time's sake.

Elektra really liked the album. "You Belong to Me" was obviously a hit single—everyone loved David Sanborn's alto sax solo—and the duet with James felt like money in the bank. For the album sleeve, photographer Deborah Turbeville shot Carly in gauzy soft focus, all lingerie and stockings in a ballet studio. Once again Carly would be portrayed as the barely dressed temptress of the seventies, the leggy fallen woman. A nipple reportedly had to be airbrushed into detumescense before Elektra would print the album jacket.

Carly and James celebrated Christmas for the first time at 135 Central Park West. It was a happy time in their occasionally fraught marriage. A week earlier a film crew from one of the syndicated midnight rock programs had caught them in their tiny wooden music room in the Vineyard house singing James's "You Can Close Your Eyes" together; James played guitar, eyes mostly closed, sitting between Carly's sheltering legs. Their new duet, "Devoted to You," was symbolic of what these two rock stars had been through together, and their hopes for the future. *This*—a creative partnership with an artistic genius whom she really loved—was what Carly Simon had hoped for, from the beginning. All things seemed to be going this proud couple's way at the beginning of 1978, with the only clouds in their coffee being the persistent fevers and constant upset of their now year-old son.

THE GORILLA IN THE ROOM

―――

*W*inter 1978. Thumping disco music still rules radio playlists, and the Sex Pistols—filth-spewing avatars of the UK punk movement— have just broken up on their first and only American tour. A new band called Blondie, starring sexy Debbie Harry from New Jersey, is spearheading (along with the Police) so-called New Wave music—pop songs with a fast beat and edgy, self-conscious lyrics.

Elektra is ruthlessly pressuring neurotic, stage-frightened Carly Simon to tour in support of her forthcoming album, and she glumly assents. Arlyne Rothberg books a dozen shows for later in the spring, mostly in the Northeast, supported by David Spinozza and the studio musicians who played on *Boys in the Trees*. James and the children will come along for the ride, and Carly vows to do her best, and not fall apart.

In February the family went on vacation to Tortola, in the British Virgin Islands. The rented house was on the beach, on the island's west end. One day James was taking the meat out of a coconut with a butcher's knife when he was distracted by a pelican landing in the water nearby. The coconut slipped out of his hand and the blade sliced his palm; he thought right away it was bad. He knew he had severed a nerve because he had no sensation in his left hand. On the thumb-edge side of his left index finger, it was a minor cut for a civilian, but a major injury for someone who played the guitar for a living. This injury would prevent James Taylor from touring that summer, resulting in what he later called "psychological effects of losing about two years of confidence off my guitar style, because of an accident to my hand."

While his hand was healing he tried to keep busy. He and Carly sang on Kate Taylor's first album for Columbia. They sang on three tracks for John Hall's solo album for the same label. James was asked to contribute a song to a new musical, *Working*, based on Chicago journalist Studs Turkel's interviews with working people. The song he came up with, "Millworker," was the first he had ever written from a female point of view. He was so excited when he finished it, well after midnight, that he woke Carly to read the lyric to her. It took her three hours to get back to sleep. "I don't exactly know who I'm giving this advice to," James later told an interviewer, "but *never* wake up Carly Simon in the middle of the night."

Boys in the Trees was released in April 1978 and became another bestselling record for Carly, reaching number ten on the album chart amid withering competition from disco queens and New Wavers. The "You Belong to Me" single topped out at number six. A twelve-inch remix of the song also sold well and was featured in the adult con-temporary charts. A few months later, the "Devoted to You" duet with James stayed in the Top Forty for several weeks. It was a wel-come comeback of sorts after the disappointing sales of *Another Passenger* of two years earlier.

In late April 1978, Carly Simon went on tour with her husband, along with their two kids, both of them sick, both throwing up in adjoining suites in rainy Boston's best hotel. Then Carly started vomiting as well. This was her first tour with a band in five years, and expectations were astronomical. In the afternoon she went to the Paradise rock club on Commonwealth Avenue for the sound check with her cracking band of New York studio pros, powered by the formidable drummer Steve Gadd, under the direction of David Spinozza, who had his own jazzy album out and would open Carly's shows with his own music. She canceled a pretour interview with *Rolling Stone* and then telephoned the writer from her hotel bed. "It's the same thing the children have had for the past two days . . . *ugh* [gurgle] . . . I can't even keep any liquids down . . . I'm so weak with hunger, I can hardly stand . . . *Ohhh* . . . Why did this have to happen—*now?* . . . I can't go on tonight, and everyone will think I'm chickening out from stage fright—again."

At the very last minute, when it was clear that all was lost, James Taylor told his wife to relax. As the dutiful and uxorious husband that he (ironically) styled himself, he would play the show instead. That night, nobody left the Paradise when the announcement was made that Carly Simon was ill and her husband would perform in her place.

David Spinozza's soft jazz set left the audience a bit cold, but the band was topflight: Steve Gadd, Tony Levin on bass, Michael Mainieri on vibraphone, Warren Bernhardt on keyboards, and old friend Billy Mernit on piano. Then James Taylor came out to enthusiastic applause, looking pretty wacked, eyes totally pinned in his head. He mumbled incoherently about Carly not feeling well, leaving the audience even more confused than before. He remarked that his guitar strings were unusually loose because he had a bad cut on his fretting hand. Staring (somewhat disconcertingly) straight into the club's main spotlight, he sang only one original song, the new "Millworker," and plugged the Broadway show it was written for. The band then joined him for an oldies set: "Hey, Good Lookin'," "Memphis," "Let the Good Times Roll." This was completely unrehearsed, and the musicians kept shooting anxious glances at one another as James plowed on. After another golden oldie crash-landed, James looked at his shoes and murmured into the microphone, "Just because . . . you've never been this close to a big star . . . doesn't mean that you can't shout abuse."

"Sing some James Taylor songs," someone yelled.

"I'm sick of that guy," James replied, and launched into Carole King's "Up on the Roof." His encore was "Over the Rainbow." James's concert at the Paradise was short, but no one asked for their money back.

Carly was sufficiently recovered to go onstage in Boston the following night. She was still nauseated, and worried that she might puke on the front row. "I hope this is a loose set," she told the sold-out club. "Anyone can go to the bathroom at any time—and so can I." The clubs and theaters Carly played on this tour all lit the first ten rows so Carly could make eye contact with the audience. In attendance that night was a large contingent from the Taylor family, including James's elusive father, Ike Taylor. Dr. Taylor, tall and imposing, was friendly. He drank a lot of beer and told people that, at home, he was known as the Doc of Rock.

Carly, dressed in a simple mauve top and a pair of slacks, frizzy long hair down her back—her body described (in a review) as "somewhere between willowy and skeletal"—opened with "Anticipation." The crowd was adrenalized by her appearance and sinuous dance moves, and they were cheering her on. Then she moved on to "No Secrets," the band expertly copying the sound of the records. Carly started forgetting about feeling ill and threw herself into the show. The first new song was "You Belong to Me," rapturously received by the audience. "De Bat" fell a bit flat, but then James Taylor came out, alone, to give his wife a breather. Again staring directly into the spotlight, he performed "Up on the Roof." (Reviewers noted that the applause he received for this was almost too thunderous, since it wasn't his show.) But then Carly took the stage again and performed "You're So Vain," as Steve Gadd played some obscenely visceral drums. Now it was a rock concert, and the applause rivaled that for

James. (This was a married couple that, on a good night, could seriously compete for audience adulation, in real time. Carly and James now found themselves in an unintended but brilliant marital game, one that no celebrity couple since Elizabeth Taylor and Richard Burton had ever experienced.)

Carly took to the piano for "That's the Way I Always Heard It Should Be." The last number of the regular set was "It Keeps You Runnin'," the band in rock-and-roll mode. Carly walked off with what a reviewer called "a phenomenally sexy bounce." She came back with James for the encore, "Devoted to You," and ended the evening with a rousing version of "Goodnight, Irene," in a rearrangement by James.

In the dressing room, the very relieved band was boozing and listening to James tell Polack jokes. Carly graciously received congrats on her stellar performance. James went out of his way to insult the *Rolling Stone* writer who was following Carly around for a forthcoming profile.

Carly received the writer at home in New York two days later. It was a spring day in early May and the trees were in bloom outside the living room window of Apartment 6S. The room was dominated by a large painting of a gorilla lounging on a beach chair. James was not in evidence; the children were in Riverdale with Andrea Simon, now "Granny Andy." Carly served chilled white wine and Perrier.

Interviewer: "A lot of your songs seem to be about adultery, and you take a traditional viewpoint that it's a bad thing. It's almost like you're trying to convince yourself."

Carly: "No, that doesn't ring a bell. I don't consider myself traditional. . . . But I've never bought that open marriage thing. I've never seen it work. But then, that doesn't mean that I believe in monogamy. I don't believe that sleeping with someone else necessarily constitutes an infidelity."

Interviewer: "What would?"

Carly: "Having sex with someone else, and telling your spouse about it. [She laughs.] It's anything you feel guilty about."

The tour continued a few nights later at the Bottom Line club in Manhattan. A masseur now joined the entourage. Each night before her set, "He massaged me into feeling very much like I was coming out of the Belgian Congo. My hair was wild by the time he had finished with me. I felt that this particular jungle of an audience seemed a lot less dangerous than the one I had just come out of." James continued to support and sing with her. The tour's backstage contract rider specified unopened packages of Pampers (disposable diapers) at every show. Arlyne Rothberg rearranged the seating chart so the record execs were on the side and the fans were down front. The audience was largely male, and they cheered everything in the eleven-song set. Carly was "gowned and frizzed like the fairy princess of patrician funk," wrote one critic. The show was flawless according to *The New York Times*. Billy Mernit did a solo piece mid-set, and James repeated his folksy version of "Up on the Roof." The two Michael McDonald collaborations got the best response, as "You Belong to Me" was pushing Carly's latest album into the platinum category. *Rolling Stone*: "She combines perfect elocution, near perfect pitch, and a vibrant, smoky timbre with one of the most powerful deliveries of any woman in rock. . . . Simon seemed to come close to satisfying her male audience's fantasies—erotic as well as musical—of what white, middle-class, woman-centered rock could and should be." After the show, Carly and James autographed unused Pampers for fans waiting at the back door.

A few nights later, at Villanova University, near Philadelphia, Carly was shaking with fright at having to perform before a large, sold-out audience. The massage didn't help. Carly: "I came up with the idea that I had to take the focus off myself and do something utterly ridiculous that would preoccupy the audience. So when I was introduced I came out onstage completely wrapped in toilet paper. I don't remember why I told the audience that I was wrapped head to foot in toilet paper. It looked like a Halloween prank, but at least they laughed at me, and that took the edge off it."

Back in New York, Carly and James taped a duet of "Devoted to You" in a TV studio for Dick Cavett's talk show. James played guitar and sang with his eyes closed. Carly sang while looking at James. The body language was tense, and it was not a relaxed performance. After the last verse ("Through the years our love will grow / Like a river it will flow / It can't die because I'm so / Devoted to you"), James looked thoughtful for a moment, and then ad-libbed, "A *sobering* sentiment."

Carly originally agreed to do seven shows, but then Arlyne booked a few more, until the total was about a dozen. After one of the final concerts, one played without her family in tow, something unusual happened. Carly remembered: "It was Memorial Day, I was up in Woodstock with my band, and I gave [one of the musicians] a ride back to the city because I had a limousine waiting for me." The limo pulled into a Howard Johnson's parking lot in the Rockland County town where the musician lived at the time, and where his wife was waiting for him. This woman exploded into a jealous rage when she saw that Carly was in the limo. "And he and his semi-estranged wife started the *heaviest* fight that I've ever seen in my life, outside of Madison Square Garden. They were just crazy. It was upsetting and fascinating and confusing and inspiring—all those things. It was an ugly scene, but I was jealous of the amount of passion between them. I was shaking, because I thought I was going to be dragged out of the limo and knocked around, too."

In fact, Carly tried to get out of the car to calm things down, but the woman shoved her back into the limo and told her to shut up and get the hell out of there.

"It made me feel, once again, that I'm a voyeur, and a sort of spy. And I'm afraid of anger, of being angry. That if I act out my real feelings, they will overwhelm me. I'll say something that I will regret for the rest of my life, or blow something terribly badly."

WE'RE SO CLOSE

———

*I*n the summer of 1978 both Carly and James were on the radio, with "You Belong to Me" and "Handy Man." Carly appeared on the cover of *Rolling Stone* in a billowy dress, shot by the Japanese fashion photographer Hiro. The article dwelt on the writer's astonishment that Carly was breast-feeding Ben (a quite large toddler at eighteen months) during the interviews. It also noted that Ben "cried uncontrollably" when the feeding stopped and Carly left the room. She was also on the cover of *People,* which reported that she lost $75,000 playing intimate venues on her recent tour, and that James Taylor's hobby was carpentry and he was building an addition to the couple's Martha's Vineyard home.

There were new people who wanted to hang out with James on the island. Comedians John Belushi and Dan Aykroyd rented houses that summer, and Belushi especially wanted to befriend James. The irrepressibly vulgar Chicago comic would drop by and take the kids for ice cream, or steal James to go fishing. Carly was both ambivalent and disconcerted about Belushi. He liked to physically pick up an astonished Carly and spin her on his shoulders. The second time he did this, at a beach bonfire one night, she was dismayed to remember that she wasn't wearing any underwear.

Belushi loved drugs—mostly marijuana and cocaine—and in no time James Taylor was a goner. The *Saturday Night Live* crowd all had JVC video cameras; by summer's end there were videos floating around that showed James and Belushi with needles in their arms, probably injecting speedballs—an amusingly toxic cocktail of cocaine and heroin. James started to disappear for a few days at a time, going on alcoholic benders with singer Jimmy Buffet, also a visitor to the Vineyard. Carly would be distraught, fearful for James, afraid also to do anything about it. It wasn't as if she could call the police and report James Taylor as a missing person, but with the current state of her marriage, that's what he was.

The next few years would be difficult ones for Carly, as her husband gradually submerged himself into old habits. He was often away, touring or recording, and when he was at home, amid the *haut bourgeois* chintz of 135 Central Park West or the spartan, unadorned walls of the Vineyard house, he was often abstracted, sitting in the shadows, looking out the window. Carly told her best friends she was raising their children as a single mother.

After losing control of himself, when he passed out at a party, when he felt he'd made a fool of himself, James would be remorseful, and Carly's heart would go out to him. "I don't have any moderation," he admitted to an interviewer. "I get intoxicated. I lose control. I black out. I make mistakes when I'm too high, which—when I finally come to—I deeply regret."

"James was an unusually guilty addict," a member of his band said. "Most drug addicts are either too stoned, or too worried about their next fix, to feel guilty about what they were doing to themselves and the people around them. But we knew that James really suffered because of his addictions."

Carly's position was difficult. James liked to snort powders with his manager's wife. What could Carly say? All these comics who wanted to hang with her husband—Belushi (and his wife), Monty Python's Eric Idle, Richard Belzer—were into drugs. When the parties got raucous, late at night in New York, Carly would appear in her pajamas and tell James and the partiers that they were waking the children.

"James was dealing with his fame and his career while trying to figure things out," Carly later recalled. He would say he wanted to quit, to change his ways. "And, in not knowing how to help him, I became even more helpless and foolish, and probably more of a deterrent to his stopping." Carly increasingly found herself going through her husband's pockets, flushing drugs, throwing away paraphernalia, checking his eyes. There were tremendous rows. Carly would throw James out of the house, or he would just flee, walking across Central Park, barefoot, and trying to check into the Westbury Hotel on Madison Avenue, where his manager had an account. The hotel would call Peter Asher's office in L.A. and say that someone—disheveled, with no identification, no shoes—claiming to be James Taylor was trying to check in.

Carly: "I lived in a state of fear—for years, and also in a constant state of denial. I didn't want to see it. I didn't want to know how serious it was. I just wanted to help, to do anything for him I possibly could. His needs always came before mine.

"Addiction really takes over everything, and we were in its power. . . . When James walked in the door, I was examining him, his expression, the size of his pupils, looking for evidence. I was nervous when he went into the bathroom. I was incredibly naïve. I thought I could actually help him. Who was I kidding?"

Eventually, James Taylor's behavior was something that Carly became accustomed to. Aside from a couple of emergency situations, it was mostly James not feeling well, sleeping late, and the stressful hassle of delayed drug deliveries to the house. Friends who knew the couple even thought that the situation might have suited Carly, who liked to be the center of attention and related well to weaker personalities.

Carly: "So I became—very much—'an enabler' [then an unknown term] and then I became 'the enemy.' And it reminded me of how I'd been treated by some of the men in my life, especially my father. It is . . . so *hard* to break those patterns! I found James incredibly intoxicating and brilliant and funny. What was devastating was how he turned so many of those things against me. And you feel so . . . responsible."

In November 1978, Carly was in Texas to perform as a guest vocalist at a gala concert given by the Houston Symphony and Burt Bacharach, one of Carly's songwriting heroes. Channeling Dionne Warwick, most of whose hit songs were written by Bacharach, Carly sang "I Live in the Woods." This was one of her first public ventures into the world of balladic standards, but the audience gave her an ovation at the end, and she was reassured.

The following month Carly began work on her next album. *Spy* would again be produced by Arif Mardin at Atlantic Studios, on Broadway, a short walk from Central Park West. She worked there through the end of the year and the first four months of 1979, composing a topical album of new songs about a failing marriage through the eyes of an angry, seriously neglected wife and mother not unlike her.

James Taylor decamped by himself for Los Angeles, where he spent that winter working on his new record, *Flag*. He didn't like talking on the telephone, and rarely checked his messages, so Carly felt more alone than she had in years. She was also suffering from severe migraine headaches. When she tried to call her husband to tell him how she was feeling, the phone on the other end just rang and rang.

The Woman Scorned is a powerful trope in art and literature, and Carly now made the most of this persona. "Vengeance," the energized rock song that begins the album and would be its first single, is a woman's yearning to be free and vowing retribution if her yearnings are stifled. Ian McLagan, who played with the Faces and the Stones, came in to play rock-and-roll piano on the verses. John Hall put on a rock guitar solo, and the full-blast horn section was the Brecker brothers and David Sanborn. Carly wanted this track to really thunder, so Steve Gadd was joined on drums by Rick Marotta, who sometimes played with James on tour. The British actor Tim Curry sang with Carly on the choruses: "That's vengeance—*vengeance*—she said—that's the law."

Carly later called "We're So Close" the saddest song she ever wrote. The lyric to this bathetic piano ballad is about a lover who takes her for granted, who meets none of her needs for intimacy or even friendship. "He says: we can be close from afar / He says: the closest people always are / We're so close that in our separation / There's no distance at all." Carly was now mining her difficult marriage for its most private and difficult material, with unusual candor.

"Just Like You Do" is a high-gloss Arif Mardin production with horns and orchestra that plead for a return to the "brave innocence we once knew." Jake Brackman's lyrics for "Never Been Gone" concern the emotional ties to Martha's Vineyard felt by Carly and her family. "Coming to Get You" is an atypical narrative about some unexplained legal situation in an Arkansas family court, certifiably one of the strangest songs in Carly's career. (The back story of the lyrics was Libby Titus's struggles with Levon Helm over custody of their daughter, Amy.)

"Pure Sin" is another big dance-rock production, a verbal threat display from a woman who won't be contained or kept down much longer. Carly wrote "Love You By Heart" with Libby Titus and Jake Brackman, and the lyrics seem aimed at a specific character: "Your habit is old / You don't need it anymore / Go on and kiss it goodbye / 'Cause you got me." James Taylor and Arif Mardin helped Carly with "Spy," a four-on-the-floor disco song. And Carly wrote

"Memorial Day" by herself. The song is a lovely and graphic account—in the form of musical episodes—of the tooth-and-nail fight she witnessed between her musician friend and his wife the year before: "Well, they bellowed / And they hollered / And they threw each other down." If all the elements of this mini-opera didn't all quite congeal, they expressed a writerly take on action and experience typical of Carly's work in this period. Steve Gadd finishes the track with a drum solo that's like a blow-by-blow reprise of the physical fight itself.

When James returned from California, he joined his wife in the studio and sang on "Love You By Heart," "Never Been Gone," "Spy," and "Just Like You Do." But, perhaps reflecting the somewhat diminished role James was playing in Carly's life in those days, engineer Lew Hahn mixed James's vocals much farther down in the track, so his voice would not be as prominent in Carly's music as in the past.

Carly wanted *Spy*'s lyric sheet to carry an epigraph from the writer Anaïs Nin: "I am an international spy in the house of love." She dedicated the album to her producer. The noirish black-and-white jacket and sleeve photographs—Carly in a slouchy secret agent's fedora—were taken by Pam Frank, a friend from the Vineyard and New York.

The album's release was set for June 1979. "Vengeance" was chosen over "Just Like You Do" as the first single release from *Spy*.

Hot Tin Roof

By 1979 many of the survivors of the American protest movements of the sixties had coalesced around the antinuclear energy issue. Atomic power was hailed as the major energy source of the future, and the government was licensing large corporations to build new nuclear power plants, some of them in risibly dangerous locations, near major population centers, especially in the Northeast. Many local alliances had sprung up to challenge the nukes, especially in rural areas where they would otherwise have been welcomed for the jobs they provided. The antinuclear activists maintained that an accident was inevitable. The government and the corporations maintained that nuclear energy was safe, period. Then, as now, nuclear energy was a controversial, contentious issue.

Later, after the accident happened in southwestern Pennsylvania, the farmers said the cows knew about it first. At dawn on March 29, 1979, dairymen found hundreds of cows lined up along fences five miles north of the Three Mile Island nuclear power station. Following no apparent signals, the cattle faced the site of the reactor hidden from view by a bend in the Susquehanna River. Later the farmers told investigators that if the cows began to bolt, they were out of there, too, no matter what the government said.

The Three Mile Island accident remains, decades later, the worst nuclear disaster in American history. The details were not that complex. The reactor's river-fed cooling system failed, and the plant's Unit 2 experienced a partial core meltdown—the nightmare of the nuclear industry. The effect on Americans, especially in the Northeast, was chilling. Half the country (already somewhat unsettled by the movie *The China Syndrome*) felt that they had been poisoned by radiation. There was a psycho-seismic wave of anxiety reflected in the screaming headlines of the contemporary media. Carly was upset, James even more so. They wondered how they could get involved. Carly later said, "People become immune to bad news. A danger like [nuclear energy] fades from peoples' minds unless it's kept alive. . . . You think, 'I am here. I could die from this. I could get cancer. My children could be affected, for the rest of their lives, by radiation poisoning.' Those are personal things. I didn't want to be scared. I wanted to stand up to them."

Not long before the Three Mile Island accident, Carly and James were visited in New York by their guitarist friend John Hall. He was upset that a power company wanted to build a nuclear reactor on the Hudson River near his home in Saugerties, New York. Hall had been a physics major in college. He wasn't a typical rock musician, but a professorial presence with interests in politics and science. He explained that nuclear plants created cancer-causing waste products that remained dangerous for centuries and were almost impossible to store safely. He said he was putting together a press conference with Bonnie Raitt to announce the formation of a group of artists and activists opposed to the spread of atomic energy. He also played the demo of a song he'd written called "Power," which suggested that solar- and hydro-based energy could do the same job without poisoning the atmosphere. James and Carly both agreed to sing vocals on the song, and appear at the press conference with Hall and Bonnie.

The press conference was put together by Danny Goldberg, then a crusading New York rock-and-roll publicist. Drawn by James and Carly's star power, a large contingent of reporters, photographers, and TV crews were on the scene. Danny Goldberg: "We were preparing the musicians for questions before letting in the media when Carly announced that her manager didn't want her to participate."

Carly seemed agitated. James Taylor sat impassively, eyes staring into space, as if focusing on a planet light-years away. Bonnie Raitt simply got up and walked out of the room. John Hall looked like he'd been slapped with a fish. Danny asked for the manager's number.

Danny: "Arlyne said that Carly had a long-standing policy of not doing political events. I snapped back that Carly had already given her permission for her name to be on the media pitch and explained that there were reporters and camera crews outside. If Carly pulled out, the story will be about that and will cause more questions than if she participates. Arlyne agreed, reluctantly, to let Carly answer questions but not make any opening statement.

"At the press conference Carly was asked the first question, and she calmly proceeded to describe the cancer-causing dangers of radiation, the questionable safety features of most reactors, and the long-term storage safety issues. Overall, Carly ended up giving the most eloquent and coherent statement against nuclear power of the day. She provided all the crucial sound bites that ran on TV and key quotes for the press."

After Three Mile Island, John Hall and Bonnie Raitt recruited Jackson Browne, Bruce Springsteen, James Taylor, and other contemporary rock stars and formed a foundation called Musicians United for Safe Energy (MUSE). The idea was to perform a series of benefit concerts later in 1979 to provide funding for antinuclear activists and grass-roots organizations opposing new "nukes" in rural communities. James Taylor would be back on tour that summer and signed on to play some of the shows with his band. When the MUSE concerts happened in September, Carly Simon would end up playing a show-stopping role herself.

Spring 1979. John Travolta knocked at the door of Apartment 6S one evening. He was staying in the building and wanted to meet James, who wasn't home. (James was with his brother Alex and Jimmy Buffett, drinking to blackout every night on the Caribbean island of Montserrat.) Carly entertained Travolta instead, and the two became good friends. When his longtime girlfriend, Diana Hyland, died a few weeks later, Travolta practically moved in with Carly and the children. To friends who asked, she described Travolta as "naïve, but with this incredible street sense."

On Martha's Vineyard, Carly was providing financial backing for a nightclub in the scrub oak forest out by the airport, a place where bands could play and people could hang out—something that had never existed on the conservative New England island. Carly had long wanted to recreate the ambience of the old Mooncusser, where she used to perform with her sister, but she wanted the new club to be more of a country roadhouse with a bar, not a coffeehouse. Her local partners, a cook and a house painter, leased two acres from the county and built the club from scratch. A local artist painted murals. The liquor license was an issue almost until the club, the Hot Tin Roof—named by Carly after one of her favorite plays, Tennessee Williams's *Cat on a Hot Tin Roof*—opened in June 1979.

The Roof, as the locals called it, was packed almost every night. John Belushi was a regular presence, along with Bill Murray and other TV stars. Deejays spun reggae records when bands weren't playing. The house drink was the Cape Codder, vodka and cranberry juice on ice with a twist of lemon. Cocaine was plentiful—it was coming in on the fishing boats from mother ships offshore—and dealt in the bathrooms. The talent booked into the club was eclectic: Dizzy

Gillespie, Tom Rush, Willie Dixon, Burning Spear. One night Carly was spotted in the club's VIP area with houseguest John Travolta, and there was a literal stampede among the patrons to get closer. The highlight of that first summer was the Jamaican reggae star Peter Tosh and his band, Word, Sound and Power. Hundreds of fans who couldn't get tickets to the sold-out shows brought ladders and heard the music from the branches of the oak trees surrounding the club. Carly Simon's Hot Tin Roof was a huge success and stayed in business for another quarter century.

May 1979. *Spy* promised to be the biggest album of Carly's career. The timing was perfect. Her last, *Boys in the Trees*, had been her best selling studio album. She had a solid body of music behind her. She had worked hard and made a good record. She had starred in a sexy video to promote "Vengeance," the blatantly commercial first single. But then nothing happened. Elektra Records' promo people started complaining that they couldn't get "Vengeance" on the radio. Programmers were locked into New Wave bands such as Blondie, the Police, Elvis Costello; the disco/rock "Vengeance" didn't fit current radio formats. Feel-good radio guys grumbled that Carly sounded too angry. No one saw the video (two years before MTV). The deejays at the Hot Tin Roof played "Vengeance" only if Carly was in the house. By the time *Spy* was officially released in June 1979, it was already considered a bomb, and Carly and her manager started thinking about moving to a new label. Carly felt certain that after eight years of relative success, her winning streak was over.

She took this hard. The single failed to make the Top Forty. *Spy* stalled at number forty-eight. She felt that she was "washed up," as she put it to friends. A Canadian reporter came to interview her on the Vineyard the day the single lost its chart bullet, stalled at number forty-five. Carly was taking this personally, asking the reporter, "Do you think people are tired of hearing me? Tired of my sound?" The critics, looking for clues about her marriage, described the album as tedious. One feminist critic wrote, "Simon is aware of her potential as gossip fodder—remember 'You're So Vain'?—but she is forfeiting emotional intensity now by offering hints, rather than insights, about her marriage. Carly Simon, in her trench coat, seems more like a flasher than a spy."

Carly remembered: "This plunged me into a major depression and a serious ego quandary. I really lost myself for a while. I thought, 'Well, Jesus, I'm not hitting the mark, am I? Is my opinion of myself totally based on what other people think? Do I even have a sense of myself?' I was just floundering. It hit me at a time when I was almost living alone with the children, and my self-esteem was precarious anyway. And it toppled it."

Her husband was away on tour for the whole summer, but it didn't mean he didn't understand her plight. "Carly's having a rough time now," he said to a writer. "She feels hurt and disillusioned and I don't blame her. But there's an attitude to adapt about this thing. It's harder for her without many other outlets, and also feeling—as she does—much more restricted by family life and raising children than I appear to be. For me to be able to go and work helps, you see. All of a sudden, I'm valid in that context. Carly doesn't have that access. So she puts out a record every two years, and when all of a sudden it doesn't get the promotion she thinks it should, and when it gets reviewed totally off the wall, if that's all she gets, that can be devastating for her."

James was promoting his new album, *Flag*, whose cover depicted the nautical signal for "man overboard." Many of the songs were confessional and angry. In one, a wife steals her husband's drugs. In another, the husband describes the petty deceits and faithlessness in a certain marriage. (Carly sings on both of these tracks, "Johnnie Comes Back" and "B.S.U.R.") There was no strong single, although Arif Mardin's orchestration helped "Up on the Roof" become a minor hit, and *Flag* sold well, helped by James's strong appearance on *Saturday Night Live* on May 12.

James wasn't shy about his anger in interviews he gave that summer. He said the new song "B.S.U.R." was a get-back at his wife for "Fairweather Father," which, he said, "seemed to paint me pretty ugly." He admitted his bad habits, allowing that his behavior was toxic, that he was poisoning himself with booze and dope. He reported that he liked to drive while intoxicated. Of his wife, he said, "My behavior threatens her. She's always worried I might harm myself."

James: "I feel strongly, and also Carly has recently—because of some real disappointments in her career, and also because of some disillusionment with the record business—that the main thing that gets in the way of our music and our growth is the industry itself. . . . Something that is successful, they want you to hold on to. I mean, they just want you to keep it coming. It gets to me."

James was on the road and missed the party that Rose and Bill Styron threw for Carly's birthday. She was renting a "secret house" on the water near the Styrons' estate in Vineyard Haven, a small cabin with a couple of bedrooms and a dock for James's boat, a place where she could get away from the armies of houseguests she invited to the island every summer. During the party, Carly showed John and Judy Belushi the cabin, and then asked the abnormally cocky Belushi a question. "I said, 'Do you ever feel unconfident?' And he said, 'Never.' And he told me that self-confidence isn't something that you wait for. It's something you've got to go after."

Still, Carly was quite undone in those days. The failure of her album was one thing, because she could always write another. But she also sensed the impending failure of her marriage to a man she truly loved. Later on she wrote of that time: "I recorded *Spy*. It contained the song 'We're So Close,' which to this day is the saddest song I've ever written. It was a song about how close you can pretend to be, when you know it's all coming undone. How you can use excuses to make it all look okay."

STARDUST

---

*L*ate in the summer of 1979, James Taylor finished his long tour and came home to Martha's Vineyard. As usual, the house and property were swarming with contractors. A pond was being dug, and a cobblestone drive was under way. James wanted the carpenters to build separate quarters for the dog, the pig, and the tractor, and there was talk of a windmill. For Carly, having her husband at home could be problematic. "James likes being loose and disorganized," she said, "and it's one of our incompatibilities. When he comes back from the road, there's always a feeling of anticlimax, of relief, followed by: 'Jesus—*now what?*' . . . Sometimes he scares people, James does. Because you never know what kind of reaction you're going to get from him. He's very mercurial. A lot of what appeals to me in James was present in my father. Because James has a kind of aristocratic elegance, even though he has some terrible habits."

In September, James was on the cover of *Rolling Stone,* with photographs by Annie Leibovitz. (One of those showed a bare-chested James carrying a half-naked Carly on his back.) The magazine's profile depicted him watching TV with his children, bored out of his mind, and listening to the *Grease* movie soundtrack—a favorite of his daughter's—over and over. (*Grease* had starred John Travolta.) "It's been devastating," James said of family life at home. He compared his daily routine on Martha's Vineyard to his youthful in-patient days at various high-end mental hospitals.

Both James and Carly performed at the MUSE concerts at Madison Square Garden September 19–23. These "Concerts for a Non-Nuclear Future" were the first major rock charity shows since George Harrison's Concert for Bangladesh early in the decade, and all the MUSE shows sold out. The Doobie Brothers, one of the biggest jam bands in the country, headlined two of the concerts. Bruce Springsteen and Jackson Browne, at the apex of his career, each headlined one. Other performers included James Taylor; Crosby, Stills and Nash; Tom Petty; Bonnie Raitt; Ry Cooder; John Hall; Chaka Khan; Jesse Colin Young; and Gil Scott-Heron, all singing together in various permutations over the four nights of shows. All the music was recorded and filmed, which created a hectic, hothouse atmosphere backstage. Carly appeared as "a special guest" in James's performances, running onstage in a shimmering greenish jumpsuit and bare feet when she heard Russ Kunkel pounding the tom-toms for the intro to "Mockingbird." Amid lusty cheering from the crowd, Carly and James danced the Lindy Hop for the movie cameras, then strolled offstage arm in arm. This always earned one of the evening's loudest ovations. Few guessed that Carly spent the last hour throwing up in the backstage ladies' room. Leah Kunkel wanted to help Carly, but kept thinking, "She's a little . . . crazy." But Carly recovered enough to join her husband and Graham Nash (one of the MUSE producers) for a stirring harmonic version of Dylan's "The Times They Are a-Changing." This, and "Mockingbird," would appear on *No Nukes,* the all-star two-LP album released later in the year by Asylum Records. *No Nukes* sold about a million copies, and eventually provided some important funding for the antinuclear movement.

In the autumn of 1979, Carly and James were only fitfully living together. It was rumored they were both close to others, outside the marriage. James was drinking heavily in public and said to be using drugs in private. He went on binges, sometimes disappearing. Carly worried that he was intoxicated when he picked the children up from school or playdates. She was afraid for their kids when they were with their father. On the Vineyard, he would take off on his bike and end up at brother Alex's house on a three-day weekend bender. James was supposed to be writing his next album, as Carly was working on hers, but he kept wandering off, blacking out, and doing stupid stuff. He later, regretful, told his biographer Timothy White, "One night, I got so drunk I blacked out a whole rampage of awful behavior. I don't even know where I got the energy for it. I was at a party, and a friend loaned me his guitar, and I started playing 'She Caught The Katy,' which I love, for something like, *hours*. And when someone finally threatened, or offered, to beat me on the head if I kept playing the song, I actually had a kind of seizure . . . and bit a big hole in the guitar—which belonged to a good friend of mine, so it was a bad thing to have done."

Lucy Simon publicly described her sister's marriage as "in turmoil."

Carly Simon still loved James Taylor with (almost) all her heart, but trying to raise their children (and write her next album of new songs) while coping with an alcoholic, drug-addicted husband and being afraid of almost everything, all the time, was starting to take a serious psychological toll on her.

But as 1980 and a new decade loomed, there were reasons to be hopeful. After ten years with Elektra, Carly signed a three-record deal with Warner Bros., one of the sister labels of the WEA empire. Warner president Mo Ostin promised Arlyne Rothberg that Carly would get a major promotional boost for her albums, the lack of which was the reason she was leaving Elektra. Carly also had a new producer, Mike Mainieri, a talented, jazz-informed musician she had met through Arif Mardin. In November 1979, Mainieri came to the Vineyard to write with Carly, working in the rented boathouse in Vineyard Haven. Early in 1980 they began working on her next record, *Come Upstairs,* at the Power Station recording studios on West Fifty-third Street, not far from her apartment. Carly sometimes walked to the studio (formerly a Con Edison electric power plant) for exercise, occasionally waving to neighbors John Lennon and Yoko Ono as they crossed Seventy-second Street to Central Park.

The *Come Upstairs* music reflects a transitional time in Carly's life. Eight of the nine tracks are love songs, some specifically about her husband, others quite explicitly about others. The singer wants love and lots of it, and isn't shy about her intentions, but she's confused about the interesting number of men in her (intimate) life. The music itself was transitional under Mainieri's direction. Warner Bros. wanted a contemporary album from Carly, who would be competing with sixties icons Fleetwood Mac and Marianne Faithfull, plus Blondie, Talking Heads, the Police, and other New Wave bands. Electronically generated backgrounds now replaced Arif Mardin's lush string orchestras. Mainieri's main instruments were the vibraphone and the marimba, but with Carly he doubled on the Oberheim and Prophet 5 synthesizers to make the songs sound more "eighties."

The album's ravenously seductive title song is very Blondie-like, synth-driven New York City power pop, a new style for Carly. The lyrics—"You can take off my clothes"—were provocative for a famously married woman to sing, an invitation to trespass, disrobing, and sin, with a joyous and apparently guilt-free chorus.

Carly's husband joined her to sing on "Stardust," a blatantly explicit homage to Mick Jagger, with whom said husband still suspected her of carrying on a long-term affair. Mick was a presence in this marriage from the beginning, and James was never satisfied with Carly's profession of innocent friendship with the Rolling Stone. Mr. Taylor's feelings about the track are unknown, but "Stardust" is pure, un-ironic hero worship, bumping and grinding along. "I told my

friends that you were just a man / Real nice . . . / I feel so important!"
(The drummer on this and other tracks is Rick Marotta, whose
rhythmic drive would be important to Carly throughout the rest of
her career.)

James also sings (with his brothers Alex and Hugh) on "Them,"
a song about aliens. And he is the subject of the song "James," an
aching ballad, a fever dream that recalls long-ago romantic exaltation
and especially the first night he played for Carly while she lay in the
warm glow of her nighttable lamp, communicating with blue chords,
soft phrasing, and improvised variations, demonstrating his genius
and his worth to her. With a soft cello sending a prayerful message,
the lyric beseeches, "Let the music speak for your heart . . . / And
bring us together once again."

Carly and Mike Mainieri worked the hardest on "Jesse," Carly's
new mid-tempo rocker slated to be the album's first single. Rick
Marotta hits the drums hard, and James, his brothers, and daughter
Sally, now six, sing backing vocals on a song about a woman's ambivalent feelings for an incontinent lover who wets the bed and needs
fresh sheets. ("Jesse" was widely assumed to be about Jesse Colin
Young, the honey-throated rock crooner.) Carly said "Jesse" was "a
song laying plain the fact that good intentions go to hell when you
are crazy for someone." By the end of the lyrics, she decides to put
fresh sheets on the bed.

The last four songs of *Come Upstairs* comprise a sort of chronicle of some of the rejection and difficult times Carly had been
through for the past year. "In Pain" is a desolate piano ballad that
devolves into operatic power chords. This is Carly as Pat Benatar (or
Dory Previn), howling fury in the third verse—"I'm in pain"—a raging emotional torrent her audiences hadn't heard from her before.
"The Three of Us in the Dark" is a clever love triangle song—with
a husband and a secret lover—asking who is just a guest and who
has to go. Session musician Sid McGinnis played guitar in the style
of Carly's husband, adding poignancy to the song. "Take Me as I

Am" is a hard-edged synth rocker, played fast, the singer's idealized version of herself and a plea for self-acceptance. The song sequence then closes with "The Desert," an arty, lovelorn self-portrait amid moonlit dunes and feelings of impending and certain loss.

James was away much of that winter, 1980, absented from his family much like his father before him. He was also working on a new album in L.A. and making appearances for the liberal congressman John Anderson, who was trying an insurgent run for the president against the floundering and unelectable incumbent, Jimmy Carter. In this period, Carly was sometimes comforted by a young recording engineer who was working on *Come Upstairs*: There was talk that the title song was about that relationship. Around that time, she sold "Haven't Got Time for the Pain" to the makers of the painkiller Medipren, and the "Pain" jingle was as omnipresent on the radio as Carly's ketchup commercial had been, years before.

In April 1980, Andy Warhol, the supremo of pop art, received a call from the ABC-TV network. They were reviving *Omnibus*, a cultural program famous from the early days of television. The producers wanted three artists to do portraits of Carly Simon. In addition to Warhol, they had recruited Larry Rivers and Marisol, a sculptor who worked mostly in wood. According to his diary, Warhol liked Carly's music and agreed to the portrait, but only if he got paid. The producers contacted Carly, who affirmed that she would buy the portrait if it weren't too expensive.

Warhol called his friend Bianca Jagger, Mick's now ex-wife, who assured him that Mick had been with Carly while he was married to her. She said that Mick was now with the American model Jerry Hall because she always gave him a blowjob before letting him out of the house. She added that the only girlfriend of Mick's she was ever jealous of was Carly, because she was intelligent and looked like Mick—and Bianca—and it was a look Mick really liked.

Warhol's diary: "They sent a limo for Carly, but when she arrived at the Factory she was too nervous to come up until we sent some wine down to the car. Then she came up and was sociable. We made her put on lipstick and then after we worked she was hungry and we sent to Brownies for health sandwiches and she loved that. I taped it all. (Brownies: $8.30, $23.44)." The finished silk-screen portrait of Carly, heavily rouged, duly arrived at Carly's apartment after the show was broadcast, and it hung in her various homes until it was sold for a fortune much later, in what Carly described as "a time of need."

In May 1980, Carly and James patched things up and took the children to England, crossing the Atlantic on the liner *Queen Elizabeth II*. James wanted to show the children where some of his songs had been written in London, and he took them by his old flat on Beaufort Street, Chelsea. Carly introduced him to old flame Willie Donaldson, now a successful author and satirist. (In his diary, Willie said he thought Carly was disrespectful to James, but only when he wasn't looking.) The family then traveled to Scotland by overnight train and toured the seacoast of Inverness. James told the children that his father had said the Taylor family originally came from around there, and that they were seafaring merchants who sailed to North Carolina and back in their own ships. Carly, James, and the kids spent a couple of happy days driving around the foggy, looming mountains and the valley glens whose landscapes were some of the most breathtaking Carly had ever seen.

BLOOD EVERYWHERE

———

*I*n June 1980, Warner Bros. released *Come Upstairs,* Carly Simon's ninth studio album. Producer Mainieri was credited with cowriting all the songs but "In Pain," and French songwriter Jacques Brel was thanked for inspiration. British photographer Mick Rock depicted Carly jiving in au courant padded shoulders, wide lapels, and gold lamé. Mainieri had given the new songs a fashionably metallic sheen deliberately unlike the softer, piano-based, singer-songwriter soundscapes Carly's fans were used to. As promised, the promo guys went to work. More specifically, the label hired independent promotion men—part of a loose (vaguely "connected") association informally known as the Network—to fan out around the country with cash-stuffed envelopes and bribe radio program directors to play "Jesse," the album's first single. (Though this system of payola was a good deal for the indie promo men, crooked radio guys, and corporate promotion vice presidents getting kickbacks, it turned out badly for the labels that created it, ending in lost profits, lawsuits, and congressional investigations later in the decade.)

Sure enough, "Jesse" got on the radio, reached number eleven on the charts, got a gold record for a million units sold, and stayed alive for six months. But when sales of *Come Upstairs* stalled and the album reached only number thirty-eight, "Jesse" was said to be a "turntable hit," a record that got on the radio but didn't sell. A Warner Bros. executive later told a reporter, "'Jesse' was legendary as one of the most expensive singles of all time, in the amount of indie promotion spent on it. I don't know the actual number, but it was probably around $300,000. It was a top ten record, got loads of airplay, but they didn't sell any albums. It was perceived as a hit record, but it was a stiff. It was only successful for the independent promoters. You couldn't blame them for taking the money."

The reviews of *Come Upstairs* were indifferent. Critics who had once championed Carly as an original now complained she was trying to be trendy, and that it wasn't working. Others said that the album was depressing, that Carly's audience wanted good news, not bad.

June 1980. Ben Taylor was now three years old and had been sickly all his life. He still cried a lot and ran fevers, and none of the doctors could explain why. The enormous child was still at Carly's breast. When teased by her friends, she answered that lactation made both mother and son feel better. But then the boy's fevers got worse, especially at night. In one account, James Taylor called his father in North Carolina. Ike Taylor called a friend at Columbia Presbyterian in New York, and Ben was finally seen by doctors who provided an accurate diagnosis: Ben had a dysplastic kidney, one that had developed abnormally and was leaking toxins into his body. The doctors wanted to remove the diseased kidney without delay, and Ben was rushed into what amounted to emergency surgery.

Carly handled this situation as best she could, since James was nowhere to be found. No one knew where he was. Arlyne Rothberg rushed to the hospital and found Carly shaking uncontrollably and in tears. Soon Andrea Simon arrived and urged Carly to pull herself together and comport herself with dignity. Arlyne called James's management, let them know that Ben was being operated on, and demanded they track James down. John Travolta tenderly comforted a distraught Carly and kept her company during the week Ben was in the hospital.

James eventually arrived at the hospital, but he didn't go up to see his family until Arlyne discovered him outside on the street— disheveled, glassy-eyed—sitting on a bench. Arlyne started shouting at him to go to his family, but James just sat there, ignoring Arlyne as if she didn't exist. Eventually he made his way upstairs and was told that the operation had been a success. Carly was furious, and felt even worse when James explained his absence by saying that he'd driven his girlfriend, a dancer, to the airport and hadn't known about the surgery. He was also playing benefits for politician John Anderson. When Ben woke up he had a fit because he couldn't find his penis, which had been taped to his body during surgery. James immediately dropped his trousers, tucked his penis into his legs, and told Ben he couldn't find his, either. Ben Taylor thought this was pretty funny and stopped crying.

Carly wanted to forgive James for his behavior, but she was so angry with him that her heart wasn't in it. When James was in residence in Apartment 6S, neighbors in the old, thick-walled building could sometimes hear the shouting. Carly wanted to hurt James so badly, really wound him, that during one battle she told him that his decade of suspecting that she had had an affair with Mick Jagger had been right all along. She regretted this almost immediately, tried later to take it back, to say it wasn't true, but the body blow had landed accurately.

One night in this period Carly and James had a fight and he stormed out of the house. Arriving at Trax, a popular Midtown musicians' hangout, he announced to his pals, "Jezebel done kicked me out, so I'm up for grabs." As for Carly's relationship with John Travolta, she told *People* magazine later that year, "John has an almost magical way of knowing when I am in need. When James couldn't be there, John came to me during that week Ben was in the hospital. [John] is sensitive, loving and very immediately there."

But when things calmed down, Carly and James stayed married for the sake of the children, although the couple was separated in all but name. Carly was privately mortified that their public image was a sham. Her once-tight bond with her husband was coming unglued, and she felt her father's abandonment returning in spades. She already realized that patching up the marriage was not going to work.

In October, Carly was on the cover of *People.* "We were both really traumatized," she was quoted regarding Ben's surgery. "I tend to get hysterical, while James is clinical and then tries to escape." After showing the reporter around the Vineyard property, as usual a bustling construction site, she allowed, "James and I have built a fairy tale house, but we don't live fairy tale lives. We were both programmed into conventional male-female roles, and we are always struggling with those. I just wish that he would do as much fathering as I do mothering." Carly's friend Libby Titus was even more revealing about the troubled marriage. "Their ship has sprung some leaks," she said, "and now they're deciding whether to patch things up or abandon ship and take to the lifeboats. The anger and frustration are just beginning to come out."

As for James Taylor, he was in L.A. making his next album with Peter Asher from September 1980 through January 1981. When production was finished, he didn't come home.

When she signed with her new label, Carly had reluctantly agreed to go on tour to promote *Come Upstairs.* This was supposed to happen during the summer, but Ben's recuperation pushed the fourteen-city tour into the autumn. The band comprised many of the musicians who worked on *Come Upstairs,* and the tour played mostly theaters. Carly was depressed, had lost twenty pounds during Ben's illness, and her nerves were shattered by the progressive unraveling of her marriage, but she tried her best to pull the tour off because people were depending on her and she'd said she would do it. Lucy Simon came on the tour to help her sister, and somehow Carly got through eight concerts in late October before arriving in Pittsburgh, where— like Three Mile Island—her cooling systems failed and she suffered a partial core meltdown.

She later described the first of two scheduled Pittsburgh concerts as the bottom of her performing career. The opening numbers went well, but then her legs wobbled and she was having trouble staying upright. Then she lost her breath and couldn't catch it. Her breathing slowed and she felt a strong series of chest palpitations. She suddenly began to menstruate prematurely, a condition related to stress. "I couldn't get the words out," she recalled. "I seemed to go to pieces in front of the audience. There was blood everywhere."

Desperate to avoid panic, Carly pondered her options. She could either cancel the concert or tell the audience the truth. She stopped the show and stammered that she was suffering from acute anxiety. Fans were shouting they were with her all the way and to keep going. She felt a little better and tried another song, but then another wave of palpitations overwhelmed her. She told the audience that she might feel better if people came onstage, and several dozen fans joined her, incredibly supportive, rubbing her back, legs and shoulders, telling her to take her time. People in the balcony were yelling encouragement, an extraordinary scene. With this support she (barely) finished the first show and staggered into the dressing room in a state of emotional collapse. Lucy Simon, appalled at what had happened to Carly, took her by the hand and said, "Carly, you don't need to do this anymore. There's no real reason why you have to put yourself through this—ever again." The second Pittsburgh show and the rest of the *Come Upstairs* tour was canceled, and Carly returned home a broken and humiliated woman in her mid-thirties, convinced beyond hope that her career was in acute jeopardy. Her doctor weighed her at 114 pounds and checked her into a Manhattan clinic, where she was fed and hydrated intravenously. She started seeing a psychiatrist again. The tour promoters sued her for canceling the final shows.

"Each person breaks down in different ways," Carly later remarked. "You could call what I had a breakdown, sure. In retrospect, it was foolish to do that tour. So, I decided that at this time of my life, when things were so difficult for me in other ways, I shouldn't aggravate my nervous system anymore by performing onstage." The Pittsburgh show would be her last for more than ten years.

Late in 1980, both Carly and James worked on *In Harmony,* an album of mostly original children's songs that Lucy Simon produced for the TV program *Sesame Street.* Carly sang, poignantly, on her own "Be with Me." James and daughter Sally contributed a very funny "Jelly Man Kelly." Lucy Simon, Kate, and Livingston Taylor all contributed, as did Bette Midler, Linda Ronstadt, Libby Titus, and Dr. John. The Doobie Brothers even covered "Winkin', Blinkin' and Nod." *In Harmony* was released in 1981 and was hugely successful, winning a Grammy Award the following year.

On December 8, John Lennon was murdered in front of his apartment building by a deranged fan. Many neighbors on Central Park West (including Carly Simon) thought they heard the shots as they were fired into Lennon at 11:00 P.M. For Carly, it was the final blow of another extremely trying year. "It was the end of an era," she sadly remembered—ten years later. "We said goodbye to Ben's kidney, to our marriage, to hit singles. Then we moved on."

FOREVER LOCKED INSIDE

---

*I*n 1981, Carly Simon and James Taylor both released albums that described in varying ways the final year of their marriage. James's came out first, in March. The album's title, *Dad Loves His Work,* was perhaps an ironic explanation to his children of why he was rarely around. The eleven songs were full of (seemingly) sincere heartache and recrimination, and many longtime Taylor fans think that *Dad* is his saddest, and hence (for them) most beautiful album. "Hard Times" tells of an angry man and a hungry woman in a last-ditch plea for stability and acceptance. "Her Town Too" (written and sung with sexy Texan troubadour J. D. Souther) describes a phobic woman, afraid of her own shadow, someone given to backbiting and gossip "on the grapevine." "She gets the house and the garden / He gets the boys in the band" was a lyric that accurately described the settlement Carly sought in an (unannounced) formal separation. James would later on swear that "Her Town Too" was about Peter and Betsy Asher, but few believed him, considering the ardent fervor of the song's cherishing last words. "Somebody *loves* you . . . Somebody *loves* you."

It went on from there. "Hour That the Morning Comes" is another vignette of the stilted family life James had been living in: he's "kacked" (junkie slang) on the sly; she's in denial that he's stoned. This puts him into despair. "I Will Follow" wants forgiveness for unforgivable transgressions. There are moody chanteys written with Jimmy Buffett and the nostalgic "London Town," about a younger man busking in tube stations, a seeker full of hope. The album ends with "That Lonesome Road," in which the singer expresses deep remorse for the way he has, for some inexorable reason unknown to himself, behaved. *Dad Loves His Work* was a farewell not only to his marriage, but also to his recording career, as Dad's work was now done, and amazingly, this prolific songwriter wouldn't make another record for almost five years.

Carly Simon, who now had no husband and two children to look after, was in no emotional shape to write an album of original songs, so she "answered" her husband's record with a compilation of standard "torch" songs that was released by Warner Bros. in the summer of 1981.

Torch songs were an enduring artistic legacy of the Roaring Twenties. "Carrying a torch" for a lost lover was a "modernist" female thing, a romantic agony personified by singers such as Libby Holman (1904–1971) who famously married the heir to a Carolina tobacco fortune and then accidentally shot him to death as he was trying to break into his own house when he'd been locked out. Torch songs were retro-noir, semidesperate expressions of female disappointment and lust, and Warner Bros. executives were understandably reticent about Carly Simon making an album of them that would be called *Torch*. They told Carly, "This is *not* your fan base. This is going to ruin your career." But she insisted, held her ground, and recorded at the Power Station, with Mike Mainieri again producing. She chose most of the classic ballads herself, occasionally contributing new lyrics of her own. She channeled her old hero, Frank Sinatra, on songs he previously owned: Alec Wilder's "I'll Be Around," and Hoagie Carmichael's "I Get Along Without You Very Well." Saxophonist David Sanborn's urgent, ungentle alto sax, with a tone between human crying and a bitter sob, is the prominent instrumental voice on the album. Orchestration is back, on Duke Ellington's "I Got It Bad and That Ain't Good" and "Blue of Blue." Jazz players—Phil Woods, Eddie Gomez, Warren Bernhardt—are featured on "Body and Soul" and the disconsolate Rodgers and Hart classic "Spring Is Here." Carly sings "What Shall We Do with the Child" as a guilt-provoking tearjerker. Her one original song, "From the Heart," is about the cold war of a failing relationship, but also carries with it a flickering ember of hope. The album ends with Stephen Sondheim's "Not a Day Goes By." Obviously moved by the song's sentiment—"I'll die, day after day after day"—Carly sings in an unusual trembling vibrato, really conveying the tortured emotions of the song. The track finishes with a final orchestral orgasm, arranged by Don Sebesky.

"They were just a bunch of songs written from the heart," Carly said later, "emotions that are easily expressed. While recording, it was rare that I got through a session without crying, because, well, they did have a lot to do with what was going on in my life at the time." For Carly the highlight of the recording sessions was the day Stephen Sondheim came to the studio as she was cutting her vocal on "Not a Day Goes By."

"I really love that song," she said. "It's from his show *Merrily We Roll Along,* and it's not really a standard, but I think it should be. I'd gone to see him at his apartment and he played me some of the songs from that show. (While he was playing, I had one of my famous anxiety attacks, and to distract myself I pinched my earlobe so the pain would be converted from my brain to my ear. While he was playing "Not a Day Goes By," blood started to fall on my crisp white shirt. He noticed it, asked if I was all right, and was incredibly kind. I suddenly remembered another appointment.) Stephen was in the studio when I recorded it. He was sitting in the control room, and I was standing in the vocal booth. I didn't want to see Stephen while I was singing because it was too scary. So I knelt down and sang the song on my knees. When I finished, I went into the control room. Stephen was crying, with his face in his hands. I thought it was because he didn't like it, but then he said he was crying because he was so moved. To this day, when I want to weep, I put on 'Not a Day Goes By.'"

When Carly walked into the Midtown studio of the prominent rock photographer Lynn Goldsmith to shoot the cover of *Torch*, Goldsmith introduced her to a young actor, Al Corley, who had a role in the arch-seventies TV series *Dynasty*. Carly was attracted to the tall, very telegenic Corley, who acted as a foil when she, dressed in a low-cut, bosomy gown, was photographed clinging in evident emotional agony to a shadowy figure of a man, who was turning away from her. In another image she leans on his shoulder, clutching at him. In another, her gown is red and tossed like a matador's cape in an arc of torrid, shameless passion. The scrawled, lipstick-red typeface on the jacket seemed to drip blood. When *Torch* came out in August 1981, Carly dedicated it to her parents and musical uncles, and also to Jonathan Schwartz, still her most ardent supporter in New York radio. She also made a video—the new cable channel MTV began broadcasting the same month *Torch* was released—where she just looks into the camera, sings "I'll Get Along," and really lets it rip.

Torch wasn't a success, reaching only number fifty. Carly heard that Warner Bros. had been told by its parent company not to push the album so she would go back to writing her own material. But now she was, almost, past caring. "Regardless of how [*Torch*] does commercially," she said at the time, "it is a success to me." And later: "[*Torch*] was so wonderful, because I was just feeling so bad. There's nothing more awful than to hide your sadness. . . . It was the summer of the breakup of my marriage to James Taylor. More emotional

Carly, James, and Sally in their living room on Central Park West.

James and Carly at home in Tisbury, Massachusetts.

Carly and James in Gay Head, Massachusetts.

James and Carly
on the window
seat at their house
on the Vineyard.

Sitting with John Updike
at a cocktail party, Sally
Taylor standing.

Cooking for charity at
the Black Dog Tavern on
Martha's Vineyard in 1973.

James, Carly, Bonnie Raitt, and John Hall backstage during the No Nukes concert at Madison Square Garden in 1979.

The No Nukes concert.

Carly and James at the Livestock '95 festival on Martha's Vineyard.

Carly and John Travolta in 1979.

Comedian John Belushi brought flowers to the opening night of Carly's club, Hot Tin Roof, in 1979.

Top: Kim Rosen, Carly, Jeremy Irons, and Sinéad Cusack. *Bottom:* Ben Taylor, Nick Rosen, Sally Taylor, and Max Irons.

Carly with close friend
Jackie Kennedy Onassis.

Carly with Taylor family
children performing "Itsy Bitsy
Spider" at her HBO concert on
Martha's Vineyard in 1987.

Carly and Jim Hart
with the Clintons
in 1993.

Carly with Jim Hart on their wedding day in 1988.

Filming a video for *My Romance* with Paul Garcia in 1990.

With Russ Kunkel in Riverdale, circa 1985.

Carly with
her mother and
sisters in Riverdale,
early 1990s.

Carly with Sally
and grandson
Bodhi, listening to
John Forté aboard
the *Alabama* off
Martha's Vineyard.

"You're So Vain,"
with Steven Tyler singing
Mick Jagger's part, on
Martha's Vineyard in 1995.

With Sally and Ben
at Carly's birthday
party in 2008.

With niece Julie Simon, Sally
and Ben Taylor, and David Saw
on Christmas Eve in 2010.

With Dr. Richard Koehler.

upheaval. They did nothing to promote it. So I had no big plans for the future anymore."

But Carly was proud of *Torch*. "I thought it was lovely. Mo Austin [president of Warner Bros. at the time] said it was one of his biggest mistakes, not seeing the potential in that record, because a little later [in 1983] Linda Ronstadt came out with *What's New* [also an album of older standards], and it was a huge success." And over time, *Torch* became a steady-selling staple of Carly's catalogue.

Carly Simon didn't want to divorce James Taylor. When he didn't return to the family after his 1981 summer tour, she issued a statement announcing the couple was separating. He went back on the road, playing concerts in Australia and Japan. Al Corley, twenty-seven, was keeping company with Carly and the kids. James gave Carly the Vineyard house in the settlement, to lessen the disruption for the children. In Manhattan, the family stayed in Apartment 6S, and James bought an apartment off nearby West End Avenue, so as to be close to the children during the school year.

Everyone was in deep shock. The children were in shreds. In the autumn of 1981, Carly tried to explain things to friends and interviewers. "There are good reasons for the decision. Our needs are different. It seemed impossible to stay together . . . James needs a lot more space around him: aloneness, remoteness, more privacy. I need more closeness, more communication. He is more abstract in our relationship. He's more of a poet, and I'm more of a reporter."

October 1981. The Rolling Stones were on tour in America. "Start Me Up" was on the radio. Mick Jagger was on the telephone, trying to get through to Carly, who was in seclusion and not returning calls. She was now writing, not songs, but prose stories. In one she describes how the endless construction and renovations of a couple's island home is a welcome distraction from the interior tensions of their family life. And when the builders finally finish their work, the marriage is over as well; memorialized by the "white elephant"—a jumble of turrets, balconies, odd windows—the couple built together. In another story, the narrator speaks to her absent husband: "My golden daughter is talking to you on the phone, saying: *'I love you so much. I miss you, where are you? When will you be back?'* Things I used to say to you, she is allowed to say to you. I am not. Sometimes I hear her words as my own."

An interviewer asked Carly if she still loved James. "Oh yes," she said. Were hard drugs the wrecker? "They were." And she added: "I think he wanted out of the marriage for a time, as did I. I also think he made himself unattractive so I would be turned off on him. And he did succeed—for a while. I didn't feel for him, except that I became very jealous of the girlfriend he was with."

In December, at the end of 1981, Carly appeared on the cover of *Rolling Stone*. This time the story wasn't about her music; it was about her life, specifically her "separation and likely divorce" from her husband after nine years. Carly shelters the children on the magazine's cover, their fingers keeping her chin up. The headline: "Carly: Life Without James." Inside, the article was titled, "Fathers & Lovers: Carly Simon Learns How to Say Goodbye." Journalist Timothy White had visited Carly on the Vineyard a few weeks previously and interviewed her about the Simon family and the endgame of her marriage. He noted that she had lost weight, was stammering, and seemed genuinely stricken. The article was one of the first to probe the mysteries of the Simon family romance, but without revealing its core issues. Carly's troubled relations with her father are, for the first time, presented as a counterpoint to those with her absent husband. The rupture of the Simon-Taylor marriage was big news in 1981 America, and Tim White was trying to make sense of it for his readers.

White (who died in 2002) was known to colleagues as a scrupulous transcriber of his interview tapes, so it's worth quoting Carly's words to him in this period. "I think James and I learned a lot about each other. When needs are not met is when you learn about what needs are. We failed in the context of marriage, but not as people.

James taught me what I needed to know about myself *and* him, and this made me a better person for the next person I'll want to love. The funny thing is, if I met James now, I would know so much more, and be a better partner, but that sounds unrealistic, huh?"

The article noted the coming and going of *Torch,* and Carly wasn't forthcoming about what she would do next. Her main concern was the children: getting them to school in the morning, being there in the afternoon, calming them later, when they asked her why—*why?*—this was happening to their family.

"I had this song [on *Boys in the Trees*] called 'Haunting,' " she told the writer. "Basically, you don't have to see someone for a long, long time for them to still be inside of you. There's no way of killing it off; it's a kind of obsession. And some people do have that effect on me. I have a good memory, especially for emotions. I never get over strong feelings."

The interview was almost over as the autumn light was failing. Sally was heard crying in another part of the house. Ben needed attention in the bathroom. The writer had a ferry to catch. But Carly continued her idea. "Sometimes, in a complete relationship, feelings have a chance to die out. But if a relationship has ended prematurely for some reason, or it can't be fulfilled for another reason, the haunting goes on, the obsessions, the dreams about the person . . ."

Carly stopped and took a deep breath: ". . . and the feeling that he is forever locked inside."

Part

III

THE SOUND OF HIS VOICE

----

*I*n 1982, though burdened with sadness, anxiety, weight loss, and the unwelcome return of her childhood stammer, Carly Simon decided to try to get back to work. In this she was helped by her boyfriend, Al Corley, who encouraged her and was a huge help with the children: playing their games, teaching them things, picking them up from school. Al was much younger than Carly, and consequently the relationship reminded her, somewhat ruefully, of her mother's transgressive affair with her brother's old tutor, also many years her junior.

Carly also looked around and saw that the music business she had grown up in was changing—fast. MTV was narrowcasting around the clock, bringing the latest talent into the cable-connected homes of affluent Americans. The new stars such as Michael Jackson, Madonna, and Cyndi Lauper would now be closer in age to their audiences; what they (and their videos) looked like, and how they moved for the camera, would now become as crucial to their careers as their music.

Around this time Carly also became interested in so-called New Age music, which appealed more to the human spirit than the heart or the groin. She was enchanted by the semi-ecstatic recordings of the Swiss harpist Andreas Vollenweider, and one day she cold-called him at home and told him she was interested in collaborating with him. He was thrilled, and Carly later helped produce his American debut at the Beacon Theater on Broadway.

In March, John Belushi died in Los Angeles of a drug overdose. Everyone who knew him was deeply shocked, none more so than James Taylor, who knew the woman—a famous L.A. heroin nurse—who had accidentally killed Belushi with an injected cocktail of heroin and cocaine. Taylor now resolved once and for all to try to free himself from addiction to heroin. He had a new girlfriend now, a strong-willed actress called Kathryn Walker, and told his few close friends she was helping him finally to get off dope.

Carly now resolved to get into making music for films. The songs could be written at home, recorded at a nearby studio, and she would only have to attend the New York premiere. There was no touring, no band to run, above all no airplanes: no fear. Carly applied herself to this, and within a few years found herself at the top of the profession, Academy Award in hand.

It started in a Manhattan studio late that spring, where Carly sang on a track called "Why," produced by Bernard Edwards and Nile Rodgers, otherwise known as Chic, the era's most sophisticated disco/pop band. The bouncy, reggae-informed tune, written by the producers, would be featured in a romantic comedy, *Soup for One*, released in 1983. "I loved the groove of that song," she said later. "I also liked that they gave me lots of suggestions on how to sing and pronounce words. I found myself being open-minded, a positive quality I'm not always associated with."

"Why" was released as a single that autumn and got only to number seventy-two in America, but it was a surprise bestseller in Europe, a Top Ten record in England, Germany, and other countries.

The song was catchy, its message sad: "Why does your love / Hurt so much?" A twelve-inch single mix was a European dance floor smash as well. Her initial foray into film music—with one of her most passionate vocals in years—provided Carly with her first big success in Europe and gave her a nice jolt of confidence as well.

Carly Simon's next album—it would be her last under the terms of her Warner Bros. contract—was recorded at the Power Station in New York and in Los Angeles during the first six months of 1983. Producer Mike Mainieri deployed his tight circle of New York studio pros, along with three Jamaican musicians: jazz guitarist Eric Gale, the famed reggae rhythm section of drummer Sly Dunbar, and bassist Robbie Shakespeare. The Jamaicans supplied a cool reggae vibration to Carly's polished presentation, especially on a lively cover of Bob Marley's "Is This Love."

The album would be called *Hello Big Man,* after its title song, which was a deftly (and touchingly) idealized portrait of her parents' marriage, beginning when the dynamic young boss of Simon and Schuster first spoke to the firm's pretty new switchboard girl. In the song, Carly erases everything but the love between Dick Simon and Andrea Heinemann, and the (wonderful) lyrics form a hopeful paean to the life they might have lived together, if destiny had only allowed them another chance. The old New York of Carly's childhood, with its carriage rides and Saturday matinees, is the backdrop to her parents' original glamorous romance. In her reimagining of their legend, Dick and Andrea Simon "still live in the house where we were born / Pictures of us kids / Hanging up all over the walls." David Sanborn plays a perfect saxophone solo on one of Carly's most vivid and mytho-biographical songs.

Epic wanted a "contemporary" sound from Carly, and so she collaborated on several new songs with Peter Wood, an English keyboardist who had worked with Roger Waters, Bob Dylan, and current MTV phenomenon Cyndi Lauper, among others. Wood cowrote (with Carly and Jake Brackman) the album's first single, "You Know

What to Do," a slice of synth-driven eighties commercial pop that features the Police's Andy Summers playing his trademark chiming pop-reggae guitar chords. Wood (whose main instrumental album credit was "Memory Moog") also worked on "Menemsha," Carly's choral tribute to the old Vineyard fishing village where she lived with Nick Delbanco in summers past. (She had also recently bought and renovated a cottage overlooking the hamlet's impossibly picturesque harbor, Menemsha Bite.) Carly missed terribly having her husband's distinctive voice on her albums—it had been a vital part of her "sound" for a decade—so now she mustered as many of her children and their Taylor cousins as she could, to sing on the song's bliss-filled choruses. For her next few albums she would often enlist James's three brothers (and sister Kate) to add that familial dash of Carolina twang to her songs.

The sessions' mood of elegy and regret is continued with "It Happens Every Day," an acoustic guitar ballad recounting an intense love not just twisted, but wrenched into a new reality. The lyrics are sorry for the spying and surveillance that turned him into a liar, a robber. But in the end, the song says, it's just another divorce. Nothing unusual, it happens every day. (This became a key track in Carly's career, much anthologized and loved by longtime fans.)

Then there are more songs about Carly's husband. "Orpheus" is another cri de coeur from an anguished wife. It's a story of a man's doubts and lost faith(s), the Orpheus legend recounted from Eurydice's point of view—in hell. "You said all your songs were gone / And the road back up was too long." He couldn't wait, couldn't save her. But despite the hurt and the disappointment she still adores him, and always will.

James Taylor and his (much older, reputedly *very* bossy) girlfriend figure in another reggae song with Sly and Robbie at the controls. The girlfriend is wearing the pants in the family, and he's asking for the keys to the car. "He asks for her permission / To get a tan / To play his hand / To blow a grand / To be a man." Et cetera. This funny put-down of a controlling shrew then gets a subversive ride-out that seems to linger with a sexy (but wishful) satisfaction. Other tracks include "Damn, You Get to Me," with youngest Taylor brother, Hugh, subbing for James (and sounding just like him), and another unhappy breakup ballad, "You Don't Feel the Same." *Hello Big Man* would eventually conclude with "Floundering," a self parody of a reggae song about an insecure woman who has put herself through every (expensive) therapy, treatment, spa, cult, exercise, and rehab in the known universe: "Then she sees her Scientologist / Gets fed by her nutritionist . . . Anna Freud's analyzed her dreams / And she's hoarse from primal screams." But in the end, she's still floundering away, but at least she's trying to laugh at herself.

And this wasn't easy for Carly, because while she was making this album her husband filed for divorce. She was half expecting this, but it came as a shuddering shock to her anyway.

Carly hadn't wanted a divorce. In mid-1983 she heard that James had gotten off drugs, and she tried several times to get him to come back home. "I beat my head against the wall and begged him to reconsider. *'Please! We're affecting the children's lives here.'*" But James stopped returning her calls, wouldn't even allow the children to pass her the phone after he had spoken to them. So she called her attorney, and the dismal legal proceedings began. She got the (Vineyard) house and the garden. He got the boys in the band. Meanwhile, to maintain a familial presence on Martha's Vineyard, James bought some prime (and very private) pastureland on the east shore of Menemsha Pond, in the town of Chilmark, and commissioned a modest, U-shaped house with a mooring and boathouse on the beach, and a long view of the spectacular island sunsets. Eventually he married Kathryn Walker, and lived with her, until their 1996 divorce, near William Styron's family in rural Connecticut, visiting his magical Martha's Vineyard house only rarely.

Talking later about her divorce, Carly blamed Kathryn Walker for orchestrating it. Carly was bitter on the subject, according to her friends. James Taylor's style was too passive-aggressive for him to have actively pursued a legal divorce. But Walker was tough and determined. She had survived the death of her lover Doug Kinney, one of the founders of the *National Lampoon* comedy empire, who had perished at thirty-two when the cliff he was standing on collapsed in Hawaii a few years earlier. Walker was also sober, and experienced in drug counseling as a member of Al-Anon. James Taylor, it stood to reason in that context, had to jettison his past in order to build his future. "She was fierce," Carly was later quoted, "a fierce woman, who wanted James at all costs. She knew exactly what she wanted."

For Carly, the idea of this clever actress succeeding where she had failed was galling. The quasi-popular notion that there was something in the dynamic of their nine-year marriage that made it impossible for James to clean up was an open wound for Carly. Jake Brackman later noted the murderous irony at work. "Carly was trying to [help James] the entire time she was with him. Then Kathryn comes in and—boom!—he's Mr. Twelve Step. What a hard thing for her to bear, whether it was the fault of their dynamic or not."

Eventually Carly accepted that James Taylor's recovery was a blessing for everyone. "The way it happened was one of those annoying things that life coughs up," she said, sighing. "But it had such a wonderful outcome, so I don't kick myself about it."

On the day in late summer 1983 that the divorce was granted, Carly slipped into the downtown Manhattan courtroom and sat behind James and Kathryn. It was the final minutes of their famous marriage, and Carly was deeply moved. "He was sitting in front of me, and I have a picture of his ankle that will stay with me forever . . . the way his ankle bone turned and where his pant leg stopped, and his sandal." Her son, Ben, now six, waiting for her at home, had the exact same ankle. "That image—it still stays with me."

When *Hello Big Man* came out in September, Carly did another round of interviews. Reporters noted the peach-colored walls of massive apartment 6S, with the killer view of New York's Central Park;

the showy floral displays; the Jane Fonda exercise videos that Carly said she watched but didn't bother exercising to. She told interviewers that she was on a spiritual path whose end she could not foresee. She said that the song "Floundering" was an accurate description of her current status. And she was often asked about the end of her marriage. She wasn't shy about letting her fans know that she was still carrying a blazing torch for her former husband. In spite of everything, Carly said, "If James walked into a room, just a look in his eye . . . his smell . . . the sound of his voice . . . could get me going all over again."

A SOURCE OF PAIN AND GUILT

––––

*H*ello *Big Man* came out in September 1983 and maintained Carly's position in what one critic called "80s pop oblivion." The pink-colored album jacket has a pretty black-and-white portrait of Carly by Lynn Kohlman. Peter Simon portrayed the session musicians on the inner sleeve. The back cover is a photo of Carly's beaming young parents and their dog on the balcony of the apartment building they used to own.

Then Carly's hopes were dashed. The first single "You Know What to Do" got minimum airplay and stalled at number thirty-six on the adult contemporary chart. The album reached number sixty-nine. The video for "You Know What to Do," featuring Carly tumbling around the woods of her house, did not make it onto MTV. A second video was made for "Hello Big Man," based on the many hours of her father's 8- and 16-millimeter home movies, which Carly had inherited, but the second single was not released, and the video wasn't seen for decades. Carly appeared on David Letterman's late night TV show, but it didn't help sell her record. Warner Bros. would not be renewing her recording contract.

In this period Carly appeared as a guest on albums by Jesse Colin Young and Nils Lofgren. She also provided a blistering vocal on "Kissing with Confidence," a track on a New Age album by Will Powers, an alias of photographer Lynn Goldsmith.

By then her romance with Al Corley was cooling off, and she was feeling lonely. Then her manager quit, another blow. Arlyne Rothberg moved to Los Angeles to manage Roseanne Barr's TV career. After a period of uncertainty, Carly signed a new management deal with talent managers Champion Entertainment. (This had been suggested to her by a close friend, MTV mogul John Sykes.) Other Champion clients included Diana Ross, John Mellencamp, and Hall and Oates. Champion's president, Tommy Mottola, was a consummate industry insider, expensively tailored, with just the right whiff of intimidating Italian connectedness. (Mottola later ran Sony Music and famously discovered singer Mariah Carey at a cocktail party.) In the late winter of 1983, Mottola and his lawyer Alan Grubman signed Carly to a one-record deal with Epic Records, a CBS subsidiary. Carly spent much of the rest of 1984 working on the album that would be called *Spoiled Girl*.

Carly had many collaborators on those sessions, which took place at three different New York studios, mostly in 1984, including Electric Lady and the Hit Factory on West Fifty-fourth Street. Nine different producers were involved in twelve new songs. The only constants in this scattered production were engineer Frank Filipetti (whose work on *Hello Big Man* had appealed to Carly) and the avuncular Epic executive Lennie Petze, who helped her navigate through this confusing period. Carly recalled: "For *Spoiled Girl*, Tommy Mottola et al. decided that I should work with some of the [famous producers] of the day, so I was partnered with the least likely bunch of characters you could ever imagine, and—*only this time*—I didn't say anything. You could say it was a character flaw on my part. I let them lead me on. I knew it wouldn't work, but I didn't say anything, just did what they wanted. In spite of this there were a few good tracks: maybe two. One of them was 'My New Boyfriend,' which got me back together with [*Anticipation* producer and old flame] Paul Samwell-Smith." This song, written by Carly, was produced by Samwell-Smith as eighties power pop, complete with sequencers and drum machines, making Carly sound something like Grace Jones channeling Duran Duran. Then there was a (Brian) Wilsonian harmonic choir in the song's bridge, consisting of Carly, her sister Lucy, Samwell-Smith, and Andy Goldmark (who had been involved in Lucy Simon's 1977 album).

Another new song, "Come Back Home," was produced by Don Was, of the commercially successful pop group Was (Not Was). A mid-tempo rocker credited to Carly, Jake, and three others, the song contains lyrics that plead for reconciliation: "Now it's December, cold and dark / No more rainbows over Central Park / In this house no window has a view / There's no love here without you." The pleading "Come back home to me" chorus sounded so much like the Doobie Brothers that radio people expected a vocal from Michael McDonald, not Carly Simon.

Carly also cut a pair of tracks with Phil Ramone, a legendary engineer who worked with Simon and Garfunkel, Phoebe Snow, and almost an entire generation of New York artists. "Tonight and Forever" is a quiet ballad, with Russ Kunkel on drums, that Carly sings with a husky tenderness. More upbeat is "The Wives Are in Connecticut," a topical narrative of bourgeois adultery. The husband is having an affair at the office downtown, but the suburban wife is fucking the entire state of Connecticut behind his back. There's a funny list of the towns the wife is swinging in: Mystic, New Canaan, Fairfield, etc.

Russ Kunkel cowrote, played on, and produced "Spoiled Girl," Carly's song about a woman who has too much, and thinks only of herself. It's one of the harder rocking tracks, brimming with staccato sequencer and synths. On the album named for it, "Spoiled Girl" would be followed by "Tired of Being Blonde," the inverse of the spoiled girl's situation, in which a newly self-liberated suburban wife leaves the credit cards and the keys to the Porsche and a good-bye note and, tired of being blond, flees a loveless existence dominated by her caddish husband. "Blonde"—a terrific, radio-friendly pop song—was written by Memphis songwriter Larry Raspberry and produced by guitarist G. E. Smith and bassist Tom Wolk, two stalwarts of the *Saturday Night Live* house band.

British producer Arthur Baker, most famous for his work with Queen, supervised two tracks. With Carly he cowrote "Anyone but Me," which summed up many of Carly's romantic obsessions and featured Carly Simon Band veteran Jimmy Ryan on guitar. Baker also produced the humorous "Interview" to a Cyndi Lauper rhythm, in which Carly turns the table and seduces her interviewer, even seemingly offering an invitation to outright oral sex. (Carly wrote "Interview" with Don Was, with whom she was close at the time. He was going through a difficult divorce, and Carly was able to console him and also helped him find a new apartment, on Riverside Drive in New York.)

Two songs produced by Andy Goldmark round out *Spoiled Girl*. "Make Me Feel Something" describes romantic numbness after the fading of love's first freshness. And "Can't Give Up" is Carly's final affirmation and celebration of love's inexorable hold over her, and her inability to stand up to the tyranny of constant desire. A third Goldmark track, "Black Honeymoon"—more jealousy and deception—didn't make it onto the album. Carly had written it with Jake and Libby on the Vineyard in the seventies. Goldmark put a new chorus on it, but the somber, marvelously jaded song wasn't released until *Spoiled Girl* was released on compact disc late in the twentieth century.

Summer 1984. Carly recorded "Someone Waits for You" by Peter

Allen and Wilbur Jennings, for the movie *Swing Shift*. She was also making videos. The clip for "My New Boyfriend," directed by Jeff Stein and Kathy Dougherty, was shot with a crew of locals and Taylor family as extras on what was supposed to be Cleopatra's barge, temporarily moored in Menemsha Pond. Carly shimmied all night for the camera like an Egyptian queen, while Alex Taylor was boiled alive in a cannibal stewpot. And then, fatefully, Carly hired Jeremy Irons to direct the video for "Tired of Being Blonde."

She had a longtime crush on the handsome English actor, dating from his role as Charles Ryder in the 1981 British TV miniseries *Brideshead Revisited*. Irons was now a full-fledged movie star, tall and ultracool, with a voice that made everyday conversation sound like poetry. His most recent role had been the adulterous friend and lover in the harrowing film of Harold Pinter's, *Betrayal*. He came to the Vineyard that summer with his wife, actress Sinéad Cusak, and their young son, Max. They stayed with Carly for weeks, enjoying the island's windblown beaches and being treated like royalty by Carly and her staff. Carly and Irons worked on the video's treatment, the idea being that they would make the film when Irons returned to the Vineyard later on.

Carly later wrote, "I was so close to him that summer we made a video together. I found him to be a sweet and funny man. Jeremy and I did have a 'special' and dramatically fun time when he came back in September. He stayed in the Menemsha house. I think it was the first time I really 'did' cocaine. Jeremy was a fiercely caring person. I won't deny that he got me pregnant."

When Carly returned to New York as Sally and Ben started school, Irons followed her. Peter Simon: "My wife Ronni and I were living in New York then, and so we hung around a lot with Carly and Jeremy. They were a great couple, very loving with each other while we were around them. He was a good man, obviously very charming, and obviously reminded her of Willie Donaldson. I think he said his marriage was pretty much over. Carly told us she was very fond of him."

After Jeremy Irons returned to London, Carly discovered she was pregnant. Whether or not she told Jeremy Irons is unknown, but she did consider having his child. Her doctors and everyone else didn't think it was a good idea, and she underwent an abortion. Eventually Irons broke up with his wife, and everyone moved on in their brilliant careers. Carly: "And however many other children he went on to sire and spend Father's Day with, I am not surprised and I wish them well. It [the abortion] is still a terrible source of pain and guilt for me."

COMING AROUND AGAIN

‒‒‒

$\mathcal{W}$ith nine credited producers, it took a long time for Epic to roll out *Spoiled Girl,* but Carly's fourteenth album finally emerged in September 1985. For the cover, Carly posed for New York photographer Duane Michals as the blasé spoiled girl in fashionably basic black. As a mid-career rethink, the album was a disaster. The first single, "Tired of Being Blonde," stalled at number seventy, but Jeremy Irons's video, with its cross cutting and parallel storylines, got into MTV's rotation and proved more popular than either the song or the album, which reached only number eighty-eight. Carly later wrote, "I had had records that didn't perform in the past, but *Spoiled Girl really* didn't perform. It was my first 'bona fide' flop—because not only did it not do well, but also because I didn't like it. If you make a record that's true to yourself, and you love the work, it can't be a flop. It can only sell poorly."

Around this time, Carly became romantically involved with Russ Kunkel. It happened one evening when her phone rang on Central Park West. Al Corley was calling from the nearby restaurant he had opened with some partners. Carly: "He said I'd never guess who just came in. It was James and Kathryn, and they were with Russ Kunkel. I told Al not to say anything and that I would shortly make an appearance, just to see what might happen." This situation was also intriguing to Carly because James and his star drummer had parted ways after James admitted to Russ that he'd had an affair with Russ's wife, Leah, when they were recording "Handy Man," which Leah sang on. Russ was angry at this betrayal and stopped playing with James, his place often taken by Rick Marotta.

Carly swanned into the restaurant, pretended to be surprised, and was pointedly not invited to join the diners, even though the fourth chair was empty. So she stood there and chatted up Russ. Kathryn was glaring daggers at her. James looked down at his supper, smoke pouring out of his ears. (He had recently asked, through management channels, that Carly stop talking about their marriage in interviews.) Just as Kunkel worried that the scene was getting too uncomfortable, Carly gave him her phone number and invited him to call her if he was in town for a while. As she began to walk away, Kathryn reached over to comfort an upset James, but her angora sweater accidentally brushed the table candle and caught fire. There was a flurry, and water was sprayed. Carly dined out on this for months.

Russ Kunkel called Carly, and she invited him to lunch. He told her she looked great, and she was attracted to him: a tall, balding, talented, and relaxed guy. He went back to L.A., rented out his house, flew to New York, and moved in with Carly and the children. By the end of 1985, Carly and Russ had announced their engagement. And that December, James married Kathryn Walker.

The problem was that the dinner Carly had crashed was about Russ rejoining James's band. Now there was major awkwardness, because James didn't want Carly at his concerts, either out front or backstage. Carly told an interviewer: "I fell in love with Russ and he with me. But he was working with James and I wasn't allowed to go to the shows. I didn't get involved with Russ to get closer to James, as some accused me of doing—talking behind my back of course. For me it was very difficult."

After some time had passed, Carly and Russ decided to see what would happen if Carly came to a show. One night they walked through the stage door hand in hand. When James found out she was there, he freaked. No one could recall seeing James Taylor that angry before. After the show, Peter Asher had to take the drummer aside for a quiet word. Maybe, James's longtime manager advised, being engaged to his boss's ex-wife was not the greatest idea in the world. "It made my boss feel uncomfortable," Kunkel recalled, long after Carly canceled their engagement the following year. (Another night, Kathryn Walker had Carly thrown out of Radio City Music Hall, where James had announced his marriage to Carly in 1972.)

But in the period she was with Russ, Carly was relatively happy and also wrote and performed some of her best music in years. Russ may have been an uncomplicated guy, but he was kind to her, always available, extremely encouraging, and not competitive at all. "He was loving and very guiding, which is something I really needed at the time, especially in my work. I can honestly say that he was more important than anyone else in my musical education. He taught me to be self-taught. He was an enthusiastic and knowledgeable audience, and he was definitely not in competition with me at all."

Russ would also prove an invaluable helper when, in mid-1985, Mike Nichols asked Carly to write the music for *Heartburn,* a new film he was directing starring Jack Nicholson and Meryl Streep.

Carly had known Nichols since the days of the Simon Sisters. The comedy duo of Nichols and (Elaine) May was one of the funniest acts in cabaret, and then Nichols had branched out into making big-budget movies for Hollywood producers. He and his wife, television personality Diane Sawyer, were Carly's neighbors both in New York and Martha's Vineyard, which gave Carly an extra comfort zone with this commission. Nichols wanted a great theme from Carly, as he privately thought the script was a little weak. *Heartburn* was originally a roman à clef by Nora Ephron—another Upper West Side neighbor—loosely based on her failed marriage to Watergate reporter Carl Bernstein. Nichols told Carly the script was a little depressing, and didn't end happily. The music had to offer some hope, an idea of redemption, and the chance that love could be reborn. Carly was thrilled by the challenge from one of the best theatrical minds in America and was determined to succeed.

Carly: " 'Coming Around Again' was the fulfillment of what the spider began. I had a nice piano part; it was rhythmic and unusual for spiders. I began singing 'Itsy Bitsy Spider,' which was the song I wanted to use over the end credits of *Heartburn*. It sounded catchy enough for me to see what else would fit over the chord progression. I thought a bookend like that would be nice for this particular movie and of course less work for me! I quizzed Nora Ephron about what Meryl's character was feeling at different points in the plot. She gave me lots of images, some of which I used or adapted, such as 'burn the soufflé.'

"Then Mike Nichols and I had a huddle over what the chorus should emotionally impart. I said, 'How do you hear the chorus as speaking? What message? What's the "thing,"—what word?'

" 'Again,' he said, *'Again.'* Then Mike said: 'Around, Around . . . you know, *Around.'* And I said, 'You mean, *around again?*' And he said 'Yes, that's it.' Then somewhere the word 'coming' was put in front of the phrase and the song started to become whole.

"Meanwhile, the spider has never been lost. Both songs ["Coming Around Again" and "Itsy Bitsy Spider"]—if you want to disconnect them—are from the myth of Sisyphus. The little chap spider is climbing up the water spout, only to be dunked down again by the rain, while the poor wife in the movie is trying and trying and trying to push this big rock called 'Marriage' up the hill, and they are constantly faltering and the rock is slipping back. But: it's *only* if you're willing to play the game, that it will be coming around again."

"Coming Around Again" and "Itsy Bitsy Spider" were recorded by Carly in New York in late 1985. Russ Kunkel was crucial in musical supervision and all aspects of production. Carly: "Russ helped me so much. He set up machines in my living room and made me play bass parts I didn't know how to play. He was a major force, someone who helped me develop some measure of self-confidence. He never got enough credit as far as I was concerned."

In all, four producers were credited. The sessions were held at Right Track and the Power Station. (Russ and Bill Payne also contributed to the film's score.) "Coming Around Again" emerged as a majestic restatement of the hope and belief in the power of love. When Clive Davis, the president of Arista Records, who once had thrown a Carly Simon demo tape across his office, heard "Coming Around Again," he signed Carly to a record deal that resulted in a decade-long creative flowering that completely revitalized her career.

When Meryl Streep and Nora Ephron heard "Coming Around Again" for the first time, they both wept. Carly's song was more than perfect. Every woman knew that there was more room in a broken heart for memories, dreams, reflections.

Heartburn was shot in New York and Washington that winter. Jack Nicholson was caddish and cool. Libby Titus had a part. So did Kevin Spacey, Milos Forman, and chanteuse Karen Akers (and John Lennon's old girlfriend May Pang). Released late in 1986, *Heartburn* was a commercial success but a critical bomb, a film too angry and distraught to be a comedy. Carly Simon's anthemic songs, evangelizing for the sake of love, were the only rays of hope in a bleak tale of adultery, betrayal, and gamely trying to move on.

The Seduction of Carly Simon

$\mathcal{I}$n early 1986, Carly consulted longtime friend Karen Thorne, who worked as an astrologer and spiritual adviser. A chart was drawn up, oracles consulted, cards read. Karen predicted that in the coming dispensation of time, Carly would have enormous professional success; her next single would be a big hit; and also that she would marry a tall man with a very high forehead. Carly took heart from these predictions. She probably already knew that the tall man she would take as a husband would not be Russ Kunkel.

Then, in late January 1985, something awful happened. A schoolteacher called Christa McAuliffe was a passenger on the space shuttle *Challenger*. She was to become the first teacher in space. Millions of children would watch the launch on television. She was also an avid Carly Simon fan and had announced she was carrying Carly's cassettes with her into orbit. Carly was watching at home when *Challenger* exploded seventy-three seconds into the flight. All seven astronauts perished, and national trauma ensued.

But Carly plunged into her work. She had to write an album for

Clive Davis now, and was out of practice. She hadn't much liked her last two albums. But now she looked around her world and family for inspiration, and ended up with one of the most successful song-books of her career.

Summer 1986. Caroline Kennedy, only daughter of the late pres-ident, married Edwin Schlossberg, a museum consultant, on Cape Cod. Carly entertained the wedding guests that evening at the Ken-nedy family compound in Hyannisport. This is where Carly became close to the bride's mother, Jacqueline Kennedy Onassis, then twice widowed and the owner of the most spectacular beachfront estate on Martha's Vineyard. Carly hit it off with Jackie immediately, and soon Mrs. Onassis was calling with lunch invitations, ostensibly to discuss possible book projects, since Jackie was by then a hardwork-ing editor at Doubleday, the old New York publishing house.

One day that summer, Carly had an epiphany at the Vineyard house. She was going through compartments in the guitar closet when she found "a little assemblage" of James Taylor's stuff: a guitar string, some twine, some burnt-out matches, wire-rimmed glasses with a lens missing, and a crumpled Polaroid snapshot of Carly. She shud-dered to remember that he had been gone from the house for five years, and yet he was so much in evidence: His fishing rod still hung above the sliding doors in the living room. The Plexiglas panels he'd nailed into the windows still kept out the winter chill. They also turned the room into a summer inferno, but Carly had never wanted to change anything because it was the last remaining part of the house James had built before she knew him.

Later Carly sat down and wrote an epistolary memoir about finding traces of her husband. The stuff she had found were the con-tents of pockets that got too full. James used to empty his pockets almost at random, anywhere in the house. These collections would turn up on top of the fridge, under a bed, or spill on a window ledge. Their contents now seemed to describe to Carly the pain her husband must have been in. "What I once saw as a sort of hectic masculine jubilee," she wrote, "I now see as something terribly poignant."

The house, Carly wrote, was a perfect metaphor for their marriage. Everyone who visited the house thought it uniquely beautiful, like a Russian church or a Bavarian castle. "Only you and I know it was a folly. . . . We were like two maniacs posted at the gates of domesticity, feverishly going about preventing anything really comfortable from happening. . . . Still I go on living in this flamboyant white elephant, and I am constantly reminded of my whole other life."

By the end of the memoir, Carly decides to take stock. She remembered how she tried to move into a new bedroom after James had gone. She renovated the children's old playroom, above the living room, and furnished it with a lilac carpet, chintzes in floral patterns, stained-glass portraits of Ben and Sally, antique lamps, and a brass bed. She hated it, and moved back into the marital bedroom.

"But I have to try again," she wrote. This time it had to be the living room that got a rethink. So the old blue guitar would go into the basement, along with the joke crèche, and the cowbells James brought home from Greece, and the broken lantern from the '76 hurricane. Same with the Plexiglas windows and his surf-casting rod. "I am sorry," she wrote. "I won't throw anything away; there's lots of room in the basement still, but there will be no inventory. No need. I'll quite easily be able to remember everything."

Carly's untitled memoir was known to close friends by its first line: "I used to have a whole other life." Later in the year, she sent the text to Jacqueline Onassis at Doubleday. Jackie called her immediately and asked her to expand the memoir into a book proposal and a sample chapter, but by then Carly and a phalanx of musicians and producers were furiously writing her first album for Arista Records. The idea of a written memoir was put aside, and Carly disappeared into New York studios for the next six months.

In early 1987, Clive Davis was at the top of his game. After being dismissed as head of CBS Records for financial malfeasance, he had founded Arista Records in 1974 with backing from Columbia Pictures. His biggest coup to date was transforming the stunning model Whitney Houston into one of the biggest pop stars of the day, someone who could stand onstage with Michael Jackson and hold her own. Melissa Manchester, a big-voiced belter, was another of Clive's successes. Arista also nurtured the careers of female talent such as Carly's heroine Martha Reeves and Diana Ross. Clive Davis was very hands-on: he chose songs, hired and fired producers, listened to every track, every remix. Now, after hearing some of the new songs Carly was bringing to the studio—"Give Me All Night," "All I Want Is You"—Davis ordered the schedule sped up. He wanted the new album out in the spring of 1987. As executive producer, Clive Davis now oversaw the work of nine different producers as Carly shuttled between Manhattan studios during the winter of that year.

Carly and those close to her realized that the quality of her music had matured into something more sophisticated, and more deeply loving, and this was reflected in the hectic recording sessions for the album that would be called *Coming Around Again*. Paul Samwell-Smith flew in from London and helped Carly and Russ remix "Coming Around Again," which would open the album and be the crucial first single. Samwell-Smith also worked on "Give Me All Night," a jaunty rock song demanding night-long lust; "Do The Walls Come Down," a plea for access to a former lover, sonically burdened with useless eighties synthesizers (Track keyboard emulator, Linn drums, Steiner electronic wind instrument, etc.); and "Two Hot Girls (On a Hot Summer Night)."

Carly: "The previous summer [1986] my friend Jenny and I got dressed to the nines and went into Oak Bluffs on Martha's Vineyard to see and be seen. ('More for a drink and to have a few eyes on us.') During the evening we were joined by a friend of mine who started hitting on Jenny so ardently that I felt invisible. I immediately began resenting a great friend with whom there'd been no previous evidence of rivalry." After a few days, Carly started singing "Me and Jenny, twinkling like crystal and pennies." She told the story of the evening in four simple verses (ABAB) with a bridge before the last chorus. "It's my narrative story form, one I'm very attracted to, like the ballads I used to sing, where the final chorus has a kind of irony, meaning something quite different when all the facts are on the table." Michael Brecker played a jazzy sax solo on the track, and Lucy Simon joined her sister to sing harmony on the song's delicate choruses.

"All I Want Is You" was written by Andy Goldmark, with lyrics by Carly and Jake Brackman. "So chase me 'round the room / Make me crazy like the moon." "That song is Stanley Kowalski territory," Carly says, referring to the iconic brutish hunk in Tennessee Williams's *A Streetcar Named Desire,* famously played onstage and on-screen by the young Marlon Brando in a wife-beater. "It is about flaming love and the lovely screams and passion that is so thrilling to me. The screams used to be misinterpreted by well-meaning neighbors who may in fact still call the police during the climax of the scene. Anyway, Andy Goldmark wrote the chord changes. Jacob [Brackman] collaborated with me on the words." The track was expertly produced by the New York musician John Boylan and featured the soul singer Roberta Flack. Boylan also coproduced (with Russ and engineer Frank Filipetti) "The Stuff That Dreams Are Made Of," another much-anthologized fan favorite. The song was an unflinching hymn to the ideals of marriage and fidelity, an affirmation of marriage addressed to a friend who was bored with her husband. Carly: "'The Stuff That Dreams Are Made Of' was written for a friend of mine who was about to leave an absolutely unhysterical marriage for the temporary relief of passion. She was my wondrously talented assistant at the time. Her husband found her love letters (as is the custom) and she was 'outed.' I was trying to reveal that she had to be partially responsible for setting the stars off in her own backyard and making the prince on the horse in the fairy tale the man she was about to become pregnant by: her husband. Of course, I rarely believe in my own best ideas, so I had to come up with some pretty nice key changes, going into the bridge." The result was some of the most heartfelt singing of Carly's career, with a stirring gospel feel at the song's climax supplied by the Reverend Timothy Wright Concert Choir.

Other tracks included a version of Joe Tex's "Hold What You've Got," produced by Richard Perry and arranged by Leon Pendarvis, with additional words and music by Carly. Clive Davis insisted Carly record "It Should Have Been Me," by Canadian rocker Bryan Adams and song doctor Jim Vallance. Adams produced a generic track for Carly, and reportedly had her in tears in the studio because he kept insisting she sing like the guy in Journey. The album was filled out with the torchy "You Have to Hurt" and Herman Hupfeld's 1931 "As Time Goes By," immortalized in the film *Casablanca*. This chestnut was produced by Ron Mounsey, a talented musician and arranger who worked on many of the album's tracks, and then began to play an increasingly crucial role in Carly's music. The album, like *Heartburn,* would conclude with the spider, still trying to get up the water spout. The kids' chorus included Sally and Ben Taylor and their cousins Alexandra and Isaac, children of James's brother Hugh.

When the new album was finished, so were Carly and Russ Kunkel. The engagement was called off. Nobody had really expected her to marry him anyway. There was a major cultural gap between the songwriter and her handsome drummer. Leah Kunkel later said that, with Carly Simon, her ex-husband was in over his head. Carly's publicist issued a statement.

Also, Carly had recently met someone else.

She'd taken the Metro North train that ran up the east bank of the Hudson River to work on lyrics with Jake, who lived upstate. He was married to a charismatic musician, Mindy Jostyn; they had a couple of kids, and Carly felt comfortable there. Carly and Jake worked on lyrics, and on Sunday evening Jake drove her to the train station. Also waiting for the train to Manhattan was a friend of

Jake's, a thirty-seven-year-old insurance salesman and aspiring poet (shades of Wallace Stevens) named Jim Hart. When the train pulled into the station, Carly and Jake said their good-byes and Carly boarded the train. Jim Hart was intrigued. (He later claimed that he hadn't known who Carly was, explaining that he wasn't a music fan. Another time, he said he thought she might have been Linda Ronstadt.) A few minutes later, Hart found Carly seated in the train reading a book. He asked if he could join her, and began chatting away.

She checked him out. He was tall, balding, quite good-looking. He was a brilliant conversationalist, with a self-deprecating Irish gift of gab. He had an ex-wife and a severely disabled child, whom he had been visiting when they were introduced. He'd studied to be a Catholic priest. He was a recovering alcoholic. His father had been some kind of gangster. He wanted to write. She took to him immediately. So did her mother, who flirted with him outrageously. Jake Brackman told Carly that Jim Hart was a good guy. Carly told her astrologer that sex with Jim was better than good. He was tall, balding, and also named James. Years later, Hart remembered that fateful journey by train: "I seduced Carly Simon. Pretty cool, eh?"

DREAMERS WAKE THE NATION

———

$\mathcal{A}$rista Records released *Coming Around Again* in April 1987. The title song got on the radio, surging to number five on the adult contemporary chart. The album sold in the millions, Carly's first record in nine years to reach platinum status. Three Top Ten chart singles followed: "Give Me All Night" (number five), "The Stuff That Dreams Are Made Of" (number eight), and "All I Want Is You" (number seven). Conventional wisdom was that Carly Simon's star had faded, but now it shone once again. This new success, in her early forties, reinvigorated Carly's muse, gave her serious new street cred in the music industry, and also firmly established her credentials as a writer whose contributions to the American songbook had to be taken seriously.

Clive Davis boasted to Arista's hard-charging promo staff that he could force Carly Simon to tour, but that didn't happen. Instead Carly was invited by the Home Box Office cable television network to star in one of their "HBO Specials." Carly didn't want to leave the

Vineyard, so HBO and an eighty-man production crew built a clever stage set that looked like a fishing shack on a stone jetty overlooking Menemsha Harbor. For two nights in June 1987, Carly Simon (dressed in flowing pastels, bobby socks and sneakers, a white duster, pearl drop earrings, and wampum jewelry crafted by Kate Taylor) performed songs from the new album and some greatest hits with an eight-man band directed by Tom "T-Bone" Wolk, with Rick Marotta on drums. For security concerns, the audiences of invited guests were bused in from island parking lots at the last minute. These were reported to be Carly's first concerts in eight years.

The weather had been terrible for a week. HBO desperately needed a balmy night in early June on Martha's Vineyard, a stone rarity. Serious sea fog was more the norm. The first night, the wind blew in hard from Vineyard Sound and the entire taped footage was unusable. It was so cold the musicians' fingers were cramping. The second night, the atmosphere was still, and the concert was shot in the golden light of a New England summer sunset. Seagulls landed on the set, pink clouds streaked the sky, and fishing boats returning to port glided through the channel behind the stage. Carly asked Ricky Marotta not to rush the beat on the rock songs. Highlights included "Nobody Does It Better," which opened the program; Jimmy Ryan's guitar solo on "You're So Vain" and great singing on "The Right Thing to Do." Michael Brecker played blistering sax on "You Belong to Me" and "Two Hot Girls." The capper was "Coming Around Again," with a troupe of six Taylor children appearing in a coup de théâtre to sing "Itsy Bitsy Spider."

The HBO special *Carly Simon Live from Martha's Vineyard* was broadcast later that summer, to unusually high ratings. The following year, eleven songs from the concert were released on VHS video and on Carly's first ever concert recording, *Greatest Hits Live.*

Carly's uncle Peter Dean died that year. At his funeral in New York, Carly and her sisters were approached by any number of attractive women of a certain age, many of them African American, who were eager to express their condolences and let the Simon sisters know how close they had been to their wonderful uncle, and how much they had loved him.

~

Late 1987. Carly and a reporter were walking down Central Park West on their way to an interview lunch. There were giant posters of Carly's smiling face along the broad avenue and everywhere in New York, an almost surreal effect for her, as the city's bus stops advertised her endorsement of *McCall's,* a venerable magazine for women. Suddenly, out of nowhere, a little man approached Carly carrying a large book. The book was a collection of photographs taken by *Rolling Stone*'s Annie Leibovitz in the seventies, and the man wanted Carly to autograph her page. This was the image of a perspiring James Taylor carrying Carly Simon, piggyback style, neither wearing much, that had been published in *Rolling Stone* in 1979. The little man handed Carly a pen, but as she was about to sign, she noticed that the autograph hound had already gotten to James Taylor. In precise lettering, James had carefully written, "A NARROW ESCAPE," and drawn an arrow pointing at himself. Carly was flustered at this, but signed the book anyway. (It was a spurned autograph hunter who had murdered John Lennon in the same neighborhood, so she preferred to take no chances.)

She married James Hart at St. Andrew's Episcopal Church in Edgartown, Martha's Vineyard, on December 23, 1987. The couple honeymooned on the neighboring island of Nantucket. The children celebrated Christmas with James and his wife. Jim Hart kept his small bachelor's apartment in New York and lived with Carly, mostly on the Vineyard. He resolved to write a novel, befriended Mike Nichols and some of Carly's other friends, and was quickly accepted into her tight social circle. Carly's old friends, who had tried in vain to start conversations with shoe-gazing James Taylor, could hardly get the new guy to shut up.

Carly took a call from Mike Nichols again in late 1987. He wanted her to score an entire film this time. *Working Girl* would star Harrison Ford, Melanie Griffith, and Sigourney Weaver. The script was a Cinderella tale of a Staten Island secretary, working on Wall Street, who attracts the company's boss. (This was Carly's mother's story as well.) Nichols wanted another big anthem like "Coming Around Again" and also wordless interludes for moods and scene changes. Carly spent most of 1988 working on the music, coming up with "Let the River Run" as her clarion paean to hope and achievement. Once "the river" in her lyrics had only referred to sexuality and desire. Now the river ran more gently through the experience of life itself. Jim Hart gave Carly the dreamers awakening the nation and the notion of a New Jerusalem, familiar to him from William Blake and almost all the Romantic poets. Producer Rob Mounsey gave the track an urban jungle feeling with big drums and a gospel choir. Big rhythms, rock guitar, and a booming vocal from Carly gave the song incredible momentum and drive. Mike Nichols loved it.

Carly wrote several pretty, sentimental love themes for use in the film, which were orchestrated by Don Sebesky. One of these, "Carlotta's Heart," has a wordless Carly vocal as well. Another has Carly singing over the famous boys' choir of St. Thomas's Church on Fifth Avenue. The *Working Girl* soundtrack is filled out with contributions from pianist Grady Tate, Rob Mounsey, vintage Sonny Rollins, and the Pointer Sisters. There was a last-minute crisis when the studio wanted to replace "Let the River Run" with something by the Eagles. Mike Nichols prevailed, and "Witchy Woman" stayed out of the picture.

Working Girl arrived in movie theaters in December 1988 and was an instant success, earning more than a hundred million dollars at the box office. The soundtrack was released by Arista in early 1989, and "Let the River Run" was a national hit single. Carly's movie music began to attract shiny statuettes: a Grammy and a Golden Globe. The Academy of Motion Picture Arts and Sciences took note and nominated her for an Oscar.

Jacqueline Onassis called Carly in early 1988 and invited her to a business lunch in Manhattan. She described to Carly her harrowing experience with Michael Jackson, then the biggest star in the world, who seemed to be reneging on a deal to publish the ghostwritten memoirs that Jackie had commissioned. Mrs. Onassis asked Carly for advice on how to deal with Jackson and his management. (Jackson's book, *Moon Walk,* was published in 1988 and became an international bestseller.)

Jackie explained that, as an editor at Doubleday, she had mostly published books about the fine arts, ballet, and décor. But her bosses were asking her to acquire autobiographies by celebrities, and Jackie said that she had a feeling that Carly had an incredible story and a great book in her. Carly later wrote: "I didn't say 'no,' but I didn't mean 'yes.' In fact, I tried because it was Jackie." In a flurry of concentrated remembrance that summer, Carly wrote eighty pages of a memoir about her parents and their family. Then she tore the pages up in a burst of self-recrimination about what she was revealing. "I could talk about my own life, with all its long and shortcomings, but not those of other people. It was impossible."

Next Jackie suggested to Carly that she write a children's book, or a series of books, that drew on her experiences as a child and the stories she had told her own children. So Carly wrote a text about a little girl who couldn't get to sleep and eventually came up with a solution that magically let her (and her mother) get some rest. Doubleday gave Carly twenty-five thousand dollars as an advance. Carly gave half of the advance to Margot Datz, a Vineyard artist who had painted murals at Carly's house and her nightclub. As Carly began working with Jackie they became good friends, sharing working lunches, occasional movies in New York, cigarettes, and confidences. (Jackie had a major crush on Massachusetts senator John

Kerry, who reminded her of Jack Kennedy if he had lived longer.) Carly found Jackie, then sixty, to be reassuring and fascinating, an idealized paradigm of her own mother. Jackie moved around Manhattan in taxis and town cars, incognito, with no bodyguards or the Secret Service protection to which she was entitled as a former First Lady. When discussing Carly's book project, Jackie made clever suggestions about the text and illustrations in a soothing, collaborative manner that Carly found flattering. Carly felt that Jackie was trying to almost bond with her imagination, because all her comments were so insightful.

Carly later said she thought Jackie was sympathetic to her because she was so incapable of hiding her feelings that Jackie could be herself—"the eighth grader she really was"—when she was with Carly. "I wasn't deferential to her. I would swear and cuss. Jackie loved naughtiness." But at first this insouciance came with a price. "I tried so hard to act the part of being relaxed around her that I would come home with a stiff neck and a migraine headache. After a while, it became much easier, especially on the Vineyard. I have a circular garden, and we would sit there and have little sandwiches—smoked salmon, watercress. Jackie loved to eat."

Carly's first book, *Amy the Dancing Bear,* was published in 1989 and sold unusually well, reportedly over a hundred thousand copies. Doubleday then asked for another book from Carly and Margot, again offering a twenty-five-thousand-dollar advance, which Carly accepted. The next time they met for lunch, Jackie asked how much the company had paid her. When Carly told her, Mrs. Onassis took off her sunglasses, looked wide-eyed at Carly, and whispered, "Carly—you got *screwwwed*!"

Carly recalled, "All the children's books had fragments of my life, to be sure. (My life as a bear, for instance.) Jackie was a wonderful editor. Over the years I did four books with her." The second book, *The Boy of the Bells,* a Christmas story, was published in 1990 and concerns a boy who enlisted Santa Claus's help in helping his mute sister regain her voice. *The Fisherman's Song* (1991) is about a girl whose lover (the illustrations made him look a lot like a young James Taylor) sadly leaves her alone on a far-off island. The final book in this collaboration, *The Nighttime Chauffeur,* is about a boy named Ben who wants to drive the Central Park carriages all night. Carly has said that the books she wrote for Jackie were high points in her career, and ended only with Mrs. Onassis's death in 1994.

In the summer of 1988, Carly took her children out of the Manhattan schools and moved the family to Martha's Vineyard full time. She and her husband redesigned the vegetable garden that she and James Taylor had planted fifteen years earlier, in 1973. A doctor diagnosed Carly's stage fright as an inner ear disorder and prescribed low doses of Inderal, one of the so-called "beta blockers" designed to combat anxiety and panic disorders.

In September, Sally Taylor went off to boarding school in Massachusetts while Ben, now eleven, was sent through the island's public school system. Jim Hart, who was now attending AA meetings, was attentive and helpful; there was little drama between Carly and her second husband, which is perhaps one reason why the next few years were very productive for her.

CARLY COMES TO DINNER

―――

*C*arly worked on two albums in 1989. The first was *My Romance,* her second album of standards from the American songbook. Clive Davis wanted an album of new songs, but Carly was written out from the *Working Girl* project. So Arista agreed to a svelte album of classic songs instead.

My Romance was recorded with a live orchestra at the Power Station in New York during two weeks in January. Carly worked on the vocal arrangements at the piano in her Manhattan apartment with arranger Michael Kosarin before the sessions, and gave the tapes to the legendary Marty Paich, who wrote the orchestrations. Most of the songs were downbeat and torchy, inspired by the albums Frank Sinatra made with Nelson Riddle in the fifties. Carly chose familiar songs by Rodgers and Hart, Rodgers and Hammerstein, Howard Dietz, and Arthur Schwartz, as well as "Danny Boy" (dedicated to Allie Brennan, who, Carly wrote, "lullabyed me with 'Danny Boy' when all else failed to pacify me"). Carly wrote one original song, "What Has She Got?" with Jake Brackman and Michael Kosarin, about being envious of a female rival. The recording ensemble included drummer Steve Gadd, two bassists, and a forty-piece orchestra.

"Let the River Run" had been released as a single at the beginning of the year. During the sessions for *My Romance*, Carly's single got to number five on the adult contemporary chart and number forty-nine on the Hot 100.

Carly and Jim went to the Academy Awards ceremony in March 1989. "Let the River Run" had been nominated by the movie industry in the category of Best Song. Carly knew she wasn't going to win, but everyone insisted that she attend the Oscars. At the hotel, she took a long time dressing and being styled, and in the end wasn't happy with her hair. But it didn't matter anyway, because no way did she think she had a chance of winning. On the way into the Shrine Auditorium in Santa Monica, she spied fellow nominee Phil Collins on the red carpet and almost fell over herself telling him that she was unworthy and that he would surely win. Carly later said she had no memory of winning, or of getting to the stage to accept the gold statuette. She managed to thank her husband by name "for the best lines in the song" before the music came up and the presenters led her off to the press room, where flash cameras strobed at her like a million suns.

Carly was dazed and exhausted. Outside the Shrine, Oscar in hand, she sat down on the curb to wait for her limousine and was nearly trampled by hordes of Hollywood types rushing to get to their limos first as the ceremony was ending. "Let the River Run" was the first movie theme to win all three major industry awards. The Oscar, the Grammy, and the Golden Globe all went up on the mantel of the Vineyard house.

Then Mike Nichols called again. He was working on his next film, an adaptation of Carrie Fisher's 1987 novel *Postcards from the Edge*. He wanted another grand theme from Carly, another compulsively listenable song to play as the credits rolled on a story about fighting addictions (and your mother). Carly came up with the slightly spooky song "Have You Seen Me Lately?" Meryl Streep recorded the version that was supposed to be used in the film. Nichols liked it, but Carrie Fisher apparently didn't, and the song was removed from the credit crawl of the (mediocre) movie at the last minute. Carly would use the song as the keystone of her next album of original songs, about which Clive Davis was already pestering her management.

Summer 1989. James Taylor took Sally and Ben on his annual tour of the nation's "sheds," outdoor suburban amphitheaters. Fifteen-year-old Sally was singing backup along with James's famous singers Rosemary Butler and Arnold McCuller. James was now an exercise buff, and he often took the children on hiking or sailing trips, and on yearly vacations to remote locations for exploration and discovery.

On Martha's Vineyard, Carly had built a large swimming pool, and a party barn for events she hosted to benefit the island's charities, and an occasional politician (all Democrats). She usually offered herself as a prize in the annual Vineyard Community Services celebrity auction run by the ancient newspaper humorist Art Buchwald. High bidders could buy a day of sailing with newscaster Walter Cronkite on his yacht, get some depressing literary advice from novelist Bill Styron, or Carly Simon would come to their houses and make them lunch. Or sing a song. (Usually both.) Carly's prizes were often the auction's top earners. This year, the auction included a tour of the *Ghostbusters II* movie set, hosted by its producer, Dan Aykroyd; a tour of *The Washington Post,* with its owner, Katharine Graham; and a picnic at Chip Chop, a famous Old Vineyard summer house formerly owned by the actress Katharine Cornell, now the seasonal home of Mike Nichols and Diane Sawyer.

Carly, looking summery tanned and rail-thin, joined Art Buchwald at the Edgartown hotel podium for the action of the item labeled "Carly Comes to Dinner." He opened the bidding at three hundred dollars and then coaxed it to five thousand and then ten. Then, cheered on by their attractive blond wives, two youngish Connecticut businessmen in blue blazers and red flannel trousers went at it ham-mer and tongs, matching bids until Buchwald stopped the bidding at twenty-six thousand dollars. After consulting with Carly, Buchwald announced that for twenty-six grand apiece, Carly would come and sing three songs in each of their homes. Carly would also bring peanut-butter-and-jelly sandwiches. "It was the least I could do," she told the venerable *Vineyard Gazette* newspaper.

One afternoon that summer, Carly was having lunch with some people at her mother's house. The other guests were her mother's neighbors, plus a prominent Chilmark selectman (a New England town official) and his wife. Andrea Simon was feeling somewhat peevish, and was suffering from diverticulitis, an intestinal disorder. (She wasn't allowed to eat anything with seeds; this removed straw-berries from the menu, which annoyed her.) Someone raised a glass and proposed a toast to Carly for winning the Oscar. Andrea raised her glass and told Carly, "You're *not* the best singer, you're *not* the best composer, but you *did* get the Oscar." Carly was very wounded by this. Later, one of the lingering guests chided Andrea, accusing her of being jealous of Carly. "You're *damned right* I'm jealous of Carly," the old woman said with a laugh. She later called her daugh-ter to apologize.

September 1989. Mick Jagger was calling. The Rolling Stones would tour America again that fall, after a disagreeable hiatus of eight years. (It had been an incredible *nineteen years* since the found-ing of the group.) Carly promised Mick she would come to one of the band's concerts when the tour arrived in New York. But her husband, Jim, had by then heard all the gossipy stories and idle speculation about the fabled relationship between his wife and Mick Jagger. James Hart was as jealous of Mick Jagger as James Taylor had been, if not more so.

Then Mrs. Onassis called. Her son, John Kennedy Jr., then twenty-nine and a recent law school graduate, had just failed the New York State bar exam—for the second time. This wasn't cool. (*New*

York Post: "Hunk Flunks!") John was a Rolling Stones fan, and now his mother asked Carly (her author) to take him to the Stones concert and introduce him to Mick Jagger, in the hope that this would pick up JFK Jr.'s spirits. Carly called John, who protested that he was too humiliated to appear in public, but Carly went into her "Auntie Carlton" mode, and persuaded the young Kennedy heir to come to the show.

The Stones' epochal 1989 *Steel Wheels* tour arrived in New York in October 1989. These stadium shows, projected to audiences via immense JumboTron video screens, were a huge comeback for the once self-proclaimed "greatest rock-and-roll band in the world." Carly rode out to Giants Stadium in New Jersey with her party. A meeting with Jagger before the show had been arranged, but as they moved through the crowded, mazelike corridors of the lower stadium, they were told that only three people—Carly, Ben Taylor, and John Kennedy—would be allowed into Jagger's dressing room.

Jim Hart waited in the hall outside and fumed. He had an acute sense of social radar, and understood that his exclusion was no accident. He was also frustrated because Carly was supporting him while he was trying to write a novel, and the writing wasn't going well. "I was out-of-my-mind jealous about Carly being with Jagger," he said later. He glared at Carly during the show, which disturbed John Kennedy. At the end of the evening, back at Carly's apartment, Hart raged at her. He had sometimes lost his temper when Carly's incessant fears and irrational phobias got the better of him, but now Hart was so angry that Ben Taylor, age twelve, dialed 911. Carly locked herself in the bedroom while two New York City cops got her husband to calm down. Carly stopped taking Mick Jagger's calls—at least for a while.

POSITIVE AFFIRMATIONS

———

Carly Simon's second album of American songs, *My Romance*, was released in January 1990 and sold respectably, reaching number forty-six on the *Billboard*'s sales chart. The record's sexy retro-noir sleeve photos were shot by Bob Gothard. The album was dedicated to Allie Brennan and Frank Sinatra. Arista executives tried to get Carly to make some concert appearances with an orchestra but were turned down. Carly, it was explained, was too busy working on her next album of original songs, her first in four years, after the success of *Coming Around Again*. Her label settled for a commercial release on VHS video, of a second HBO Special studio concert Carly performed, supported by the New Orleans singer-pianist Harry Connick Jr. (This was titled *Carly in Concert: My Romance*.)

Carly spent the winter of 1990 working on songs with producers Paul Samwell-Smith and Frank Filipetti at the Power Station, using Steve Gadd and Will Lee on bass and a cast of New York studio pros. There had been a falling-out with musical collaborator Rob Mounsey, who reportedly felt deprived of credit (and perhaps a share of the

Oscar) for "Let the River Run." Now Carly turned to Swiss musician Matthias "Teese" Gohl, an associate of Andreas Vollenweider. Gohl would work with Carly on her recordings for much of the next decade.

The new songs were some of her best in years. "Better Not Tell Her" is a subversive song of romantic betrayal, inspired by Carly's affair with a Manhattan media mogul who was engaged to another woman. Carly: "This guy was courting his next wife, and I thought I would offer him a few words of wisdom even though, frankly, he was not a 'love' in any sense. And, more importantly, we never went to Spain like we do in the song. In fact, he went on to become my manager for some short, unworthy span of time, lost me a hundred thousand dollars, and disappeared back into the heavy mogul world."

With swirling flutes and Brazilian inflections, Carly reminds a former lover of their former rapture together. Guitarist Jay Berliner plays a Spanish guitar solo that conjures a forbidden tryst in the gardens of ancient Grenada.

The album's title song, "Have You Seen Me Lately?," was recycled from Carly's rejected movie theme. The mysterious song seems to move in and out of reality as a contented sleeper is reluctantly awakened from dreamtime, the way a recovering addict moves between levels of consciousness. The lyric asks, "Was I crazy?" and the listener already knows the answer before the question is asked.

The new album's main anthem is "Life Is Eternal," a philosophical meditation on approaching death in the raging age of AIDS, written with Teese Gohl. The eighties and early nineties were plague years for homosexual men, with many important artists of the period (among them Queen's Freddie Mercury and photographer Robert Mapplethorpe) dead or dying of an illness that destroyed the human immune system. New retroviral drugs had not yet come online, so hope and prayer were the (almost often futile) attempts to prolong the lives of sufferers whose only fault had been careless love and unprotected sex. Carly's lyrics had come from discussions with

Reverend Bill Eddy, a compassionate Vineyard minister who was friends with Carly. The song featured a synthetic but soulful solo by Michael Brecker and a soaring choral round—aimed at a far horizon—by a choir of Carly, Sally and Ben, niece Julie Levine, and Will Lee. (This song would become a beacon of hope in the nation's hospices as AIDS continued to be a scourge of the gay community.)

Carly's original plan was to name the album *Happy Birthday,* after one of the early songs she wrote for it. "Happy Birthday" is a bittersweet ditty about aging: feeling unwell, not having much sex, blown-out candles sputtering smoke and spoiling the birthday cake. She name-checks her brother and her mother and complains that now, growing ever older, "we're too good to be bad." Other songs include "Waiting at the Gate," about a woman married to an addict; "Holding Me Tonight," a Sting-like adultery-contemporary pop song; "It's Not Like Him," a New Age soap opera; "Don't Wrap It Up," in which a woman asserts her emotional needs, with no apology; "Fisherman's Song," featuring Lucy Simon and Judy Collins on backing vocals; and "We Just Got Here," a sweet lullaby about returning home to an island in hurricane season.

Carly also worked on other material in the summer of 1990. "Raining" is a pretty jingle written for her children to sing at the Chilmark Community Center on the Vineyard. (It would later be recorded for inclusion in Carly's 1995 anthology *Clouds in My Coffee.*) She and Andy Goldmark wrote "A Man Who Isn't Smooth" for an album by soul singer Thelma Houston, produced by Richard Perry. And Nora Ephron once again recruited Carly to work on music for the movie *This Is My Life,* which Ephron was directing, based on her script about another upwardly mobile New York woman.

Jackie Onassis called Carly late in August and invited her for a swim at her Chilmark estate. Over iced tea and salad, Jackie again pressed Carly for an autobiography, but again Carly explained that revealing her family's story was too much for her. Later, they were swimming in Jackie's pool when a helicopter flew over and hovered while photographs were being shot. "I guess they know *you're* here," Jackie quipped.

Have You Seen Me Lately? was released in September 1990 and was judged a success in terms of sales and reviews, which noted that the new album was better than *Coming Around Again*. The cable music channel VH-1 sent a crew to interview Carly, who described employing "positive affirmations" to avoid falling into "mental traps" of her own making. Jonathan Schwartz arrived on the Vineyard to interview her for a magazine profile. She explained that she felt most comfortable at home, and was reluctant even to leave her family's fenced-in compound. "I've got a lot of limitations in the outside world," she told Jonno. "I'm a hypochondriac. I'm claustrophobic. But I have a lot of interior life going, and that's what saves me." When Jonno asked about the novel her husband was supposed to be writing, Carly only rolled her eyes. Jake Brackman was also interviewed, and described Carly's relationships to that of a luxury hotel, where guests could be shuttled between floors at the whim of the management. Friends could find themselves in the penthouse one week and in the basement the next.

Arista released "Better Not Tell Her" as a single, which reached number four on the adult contemporary chart in October 1990. Carly, wearing a flowing red dress, appears in a flamenco-themed video for the song, which got into "heavy rotation" on VH-1. Early in 1991, "Holding Me Tonight" got to number thirty-six on the adult contemporary chart.

Whatever success the new album achieved for Carly, it was tempered by her daughter's leaving for boarding school on the mainland. Sally, now sixteen, went off to Tabor Academy on the southeastern Massachusetts coast. This left Carly feeling bereft, and she drew her son, Ben, even closer to her. (Ben, fourteen, was unhappy at the various schools he attended, and would later be diagnosed with dyslexia.) Carly's spirits were raised when she was asked to sing with the great operatic tenor Placido Domingo for an album of classic show tunes. She recorded "The Last Night of the World" from the musical *Miss Saigon* with Domingo in New York, and the duet was released on his hit compilation *The Broadway I Love*.

Carly spent much of 1991 working on the music for another Nora Ephron movie, *This Is My Life*. This wasn't easy, because the story line was weak and Ephron's script was lightweight. (Mike Nichols had declined any involvement.) Working mostly at home, Carly came up with the main theme, "The Love of My Life" (based on her feelings for Sally and Ben), and various instrumentals inspired by her uncle Peter Dean. These involved Peter's favorite instruments— ukulele, harmonica, whistling through the teeth—and were intended by Carly as an homage to the uncle who had had the greatest influence on her career. In August 1991, Carly was working on the movie music at home with Teese Gohl, Jimmy Ryan, Will Lee, and Russ Kunkel when the island was slammed by Hurricane Bob, a storm so violent that all the leaves were blown off the trees. The power went out, but Carly had a deadline, so Frank Filipetti ran the gear through a gas-powered generator and the musicians worked by candlelight. Carly told the band about how Uncle Pete had retired as a talent manager at sixty-eight to go back to work as Peter "Snakehips" Dean, performing in clubs and cabarets. They listened to his old albums for inspiration. The songs they worked up on the island were then recorded by Filipetti in New York, including "The Show Must Go On," a faux-Broadway showstopper (that took Carly three weeks to write), and "The Night Before Christmas," a Hollywood carol with Sally and Ben chiming in on the chorus. Harmonica virtuoso Toots Thielemans (who had known Peter Dean well) contributed some of Uncle Pete's characteristic funkiness.

This Is My Life was released in early 1992 and promptly bombed. The reviews were gruesome, and the movie studio pulled the film from theaters as an embarrassment. But the legendary producer

Quincy Jones (who had worked with Uncle Pete) had been following the project and released Carly's soundtrack on his Qwest/Reprise label in April. The single "Love of My Life" got some airplay and charted at number sixteen, so for Carly the project wasn't a total loss.

Carly saw a lot of Jackie Onassis in New York that spring. They often met in the afternoon for movie matinees. Jackie, ever shy, would wait for Carly in the ladies' room if she arrived at the theater first. A couple of times they were spotted and asked for autographs. Jackie always demurred and turned away, while Carly gamely signed and chatted with the fans. When asked when her next album was coming out, Carly replied that any new record was on hold because she was working on an opera.

Actually, Carly and Jake Brackman had been working on this project for about a year, after she had received a commission from the Metropolitan Opera Guild, in association with the Kennedy Center for the Performing Arts, in Washington, D.C. Carly's brief was to write a family-friendly work that would attract both her fans and especially their children. She and Jake came up with an opera about a child of divorced parents. The libretto, cowritten by Carly and Jake, concerns a twelve-year-old New Yorker, Romulus Hunt, who tries to trick his estranged, incompatible parents into reuniting. Romulus teams up with his imaginary friend, a Rastafarian called Zoogy, who uses his knowledge of Jamaican voodoo to this end. Of course this doesn't work, but in the end, Romulus earns the love of his feckless bohemian father by making him recall his own father's indifference.

Romulus Hunt was an ambitious project and called for more collaboration than Carly had ever been used to. Teese Gohl worked on the orchestration and arrangements. Executives from the record label Angel/EMI Classics offered suggestions. Director Francesca Zambello and choreographer Carmen De Lavallade worked on the production. Carly consulted her operatic sister, Joanna, on various aspects of the work, and then named Romulus's mother (a prim Upper East Side matron) after her. When prerehearsal run-throughs began in New York that summer, Carly worried that her main leitmotif, "Voulez-Vous Dancer?"—Rom's father was a choreographer—sounded tepid. The five singers, none of them opera stars, seemed unsure of themselves. The ten-piece band was having a hard time with the reggae rhythms required for Zoogy's music. Then came a series of legal skirmishes over who owned the rights to the production, which got the lawyers involved. Despair set in, but Carly was determined to press on and make it work.

Summer 1992. Carly took a call from her old flame Willie Donaldson in London. Willie, now sixty-two, was a bestselling author in England (*The Henry Root Letters*) and a columnist for *The Independent* newspaper. (The column trumpeted his sleazy experiences as a Chelsea pimp and cocaine addict and was very popular with the daily broadsheet's politically liberal readers.) Willie told Carly that the paper was sending him to New York to cover a benefit at the Ritz nightclub, starring Elizabeth Taylor and the hip-hop group Salt-N-Pepa. Willie invited Carly along as his date.

Carly replied that she wasn't able to leave her apartment at the moment because she was waiting for a phone call. She explained that she'd heard that James Taylor was again recovering from some addiction, and was going through the twelve-step recovery program associated with Alcoholics Anonymous. The final step required him to make amends to all the people harmed by his addiction. "I certainly want to be in when he finally gets to me," Carly told Willie. "I don't even leave the apartment to go shopping." When Willie phoned again a few weeks later, Carly reported that James had never called her to make amends.

Late in 1992, the Christmas holidays were approaching, and the children would be coming home. Carly asked her husband to leave because he was using cocaine and she didn't want him around the children. He moved to the apartment he had kept in New York until Sally and Ben returned to their schools early in the new year.

Unsent Letters

$\mathcal{I}$n February 1993, Carly's opera, *Romulus Hunt,* had its first performances at the John Jay Theater, on Tenth Avenue in New York. Carly told friends that the music was by far the hardest work she had ever undertaken, that it had been an honor to have been asked to compose it, and that she really loved (most of) the way it turned out. Carly: "It was a real challenge and it got pretty well panned, except by a very nice man in *Stereo Review,* who said it was the best American opera since Gershwin's *Porgy and Bess.* This was a man I had paid a great deal of money to." Other critics were less kind. *The New York Times* called the opera "a peculiar, well-meaning and misguided failure." The libretto was described as emotionally pallid and the whole production generally depressing. But the hour-long opera completed its New York run before moving to Washington in April. Teese Gohl and Frank Filipetti produced an album of the *Romulus Hunt* music, which was released by Angel Records that spring, but it failed to make much of an impression on its own.

Meanwhile Carly kept working. She recorded the standard "Wee

Small Hours of the Morning" for the hit movie *Sleepless in Seattle* (another Nora Ephron project), and then repeated the song, intercut with "Guess I'll Hang My Tears Out to Dry," with Frank Sinatra for his *Duets* album. (Carly and Sinatra never met, both recording their parts in separate studios.) When *Duets* was released that year, Carly's contribution was critically hailed as the best music on an album that most critics and fans agreed was one of Sinatra's worst. In this period Carly also collaborated with Andreas Vollenweider, contributing the song "Private Eyes" to his album *Eolian Minstrel*.

And Clive Davis was calling. Arista wanted another album of original songs from Carly. Seeking inspiration, she was rummaging in a closet one day that spring, looking for an old notebook, when she reached up and found a cardboard box on a high shelf. It contained a sheaf of notes and letters she had written to various people, including her first husband and some old lovers, but never mailed. She remembered that her mother once told her that a good way to purge negative feelings toward someone was to write to them, but she should *never* actually mail the letter. Now Carly began to read some of this material, some of it dating back more than twenty years, and she realized that some of the contents could work as song lyrics. But this was derailed when Andrea Simon suffered an aortic aneurism and was hospitalized in Boston. Carly and her sisters camped out by her bedside, and after a few weeks Carly was able to take her mother home to Martha's Vineyard. They almost made it to the island's ferry in Woods Hole when Andrea declared a bathroom emergency in the adjacent town of Falmouth. Carly had the driver stop outside a quaint roadside inn and half-carried her mother into the bathroom, "shit stained, if you want to know the truth. I really forgot myself amid her pain and anguish." As the exhausted pair emerged from a long siege in the bathroom, Andrea called out to the bewildered innkeepers, "Do all of you know my daughter, Carly Simon, the singer?"

Jim Hart was living with Carly again during the summer of 1993.

It was a fraught time for Carly. Her mother was diagnosed with lung cancer, and given about a year to live. This was devastating enough, but then Jacqueline Onassis confided to Carly that she, too, had cancer, but her doctors were more hopeful in their prognosis. Alex Taylor, James's older brother, drank himself to death the night before entering rehab in Florida. The Taylors, Carly's children included, went into shock.

In an attempt to put on a brave face and salvage the summer, Carly decided to throw a party. Early in July, invitations to "A Moon Party" went out to the island's elite, from the usual summering celebrities to star-quality local artists, fishermen, lighthouse keepers, and plumbers. Guests were asked to wear only white, since the party celebrated July's luminous full moon. RSVPs included Mrs. Onassis and her companion, financier Maurice Tempelsman, Katharine Graham, Mike Nichols and Diane Sawyer, every important writer and musician on the island, the entire Taylor family except James, and almost everyone who'd been asked. After cocktails by the shimmering pool and a sumptuous catered dinner in the party barn, several of the guests performed skits at different levels of cringe-worthiness. Then Carly and her increasingly frail mother sang a song, to rapturous applause at the sense of the occasion's history. Sally and Ben played a duet and got lost in the middle. Then Carly and a band played a relaxed set of oldies while the younger set danced until the full moon sank westward into the Vineyard sound.

In August 1993, President Bill Clinton brought his family to Martha's Vineyard for their summer holiday. Clinton had been elected the previous November and was settling into his first term with a large popular mandate. On the Vineyard the First Family settled into a borrowed pond-side mansion and tried to relax. The president told his host that the one person he wanted to meet on his vacation was Cary Simon, so Carly invited the Clintons to a casual dinner. Peter and Ronni Simon were there as well, so Peter could document the visit with his camera. They waited and waited, and eventually the First Family arrived—almost three hours late.

Carly and Jim Hart received the casually dressed Clintons in the driveway of her home. As Hillary Clinton was introducing her daughter, Chelsea, to Carly, the president gripped Jim Hart by the elbow. "I can't believe you didn't know who she was," Clinton whispered.

Hart was taken aback. Clinton: "I read somewhere that you said that when you and Carly met, you didn't know who she was."

"Actually," Hart said, "I thought she might have been Linda Ronstadt."

Clinton laughed. "I think I read that too," he said. He went on the say that he and Hillary were big fans of Carly's. Then, sort of randomly, the president mentioned that they had named their daughter after Joni Mitchell's song "Chelsea Morning." At that point Peter asked the two couples to pose together for a photograph. Bill Clinton moved in on Carly, put his arm around her waist, and drew her to him. She edged away for the sake of propriety, but later said she was flattered by the attention. (The next day, Carly's mother called and said no one she knew could *believe* that Carly hadn't invited her to meet the president. Andrea later complained to Lucy that she had missed a golden opportunity to tell Bill Clinton how to save the country.) For the next seven years, through reelection and impeachment, the Clintons returned to the island almost every August and usually exchanged visits with Carly when there was time.

Carly kept working on new songs for her next album, but her mother was dying and Carly tried to stay as close to her as possible. Andrea Simon fought her cancer with great bravery, but Mrs. Simon and Schuster died in February 1994. The funeral was held on a snowy night a week later at the Riverdale Presbyterian Church. The eulogies hailed Andrea Simon's work for civil rights and the mental health charity she promoted. Then her three daughters—Joanna, Lucy, and Carly—sang "May the Lord Bless You and Keep You" in the three-part harmonies they had been singing since they were children. When this was finished, an obviously distraught Carly stepped forward and addressed the crowded church. "I j-j-just want to say," she stammered, "that I feel like my heart has been . . . *torn from my chest.*" There was a reception afterward in the Simon house on Grosvenor Avenue, where some guests were deeply touched by the dozens of family photographs that hung on the walls. Many would carry loving memories of the years of parties and laughter and conversation in that house, for the rest of their lives. The three Simon sisters decided they would never sing "May the Lord Bless You and Keep You" ever again.

But for the four Simon children, the next few months of 1994 were a nightmare of discord. The terms of their mother's will were shocking to Carly, who had been left less than her sisters and brothers. (Andrea had taken into account Carly's considerable fortune from her recording career when planning the disposal of her estate.) Then there were the contents of Andrea's houses—artworks, antiques, rare books, family heirlooms. Andrea's jewelry was up for grabs, and it didn't go well, especially between Carly and Joanna. Lucy, always accommodating, wanted only her father's piano. Carly wanted it, too. In the end, Lucy got the Steinway and Joey got the double strand of Tiffany pearls—and Carly felt that, once again, she had gotten screwed. Relations between the Simon sisters would be strained for the next several years.

Through all this, Carly occasionally took various medications prescribed by her doctors. One of these was Fioricet, used to control migraine headaches, to which she was prone. After a while the headaches increased, and her husband told her that she was taking too many pills, and persuaded her to enter the Regent rehab clinic affiliated with New York Hospital. Before she checked in, she gave Jim a letter to post to Jackie Onassis across Central Park.

Carly: "Group therapy at the rehab was me and fourteen ex-cons, all guys, all black. All had awful backgrounds; one had killed his mother. At first they attacked me for being no better than they were,

[but] most of them came around and then embraced me as they became my backup singers in the smoking room. I always thought this could be a great premise for a musical, but unfortunately it only lasted six days and I came home to find that Jim hadn't mailed my letter to Jackie O, which was the only personal thing I'd asked him to do in my absence."

Then, as the winter of 1994 turned into spring, the lunches and movie dates with Jackie Onassis dwindled and then stopped. Jackie told Carly that her prayers had gone unanswered, but that she still had hope. She often called Carly if she saw James Taylor on TV. Carly: "She would say, 'You know, he just doesn't look happy.' Then she always would ask me, 'Are you blossoming?'" Jackie kept insisting, "Just four more weeks and I'll be myself again." Carly was upset, but the news triggered a creative surge, and she wrote one of her greatest songs, "Touched by the Sun," as an homage to her editor and friend. At the end of their final lunch together, Carly presented Jackie with the lyrics to the song, which recognized the epic grandeur, the bravery, and the heartbreak of Jacqueline Bouvier Kennedy Onassis's life. "This is for you," Carly said. "You inspired it." They never spoke again.

Jacqueline Onassis died in May 1994. A few days later, the Kennedy family held a wake at her apartment at 1025 Fifth Avenue. Carly arrived by herself and was amazed to find a full-blown Irish wake in progress. Jackie's apartment was packed with people eating and drinking and smoking. Senator Ted Kennedy was holding court by the windows overlooking Central Park, downing cocktails and laughing at old jokes. Carly was taken aback by this irreverent scene. Noting that the coffin was alone in the bedroom, Carly tried to go in, but was told only family members were allowed. She explained that she wanted to place a memento in Jackie's coffin, but was again told that this was only allowed to members of the immediate family. Carly became distraught, and began to stammer. Caroline Kennedy's husband took her by the arm, told her it was time for her to leave, and ushered her into the elevator. Once on the street, Carly felt a little better and walked home across the greening park.

Then she rallied, and went to work. "I had lost the two most important women in my life," she said later, "my mother and Jackie. I could either fall apart, or I could make the grieving energy into something positive. I wrote 'Touched by the Sun' for Jackie when I first heard she was gravely ill. It was based on a wonderful poem by Stephen Spender—'*I think continually of those . . .*'—that supposedly was one of Jack Kennedy's favorites. Both the words and the music came very quickly, as did 'Like a River,' written the same year, after my mother had died. For the first time in many years, I had no trouble translating the emotions I was feeling—and they were intense—into words and music."

Carly was on a roll now, writing for her next album, which everyone kept reminding her was overdue. Some of the new songs were informed by the news, brought to her by her children, of a serious rift between James Taylor and his second wife. Neither of the kids gave their father's marriage much longer to last.

LIKE A RIVER

———

After Andrea Simon passed away, one of the family treasures coveted by her three daughters was the silver-framed photograph of George Gershwin, signed by the composer with a dedication to their father, Richard Simon. (Lucy got it.) Then, later in 1994, it was Carly's turn to have a run at the Gershwin legacy. She recorded a version of George and Ira Gershwin's "I've Got a Crush on You" for the compilation album *The Glory of Gershwin,* working with Beatles producer George Martin. She asked the famously protective Gershwin estate to allow her to make a small lyric revision in one verse of the song, and the estate agreed, the only time this request had ever been granted. Then Carly—to her amazement—was inducted to the Songwriters Hall of Fame, whose first inductee (in 1969) had been George Gershwin. Carly thought about her father when this happened, and all the ironies involved, and hoped that he would have been proud that his awkward youngest daughter had been accepted in the same exalted company as his old friend.

Also in 1994, ex-Brooklyn Dodger mascot Carly recorded "Take

Me Out to the Ballgame" as the main theme for *Baseball,* a multipart series produced by Ken Burns and shown on public television that year. Inflected with gospel piano, Carly's rendition has a smoky quality that goes well with Burns's use of old photos and newsreels of classic baseball players and home runs.

After Jackie Onassis died, Carly rallied. She called the builders back to Hidden Star Hill, as her Vineyard property was now called, and ordered a cherry tree moved to accommodate a new conservatory, where she could paint. She commissioned murals and new stained-glass windows depicting Sally and Ben. An addition was built onto the guesthouse that Carly called Honeymoon Cottage. The circular garden was replanted with perennials and annuals, surrounding a core of herbs for the kitchen. She also recorded thirteen new songs with Frank Filipetti in her neighborhood recording studio, Right Track. These were released as *Letters Never Sent,* Carly's first album of new songs in four years, in mid-November 1994. The album cover was a *Sgt. Pepper's*-like collage of faces compiled by Carly and friend Tamara Weiss, augmented with new photography by Bob Gothard.

Carly may have been grieving for her mother and her friend, but she managed to channel her emotions into some stirring original songs. "Letters Never Sent" (written with Jake Brackman) is about lingering regrets, with a dreamlike middle section and rhythmic voodoo chanting. "Lost in Your Love" is an Arif Mardin production, an homage to the late Otis Redding, with his sons on backing vocals. Then came "Like a River," an extremely touching letter addressed to Carly's late mother.

The genesis of the song was "the grab," the dividing of their mother's things with her sisters at the emptied Riverdale house. Afterward, Carly returned to her own apartment, feeling ripped off, and then ashamed that she was preoccupied with material things more than with the loss of her mother. She sat on the plush maroon velvet-covered sofa in the apartment's big living room. The lights of Fifth Avenue twinkled across the darkened park. Carly remembers her mother trying to breathe in the final stages of lung cancer. Then, possessed by an urgency to write something, she took up her pen and wrote the first verse of "Like a River." The verse describes her mother's empty house and the empty feeling of being in it. She asks her mother questions about the next world, and describes how she fought over the pearls with the other girls. Carly read this over and then called her sister Lucy and said, "I've written something I want you to hear." Encouraged to keep writing, Carly questions Andrea in the afterlife. "Have you reconciled with Dad?" she asks her mother's spirit. Is Andrea dancing with her idol Benjamin Franklin on the face of the moon? The song began as a stately kind of funeral march and then swelled with thrilling chord progressions and even hard rock. (The song's coda quotes from *Romulus Hunt*'s theme, "I'll Never Turn Away.")

"Time Works on All the Wild Young Men" is a forty-four-second interlude between tracks, sung with her son, Ben Taylor. It is followed by the resounding tribute to Jackie Onassis, "Touched by the Sun." This fierce paean, ambitious and epic in scale, deploys Rick Marotta's volcanic drums as the lead instrument of the recording ensemble, and a Carly Simon vocal that goes over the top, sounding a little crazed, as if she were grieving at a private wake of her own.

Letters Never Sent continues with "Davy," a collaboration with Andreas Vollenweider's transcendent electric harp, and "Halfway Round the World," a sailors' song performed with blues singer Taj Mahal and Dave Stewart of the Scottish band Eurhythmics. Carly is hot and in heat on "The Reason," a rock song about courtship featuring the great session drummer Steve Ferrone, coproduced by Danny Kortchmar. "Private" is another unsent letter that is sung falsetto, something of a departure for Carly. "Catch It Like a Fever" is a bongo beatnik song that seems to be about a sex act beloved of many males of the species. "Born to Break My Heart" is a great country/pop song done with Roseanne Cash, a portrait of a maturing woman "cursed to seek love again from another cold heart." That woman reappears in the album's finale, "I'd Rather It Was You," a George Harrison homage with Jimmy Ryan on guitar.

With its brief, quirky interludes between longer songs, and no obvious singles, *Letters Never Sent* was released in late November 1994. The label didn't release a single, despite a certain amount of agitation for "Born to Break My Heart." Carly couldn't get Arista to fund a new video. (She heard that one of the label's executives was referring to her as a "heritage act," and this bothered her.) The album barely sold enough to chart, reaching number 129 early in 1995. Now Clive Davis told Carly she had to tour that summer and make other appearances. New manager Brian Doyle told her that her career was at risk if she refused. Reluctantly, Carly Simon agreed to form a band and face the music.

The band was drummer Rick Marotta, Teese Gohl, T-Bone Wolk on bass, Peter Calo on guitar, and Curtis King on vocals. A friend of Carly's, Dirk Ziff (who was investing in her Vineyard nightclub), also played occasional guitar with the band. One of their first gigs—augmented to twelve musicians, with Doug Wimbish on bass— was a late-morning set in April 1995, on a stage built over the west stairs of the main hall of Grand Central Station as bemused travelers streamed through the terminal and spring sunlight seeped through the massive eastern windows. Carly was performing in a white shirt and a small black skirt over her long legs. This show, *Live at Grand Central,* was filmed for broadcast on the Lifetime cable channel. The band, augmented by Jake Brackman's charismatic fiddler wife, Mindy Jostyn, burned through "Touched by the Sun," "Haven't Got Time for the Pain," "Letters Never Sent," "I've Got to Have You," "Anticipation" (huge cheer from the commuters); the upbeat, clapping energy of "Jesse"; "Coming Around Again," with its emotional surge; "That's the Way" (Carly on electric piano); "Let the River Run"; and "No Secrets." Toward the end of the set, Carly's voice gave out, and she had to dub in her vocals later. After the last song, Carly told the crowd, "We gotta go, we gotta make our train." Later the film editors realized that Mindy Jostyn—given a broad mandate to entertain the crowd by stage-shy Carly—had completely stolen the show. Mindy figured in almost every good shot, so veteran video director Andy Dick had to work overtime to produce a film that ensured that Carly was the only star of her own show.

This band also played a late spring show at the Avalon nightclub in Boston, across from Fenway Park. A reporter joined Carly in the lobby of the Four Seasons hotel, noting her leather jacket and flowing chiffon skirt. On the drive to the club, Carly explained that she had originally checked into the Charles Hotel in Cambridge, but there was no piano in her suite. At midnight she moved to the Four Seasons, but the suite had no heat. By seven in the morning she was wandering on Boston Common, struggling with a sudden anxiety attack. It hadn't helped her confidence when she stopped her tour bus in Providence, Rhode Island, to visit daughter Sally at Brown University. Carly was somewhat unnerved at Sally's dorm room, which displayed dozens of photos of her father, James Taylor, and exactly one of her mother. "I felt so deflated," she told the reporter.

An hour into that night's show, Sally Taylor walked onstage and Carly stepped aside as her sexy young daughter belted out Wilson Pickett's "Mustang Sally." It was a sassy and funny performance that got the audience up and dancing for the first time that night. After Sally left the stage, Carly spoke to the audience: "I'm happy tonight," she said. "I'm really happy."

Carly and her husband attended the 1995 Rock and Roll Hall of Fame induction ceremony in the ballroom of the Waldorf-Astoria Hotel in New York. That year's inductees included Led Zeppelin, Neil Young, and the late Frank Zappa, but Carly was there to see her old heroes Martha and the Vandellas safely into musical Valhalla. An old friend asked Carly when she thought her turn would come. She smiled and said, "Probably never."

Summer 1995. Carly Simon and her band played sixteen concerts with Philadelphia (blue-eyed) soul singers Hall and Oates opening the concerts. (Carly often joined them for their big hit "Every Time She Goes Away.") This was her first serious tour since 1981, when she had hemorrhaged onstage in Pittsburgh amid her breakup with James Taylor, and now her fans turned out in droves. The tickets (for mostly club-size venues) were expensive—sixty dollars was typical—but many of the concerts sold out in half an hour. Carly played all the hits—"You Belong to Me" and "You're So Vain"—and some new songs, including "Touched by the Sun," which she always dedicated to Jackie. "She was as *exquisite* as you think she was," she told her audience in Boston. Darryl Hall and John Oates always joined Carly to sing "Anticipation" toward the end of the set. The final shows were in California, with Carly trying to channel Al Green's impression of cool Memphis soul. The last audience of the tour, in Concord, California, called Carly back for encores three times.

Carly arrived home on the Vineyard on August 25, 1995, and began rehearsing with James Taylor's band for a benefit concert on August 30. This was Livestock '95, a big semiprivate concert whose proceeds would help build a new (and sorely needed) hall for the local Agricultural Society. James Taylor had agreed to appear with Carly Simon for the first time since the No Nukes concerts in 1979. A stage was built on the county fairgrounds in West Tisbury. Local musicians were recruited to play. Ten thousand tickets sold out in four hours. National media was blacked out. Both Carly and James performed solo sets as news helicopters hovered overhead and interfered with the sound system. Carly dedicated "Nobody Does It Better" to James. (And Aerosmith's scarf-laden Steven Tyler popped out to sing Mick Jagger's part on "You're So Vain.") Then Carly joined James for "Shower the People" during his closing set, which ended with Carly and James dancing the Lindy Hop to Russ Kunkel's pounding beat during a long, rollicking "Mockingbird."

Carly had been worried about how James would react to her, but he wasn't around much until the day of the show, and then he was cordial, if distant. The only problem occurred some weeks later, when *Martha's Vineyard* magazine ran Peter Simon's photo of Carly and James dancing on the cover. Carly was radiant, but James looked like a cretin, with hair akimbo, wiry specs way down his nose, and a crazed grin on his wrinkled features. His mother, Trudy Taylor, saw this and blew up, which got James upset. Carly and her brother were accused of making James look bad. "Other than at Sally's wedding," Carly later said, "James has hardly ever spoken to me again."

Carly was also blamed for a sleazy magazine profile of her that appeared in *Vanity Fair* that summer. "I Never Sang for My Mother" was written by an ex-wife of Jonathan Schwartz, so the Simon family's secrets tumbled out of the glossy monthly like spoiled fruit. The "Ronnie Material" was given a national platform, and the author also implied that Andrea Simon had callously allowed her husband to die alone, which was far from the truth. Carly's sisters, and her mother's friends (including Jackie Robinson's widow, Rachel), were upset by what they saw as a hatchet job on Andrea Simon. To some, it seemed that Carly was dishing dirt on her family to sell more copies of her new album.

Autumn 1995. The British music press reported that Tori Amos was performing "Boys in the Trees" in concert and was telling her audiences that she wished she had written the song. Carly worked on *Clouds in My Coffee,* a three-CD boxed compilation of her top music to date. This involved locating old demo tapes in her basement archive and negotiating with record labels Elektra, Epic, United Artists, Reprise, Angel, and even back-office elements at Arista. (Getting the rights to include "Nobody Does It Better" from UA was a Bond movie in itself.) The package included an essay by a young accountant Carly had met when she started surfing on AOL the previous year. Carly contributed her own notes as well: "Even when I am in a state of self-loathing, I can write something that I fall in love with. . . . The reasons for choosing the songs I did had to do sometimes with availability. Politics played an unavoidable part. There are songs that are missing, not too glaringly, I hope." Some of the earlier songs—recorded with tubes and then transistors from 1968 to 1972—were also tweaked by Carly and Frank Filipetti (employing a Neve Capricorn digital desk) at Right Track for sonic equalization in the postmodern age. The *Clouds* box was released late in the year, and Carly visited radio stations in important markets to help it onto the sales charts. But, she says, there were also some serious reservations about her manager, her lawyer, and her label at the time, and what she described as bad decisions that cost her almost two million dollars.

October 1995. The president of the United States and his wife, Hillary Rodham Clinton, flew into Martha's Vineyard to attend the wedding of two island summer celebrities, the actors Mary Steenburgen and Ted Danson. Carly wasn't invited (reportedly) because the bride and groom were friendly with James Taylor. But after the festivities and a few glasses of champagne, on the way back to the plane, Clinton ordered his entourage to detour to Hidden Star Hill, and surprised a delighted Carly Simon with an impromptu presidential visit.

FILM NOIR

———

*I*n early 1996, with *Clouds in My Coffee* selling well, Carly signed a two-book deal with her father's old company, Simon and Schuster. The contract called for another children's book, and then a compilation of lyrics and family photographs. Movie commissions continued, with themes for the Hollywood film *Marvin's Room* and an adaptation of Ludwig Bemelmans's classic *Madeline.* For the former, Carly wrote "Two Little Sisters" and sang it with Meryl Streep, one of the film's stars. Carly had also taken up painting as a serious pastime, and that year she visited Santa Fe, New Mexico, and was inspired by the same arid, southwestern landscapes that had inspired Georgia O'Keeffe and D. H. Lawrence, among legions of other artists.

Her record company wanted another album, but Carly wasn't in the writing zone. Instead, she delivered *Film Noir,* her third album of American songbook classics, a tribute to the music of the genre movies of her childhood: "B pictures" featuring Bogart, Lauren Bacall, Robert Mitchum, and Lana Turner, among others, which now, in the late twentieth century, had a glamorous retro allure—gangsters, gun molls, and cops—recently repopularized by the American Movie Channel cable TV outlet. Carly plunged into this glam project with fellow Hall-of-Famer Jimmy Webb, who helped choose the songs, played piano, sang, and cowrote the neo-standard title song, "Film Noir." Van Dyke Parks also helped, with orchestrations.

The album leans heavily on songs with strong themes, and works by American masters such as Cole Porter, Frank Loesser, and Hoagy Carmichael. "Lili Marlene" channels Marlene Dietrich with Webb on piano. Carly sings with son Ben—sounding like a clone of his father—on "Every Time We Say Goodbye." "Last Night When We Were Young" had been almost owned by Frank Sinatra, but Carly and Jimmy give it a spooky, filmic twist of their own. "I'm a Fool to Want You," cowritten by Mr. Sinatra, was often identified with his love for Ava Gardner, a film noir heroine early in her career. Carly sings the (male-voiced) lyrics of "Laura" as written by Johnny Mercer after the movie *Laura* came out with its magnificent instrumental theme, here reimagined by Arif Mardin. Noirish 1950s TV is also invoked, in "Somewhere in the Night," better known as the *Naked City* theme. Van Dyke Parks arranged and conducted the orchestra in the clever divorce note "Don't Smoke in Bed." The album's highlight is Carly's duet with John Travolta on "Two Sleepy People," about lovers too tired to carry on, but too much in love to go back home. It is a passionate performance of one of the greatest songs of its generation.

Film noir is characterized by suspense leading to violence, always shot in shadowy black and white. The movies are tense and foreboding, often informed by injustice, tragedy, and deceit; populated by jaded femme fatales and a new kind of hero, the anti-hero, who battles criminals, murderers, the police, and existential despair. Carly and Jimmy Webb took this into account with the song "Film Noir," which became a drama-laden rock ballad, another sad story about a dramatic heroine who loses control and fades to black.

Film Noir was released by Arista in September 1987, with booklet notes by noir-obsessed director Martin Scorsese and glamorous studio photographs, taken by Bob Gothard, of Carly in the glorious penumbra of black and white. Reviews now ran (highly positive) in fashion magazines, not the rock press. The album sold well and reached number eighty-seven on the *Billboard* chart. Carly and her label made a short film about the album, *Songs in Shadow,* which was shown on the AMC channel that autumn.

Also around this time, Carly published her fifth book for children, and her first for Simon and Schuster. *Midnight Farm* is a tale (in verse) of a magical farm that comes to life after sunset. Midnight Farm was also the name of a classy dry goods emporium in the town of Vineyard Haven that was a joint venture between Carly and her friend Tamara Weiss.

October 1997. Carly and her husband were living apart, although she still supported him as he tried to morph into a published poet, having given up on the novel long before. As Carly was working on her new album that year, she noticed that a small lump in one of her breasts was changing. It had been there for some time, but the doctors said not to worry, because they were watching it. Carly: "I didn't insist on it coming out because I don't like operations, but toward the end, it [the lump] started to talk to me. I'd be reading Tolstoy or cooking or exercising and I would hear it going, 'Get me out of here!' . . . Then one doctor looked at my mammogram and said he'd rather see the lump in a jar than in my breast. So he took it out, and it was cancer. Fortunately it had not spread to my lymph nodes. I was a little angry at myself [for waiting so long]."

For years, according to Jim Hart, Carly Simon had woken up every morning with the fear that something or someone was trying to cause her harm. And here was this fear, made palpable in her very flesh, in the form of stage-one breast cancer. Something really did want to kill her. But instead of falling apart, Carly decided to fight back. She overcame her fear of surgery and underwent a mastectomy in November 1997. While recovering, she focused on the bravery her mother had shown in her last months. Carly: "My mother was a great role model for me then. I remembered that she'd had severe arthritis in her fingers, even when she was my age. But she used to look at her hands and say, 'Isn't this *beautiful*? Look at the shapes—don't they looked like gnarled tree trunks?' And whether or not she really felt that, that's what she did for us."

After the operation, when the dressings were removed, Carly discovered a long scar where her breast had been. She was amazed to see that the scar was shaped like an arrow. In the way she then had of embracing her current reality, she took to the scar immediately. "My scar is *beautiful*," she told an interviewer. "I didn't bother rubbing things into it, or having silicone injections. I just kept it that way, because I liked it."

One night, while she was recovering, James Taylor came to see her in their old apartment. Their children urged him to visit Carly, and he did. At the age of fifty, James now lived somewhat more easily within himself, and was courtly and encouraging to Carly, having been divorced by his second wife. As he was leaving, she asked him to give her a call if he ever thought of her, and James replied that if he called her every time he thought of her, there wouldn't be time for anything else.

Carly's oncologist advised her to try to forget about the surgery, and not even speak about it for a while. So, before the onset of a year of chemotherapy, Carly took Sally and Ben for a winter vacation on Tortola, in the British Virgin Islands. (Jim Hart's support of Carly had reportedly been less than heroic during the cancer ordeal, and the couple never really lived together after that.) The rest of 1998 was spent in a fever of chemotherapy and severe depression, a slough of despond the depth of which Carly had never experienced, a mental illness that famously depressed Bill Styron described as a "total shit storm."

To get through it, Carly knew she had to keep working. Living large, between two households, meant that she had a legion of people—assistants, household staff, gardeners, caretakers—who were financially dependent on her continuing largesse. She made a deal with Clive Davis for another album, which she decided she would record herself, at home, where she was comfortable. Frank Filipetti helped her install a digital recording studio in the living room of her place in New York.

One day in this period, Carly was having tea with a friend, a fellow cancer survivor, at the Carlisle Hotel on Madison Avenue. She and the friend had both decided to have reconstructive surgery, and were feeling upbeat and hopeful. Then Carly ran into Warren Beatty in the lobby. They spoke for a moment, and Carly told him about the cancer and the surgery. Beatty turned a little gray, mentioned he had an appointment, and was out of there. Cancer, someone told Carly, let you know who your real friends were.

Then she lost her inexpensive, rent-stabilized apartment on Central Park West, when the landlord was able to prove that the massive flat was no longer Carly's primary home. Carly was forced to vacate. Her furniture and instruments, the recording gear, and the children's belongings were packed up and shipped to Hidden Star Hill. Carly took this traumatic excision from her past very hard. The loss of apartment 6S, the home she'd shared with James Taylor and their children, was almost as much a loss to her as her breast.

Bedroom Music

---

*W*hile Carly was installing a home studio in Sally's old bedroom upstairs in the Vineyard house, Sally Taylor was releasing albums herself. *Tomboy Bride* and later *Apt #6S* were indie CD productions recorded in Colorado, where Sally had settled after college. Ben Taylor had released his first single a year earlier, and was recording demos with friends in New York. Then a nineteen-track compilation from *Clouds in My Coffee* was released in Europe by Warner Global as *Nobody Does It Better: The Very Best of Carly Simon,* and sold well in European markets where Carly had never performed.

Carly also sang the vocal on "Your Silver Key" on Andreas Vollenweider's *Cosmopoly* album.

In mid-1999, Carly was recovering to the extent that she started recording demos of the songs she had written during the long days of chemo and depression. Her favorite new song was a tribute to George Gershwin as a beacon of inspiration and hope. Later she wrote that she had been in a miserable state of writer's block and had all but decided to give up writing songs. One day, she was in the Lee

Side tavern in Woods Hole, waiting for the ferry to the Vineyard, when Gershwin's classic "Embraceable You" came on the jukebox. She imagined the young Gershwin writing timeless music on Riverside Drive in New York. For a melody, she chose a reverie-like variation on the chorus of "Embraceable You." Carly's lyrics described "one note that weeps the truth / And makes my life mean something." Carly titled the new song "In Honor of You (George)." Carly: "It may have been the process of writing and arranging the song with Teese Gohl that got me unblocked. I'm not exactly sure, as everything was complicated by the emotional requirements of being a patient during that whole period."

Carly spent eight months working on her next album—usually alone. The instruments and microphones were in Sally's room because they didn't fit in Carly's bedroom, down the hall. The small space was filled with guitars and machines, lyrics written on scraps of paper, phone messages, bits of clothing. No one was allowed to clean. Carly learned to program the drum machines. Musician neighbors, including Jimmy Parr, helped install a recording studio in the basement. Carly grew to be fond of this arrangement, where she was able to experiment in private. "I could fail—over and over," she remembered. There were no label executives or hired producers suggesting that she sound more like Christina Aguilera, Natalie Imbruglia, or Debbie Harry. Carly realized that she was writing the way she'd begun in 1970: "Making sounds that I liked. Not thinking in an orthodox way about the songs." In this period, she wrote about twenty new songs, and recorded them as demos on her 8-track-tape machine.

Gradually the chemotherapy ran its course, and Carly's energy began to return. She missed having an urban base now, so in 1999 she bought an early nineteenth-century Georgian house on Beacon Hill, Boston's most historic and exclusive residential neighborhood. The old house on West Cedar Street needed extensive renovation, and Carly figured that the project would be a welcome distraction from working, and an outlet for her fervid interest in home design and décor. In the winter, she thought, the cozy Boston house, with its many fireplaces, would be a welcoming retreat from the damp Vineyard.

But the renovation problems started right after the deal closed. The builders told her that the main staircase was two hundred years old and rotten. The house's original sash windows were crumbling and were replaced by modern French windows. A roof deck was installed to provide stunning views of the Boston skyline and the Charles River Basin. Carly shopped for furniture at her favorite stores on Newbury Street, and the house was expertly fitted with sofas and antiques that reminded old friends of her mother's rooms in Riverdale. It took a full day for workmen to get the piano into the house.

Finally, Carly moved in. One day she threw open the French windows, sat at the piano, and started to sing. The neighbors thought this a nuisance and called the police, who were polite but firm: no singing. Then the building inspectors swarmed. The roof deck was a code violation and had to go. The new French windows contravened Beacon Hill's rules for building exteriors in the historic district and had to be replaced. Carly tried to light a fire on a chilly morning, and the house filled with smoke because the chimneys had been plugged years before, when the city banned working fireplaces on the densely populated hill. The final straw may have been the three rats found cavorting in the fruit bowl when Carly came down to breakfast one morning. She put the house on the market, moved everything she wanted to the Vineyard, and was relieved to be exiled from Beacon Hill. Later on, she remembered, "chemotherapy *paled* in comparison to the problems I had with that house."

In the new year, 2000, Carly began production on the new album she was calling *Manhattan Was a Maiden,* after a new song that was eventually left off the record. Drummer Steve Gadd was reenlisted, along with bassists T-Bone Wolk and Tony Garnier, Bob Dylan's musical director (and a Vineyard neighbor). Teese Gohl was orchestrating three of the songs, including the big Gershwin finale.

Microphones were installed in Carly's barn, and Mindy Jostyn arrived to play her fiddle and sing backup. There was a long weekend when the Irish singer Liam Ó Maonlaí and the Rankin Sisters sang backing vocals. These musicians ended up on seven of the eleven tracks of the album called *The Bedroom Tapes.*

Carly's tapes were mixed at Right Track Studios in New York by Carly and Frank Filipetti. Instrumental and vocal tweaks were added for new colors, but Carly wanted most of the album to be true to the original concept of her working alone in Sally's bedroom. One night, she needed some funky backing vocals for the song "Big Dumb Guy" (said to be about a Boston newspaper reporter). Ben Taylor brought along his friend John Forté, twenty-five, a talented black musician from Brooklyn, who had won a full scholarship to Phillips Exeter Academy and then produced tracks for the multiplatinum group The Fugees, and other hip-hop luminaries. Carly and Forté became good friends—he called her "Mama C"—and Forté often stayed with Ben during long sojourns on the Vineyard. The boys nailed the vocal in a couple of takes, after they were able to stop laughing at the song's goofy lyrics.

The Bedroom Tapes compact disc was released in early May 2000. The new music spoke to the trauma of postcancer therapy and the (for Carly) joyous release of retail therapy, or shopping. The CD booklet was photographed by Bob Gothard and contained a short essay by Carly thanking all the producers she had worked with, by name, for inspiring her to produce this new album, by herself.

The lead track, "Our Affair," is an old-fashioned, seductive Carly Simon song that could have been on *No Secrets* or *Hotcakes.* "So Many Stars" is about yearning for love in Manhattan. "Big Dumb Guy" is a loosey-goosey rap, partly on life in front of a computer screen, partly on God knows what. "Scar" is like a mastectomy two-step, with a wonderful chorus about the old wise woman who could have been her mother, Mrs. Onassis, or about Carly herself, now in her mid-fifties. ("Scar," Carly wrote, took six months to get a complete lyric, and another six months "to make it emotionally true.")

The album continues with "Cross the River," a surreal narrative (Carly described it as "South American fantastic realism") of a boat ride on the Hudson River. "I Forget" is a torch song of illness, anguish, and recovery. "Actress" is pointed and uncomplimentary. The confessional "I'm Really the Kind" has intimations of seriously low self-esteem. The faux-paranoid rock song, "We Your Dearest Friends," is about the hordes of freeloading guests who descended on Hidden Star Hill every summer: clogging the guest rooms, lounging by the pool, fueled by pills and powders, bugging the staff, charging unauthorized restaurant meals to Carly's account, and then talking behind her back about how horrible she was. (Friends whispered that the song was partly about Libby Titus, with whom Carly had fallen out, but Carly wasn't saying.) Mindy Jostyn plays violin on a wistful song, "Whatever Became of Her." The album ends with Carly's epochal tribute, "In Honor of You (George)," the song that begins in self-pity and ends in a surge of hope amid the swooning orchestration, courtesy of the track's producer, Teese Gohl. (When the album was reissued later, it contained two more songs: "Grandmother's House" and the Brazil-flavored "Sangre Dolce." In this period, Carly also wrote the lovely song "Amity," for the movie *Anywhere But Here,* and recorded it at home with Sally Taylor.)

Clive Davis couldn't identify a single from the new album, so Arista didn't release one. There were no concerts, and no video. Carly and Jim Hart took to the road in a van with a driver and did a radio tour of her major markets. She performed "Big Dumb Guy" with Andreas Vollenweider and the house band of David Letterman's late night TV show on CBS. Album reviews were mostly good, especially for the song "Scar," but some critics said the album was depressing, and that Carly didn't sound like herself on some of the tracks. (Although, a prominent English critic called the album a masterpiece.)

The Bedroom Tapes stalled at number ninety. Then Clive Davis was fired, and Carly's years at Arista came to an abrupt end. Carly: "What a fiasco. Here is my personal best, coming off the press, and Clive Davis gets fired from Arista."

This was another in a long series of traumas. Arista's parent company, the German-owned Bertelsmann Music Group (BMG), had a mandatory retirement age of sixty-five, and Clive Davis was sixty-seven. When Davis refused to designate a successor, BMG terminated his contract and hired super-hot executive Antonio "L.A." Reid as president of Arista Records. Reid was known for signing "urban" pop stars and ultracommercial, teen-oriented acts. Carly went to see him, and came away with the distinct feeling that L.A. Reid didn't care about her. It was a blow. Carly felt that this new collection of songs was extremely important to her because she had been unusually honest in the lyrics, and she also realized that the music didn't conform to any contemporary modes of what was hip. This, to her, made *The Bedroom Tapes* even more meaningful.

Carly: "That album was only out a short while when Clive left the label. I made a deal with L.A. Reid for me to take *The Bedroom Tapes* back, in exchange for the second album due to Arista under that contract. So, it basically cost me—no marketing for the CD and a truncated end to its sales—the reputation of that music and those songs. It's a reputation which I felt would have flourished had it not fallen into the arms of a silly man—L.A. Reid—and his fragmented, overtaken company—Arista, post Clive—. . . I still own that album, and someday I'll re-release it."

Carly ended her relationship with her then-manager, Wendy Laister, not long after this.

Carly later wrote that those days—in 1999 and 2000—were the hardest times of her life. She didn't want to invite her fans to a pathetic pity party, she said, but at the very least she'd learned that she "had the 'stuff' to travel alone, and lightly." She remembered the long, dark nights of terror when she was able to go into Sally's room and lose herself in her music. Not everyone had wanted to go through this with her, she said. Her raw emotionality produced what she described as "turmoil" in everyone around her. She felt guilty about this. Certain friends disappeared and were no longer friends. She told people close to her that she could have become quite bitter, but felt that bitterness was "all too predictable." She'd rather be like the guy on the Vineyard who'd been attacked by a shark, and survived, and then had become an implacable advocate for not killing them.

CARLY HART

———

One day in the summer of 2000, Ben Taylor's friend John Forté was arrested at Newark International Airport with a briefcase containing $1.5 million worth of liquid cocaine. The federal narcotics agents told him he was entitled to one phone call, and Forté called Carly Simon.

Carly took the call on her cell phone as she and her husband were riding home from her radio tour promoting *The Bedroom Tapes*. After she found out where Forté was being held, she told the driver to pull over, and was sick to her stomach. The next day, she and Jim went to the jail, where Forté tried to make them believe that he thought the briefcase contained only money. (Jim Hart later remembered that the only time Carly had ever used her married name—"Carly Hart"—was when she and he were signing into various jails and prisons to visit Forté.)

Carly told Forté she would do everything she could for him, but he was quickly tried and convicted of massive cocaine possession and conspiracy with intent to distribute. Due to the large amount of drugs involved, the sentence was a mandatory fourteen years under the Reagan-era "War on Drugs" legislation that removed a federal judge's discretionary powers in a major case. Forté was sent to prison in Pennsylvania, while Carly desperately tried to call in favors. She lobbied the Clintons, then still in office, to no avail. The Kennedy family was of no help, either. Senator John Kerry of Massachusetts said sorry. She asked her friend Alan Dershowitz, the famous attorney and Harvard law professor, to look into the case, but he reported that there was simply not much that could be done.

Eventually Carly was steered to Senator Orrin Hatch, a conservative Republican from Utah who was (famously) an aspiring songwriter, and an admirer of Carly. Hatch was also the chairman of a senate committee on prisons, and it was presumably his considerable influence that caused Forté's transfer to a minimum-security prison in Fort Dix, New Jersey, in 2001. For the next seven years, Carly continued to lobby for a lesser sentence and better prison conditions for John Forté, and eventually her tactics and stamina would result in an outcome that many regarded as a miracle.

In 2001, Carly appeared on Janet Jackson's *All for You* album, which sampled "You're So Vain" in a new mash-up called "Son of a Gun." She sang on Mindy Jostyn's album *Blue Stories*. After the murderous jetliner attacks on New York and Washington on September 11, which killed more than three thousand Americans, Carly allowed the government to use "Let the River Run" in a national public service TV advertising campaign to raise public morale in the wake of 9/11 and the subsequent anthrax poisonings that had killed several postal workers. Carly's dramatic anthem was seen as a fitting balm for the grievously wounded American spirit, at the dawn of the new millennium.

Carly celebrated Christmas 2001 at home on the Vineyard with her children and close friends. Something about Christmas that year—the season, the music, the national traumas, the ghosts of Christmases past—was very moving for her, and she resolved to make a new album of songs that would reflect her own, often wistful, take on the spirit of the closing days of the year.

⟶

January 2002. Carly was in Los Angeles to sing with Ben Taylor at a party for the Winter Olympics, held in Utah that year. Afterward, not really wanting to return to an empty house, she called her old friend Don Was and asked him if he wanted to help her make a Christmas album. Don explained that he was leaving for Paris in five days to produce the new Rolling Stones album. Carly said she could do the album in four days. Soon Don Was arrived at the Peninsula Hotel, where Carly was staying, and turned her room (number 139) into a modern rehearsal hall merely by opening his laptop computer. Engineer Bob Clearmountain arrived a day later with some micro-phones. Carly and Don went to Tower Records on the Sunset Strip and bought every Christmas album they could find. For the proper atmosphere, Don's wife, Betty, decorated the room with twinkly lights, stuffed Santas, plastic elves, and jingle bells. To get in the proper mood, Carly went shopping at some of her old Beverly Hills and Melrose Avenue haunts for a new wardrobe. Over the next three days, many of L.A.'s great session musicians—plus Willie Nelson and entourage—trooped through room 139 to play on the tracks. After the fifth day, Don Was vanished into the Stones' milieu, and Carly mixed the album later on Martha's Vineyard with friend Jimmy Parr.

But Carly's main project that year was compiling, and remixing, back catalogue songs for a new compilation album, her greatest hits on digital compact disc. This had been a project for Rhino Records, a respected independent label that had evolved from a famous record store in L.A.'s Westwood section, but it had since been subsumed by Warner Music. Rhino's market research had identified Carly's core audience as millions of soccer moms in CD-equipped SUVs and minivans who loved her music but no longer had record players to access the music at will. The result was the *Anthology* album, released in November 2002. It contained eighteen digitally remastered versions of Carly's songs, some of them cleverly sourced from the rare, radio-friendly versions of hit singles such as "Anticipation" and "You're So Vain." These were generally "brighter" (and slightly shorter) versions; punchier, with the drums more prominent, plus new echo and reverb. *Anthology* was the first time some of these tracks had appeared on compact disc, and the set sold well in the run-up to Christmas 2002.

Carly played the Christmas music she'd recorded for Rhino executives, and the label agreed to license the album for release that year. Carly and her team (barely) made Rhino's deadline for the new seasonal album, *Christmas Is Almost Here*. But Carly's was a different kind of Yule fare, which usually relied on hoary clichés about the religious events of late December. Instead, Carly's album falls into the bohemian tradition of Miles Davis's classic "Blue Christmas"—recognizing that the holidays were a difficult, lonely, and (sometimes) despondent time of year for those without love or familial comfort in their lives.

Christmas Is Almost Here proved to be one of Carly's most interesting (and personal) recordings. The title track is a duet with its composer, Livingston Taylor, the singers seeking solace in the short days of the winter solstice. The folkloric "O Come, All Ye Faithful" features Bon Jovi's ace guitar hero, Richie Sambora, on electric Dobro. Another original song, "The Land of Christmas" (written during a migraine headache the night before the recording began), is a prayer to the Blessed Mother for pain relief. "Silent Night" features Ben Taylor in a quiet madrigal, hymnal and incantatory, with a beautifully hummed third verse. "The Gates to the City" is pure soul-gospel, with legendary Stones/Beatles collaborator Billy Preston on organ. Lucy Simon's beautiful song "Heaven," written much earlier, is emblematic of the idea—important to both Carly and Don—that the Christmas spirit is not for Christians only.

The old standard "I'll Be Home for Christmas" has additional (wistful) lyrics by Carly. Star L.A. session drummer Jim Keltner helps Carly with a reggae-informed "God Rest Ye Merry, Gentlemen." "Pretty Paper" is a clever/corny duet with its composer, country star Willie Nelson. The album ends with a version of John Lennon's "Happy X-mas (War Is Over)."

Christmas Is Almost Here was released in December 2002. Critics described it as a sophisticated, if unusually somber, variation on the traditional Christmas album. Rhino was good with promotion, and in New York that month Carly sang carols (with Ben Taylor and Mindy Jostyn) on NBC television during the lighting ceremony for Rockefeller Center's iconic Christmas tree. *Christmas Is Almost Here* (with some saucy photos by brother Peter Simon) was released too late in the season to make the sales charts, but *Anthology* did very good business, and repositioned Carly's music into America's digital culture. (The Christmas album was reissued the following year with two more tracks: "White Christmas," with Burt Bacharach; and "Forgive," a new song by Carly and Andreas Vollenweider.)

In 2003, Carly worked on songs (again in Sally's bedroom) for *Piglet's Big Movie,* the Walt Disney Company's latest animated exploitation of *Winnie-the-Pooh,* A. A. Milne's beloved children's stories. The soundtrack CD, featuring the voices of Carly, her children, the opera star Renée Fleming, and a full orchestra, was released later that year on the Walt Disney Records label.

In 2003, Carly's husband, Jim Hart, had been absent from her for some time. She knew that he was using cocaine when he was at home in New York. She told him that she needed more love and affection in the marriage. He admitted that this was difficult for him after her illness and surgeries. But he also said he was now more interested in leading a gay lifestyle. This was rough for Carly. Later she confided to a reporter for a London newspaper, "I can tell you that being married to a gay man made me feel unattractive again."

Carly wanted to buy a place to hang her hat in Manhattan. An apartment was available in the Dakota, the exclusive gothic pile on Central Park West where John Lennon had lived and been murdered in 1980. Carly enlisted her sister Joanna, now a prominent real estate executive, in a campaign to get past the cooperative building's notoriously difficult vetting committee. A letter to the Dakota on Carly's behalf was sent by legendary newscaster Walter Cronkite, supposedly one of the most trusted men in America, who described Carly as "an ideal neighbor and co-op member." A similar encomium was written by Joanna's friend Beverly Sills, then chairman of the board of the Metropolitan Opera. But Carly's bid was rejected anyway, without explanation.

Instead, she bought two apartments in an antique building in the West Village, near where she had first lived with her family on West Eleventh Street. This she turned into an eccentric Village duplex apartment, with a couple of bedrooms, a piano in the bathroom, and a tiny kitchen, and it became her favored pied à terre when in New York.

Spring 2003. Sally Taylor—now almost thirty years old—told her mother that she was going to marry her model-handsome beau, Dean Bragonier, in September. Carly envisioned a ceremony on her rose-covered bridge, over the stream by the gazebo. She was "crushed," she told friends, when Sally said that wouldn't work for her father, and that she was planning to marry at James's house in Chilmark, overlooking Menemsha Pond, at sunset on Labor Day weekend. Carly seethed about this all that summer.

Carly did her bit at the island's celebrity charity auction that summer. The high bidder for her prize would be told, by Carly, whom "You're So Vain" was about. Then the person would pledge to keep the identity secret. The high bidder was Dick Ebersol, a sports executive at NBC television. On the appointed day for the revelation, Ebersol arrived at Carly's house with six friends. Carly thought this rude, but told them some version of the secret. If it got out, she said, she would simply deny it. Later she told an interviewer that Dick Ebersol was a jerk.

Sally's wedding was a big deal. At James's house, Carly sniffed at the gauche line of portable toilets for guests. The lawns had been mown too short and had turned brown. Poison ivy trailed through the property, which was mostly unoccupied, since James Taylor now lived with his third wife, Kim Smedvig, and their kids in western Massachusetts. (He and his wife had met ten years earlier, when James was performing at Tanglewood, the summer home of the Boston Symphony Orchestra, where Kim Smedvig worked as a publicist. They married in 2001 and had twin sons—half brothers to Sally and Ben.) Wedding guests were shown down a path to the shoreline of Menemsha Pond, where they waited with their backs against the sun. Carly: "The father and I led the magnificent Sally down to her husband-to-be and the rest of the wedding party. Then there was dancing and a modicum of alcohol. Spirits were high—a nice chance to get together with both the Simon and Taylor families." James Taylor was careful to introduce his wife to Carly's various siblings and cousins.

There were many toasts as the sun sank into the Vineyard Sound and the champagne flowed. Livingston Taylor got up and offered a heartfelt appreciation of the mother of the bride. Then Carly delivered an impassioned toast/screed that was in turn passionate, articulate, stammering, and cringe-worthy. She sat down to prolonged applause and general relief. The party then turned into a bonfire on nearby Lobsterville Beach, and the happy couple was reportedly not seen for several days.

This was, in 2003, the last time Carly Simon spoke to James Taylor.

REALITY SANDWICH

———

$\mathcal{I}$n 2004, Carly edited another compilation of her songs, *Reflections*, a joint enterprise between the Bertelsmann Music Group, which had swallowed Arista, and Warner Music, which had subsumed Electra Records, Carly's original label. This was a single CD, and therefore required considerable pruning of Carly's oeuvre. Don Was helped produced the song "Amity," which Carly had recorded with Sally Taylor some years earlier. Carly dedicated the album to all the various drummers she had known, been inspired by, and in some cases loved. Released in May 2004, the compilation was a success for Carly, reaching number twenty-two on the *Billboard* chart. A slightly different version of *Reflections* was released in June, mostly for the British market, and sold well in European markets as well.

Meanwhile, Carly's brother, Peter, was arrested several times for drunk driving on the Vineyard. Carly dutifully attended his legal sessions at the county courthouse in nearby Edgartown, and supported him as he resolved to get treatment for alcohol addiction. Peter spent that summer in the island's jail, visited by his sister and various island luminaries. (When TV comedian Larry David visited Peter [with Alan Dershowitz], he was mobbed for autographs by jail employees.) Sally Taylor was on her honeymoon in darkest Cambodia, sending her worried mother bulletins via e-mail.

Then there was her husband in New York, struggling with drug use and dependent on a network of dealers to keep him going. Needing some distraction from these travails, Carly accepted an offer to appear as herself in a cameo role in the movie *Little Black Book,* for which she'd written some music. The difficult year 2004 ended with two gospel-flavored Christmas concerts at the Apollo Theater in Harlem, with Carly's children, Lucy Simon, Liv and Kate Taylor, gospel star Bebe Winans, jazz star Christian McBride, and a big, full-throated gospel choir. Carly described the concerts' atmosphere as uninhibited and the carols this group produced as "rousing."

Carly Simon pulled out of this period in early 2005 by once again turning to the music of her past. She had been contacted by her old friend Richard Perry, who had produced Rod Stewart's recent best-selling albums of standards. Perry had a bunch of songs in mind that Stewart hadn't used, and Carly said she would do them. Perry recorded the orchestra in Los Angeles, and Carly sang her vocals in New York and on Martha's Vineyard. The songs included classics such as "I've Got You Under My Skin," a samba-like "Alone Together," the always spooky "I Only Have Eyes for You," the Gershwins' "How Long Has This Been Going On," and Cole Porter's "In the Still of the Night."

"We had fun," Carly later said of these sessions. "We recorded more cheaply than ever before. Richard and I knew each other well enough to allow the jibes to turn into warmly taken, non-bristly affairs." The eleven tracks they recorded—Carly's fourth collection of timeless tunes—were released by Columbia Records in July 2005 under the title *Moonlight Serenade.* Carly appeared on the CD package in elegant silken evening gowns, in photos taken by Bob Gothard.

To everyone's amazement, *Moonlight Serenade* was an instant smash, hitting the charts at number seven on the day of release. It was Carly's first Top Ten recording in thirty years. "I was very shocked," she told the BBC. "Then incredibly happy, and then I was thinking, 'I'm only gonna get killed now.' As soon as you do anything successful, everybody hates you as somebody who has 'legs' in their career. . . . Not that I didn't call everybody I knew [about the chart position], saying, GUESS WHAT? like a teenage girl." *Moonlight Serenade* sold well for the rest of the year and was nominated for a Grammy Award. Critics opined that Carly's success was due to the rapidly aging baby boom generation's nostalgia for the music of their parents. *New York Times* headline: "Sex Symbols of the 1970's Doing Lawrence Welk for Hip Seniors."

Carly swerved when her friend Mindy Jostyn died of cancer in March 2005. This was a terrible time. Peter Simon: "The issue of Mindy's death that made it so rough on Carly was that Mindy was a practicing Christian Scientist who refused treatment for her cancer altogether. Mindy just asked for prayers, so when she died, there was this terrible feeling of helplessness that just engulfed everyone."

Mindy's husband, Jake Brackman, tried to hold things together for their children, but Carly fell apart and stopped eating. When she got down to a skeletal 110 pounds, she was persuaded to enter McLean Hospital for treatment. On the night she checked into the hospital's unlocked facility for patients who weren't a danger to themselves, she was told there was a sandwich for her in the refrigerator down the hall. Carly wasn't hungry, but the nurse said she had to get the sandwich. When she opened the fridge, there was indeed a sandwich with her name on it, next to another one labeled "James Taylor." Carly froze. But she found out the food was for another patient with the same name. "I think someone just wanted to zap me," Carly said later. "And no, I didn't eat the sandwich."

Later, she heard that her old London flame, Willie Donaldson, had also expired after a long career as a public reprobate. She mourned for Willie, too.

When she felt better and had gained some weight, Carly went to work promoting her big hit album *Moonlight Serenade*. She gave a lot of interviews and spoke about living in her sixth decade. To the London daily *The Independent*: "It's very odd turning sixty. I thought I'd be much better about it than I am. I thought that I'd just kind of float into it and be a great older woman—my new identity—and then all of a sudden the shock of the number: SIXTY!"

On menopause: "My mother used to say, 'It's such a relief not having that constant thing [menstruation] that makes you feel like an animal in heat.' If I want to feel sexy, I know how I can feel sexy. But now it's got to be about someone *very* appealing, because you don't have random thoughts about sex that—like when you were in your teens or twenties—make you want to get into bed with just about anyone. Actually, for me, that was most prevalent in my forties. I think it was Mother Nature's way of saying, 'This is your last chance, so I'll give you a little bit of extra steam right now.' So I had a very active love life in my forties."

Autumn 2005. Carly and her daughter, Sally, filmed a special for PBS aboard the Cunard Line's new luxury ship, *Queen Mary II*. Jim Hart came along, looking elegant in black tie. Carly and Sally were both resplendent in gowns and stoles. A tour was planned for later in the year, so Carly rehearsed with a new band (most had played with James Taylor on his annual summer tours) at the Hot Tin Roof, the Vineyard nightclub she'd founded, and which had been sold out from under her by her business partners while she was in the hospital. (She first heard about this in the local paper, the *Vineyard Gazette*.) Carly had registered copyright for the club's name, so when it reopened the next summer, it was called Outerland.

The tour began in Boston on November 19, 2005. Every show sold out immediately. The band was hot, and Carly shared the stage with Sally, Ben, and her little dog, Molly. Carly mixed hit songs and deep album cuts with atmospheric songs from *Serenade*, especially "I Only Have Eyes for You," that brought her ovations almost every night. "Jesse" was a big rocking jam that often got the audiences up and dancing. Carly's troupe motored through the tour in a pair of deluxe buses. After the concerts, Carly had the intense satisfaction of trying to go to sleep, as the buses rolled through the night to the next show, with both her children resting in their curtained berths across the aisle from where she lay.

Some nights were funky. Some nights Carly was helped onstage. Backup singer Carmella Ramsey hit the high notes on "Coming Around Again" and other songs. Carly would forget lyrics and appear disorientated. In New York, the drummer motioned to a stagehand to help her get up from the piano. At some shows, people murmured that she seemed medicated. Before some (delayed) shows, Sally told audiences that her mother was very nervous, but would hopefully be joining them soon. Other shows were nailed, almost perfect. In Washington she beamed at a special guest, Senator Orrin Hatch, a crucial ally in the continuing campaign to spring John Forté from prison.

Christmas was weird that year, 2005. Everyone was burnt out. Jake Brackman and his children came to the Vineyard, devastated. Kate Taylor, who'd lost her husband to cancer, came around and looked after everyone. Carly and her people got through the holiday season as best they could.

INTO WHITE

_____

$\mathcal{I}$n 2006, Carly Simon divorced her second husband, with whom she remained on friendly terms. She had a spacious new kitchen built at Hidden Star Hill, which still bristled with assistants and caretakers and also served as an upscale boardinghouse for various musicians and friends of her son. Columbia wanted a follow-up to *Moonlight Serenade,* so Carly proposed an album of R&B covers with soul bandleader Booker T. Jones. The label asked for another plan. Carly suggested an album of soothing songs and lullabies, a sort of evening raga, and Columbia gave this a green light.

Carly recorded about twenty songs at home and at local studio Parr Audio that summer. With Jimmy Parr producing, the basic ensemble consisted of Carly, Teese Gohl, Peter Calo, and Ben Taylor's friend David Saw, one of the property's resident songwriters. All the songs were important to Carly, emotionally and historically. All had some meaning or intimate connection to her past. Cat Stevens's visionary "Into White" begins the album. The Beatles' "Blackbird" has a beautiful cello descant. Carly sings James Taylor's "You Can

Close Your Eyes" with their children. Her take on Luis Bonfá's "Manha De Carnaval"—the theme from the movie *Black Orpheus*—is lilting and redolent of a quiet night in Brazil. Lord Burgess's "Jamaica Farewell," made famous by Harry Belafonte (and a favorite of the Simon Sisters), has a beautiful Dobro solo and ends with a hypnotic fade into "You Are My Sunshine." There is an Everly Brothers medley, and a melancholy "Over the Rainbow."

Stephen Foster's "O! Susanna" is hushed and very haunting, softly lit by kalimba and flute. The traditional "Scarborough Fair" is given new lyrics by Carly. "I Gave My Love a Cherry" is tucked into bed by a lovely cello played by Jan Hyer. Carly reworked the lyrics to "Love of My Life" from the *This Is My Life* soundtrack. (The reference to loving Woody Allen is changed to loving Mia Farrow, his ex-wife.) David Saw contributed two new songs, "Quiet Evening" and "I'll Just Remember You."

Fourteen of these tracks were released late in 2006. The album, *Into White,* received very good promotion from Columbia and entered the sales chart at number fifteen. (A bonus track, "Hush Little Baby"/"My Bonnie," appeared on CDs sold at the Barnes and Noble bookstore chain.) Carly dedicated the album to Paul Samwell-Smith, her erstwhile producer and friend. Most of the album's photographs were taken by Sally Taylor. In a booklet note, Carly writes that *Into White* is music of the kind "grown-ups like me can get a little weepy over." If the album does its job and lulls the listener to sleep, she hoped that "you won't notice if you have tears on your pillow." Explaining the ideas behind the album to an interviewer from a Chicago daily, Carly said, "I've reached the age of wisdom, now, and I feel strongly that I want to report on that."

For about a year Carly had been working on a book for Simon and Schuster titled *Lyrics.* She chose about a hundred of her favorite lyrics, and added about as many photographs from her private archive. She found many of the original handwritten manuscripts of the songs, and also wrote a serious introduction concerning her views on the art of songwriting. Simon and Schuster put *Lyrics* into production and sent proof copies to booksellers and reviewers. When Carly saw the finished copies, she found the production values—especially the inexpensive paper stock and the way the photographs were reproduced—to be way below her standard. It looked to her as if S&S were trying to publish her on the cheap. When the editors said it was too late to change the print run, Carly threatened legal action, which stopped *Lyrics* for good. All available copies were pulped, and a year's work went for naught.

Autumn 2006. Carly worked with Andreas Vollenweider on a Christmas album, *Midnight Clear,* appearing on four of the tracks.

One day that fall, an old reel of audio tape arrived in the post from Woodstock. Albert Grossman's widow, Sally, had closed down her husband's famous Bearsville recording studio. When the studio archive was opened, one of the surprise discoveries was the tape Carly had made with members of the Band when Grossman was trying to brand Carly as the female Bob Dylan. The tape included "Baby Let Me Follow You Down" with lyrics rewritten for Carly by Bob Dylan, and the other demo that had been written by the producer. Carly had been looking for this tape for forty years, and here it was at last: Robbie Robertson's stinging guitar, Garth Hudson's droning organ, Levon Helm on drums, and Carly singing from the heart, in the pocket. Everyone Carly played the tape for loved it.

Carly Simon was able to divorce her husband that year because she was involved with a new love. His name was Richard Koehler, a surgeon who had until recently worked at the Martha's Vineyard Hospital. Dr. Koehler's marriage was breaking up, and one day he was talking about his situation to Carly's brother. Peter suggested that he give Carly a call, since Richard already had her phone number. He called, and they hit it off. He was handsome, blond, charming, attentive, and a decade younger. He was a doctor, and Carly needed a doctor, she told friends, preferably around the clock. Some of their early dates were drives around the Vineyard. One day she took him up to High Mark, the hilltop house where her mother had lived, to show him the stupendous view of the sea. The present owner was there, and invited them in to see the changes that had been made to the property. A wave of memories washed over Carly, and she was very moved. Outside, she stood between the trees where her mother's hammock used to be, where she'd rocked for hours with baby Sally in her arms on summer evenings when James was away on tour. She looked at the lichen-covered stones that dotted the lawn. She knew those stones so well, she told her new beau, that she almost remembered their names.

THIS KIND OF LOVE

─────

$\mathcal{I}$n early 2007, Carly Simon sent almost fifty sets of lyrics to Jimmy Webb in California to see what he could come up with. After two successful albums of covers, it was time to make an album of new songs. The problem was that the recording industry was in a state of endemic collapse following the digital revolution, whose file-sharing applications made buying recordings completely redundant. The closing of Tower Records' flagship store on Sunset Boulevard in 2006 was emblematic of the thousands of other record shops around the country shutting down for good.

In the spring of 2007, Carly joined a few other major artists who were licensing their recordings to Hear Music, a record company whose products were sold exclusively in Starbucks coffee shops nationwide. Hear Music had made a hit out of Paul McCartney's *Memory Almost Full* album, and Joni Mitchell was currently enjoying success with Starbucks as well. Carly liked her meetings with Hear's executives, who offered Carly up to one million dollars in advance, and made her a lot of marketing promises (CDs stocked by the cash registers, album tracks in heavy in-store rotation), and so she decided to sign up with them. She thought she was working with Starbucks, one of the biggest retail chains in America, and the deal had been presented to her as a sure thing. By summer 2007, Carly was planning to make this album, and then she was planning to retire.

In August, she was joined by Sally and Ben Taylor at a campaign event on Martha's Vineyard for Hillary Clinton, who was running for president. They sang "Devoted to You" for a crowd of almost two thousand.

Then Carly and Jimmy Webb embarked on a working journey to Brazil. Carly had been in love with samba and bossa nova music since she first heard the epic collaborations between Joao Gilberto and Stan Getz in the early sixties. Now she was eager to put a Brazilian spin on her new album, to capture both the ecstasy of the music and its *saudade,* the untranslatable Portuguese term for the feeling of sorrow transmitted through some of tropicalism's most beautiful songs. The original aim of the Brazilian trip was to link up with Caetano Veloso, the reigning high priest of Brazilian jazz, but Veloso's schedule was full when they arrived. This was a disappointment but they soaked up as much local color as they could. When they got back to America they began writing songs. By September 2007, Jimmy Webb was recording with Carly and producer Frank Filipetti in her Vineyard kitchen studio, while, in another wing of the house, her daughter, Sally, was beginning to go into labor. Carly Simon's grandson, Bodhi, was born that month on Martha's Vineyard.

February 2008. Headline in the scandal sheet *National Enquirer*: "Carly Simon Banned from Seeing Her Grandson/Feud with Son-in-law EXPLODES." The article reported that "people close to Carly" said that Sally's husband was being difficult. The tabloid reported that Carly's son-in-law became angry when Carly refused to give up some property he wanted. Sally and her family had left Hidden Star

Hill and moved to Boston, leaving Carly somewhat bereft. "I'm sorry," she was quoted, "but I just can't comment on any of that. All I can say is that I adore my daughter and cherish my grandson. I only got to hold him once, and that hurts."

Later that spring Carly played her first ever concert in Miami with her son, Ben (who dedicated his song "Island" to his "stubborn sister," who was absent from the band). The concert was part of a Carly Simon weekend at Florida International University, whose theater department was mounting a full-length revival of Carly's "family opera," *Romulus Hunt*, featuring all-local performers. This was paired with a nonprofit care center for abandoned or neglected children, and the two benefit performances were complete sellouts. Carly and her band were putting a lot of new spins on familiar songs such as "You're So Vain" and "Anticipation." As she introduced "Coming Around Again," she told the audience, "These songs have different meanings for me because I'm so old now."

The new songs Carly put together with Jimmy Webb were released by Hear Music in May 2008, on an album titled *This Kind of Love*. Carly's hard-won new record was dedicated to the Brazilian songwriter Antonio Carlos Jobim, and to Art Buchwald, who had recently died. The music is some of the most eclectic of Carly's career, the songs reflective of varying colors and shadows in the sixth decade of her eventful life. "This Kind of Love" is another of Carly's transgressive love ballads, but with a vibrant Brazilian hook at the end. "Hold Out Your Heart" reflects immediate conflicts within Carly's family, as her children began breaking away from the fierce embrace of their mother's uber-maternal love. "People Say a Lot" is a sinister funk-rap on the perils of employing personal assistants: initially competent but later unstable personalities who soon might know too much; who might, sometimes, be driven to blackmail and threats.

Ben Taylor's song "Island" owes a lot to Bob Marley. "Hola Soleil" is a sun-worshipping samba jam with the band and a kids' chorus. "In My Dreams" is Carly—sounding her age—soloing with

Jimmy Webb on cabaret piano. One of the highlights of the set is a cool bossa nova—"When We're Together"—written by Sally Taylor in the style of the current Brazilian star Bebel Gilberto. Carly's friend Peter Calo contributes expert and apposite Dobro and guitar.

Another highlight, and the most typical Carly Simon song on the album, is "So Many People to Love," a collaboration with Carole Bayer Sager, sung with an endearing stutter that speaks of Carly's worries about the people she felt were depending on her continued success. A similar sentiment runs through "They Just Want You to Be There," another musing on adult responsibilities. Jimmy Webb and Carly cowrote "The Last Samba," actually more a bossa nova, as their shared tribute and soft elegy for the pure pleasures that Brazilian music had brought to their artistic lives. The album concludes with "Sangre Dolce," a portrait of an immigrant woman stranded between loves and loyalties, and "Too Soon to Say Goodbye," a corny summer carousel with Jimmy Webb on his typically haunting piano.

For Carly, a lot was riding on her new album in the spring of 2008, and she plunged into promo mode. She played a show for an invitation-only crowd of fans at Joe's Pub in Manhattan. (Introducing her son: "I'm his mother, James Taylor is his father, though James doesn't always connect the dots." The audiences laughed, as if they were old friends.) She received a reporter for London's *Telegraph* newspaper at her Greenwich Village duplex wearing a stylish pinstriped Ralph Lauren blazer. First stop was the bedroom, with sheer golden and damask drapes hanging from the frame of an antique four-poster. The pale pink quilt, made of silk, had belonged to Carly's mother. The interview was conducted in the candlelit, piano-equipped library/bathroom, the reporter seated in a green armchair wedged between an old desk and a claw-footed porcelain bathtub. Carly pulled up a stool. Downstairs, Ben Taylor and David Saw were rehearsing guitar parts for a possible tour to support *This Kind of Love*.

When the reporter pointed out that this was Carly's first album of new songs in eight years (since *The Bedroom Tapes*), Carly explained, "It's like meeting a man, this album. As you get more and more into him, it turns out that there's a chemistry there after all—even though he has shades and tones and attitudes and looks and feelings that were much different from those you were used to." She explained that her current lover, Dr. Koehler, was a new kind of love for her. "He's really different from the other men I have known. I didn't think he was my type, at all." Then Carly drifted into a lyric: "But I was stranded, with no light home, and we drove the beach road together. He's the magician who sings the sun down, his face in silhouette." Carly also noted that her sister Joanna was now living with Walter Cronkite, whose wife had passed away. And that her oncologist had recommended peas as a healthy midnight snack, so she could sometimes be found, late at night, staring at the microwave oven, watching little green cups going around and around.

May 14, 2008. In New York, Carly appeared on the syndicated TV talk show hosted by Tavis Smiley, looking great in long blond hair and black-rimmed glasses, nursing a mug of tea. Smiley asked about the songs about her children on *This Kind of Love*. She explained that "Hold Out Your Heart" began when Ben told her he was going surfing at midnight in February, which made her crazy. Then there were difficulties with Sally and her husband she didn't want to get into. But she allowed there'd been "a recent set of problems with my daughter that really makes it very, very difficult to talk to her about them, because there's a kind of . . . vacuum of silence . . . a kind of impenetrable wall that we can't seem to blast through. And so I wrote about it in the second verse of that song."

June 2008. Copies of the *This Kind of Love* CD disappeared from Starbucks outlets and were not replenished. The album didn't chart. Carly couldn't find out what was going on. Then Hear Music suddenly announced that the company was shutting down. The president of the company and key executives were reportedly escorted out of their offices by security guards. Starbucks announced it was pulling back from the music business, and sales management of *This Kind of Love* was handed to a partner, the Concord Music Group. Carly Simon was dumbfounded. In her mind, she could once again hear Jackie Onassis saying, "Oh, Carly—you've been *screwed*."

Retirement, Carly realized, had to be indefinitely postponed. And there were financial problems as well. She owed money on her island home, and had tried to sell her Manhattan apartment, without success. Her financial manager, Kenneth Starr, reported losses in the stock market. Hear Music had never paid her the full advance for the album, and there was no lift in catalogue sales or radio royalties that usually come with a successful new album. Carly quietly sold the portrait Andy Warhol had painted of her, and some other things, to cover costs.

She huddled with lawyers. Then she sued Starbucks for ten million dollars, alleging breach of promise and fraudulent business practices. This case, which made national headlines and was also reported in the European press, dragged on for a couple of years, until a judge ruled that Hear Music had never been a legal division of the giant coffee company, so Carly's suit against Starbucks had no legal standing. Carly appealed. Her lawyers argued that she had been grossly misled and that facts had been concealed from her. A judge in the appellate court in California ruled against her, based on the wording of contracts and other documents she had signed with Hear Music. (By this time, *This Kind of Love* had sold about 125,000 copies through normal outlets.) Carly's high-priced attorneys then filed an amended appeal, and in 2010 another California judge also ruled against her. "We couldn't break the judge's heart," she ruefully told a friend.

Autumn 2008. Carly's friend Pam Frank, the photographer who'd shot the cover of the *Spy* album, married Harry Belafonte. Carly and her band (again without Sally Taylor) played a sold-out show at the Borgata Hotel in Atlantic City in October. Barack Obama's campaign was broadcasting Carly's "Let the River Run" as one of the major themes in his successful run for the American presidency. And, after the election, on November 24, 2008, President George Bush sat down at his desk in the White House and pardoned fourteen individuals, and commuted the prison sentences of two others convicted of offenses related to the sale of cocaine. One of these was identified in the press as John Edward Forté of North Brunswick, New Jersey. Carly's friend Senator Orrin Hatch had come through for her, after seven years of promises. (*New York Post* headline: "Rapper Is Free to Yo.") John Forté was released from prison four weeks later, just before Christmas, and joined his friend Ben Taylor's household at Hidden Star Hill.

Carly was flushed by the success of John Forté's release. She told the Associated Press that Orrin Hatch "is not just a Republican, but a great human being. He was always very impressed with everything I brought to his attention regarding John." Then Carly's early hero Odetta died on December 2, 2008. Carly wrote a glowing encomium for one of the last great figures of the civil rights movement of her youth, a fond farewell that was published on the *Huffington Post* website.

NEVER BEEN GONE

———

$\mathcal{I}$n 2009, Carly told *The Wall Street Journal* that her attempt to make a final album, and then retire, had been a total bust. "My thrilling comeback," she allowed, "was no such thing." She told the newspaper that she was in litigation with Starbucks; she claimed that she was three million dollars in the red; and that she was forced, at her advanced age, to keep working. She wanted, she said, to write serious music: concertos and symphonies. Instead, she decided, for business reasons, to rerecord some of her most important songs.

A lot of her generational peers were doing it, too, because most veteran songwriters didn't own the master recordings of their old songs. These tapes tended to remain the property of the (often defunct) record labels that originally released the songs, so their creators earned only a relatively small amount from back catalogue sales and other revenue streams. Trying to recover master tapes, through legal means, from the giant corporations that had swallowed the original labels was expensive and even risky. But if songwriters such as Carole King, Suzanne Vega, or John Prine rerecorded their old songs, they could retain ownership of these new versions and garner a majority of any future income through licensing and other means. (*The Wall Street Journal* described this gambit as an astute business move for popular recording artists past their peak, in terms of sales.) Also, Carly was still under a contractual obligation to some now-hated and amorphous corporate entity—Hear Music/Starbucks/Concord Music Group/Universal—not to record any new music until a specified period of time expired. The downside of releasing new versions of old songs is that the original fan base just wouldn't care enough to purchase them.

According to Carly, it was her son Ben who suggested, "Let's make an album at home for no money." This took much of 2009. Carly: "We forged ahead in fits and starts. Ben would go on tour and then come back, and we'd do some things. And for a lot of the recording I was saying, 'Huh? What is this going to be about? I'm dealing with a lot of other things in my life, and this isn't necessarily something I need.'" Ben Taylor, then thirty-two, was trying nothing less than to reimagine his mother's major work with new arrangements, different rhythms, and resettings of Carly's classic material. Mother and son fought over the direction this new music was taking, but both also described themselves as "serial capitulators" in the creative process. Carly said later that they must have spent a thousand hours working on the new "Boys in the Trees" alone.

Summer 2009. Jim Hart's son, Eamon, died, and Carly was affected. Eamon had never lived with Carly and Jim, but he had been her stepson for eighteen years. Carly got back in touch with Libby Titus after hearing that Libby's son, Ezra, had also died. A guy who claimed he had fixed the fence around Carly's property was sending her hate mail. In August, President Obama brought his family to the Vineyard, but Carly had had enough of politicians by then. She sang onstage with Ben and John Forté at her old nightclub and was dazzling. Then she appeared at a book signing party at the Midnight Farm store looking glazed over and unsteady. In fact, she really wasn't feeling well at all, and was occasionally hospitalized for various ailments. She probably had some work done on her facial presentation. A British writer who'd published a book about Willie Donaldson approached Carly with the idea of writing her biography. Carly e-mailed back that he'd be wasting his time. To another would-be biographer she wrote, "I would pity you, having to re-live my experience, I would say, 89% of which was painful. There's very little of show business that is fun for anyone who doesn't have the cunning of Anne Boleyn's father. (You could substitute that with Beyoncé's father.)" At the end of August she traveled with her completed tapes to Portland, Maine, where they were mastered by Bob Ludwig, the legendary recording engineer who always completed the final stages of turning Carly's late-period music into a finished product.

Carly was fighting with Simon and Schuster. Her father's old firm was demanding twenty-six thousand dollars in production costs for the pulped *Lyrics* book, and no way was Carly going to pay. S&S was also turning down Carly's ideas for another children's book, which would have completed her deal with them. She told friends that problems with Simon and Schuster was like being rejected by her father all over again. She also said she was being victimized by a financial manager who operated in the mold of the notorious schemer Bernard Madoff and was in the process of losing millions of her money. On September 11, 2009, Carly sang "Let the River Run" with Sally and Ben at a memorial at the site of the former World Trade Center in Lower Manhattan.

Never Been Gone, the album of rebooted Carly Simon songs, was released in October 2009 on Iris Records, a label partly owned by her son, which licensed the tracks from Carly on a temporary basis. Carly described the album as "the gateway to the rest of my life" and she dedicated it to her lyricist, alter ego, and friend Jacob Brackman. The new versions of the old songs were chiming, shining, tingling: the old analog music buffed for the digital age. "The Right Thing to Do" is all sweet and lulling acoustics and new, passionately jamming lyrics. "It Happens Every Day" has a funky R&B tempo. Teese Gohl plays piano on the title track, from a foxtrot to a waltz. "Boys in the Trees" has a spooky orchestration and Sally Taylor and John Forté on vocals. "Let the River Run" has buttery new, choirlike vocals. "You're So Vain" is a mash-up of bass elements with (Brian) Wilsonian variations.

"You Belong to Me" is transformed by her son and John Forté into cool, adult-oriented hip-hop. The heavily orchestrated "That's the Way I Always Heard It Should Be" seems both haunted and haunting, as its ancient suburban values are exposed to the light of a new century, and much newer attitudes. Carly wrote an intense new verse for "Coming Around Again," now presented as more of a meditation on the broken heart than the anthem of romantic hope it once was. David Saw's resetting of "Anticipation" is somewhat tepid, and the album concludes with the obscure "Songbird," with the twin images of a young Carly Simon at her piano and the current model dealing with aging and maintaining a reckoning with the world: stoic, always heroic.

Carly went to work that autumn, promoting her album on TV's *Good Morning America* and Jimmy Fallon's late night comedy show. Carly and the band worked up a hot slice of "You Belong to Me" with John Forté rapping and DJ Logic scratching. "You're So Vain" was given an updated, staccato feel. Carly's team also worked on maximizing her online presence at her website (carlysimon.com), enticing her fans with impromptu home performances, personal observations, and funny video blogs. Her son told *The Boston Globe*, "We mean to go micro, and make her own universe so provocative that every Carly Simon fan wants to go there and have a more personal connection. She's used to such a different paradigm, a big corporate music situation, and we had to keep spelling it out. She kept saying, 'Do I *really* get to keep 60 percent of everything?'"

Nevertheless, sales of *Never Been Gone* were initially disappointing.

Thanksgiving 2009. In New York, Carly rode on the Care Bears float in the Macy's parade, which she used to watch with her kids from their perch at apartment 6S, on Central Park West. When Carly's float reached the main department store on Thirty-fourth Street, she lip-synced "Let the River Run" for the huge national TV audience. Then she took the rest of the year off. She sometimes scrubbed with her surgeon boyfriend, and then sang loving songs to his recovering patients at the Plymouth, Massachusetts, hospital where he operated.

In March 2010, Carly and Ben flew to England, where *Never Been Gone* had just been released. She played her first-ever concert in the UK, at the BBC's Maida Vale studio, and chatted about some of the stories behind the songs. Asked by several British interviewers who "You're So Vain" was about, she replied, tongue in cheek, that the song was about David Geffen. Asked about James Taylor, she answered, "He won't talk to me." She told another reporter that her children weren't allowed to give her James's phone number. "But I don't have many regrets," she added. "I chose pain, too, and I don't blame James for any part of it."

By Easter 2010, Carly was back on the Vineyard and being more of a grandmother to Sally's little blond boy, Bodhi, having reconciled with his father and mother.

In May, Kenneth Starr, who managed Carly's financial affairs, was arrested in New York by government agents. They found him hiding in a closet in his multimillion-dollar apartment, his shoes sticking out from under the door. Carly was among his celebrity clients, who included Sylvester Stallone and photographer Annie Leibovitz. He was charged with stealing fifty-nine million dollars from his clients and was imprisoned. One source estimated that Carly possibly lost several million dollars. Asked by a reporter how she could credit Starr's standard promise of 28 percent returns, she replied, "I'm just that naïve and stupid. I thought that it was possible." About her Vineyard estate: "If I sold this house, which is our family compound, if I sold that and lived in a trailer, we would have plenty of money." Asked why she hung on with Starr after allegations had been made against him, she replied, "I remember thinking that they wouldn't dare fool with me, because now they're under investigation."

June 2010. James Taylor and Carole King were touring together in a nostalgia bath of singer-songwriterness. Almost every arena their Troubadour Reunion tour played sold out. (It was the second biggest grossing tour of the year, after Bon Jovi's.) Judy Collins played her cabaret show at the Café Carlisle for five weeks, also a near sellout. Carly Simon was added to three concerts of the revived Lilith Fair, a woman-centric traveling summer festival, but had to pull out when she injured her foot. One day that summer, she appeared at the island's ferry landing handing out a two-song CD from *Never Been Gone* as a teaser to the tourists.

That summer she worked with the Brazilian soccer hero Pelé on a project related to the 2012 Olympic Games. In September she appeared onstage with her son and John Forté in a benefit for the victims of Hurricane Earl, which actually failed to reach Martha's Vineyard. She and her children sang at a memorial service for the actress Patricia Neal, a longtime Vineyard resident. She lost her final appeal in the lawsuit against Starbucks. Guests at Carly's Christmas Eve party included Sally and her family, Ben and his girlfriend, her niece Julie Levine, Peter and Ronnie Simon, David Saw, and Jake Brackman and his children.

In January 2011, Carly signed a half-million-dollar music publishing deal with the Bertelsmann Music Group. She accepted an award from Our Time, a charitable foundation dedicated to those who stutter and stammer. (The recent film *The King's Speech* had brought massive attention to this malady.) On March 2, she saw on the news that President Obama had bestowed a National Medal of Arts on James Taylor at a White House ceremony. The next month James, now sixty-three, played four sold-out nights at Carnegie Hall. (James at the White House: "I always felt like such an outsider. There's an element of alienation in my approach. I wonder when all this stuff is going to sink in.") That summer, Ben Taylor opened shows on his father's annual tour.

Carly toyed with making another album of standards with Richard Perry, trying to capture the large audience that *Moonlight Serenade* had attracted. One day, Warren Beatty called her, seemingly out of the blue, and urged her to make this record with Perry. Carly told her old friend Warren that, like always, she was keeping her options open.

Summer 2011. Carly sang with the Boston Pops at a benefit for the Nantucket Cottage Hospital. She sang at a birthday party for Bill Clinton on the Vineyard. At another venue, she appeared onstage with Ben Taylor and John Forté. She collaborated with playwright Ernest Thompson on a new song, "The Father-Daughter Dance," for a revival of *On Golden Pond* in New Hampshire. *The Boston Globe* sent a reporter to the Vineyard to interview her. Carly explained that in general she was feeling better but was still prone to depression, due to some hormonal losses after her bout with cancer. Asked if she still thought about retiring, she answered: "I want to make the most of my time. I'm into writing poetry now, and piano concertos. My weakness is my tendency for laziness. But I'm determined to remain a body in motion. I want to rev it up!"

The reporter remarked that Carly's voice still sounded very strong, and asked her secret.

"Letting love come into my life," she replied. "Feeling love makes me feel like I want to shine."

As of this writing in 2012, Carly Simon hasn't retired. She's still moving between her homes in New York and Martha's Vineyard; still nurturing friends and family; still carrying a major torch; still worrying about the state of the world; and still creating when her faithful muse visits her, in the wee small hours of the morning.

Acknowledgments

The author wishes to thank the Simon family for decades of inspiration (and fun). Thanks also to the Davis family, for the same. Christopher B. Davis contributed research and maintained editorial standards. Everyone who was interviewed is a gem. Thanks to the great journalists who covered the Carly Simon story in the past. To my colleagues at Gotham Books in New York, I'm sorry this took so long, but like many things, it was too much fun to stop. Special thanks to editors Lauren Marino and Cara Bedick, plus publisher Bill Shinker. Cheers to David Vigliano and John Pelosi, Esq. As mentioned in the introduction, this biography is unauthorized. Thanks to Carly for her help. *Bonum quo antiquius eo melius.*

    —STEPHEN DAVIS